Informal Order and the State in Afghanistan

Despite vast efforts to build the state, profound political order in rural Afghanistan is maintained by self-governing, customary organizations. Informal Order and the State in Afghanistan explores the rules governing these organizations to explain why they can provide public goods. Instead of withering during decades of conflict, customary authority adapted to become more responsive and deliberative. Drawing on hundreds of interviews and observations from dozens of villages across Afghanistan and statistical analysis of nationally representative surveys, Jennifer Murtazashvili demonstrates that such authority enhances citizen support for democracy, enabling the rule of law by providing citizens a bulwark of defence against predatory state officials. Contrary to conventional wisdom, it shows that "traditional" order does not impede the development of the state because even the most independent minded communities see a need for a central government— but question its effectiveness when it attempts to rule them directly and without substantive consultation.

JENNIFER BRICK MURTAZASHVILI is an Assistant Professor at the Graduate School of Public and International Affairs at the University of Pittsburgh. She earned her PhD in Political Science from the University of Wisconsin-Madison.

Informal Order and the State in Afghanistan

JENNIFER BRICK MURTAZASHVILI

University of Pittsburgh

CAMBRIDGE
UNIVERSITY PRESS

CAMBRIDGE
UNIVERSITY PRESS

University Printing House, Cambridge CB2 8BS, United Kingdom

One Liberty Plaza, 20th Floor, New York, NY 10006, USA

477 Williamstown Road, Port Melbourne, VIC 3207, Australia

314-321, 3rd Floor, Plot 3, Splendor Forum, Jasola District Centre, New Delhi - 110025, India

79 Anson Road, #06-04/06, Singapore 079906

Cambridge University Press is part of the University of Cambridge.

It furthers the University's mission by disseminating knowledge in the pursuit of education, learning and research at the highest international levels of excellence.

www.cambridge.org
Information on this title: www.cambridge.org/9781107534582

© Jennifer Brick Murtazashvili 2016

First published 2016
First paperback edition 2018

A catalogue record for this publication is available from the British Library

Library of Congress Cataloging in Publication data
Names: Murtazashvili, Jennifer Brick, author.
Title: Informal order and the state in Afghanistan / Jennifer Brick Murtazashvili.
Description: New York, NY : Cambridge University Press, 2016. | Based on author's thesis (doctoral - University of Wisconsin-Madison, 2009) issued under title: The Microfoundations of State Building: Informal Institutions and Local Public Goods in Rural Afghanistan | Includes bibliographical references and index.
Identifiers: LCCN 2015042017 | ISBN 9781107113992 (Hardback)
Subjects: LCSH: Local government–Afghanistan. | Central-local government relations–Afghanistan. | Afghanistan–Politics and government–2001– | BISAC: POLITICAL SCIENCE / General.
Classification: LCC JS7442.2 .M87 2016 | DDC 320.8/409581–dc23 LC record available at http://lccn.loc.gov/2015042017

ISBN 978-1-107-11399-2 Hardback
ISBN 978-1-107-53458-2 Paperback

For my loves: Ilia, Leo, Zoe, and Eve

Contents

Contents   ix

Tables

Glossary

Many of the terms below are common among all languages spoken in Afghanistan. Some of the terms have their origin in a specific language, but are used by multiple groups in the country. Because the materials in the book are based primarily on vernacular sources, the spellings reflect such uses rather than standardized transliterations.

adat	Customary law
alaqadari	Sub-district
amir	Leader or Commander. Some Afghan monarchs used this title in lieu of *Shah*.
amir al-mominin	Lit. Commander of the Faithful (Arabic). A ruler who claims legitimacy to rule from divine authority.
arbab	Customary village leader
aylaq	Pasture land used during spring/summer (lit. 'summer settlement')
Bibi haji	Female who has completed pilgrimage to Mecca
deh	Village
gozar	Neighborhood or settlement
Haji	Muslim who has completed pilgrimage to Mecca
hambastagi	Solidarity
Harakat (Harakat-e Islami-yi Afghanistan)	A Shia political party aligned with the Northern Alliance (Dari, lit. 'Islamic Movement of Afghanistan)
hashar/ashar	Collective, voluntary community labor

Hezb-e Islami	Islamist party in Afghanistan led by Gulbuddin Hekmatyar. Active in anti-Soviet, anti-Communist resistance (Dari, lit. 'Islamic Party')
imam	Formally trained religious leader
jalasa	Meeting
Jamiat-e Islami	Political party that fought the Soviets during the anti-Soviet jihad, part of the Northern Alliance. Led by Burhanuddin Rabbani (Dari., lit. 'Islamic Society.')
jerib	Islamic measure of land used in Afghanistan
jihadi	A person who fought against the Soviet invasion of Afghanistan
jirga	Customary village council, tribal council (Pashto, lit. 'circle')
jizya	Tax assessed on non-Muslims living under Muslim rule
kalantar	Customary village leader, elder (lit. 'the biggest')
Karbalayi	Shia who has completed pilgrimage to Shia holy city of Karbala, Iraq
karez	Customary irrigation system
kelay	Village (Pashto)
Khalq	Faction of the People's Democratic Party of Afghanistan (lit. 'people' or 'masses')
Khalqi	Follower of the *Khalq* faction
khan	Historically a large landowner or tribal leader. In some contemporary contexts, a khan is simply a village leader rather than a large landowner or tribal leader.
Loya Jirga	National-level council of customary leaders (Pashto, lit. grand council)
madhab	School of Islamic religious interpretation
madrasa	Religious school
mahalla	Neighborhood
mahram	Title given to male escort (a relative) who accompanies a female in public. Taliban required that all women leaving their homes be accompanied by a mahram.
majlis	Council
malang	Wandering mystical Islamic preacher
malik	Customary village leader; sometimes Pashtun clan leader
maliya-ye mutaraqi	Tax enforced by Daud in 1970s (Dari, lit. 'progressive tax')
manteqa	Region or collection of villages (Dari)

maraka	Meeting
mardomi shura	Community council (Dari, lit. 'People's council)
mardikar	Day laborer
mashran	Elders (Pashto)
mawlawi	Religious teacher or scholar
mehmankhana	A receiving room for guests
Meshrano Jirga	Upper house of Afghan National Assembly, also name for council of elders in a village (Pashto, lit. Council of Elders)
moween	Deputy leader
mir	Leader (equivalent to malik)
mirab	Customary manager of water resources
mujahid	A *jihadi*. A person who fought against the Soviet invasion of Afghanistan
mujahideen	Plural of *mujahid*
mullah	Village religious leader
musaseh	Organization; Term used to describe non-governmental organizations (NGOs) (lit. organization/institution)
muslehin	Local third-party negotiator
mu-ye safidan	Elders (lit. white hairs)
nahia	Neighborhood
namayenda	Customary village leader (lit. representative)
oq soqol	Elder (Uzbek) (lit. 'white beard')
padshah	King
Parcham	Faction of People's Democratic Party of Afghanistan (lit. 'flag' or 'banner')
Parchami	Member of *Parcham* faction of PDPA
Pashtunwali	Pashtun tribal law
pir	Sufi religious leader
qarya	Village
qaryadar	Customary village leader
qawm	Tribe, clan, or ethnic group. Could also mean area of geographic origin. Most important signifier of social identity in Afghanistan; has flexible meaning. In some context means ethnic group (between two people of different groups); among people of same ethnic group, but two different tribes, signifies tribe; among people of the same tribe, signifies sub-tribe.
qawmi qhura	Village or tribal council
qazi	Islamic judge (can also be state judge)
qishlaq	Village (lit. 'winter settlement')
rais	Leader
rawaj	Customary law

rish safidan	Elders (Dari, lit. 'white beards')
sadaqa	Charitable contribution as prescribed by Islam
sayed	Individual claiming relations to the Prophet Muhammad
shariat	Islamic law
shaykh	Man respected for religious training or knowledge, Sufi leader
shura	Council
Shura-ye Enkeshafi Mahalli	Community Development Council (CDC) (Dari)
shura-ye mahal	Council of neighborhoods (Dari)
Shura-ye Nazar	Title given to coalition of anti-Soviet commanders, mostly from Northern, Central, and Western Afghanistan, led by field commander Ahmad Shah Masoud. In English, commonly referred to as the Northern Alliance (Dari, lit. 'Supervisory Council').
shura-ye rish safidan/ shura-ye mu-ye safidan	Council of elders (Dari)
shura-ye ulama	Council of religious scholars, leaders (Dari)
spinzheri/spingeri	Elders (Pashto, lit. 'white beards')
tanzim	Refers to one of the seven Afghan political parties (mujahideen factions) that received funding from the United States through Pakistani intermediaries to fight the Soviet Union in the 1980s (lit. 'organization').
tazkera	Government issued identification card
ulama	Religious scholars
Wahdat (Hezb-e Wahdat-e Islami Afghanistan)	Political party and anti-Soviet mujahideen faction that represents Hazaras
wak	Oath
wakil	Customary village leader (lit. 'representative')
Wahhabi	Individual who ascribes to the conservative Wahhabi Islamic madhab, which has its origins in Saudi Arabia
wali	Provincial governor (in some instances a village leader)
waqf	Islamic endowment
wilayat	Province
Wolesi Jirga	Lower house of Afghan National Assembly (lit. 'House of the People')
woluswal	District governor
woluswali	District government administration
zamindar	Land owner

Acronyms

ANDS	Afghan National Development Strategy
CDC	Community Development Council
CSO	Central Statistics Office
DCC	District Coordinating Council
DDA	District Development Assembly
GIRoA	Government of the Islamic Republic of Afghanistan
I-ANDS	Interim Afghanistan National Development Strategy
IDLG	Independent Directorate of Local Governance
INGO	International NGO
MAIL	Ministry of Agriculture, Irrigation, and Livestock
MoI	Ministry of Interior
MRRD	Ministry of Rural Rehabilitation and Development
NATO	North Atlantic Treaty Organization
NGO	Non-Governmental Organization
NRVA	National Rural Vulnerability Assessment
PDPA	People's Democratic Party of Afghanistan
PRT	Provincial Reconstruction Team
NSP	National Solidarity Program
UN	United Nations
UNDP	United Nations Development Program
USAID	United States Agency for International Development

I do not wish to trouble my readers with too much detail, but the book would be incomplete if I omitted any information as to the many ways in which progress has been made during my reign. The fact is, that so little really accurate information about Afghanistan is possessed by the world generally, that very much that I shall tell them will be perfectly new, and heard of for the first time. It is plain to me that some foreigners who have visited Kabul from time to time have given the world false impressions, by posing as great authorities on Afghan affairs, internal and external. I am very often amused by reading articles written by them, because it is quite evident that they have never approached the borders of Afghanistan nearer than 500 miles. It is therefore necessary that I should give true information, if not in detail, yet as much and as varied as possible. My time is very fully occupied, but I will spare a little for this purpose from my numerous duties and engagements.

– Abdur Rahman Khan, Afghanistan's king from 1880 to 1901, in his
autobiography *The Life of Abdur Rahman, Amir of Afghanistan*

The small-holding peasants form an enormous mass whose members live in similar conditions but without entering into manifold relations with each other. Their mode of production isolates them from one another instead of bringing them into mutual intercourse. The isolation is furthered by France's poor means of communication and the poverty of the peasants. Their field of production, the small holding, permits no division of labor in its cultivation, no application of science, and therefore no multifariousness of development, no diversity of talent, no wealth of social relationships. Each individual peasant family is almost self-sufficient, directly produces most of its consumer needs, and thus acquires its means of life more through an exchange with nature than in intercourse with society. A small holding, the peasant and his family; beside it another small holding, another peasant and another family. A few score of these constitute a village, and a few score villages constitute a department. Thus the great mass of the French nation is formed by the simple addition of homonymous magnitudes, much as potatoes in a sack form a sack of potatoes ... Insofar as there is merely a local interconnection among these small-holding peasants, and the identity of their interests forms no community, no national bond, and no political organization among them, they do not constitute a class. They are therefore incapable of asserting their class interest in their own name, whether through a parliament or a convention. They cannot represent themselves, they must be represented.

– Karl Marx, *The Eighteenth Brumaire of Louis Napoleon*

Acknowledgments

This was never supposed to be a book solely on Afghanistan. As someone who had spent many years in former Soviet Central Asia, I began exploring the possibilities of doing research in Afghanistan because I was interested in placing Central Asia back into comparative context with its neighbors. As the post-2001 Government of Afghanistan began to take shape, its approach to local and community governance – from the second-hand accounts I had read – appeared to be innovative. Political events in the region moved faster than the flexibility of my research design and the comparative project, which was to look at Afghanistan, Uzbekistan, and Tajikistan, never came to fruition. Visa problems resulting from political events in Uzbekistan stymied these efforts. Once-eager funders pulled the plug on research in Afghanistan just weeks before my intended departure, unwilling to accept liability for the risk such research entails. The obstacles I encountered quickly translated into possibilities. These opportunities would never have happened without the support and assistance of so many people all over the globe.

I am grateful for the openness and warmth of hundreds of Afghan families who let me speak to them as part of this project. Doing this research required knocking on the doors of hundreds of strangers in dozens of villages in rural Afghanistan. Amazingly, I can't recall a single interview request being turned down. Such a high response rate is unthinkable any other place. Not only did families open up their doors, they were willing to spend hours sharing very personal information about their lives during conflict. They also shared a relentless hope for the future. Afghan government officials at the national, provincial, and district levels were similarly generous.

This project was the product of the outstanding training I received at the Department of Political Science at the University of Wisconsin–Madison where the dissertation upon which this book developed. My dissertation chair, Melanie Manion showed me the enormous power in applying the insights of formal institutional analysis to informal institutions. She has also served as a role model and friend. I am eternally grateful for her wisdom and the endless time she put into shaping this project. Scott Gehlbach provided patient but rigorous guidance and always found new insights hidden in my own evidence that I had not considered. Ed Friedman, Dave Weimer, Tamir Moutafa, and Dan Bromley made enormous contributions to shaping the argument. Mitra Sharafi and Marc Galanter shared insight into customary law in South Asia. Asifa Quraishi guided me through the intricacies of Islamic Law. Fellow grad students Marc Ratkovic and Meina Cai also read drafts and provided feedback on my empirical models. Donald Downs served as an unfailing mentor during my years in Madison. Without him, Madison would have been a far less interesting place to call home.

Support for this project was provided by several organizations. Field research was supported by the Afghanistan Research and Evaluation Unit (AREU) with financial support from the Japanese International Cooperation Agency (JICA). Short-term trip while a graduate student at the University of Wisconsin–Madison were supported by the Graduate School and the Bradley Foundation. Several subsequent follow-up trips were supported by the Center for Global Studies at the University of Pittsburgh, Democracy International (DI), and the United States Agency for International Development (USAID). I am grateful for feedback on this research during presentations at the University of Wisconsin–Madison, Yale University, the University of Michigan, American University, Indiana University, the University of Pittsburgh, and Australian National University.

David Altus Garner kindly shared with me the network of friends and contacts he amassed during the almost fifty years he has been working on Afghanistan. David has been an extraordinary mentor, guide, and friend who gave me tremendous support during months of sometimes grueling fieldwork in Afghanistan. David also introduced me to Minister Mir Sediq and his energetic wife Fatima who, by chance, were my next-door neighbors in Kabul. David, Mir, Fatima and the rest of their family cared for me as a member of their own while I was so far away from mine. Without David's extraordinary efforts on my behalf, I never would have met those groups who ultimately supported this research. In addition to his friendship and support, he has been a constant constructive critic and source of encouragement.

I am also particularly grateful to friends and colleagues at AREU who gave me the opportunity to use data I collected for a research project funded through them for my own work. Data for this project were collected by an extraordinary team of committed Afghan colleagues at AREU. Both the design of the research and the collection process was a truly collaborative effort. Many of the ideas in this book reflect their keen insights. Ghulam Sakhi Frozish served as a senior research assistant who worked closely with me to design, field test, and craft interview guides. He also worked tirelessly to mentor our colleagues on interview skills and provided unparalleled leadership throughout our fieldwork. Nasreen Quraishi, Abdul Hadi Sadat, Hussein Wafaey, Gulalai Karimi, and Fauzia Rahimi all spent months at a time away from their families dedicated to this project. They endured difficult conditions and traveled to unfamiliar places and in some cases, risked their safety and security for this research. One of the real thrills of this research was triangulating with this group of enormously talented and diverse colleagues. After days of work in the field, we would return to provincial centers only to disagree about how to interpret results. These disagreements led to return visits to communities to help figure out the "truth." Despite hardship of long months away from home in distant communities, we shared laughter and learning. This book is very much a reflection of their curiosity, sincerity, patience, and magical abilities to put people at ease during interviews that often dealt with very sensitive topics.

Hamish Nixon and Paul Fishstein deserve special recognition for bringing me into the AREU family and entrusting me with this research project. I benefited enormously from their guidance and wisdom. Paula Kantor, who was killed by the Taliban in a violent attack just as this book was coming to press, served as a wonderful colleague, role model, and mentor whose dedication to research will live on in the hundreds of researchers she trained in Afghanistan (both foreign and Afghan). Deborah Smith at AREU went above and beyond her call of duty to help me organize and plan fieldwork, hire and manage researchers, and deal with the challenges and blessings that work in Afghanistan entails. At AREU, Adam Pain, Mamiko Saito, Asif Karimi, Ibrahim Mahmoudi, Abdul Shakir, Zalmai Sultani, Sonita Sahab, Nasrullah Baqi, as well as Nazir Khamosh also provided support to this project. Brave and patient drivers labored through long hours in hot, dusty, and sometimes dangerous conditions to get us to distant villages over mighty mountain passes; these include Luqman, Sayedpadshah, Turab, Faroq, Shaqib, Ghulam Ali, and Nazir.

George Varughese at the Asia Foundation in Kabul shared with me the Asia Foundation survey data used in this book. Andrew Beath at the World Bank shared with me the NRVA survey data. Both George and Andrew helped me think through many analytical issues I confronted while doing fieldwork. Glenn Cowan, Jed Ober, Terry Hoverter, Daniel Murphy, Rachel de Santos, and Min Zaw Oo, at Democracy International also provided support for several return research trips to Afghanistan in 2011 and 2012.

Several individuals in the Government of the Islamic Republic of Afghanistan played an important role in shaping and guiding this research. In particular, Mir Wais Barmak, former Minister of Rural Rehabilitation and Development provided guidance on the initial design of the research and shared comments and critiques at its conclusion. Asif Rahimi, former Minister of Agriculture, Irrigation, and Livestock also provided feedback on preliminary findings. Barna Karimi, former Deputy Director of the Independent Directorate for Local Government, opened up his agency to me in search of data and interviews. Special thanks to former government servants Daoud Yaqub and Aarya Nijat.

I owe a particular debt to Jan McArthur, former Country Director of Internews in Afghanistan, for supporting me during pre-fieldwork trips to Afghanistan. Paul Lundberg, formerly the country manager for the United Nations Development Program/Assistance to Sub-national Governance Program (UNDP/ASGP) shared his encyclopedic knowledge of local governance issues around the globe as well as a fascination with self-governance. Likewise, J. David Stanfield, a researcher from the Land Tenure Center at the University of Wisconsin–Madison (who I met in Kabul of all places), guided me through the complex land issues in the country and helped me place them in comparative perspective. R.J. Ennis, Megan Asdorian, Paul King, Sean Gralton, Demetrios Karoutsos, and M. Yasin Safar also provided friendship during fieldwork.

Colleagues and friends at University of Pittsburgh most notably Kerry Ban, Sabina Dietrick, Bob Hayden, John Keeler, Pierre Landry, David Montgomery, Lou Picard, Scott Morgenstern, and Phil Williams provided vital feedback and support as I drafted this manuscript. I am also grateful to graduate students Torsten Jochem, Leslie Marshall, and Ronald Alfaro Redondo for comments on the manuscript.

Anthropologists working on Afghanistan over the course of the past several decades have taught us more about the country than any other group of scholars. I am deeply indebted to Thomas Barfield who kindly read through the manuscript, as well as Alessandro Monsutti, and David Katz who were kind enough to help me navigate this perilous terrain.

It was an enormous honor to present earlier versions of this project at Elinor Ostrom's Policy Workshop at Indiana University just a year before she passed away. The project benefitted enormously from her insights. Her refreshing approach to the world – so grounded in deep understandings of local realities yet at the same time motivated by theory – influenced generations of social scientists.

At Cambridge University Press, I am thankful for the faith Lew is Bateman had in this project and his careful stewardship of the book. Shaun Vigil, Elda Granta, and Rachel Cox also guided the project along the way. Oxford University Press granted permission for portions of my previous article "Informal Federalism: Self-Governance and Power Sharing in Afghanistan." *Publius: The Journal of Federalism* 44, no. 2 (2014): 324–43, to appear here. Replication files of the statistical analysis in the book can be found at: http://jen.murtazashvili.org/ioatsia. Of course, all errors are my own.

None of this would have been possible without the wisdom and love of my parents, Geraldine and Stanley Cutler, who always encouraged me to learn about faraway places and pursue my fascination with languages and politics. I can't begin to thank them enough. A special thanks to my brothers and sisters who worked to assuage the natural concerns of my parents during my long months away.

Finally, this book could never have been imagined without the love and patience of my husband, Ilia. He tolerated long months apart where we could not even speak as I was working in very remote areas. He never blinked when I told him that I had to go back to Afghanistan for two follow-up trips while pregnant with our second child and when she came into the world, supported me to return to Afghanistan to collect more data. He read drafts of this book and watched our kids while I worked to finish the manuscript.

In the short time between the completion of the dissertation and its transformation into a book manuscript, we were blessed to welcome our three beautiful children into this world: Leo, Zoe, and Eve. This book is dedicated to my family. I hope that one day my children will be able to visit Afghanistan as a country in peace and experience the enormous kindness shared with me by countless strangers who were so willing to share with me their hopes for the future.

Preface

On Saturday mornings in a district in northern Afghanistan the district governor meets with customary representatives from villages in his district. At such meetings these representatives, called *qaryadars* in this region, bring up issues of community concern. They discuss needs for public goods and services, such as clinics and teachers, and talk about conflicts boiling in their communities that beg for outside mediation. Some of them discuss threats from the Taliban insurgency. The district governor, or *woluswal* in the local language, listens to these concerns and informs the qaryadars, who are appointed by their communities to represent interests of villagers to the state, of visits by NATO officials or about aid projects that are scheduled to commence. The most pressing concern of the woluswal is security. To survive, both politically and physically, he requires information from the qaryadars about events in their communities. Are the Taliban traveling through the area? Are villagers harboring insurgents? Are there community conflicts that may spill over and threaten district stability?

As one such meeting ended on a hot Saturday morning in June, the qaryadars poured out of a room in the district administration building. Among them was a middle-aged woman who was deeply engaged in conversation with the men. She introduced herself as Fatima.[1] It turns out that she was the qaryadar of her community.

Fatima invited me to visit her village. She wanted to show me what she had been able to accomplish in the past few years. Although her community only recently selected her to be its "official" representative she had been very active in local affairs for years. In her position, she was responsible for resolving

---

[1] This is a pseudonym used to protect her anonymity. All identities in this book – of both research sites and individuals interviewed with the exception of some public officials – are similarly concealed.

community disputes, handling small bureaucratic issues that involve the state, and representing community interests to the woluswal.

Upon visiting her home it was clear Fatima was not wealthy, although she was not among the poorest in her community. There was nothing remarkable about her home, except for one thing: her bright pink *mehmankhana*, the room used to receive guests. In this room, she greeted men and women from her community who approached her with problems. On the day I visited with her I saw mostly men visit her home. Some sought her assistance so that they could receive their government-issued *tazkera* (identification cards). Others had questions about how to register their customary land titles with district authorities. Her husband, who was always close by, appeared to be a bit older than Fatima. She was assertive and strong, while her husband was far more soft-spoken.

When I told Fatima that I was there to do research, she could not quite process my request. Like many others I had interviewed over the past several months, Fatima assumed that I was an aid worker conducting an assessment for a new project for her village. Regardless of attempts to explain that my research would not result in material rewards or projects for her community, she took the occasion of my visit to show me all the important unresolved infrastructure issues in her village. She also sought to show off her achievements.

Her most pressing concern was the construction of asphalt roads. At one point, she jumped up on a rusty Soviet-era tractor and showed me how she had flattened mud paths in the community to prepare them for paving. It was beyond the financial means of the community to afford the asphalt, but she said everyone could help with construction.

After the village tour, I spent several hours in her mehmankhana learning about her family history and how she came to be the qaryadar. She said that her husband had once held the position and was a "respected" person in the community. The community held her family in high regard as fair brokers, a reputation largely gained by virtue of the fact that her deceased father was a revered religious leader who had counseled almost every family in the village. After her father's death, both men and women began approaching her to resolve the kinds of issues her father once handled. As she was able to mediate conflicts and organize to achieve small things, it became increasingly clear to the community that Fatima was a doer. Eventually, the community suggested that Fatima serve as the qaryadar and move out of her husband's shadow. I sensed that she had been serving in this position behind her husband's name for many years.

As qaryadar, her time was spent resolving domestic and other community disputes, working alongside village mullahs to resolve inheritance disputes and other issues. She also spoke about her relationship with local elders, called *shura-ye rish safidan* ("council of white beards"), that met on occasion to resolve more tenuous issues requiring broader community consensus. Her proudest accomplishment, she said, was convincing the government to connect an electricity line into the community off a nearby power grid. Gaining access to the grid required more substantial capital investment than anything her community could afford on its own.

Fatima said that her work in the community did not begin when her neighbors selected her to be the qaryadar. She had been active in the community for the past twenty-five years. Unlike many of her neighbors who had fled to Kabul or neighboring Pakistan or Iran after the Soviet invasion or during Taliban rule in the 1990s, Fatima stayed in her village. When the Taliban controlled the government in Kabul, they did not allow women to leave their homes without accompaniment of a male relative or *mahram*. During this period, she taught women how to embroider as a way to keep their minds occupied away from thinking of the pains and loss of war. After the fall of the Taliban government, she ran for a seat in the new National Assembly in 2005 but lost to another female candidate (there is a 25 percent female quota in the National Assembly). According to Fatima, a wealthy man "bought" votes in the area for his own wife. During our conversations, she cast suspicion on the country's new class of female politicians who she felt represented a new urban elite. This emergent class often spoke English and knew how to handle themselves in donor-sponsored soirees in Kabul or in her provincial capital, but they often had difficulty relating to rural women. Fatima lost the election but was not discouraged.

From spending just a couple of days with Fatima, it was clear why her community selected her to lead and represent them to the outside world. Her joyous energy was infections. Fatima believed that by changing her community she could change the country. Her politics were not ideological, but instead based on a conviction that her community work could inspire others in her district – and eventually the country as a whole. She did not think of herself as a female leader. In her eyes, she was just a qaryadar.

Fatima was a paradox: a female who climbed the ranks of "traditional" authority.

A few years later, I returned to her district to catch up. The security situation in the area had deteriorated significantly, so I was not able to travel to her home. The woluswal of her district arranged for Fatima to visit his office, at my request, so that we could have a safe place to meet. I was excited to learn about all that Fatima had achieved during the couple of years since we had first met.

As I was discussing local affairs with the woluswal, Fatima entered the office. Her smile remained unchanged, but the spirit behind it seemed different. After exchanging greetings, the woluswal brusquely excused himself. He said he had another meeting to attend. As soon as he left the room, tears began to swell in her eyes. She said that I would not believe what had happened to her since we last met. She was right.

Several months before this meeting, she was traveling from her village in the north of Afghanistan and over the Hindu Kush into Kabul – an eight-hour drive in good weather. She had hired a driver from her village (a distant relative) that was to take her. Immediately before entering the Salang Tunnel that connects the north of the country to the rest of Afghanistan, Fatima and her driver stopped to have lunch at a famous restaurant that is well known for serving kebab with a wonderful mountain view.

After they had eaten, Fatima and her driver returned to their car. At that point, she said, two men who were hanging out inside the restaurant approached them as they were leaving. They forcibly separated Fatima from her driver. She said she was "beaten" and "robbed." I did not ask about the details. I simply let Fatima tell her story, which gushed as swiftly as her tears.

After several hours of begging for her life, the assailants bound Fatima's hands and legs and threw her in the trunk of a car. They told her they were taking her to a safe house.

Instead, they threw Fatima into a nearby river.

After plunging into the water, Fatima believed death was imminent. She said, "I prayed to Allah. I asked, 'Why is this happening to me? I have worked all my life for others. I have taken my family inheritance and spent it on the people in my community. I have never asked for a single penny of help and have just given to others. Why is this happening to me?'"

Miraculously, she said she was able to position her body so that she could float down the river. She floated until eventually her arms caught on a branch. As soon as she stopped, she said she began screaming for her life. Thankfully, there was a village nearby. Instead of saving her immediately, she said, the villagers called the Afghan National Police who patrolled this strategic area around the tunnel. She was shocked that the villagers had not immediately come to her aid upon hearing her pleas. She said they were afraid that she was with the Taliban or an insurgent group.

After an hour or so, the police rescued her. Exhausted and cold, they immediately took her to the famous mountaintop restaurant from where she was kidnapped. As she reentered the restaurant, she said, she found the assailants who looked as if they had just seen a ghost. They were shocked that she had survived. After she identified them, the police arrested her attackers.

A few moments later, Fatima learned the assailants had killed her driver. They confessed that they were motivated by an opportunity to steal his car. Upon returning to her village, Fatima incurred the wrath of her driver's family. They blamed her for what had happened. Her troubles, however, did not end on that day.

The criminals who assaulted her and killed her driver were allied with a criminal gang from the area around the Salang. Although they were in jail, Fatima received regular death threats from the criminals and their associates. They demanded she recant her story and pay a bribe to the police to ensure their release. If she did not heed their warnings, they wrote that they would kill her and her family. Not knowing what to do, Fatima used the opportunity of our meeting to ask for help. Feeling utterly helpless, I discussed her case with several policymakers in her region, including with a United Nations office and with officials in Kabul. The only solution the international community could offer was an application for political asylum abroad.

Asylum was not a solution for Fatima. She had no desire to leave Afghanistan. She wanted to continue to serve the people in her village.

The story of Fatima, the female qaryadar, on its face appears to be atypical of Afghan politics. A female village leader is almost unheard of in popular accounts of the country. In fieldwork I conducted across six provinces, she was the only female village leader I had heard about, although the provincial government official I spoke to in her province said there are at least seven that he worked with in that province alone.

Although female representatives may be uncommon, I found the legitimacy of customary authorities who lead communities to be almost ubiquitous. Like many other qaryadars – or *maliks, wakils, arbabs, namayendas,* as they are called in different parts of the country – Fatima was selected by her community through a more or less deliberative process to represent their interests to the government and the outside world. Her position is permanent as long as she is willing to respect the will of the people in her community. This means that she should not collude with the government against the interest of her constituents. She should not steal, cheat, or charge excessively for services she provides. If she comes from a wealthier family (as she does), then she should not charge villagers at all for the small services she provides liaising with the state. It is her responsibility to advocate on behalf of members of her community to neighboring villages and to outsiders.

Fatima did not come to power through the help of an international aid program or a non-governmental organization (NGO) seeking to promote "gender empowerment" in rural Afghanistan. She did not attain her reputation with the assistance of well-intentioned foreigners. Since 2001, it has proven almost impossible for outside actors such as NGOs, aid programs, or even the Afghan government to establish the sort of legitimacy Fatima clearly had among her constituents.[2]

Her story illustrates the evolution and persistence of customary governance in rural Afghanistan. Historically, customary governance was the exclusive purview of men. In some parts of the country, large landholders known as *khans* once dominated such authority. Although Afghanistan never had the scope of feudalism present in Europe or even neighboring states of Pakistan or Iran – landholdings have always been small and relatively equally distributed – in some instances, land and power were concentrated in villages. Yet as the patronage-based khan system declined in significance, it left village-based customary authority – which is not always based on patronage, but rather consent – as a main source of

---

[2] Julie Billaud, *Kabul Carnival: Gender Politics in Postwar Afghanistan* (Philadelphia:University of Pennsylvania Press, 2015).

governance in rural parts of the country. In my fieldwork, informants in rural areas described how customary governance had become far more participatory and inclusive than it had ever been, as Fatima's story vividly reminds us. Through oral histories, I understood that it had evolved during decades of war in most areas to become more responsive to the demands of the citizens it serves.

Although it had evolved to address the new demands of citizens who seemed no longer tolerant to be subjects to a distant monarch in Kabul, customary authority is neither a perfect system of governance, nor is it completely democratic. It is by no means an ideal form of social control. In several villages I visited people felt their current or recent customary leaders were ineffective, biased in the way they resolved disputes, or machinated with government officials or local commanders to steal international assistance planned for their communities. In most communities where representatives told of stories where customary leaders no longer worked on behalf of the community, citizens would eventually replace them with someone else. Sometimes, they had to wait to find the right opportunity to do this, mainly to avoid shaming the incumbent too badly. In some communities where local leadership was captured by such interests, customary leadership dissimulated and operated underground. Of course, women remain largely missing from such governance. From my research, I found that while these seemingly "old" organizations had remained in place (although sometimes their names had changed), citizen expectations about how these organizations were to perform had changed dramatically as a result of war.

Fatima's story illustrates the evolution of such authority, but also underscores its fundamental limitations. Although Fatima and others in her position were able to promote order and solve a wide range of problems within communities, there are many important issues that a single village leader – even with enormous constituent support – cannot solve alone. Large-scale security threats from neighboring provinces, like the criminal gangs tormenting Fatima, are the most common example. Similarly, provision of costly public goods, such as building and staffing clinics or constructing an electricity grid, are beyond the means of a single village. Such goods typically require cooperation of several communities or external intervention to produce. Finally, some customary leaders colluded with local warlords and commanders, extracting a heavy toll on citizens. Although customary organizations may govern a village effectively, they are not a panacea.

Yet the persistence and resilience of customary order might surprise some observers. In conducting fieldwork, I did not expect to find such broad effectiveness of customary organizations at the village level. Many scholars and journalists reporting on post-2001 Afghanistan described how "traditional" structures in rural Afghanistan had withered away during thirty years of war. Therefore, I was truly surprised to find them so active in village after village.

After weeks of fieldwork across the country became months, I began to realize that the observers who described the demise of customary order were half-right. Many of the larger-scale customary leaders, such as khans, were no longer as important as they once were. However, a khan typically operates at a level above the village, imposing order over wide swaths of territory. Furthermore, khans were never ubiquitous, but were a convenient stereotype used to describe "traditional" authority. Did the decline of the khan system lead to anarchy and disorder?

As it turns out, as the khan system may have weakened in some communities, customary leaders found a renewed sense of importance at the village level because they filled a governance deficit that widened during decades of conflict. Despite heavy assistance to build the Afghan state after 2001, the state never extended to rural areas. Thus, the customary system appeared to strengthen during the precise period when state-building assistance reached its apogee. In fact, despite ethnic and regional differences I found the organization of customary village governance to be quite similar in communities across the country.[3] Most villages are governed by a constellation of three informal political organizations: village councils (shuras, jirgas, or simply "elders"), village representatives (qaryadars, maliks, and several other titles), and religious leaders (mullahs). These organizations have evolved over time, adapting to deal with new problems and taking advantage of new technologies of governance. In several villages I visited, for example, villagers used ballot boxes and secret ballots to select their customary leaders.

Despite their ubiquity, in the early days after the fall of the Taliban government in 2001, it remained common for outsiders – the Western-trained senior Afghan ministry officials in Kabul and members of the international donor community who came to bring the state to rural areas – to assume that customary and other forms of self-governance had withered. This was due to the fact that many of these leaders had been killed over the past thirty years and – as I found – villagers were no longer using titles they used before the war to describe their systems of self-governance. The death of an individual or the change in title of a customary representative, did not result in the complete obliteration of a system of self-governance and a set of social norms that enabled it. In some parts of the country, villages discarded old honorifics and began describing their leaders as namayenda ("representative"), wakil ("representative"), or rais ("leader") in lieu of the old titles such as khan or arbab. One of the contributions of this book is describing how the "old" system

---

[3] In his seminal analysis of grassroots political life in Afghanistan during the anti-Soviet conflict, Olivier Roy hints at this possibility by noting that due to the breakdown in the khan system among some Pashtun groups, political life in the "north and the south are becoming more alike, since the disappearance of the aristocracy and the most powerful khan has left behind individuals of moderate but not excessive influence." See *Islam and Resistance in Afghanistan* (Cambridge: Cambridge University Press, 1990), 152.

regenerated itself after the fall of the Taliban, albeit under new titles, as well as the ongoing significance of the customary system of governance.

In the first few years after 2001, another narrative took shape among some in the international donor community and among some Afghan urban elites. With a desire to promote "Millennium Development Goals" and gender equality, this group believed that customary governance was alive and well and that its continued presence served as a threat to modernization and democracy. For these groups, Western NGOs and their aid programs became important vehicles for social change from the bottom-up. There is no better poster child for the injustice of customary governance in Afghanistan than horror stories of women being traded as chattel to resolve blood feuds or the execution of women who had dishonored their families, ostensibly under the Pashtun tribal code *Pashtunwali*, which guides decisions in many communities. Often motivated by these stories of gendered atrocities, many in the international donor community – especially in the first five years after the fall of the Taliban government – believed that Afghanistan could only achieve a fighting chance at prosperity by lessening the influence of customary justice dispensed in villages.[4] Traditional leaders became synonymous with Taliban-style repression of women despite the fact that customary leaders were among the first targets of the Taliban as they seized new terrain. As a result, there are no shortage of studies explaining how gender relations can be improved by replacing traditional decision-making with new forms of democratic decision-making.[5]

After five years of the international effort, a new narrative emerged from rural Afghanistan. Liberal peacebuilding in Afghanistan was not producing stability or democracy, but instead a resurgence of the Taliban. Some scholars argued that this was due to a profound neglect of the customary system of self-governance that existed throughout rural Afghanistan.[6] Some foreign soldiers serving in the countryside explained the failure of military and development

---

[4] Valentine M Moghadam, "Patriarchy, the Taleban, and Politics of Public Space in Afghanistan," *Women's Studies International Forum* 25, no. 1 (2002): 19–31; World Bank, *Afghanistan: National Reconstruction and Poverty Reduction, the Role of Women in Afghanistan's Future* (Washington, DC: The World Bank, 2005); United Nations Assistance Mission in Afghanistan and United Nations High Commissioner for Human Rights, "Harmful Traditional Practices and Implementation of the Law on Elimination of Violence against Women in Afghanistan" (Kabul, 2010).

[5] For example see, Andrew Beath, Fotini Christia, and Ruben Enikolopov, "Empowering Women through Development Aid: Evidence from a Field Experiment in Afghanistan," *American Political Science Review* 107, no. 3 (2013): 540–57; Chona Echavez, "Does Women's Participation in the National Solidarity Programme Make a Difference in Their Lives? A Case Study in Kabul Province" (Kabul: Afghanistan Research and Evaluation Unit, 2012).

[6] Ali Wardak, "Building a Post-War Justice System in Afghanistan," *Crime, Law and Social Change* 41, no. 4 (2004): 319–41; M. Nazif Shahrani, "Afghanistan's Alternatives for Peace, Governance and Development: Transforming Subjects to Citizens and Rulers to Civil Servants," The Afghanistan Papers (Waterloo, Ontario: The Center for International Governance Innovation, 2009).

strategies by presenting a picture of a neglected "traditional" authority that they argued should serve as the primary ally of NATO in Afghanistan. In their view, maliks and other "traditional" leaders had suffered terribly at the hands of the Taliban and mujihideen groups over the past decades. Rather than obstacles to state consolidation, they saw traditional authority not as an enemy of the state but an important source of defense against a growing Taliban insurgency. Some in the U.S. military, due in part to the fact that its soldiers were serving in some of the most difficult rural terrain in the country, seemed to have a far more nuanced understanding of the realities of rural Afghan life than many humanitarians in the donor bubble of Kabul. For soldiers, understanding context was not simply a matter of furthering modernization or project object-ives, but was a matter of life or death. As they patrolled villages, they described the centrality of customary leaders that many Kabul-based modernizers who focused primarily on forging national-level institutions, seemed to ignore. Soldiers in the field began setting up blogs and websites describing the import-ance of "tribes."

These soldiers on the ground helped inform a new U.S. counterinsurgency strategy that centered on the village. Unlike the work of many aid groups who intentionally set up parallel community structures so as to avoid being "cap-tured" by elders, soldiers began to engage directly with customary authority. The counterinsurgency mantra "clear, hold, build," meant that after villages had been cleared from insurgents and then held security for a given period, it was the job of the military together with aid contractors and local partners to build things for villagers, thus buying their loyalty to the state.[7] Like the NGOs before them, this military strategy hoped that service delivery would demon-strate to rural Afghans the gains to be had from supporting the state. Much of what was built once again came in the form of village-level infrastructure. U.S. and NATO strategy believed outsiders could create a legitimate Afghan gov-ernment by funding countless "shuras" to bring traditional leaders to the government. Military actors, however, repeated a similar diagnostic error that the NGOs had made: that hearts and minds in Afghanistan could be won through the provision of "community development" and that somehow "governance" implemented and funded by foreign aid organizations would somehow convince the people of Afghanistan to swear loyalty to the govern-ment in Kabul.[8] They also believed that fora of traditional leaders summoned and paid for by NATO would seem legitimate to citizens.

Both civilian and military efforts seeking to build the Afghan state treated such efforts as a technical problem by providing trainings to villagers on issues like community mobilization and procurement but seemingly failing to

---

[7] This approach to counterinsurgency strategy can be found in John Nagl et al., *The U.S. Army/ Marine Corps Counterinsurgency Field Manual* (Chicago: University of Chicago Press, 2007).

[8] For a superb, field-based account of such efforts see Malkasian, *War Comes to Garmser: Thirty Years of Conflict on the Afghan Frontier* (New York: Oxford University Press, 2013).

understand that efforts to extend the state into rural Afghanistan was an inherently political project.[9] The Afghan state had never in its history ruled villages directly, so it should be no surprise that efforts to "harmonize" the state even by the friendliest of Western NGO workers would be met with suspicion by citizens.

The chapters ahead demonstrate that many of the vital assumptions made by the international community, both by development agencies and military strategy, did not have a strong empirical foundation. Strong customary governance in Afghanistan did not mean a central state was unneeded or unwanted. In other words, the relationship between the state and customary order is not zero-sum. Although Afghanistan is often depicted as the "Wild West" where people seem to prefer disorder to intrusions by the state into their affairs, I found a more nuanced situation. In most of the country, there is demand for some state services, especially for larger-scale public goods and services that communities struggle to provide themselves. At the same time, self-organized customary organizations are often effective and responsive, providing an essential source of some public goods and services in the context of an otherwise weak state. Within their villages, however, most individuals I spoke with preferred less intrusion from the outside. This is not because rural Afghans reject centralized authority; rather, it is primarily because many of them have been subjected to some of the worst governments imaginable throughout their modern history.

More than a decade after state-building efforts in Afghanistan began in earnest, enormous changes swept Afghan society. More children had access to education than anytime in Afghan history. Disease rates and maternal mortality declined. Private enterprise began to flourish compared to its dismal state under the Taliban. Yet the goal of "state building" seemed more elusive than ever. In post-2001 Afghanistan, it was not clear who governed the countryside.

The question of local governance after 2001 was never settled because liberal peacebuilding and state-building efforts crowded out or delayed domestic debates concerning the role of the state in society.[10] Most informants I talked with were eager for access to some public goods and services provided by the state, but were not willing to sacrifice community autonomy as part of this bargain. Instead of helping communities with the things they cannot do well, vast assistance was channeled to the community level in an effort to either fill a "vacuum" of governance or replace "traditional" structures. At subsequent junctures, the international community recognized the importance of customary authority and momentarily sought to pump billions of dollars into "tribes"

---

[9] James Ferguson's classic book brings this issue to light in the context of World Bank projects in sub-Saharan Africa. See *The Anti-Politics Machine* (Minneapolis, MN: University of Minnesota Press, 1994).

[10] Jennifer Brick Murtazashvili, "Bad Medicine," *Central Asian Affairs* 2, no. 1 (2015): 10–34.

and "elders" creating enormous distortions as NATO forces and aid projects sought to strengthen society to fight a resurgent Taliban.[11] As aid projects came to villages, in all shapes and sizes, villages became a donor obsession. Yet according to my conversations with hundreds of people in rural Afghanistan, the demand for larger-scale public goods – goods that transcended individual communities – largely went unmet or was muddled through endless cycles of corruption at the hands of international donors, warlords, NGOs and their sub-contractors, and the state.

Commentators and some officials believed efforts to strengthen the state failed due to Afghan support for religious fundamentalists or because the medieval and "backwards" country has tribes and village elders who wish to live in the "stone ages."[12] In this view, foreigners and their ideas were unwanted, reflecting the perception that Afghanistan is the quintessential quagmire for foreign invaders. Thus, the failure of the state-building effort was not a failure of liberal peacebuilding, but because the people of Afghanistan are simply *ungovernable*.

This book shows that Afghanistan is neither ungoverned nor is it ungovernable. Although there are many reasons why liberal peacebuilding efforts fell short, primary among them is that such efforts made two contradictory assumptions about the nature of Afghanistan. First, some assumed the country was a tabula rasa and that after thirty years of war the country and its political institutions had to be completely rebuilt. A second – and contradictory – assumption is that traditional norms and values remained steadfast and that they must be replaced by "modern" democratic norms in order for the country to attain prosperity and peace. According to this second perspective, new political institutions needed to sweep away those that represented an archaic, traditional, and informal order.

Neither of these perspectives captures how Afghanistan is governed or what the vast majority of people I spoke to seemed to want from their government. The findings in the pages ahead suggest that rural Afghans desired a state that was strong enough to do a few things their communities cannot do on their own, such as provide health care, education, and national security, but they did not want the state to tell them how to live their lives, how to organize their families, or how to organize community life or politics. Most importantly, they seemed unwilling to sacrifice community autonomy for hollow promises made by a state widely perceived as corrupt and that – at no time in modern history – had a track record of true accountability. Yet the state that the Afghan

[11] David Kilcullen, *Out of the Mountains: The Coming Age of the Urban Guerrilla* (New York: Oxford University Press, 2013), 119; Wimpelmann, Torunn. 2013. "Nexuses of Knowledge and Power in Afghanistan: The Rise and Fall of the Informal Justice Assemblage." *Central Asian Survey* 32 (3): 406–22.
[12] Tom Coghlin, "Afghans Accuse Liam Fox of Racism; Karzai Angry at Reference to 'Broken 13th-Century Country,'" *The Times*, May 24, 2010.

government and international donors attempted to build took no account of such expectations. It was premised on the basis that provision of public goods and the extension of the state can win hearts and minds. At the height of the surge in 2010, the U.S. government sought to bring "government in a box" to areas contained by U.S. military forces. This was a recipe for disaster and a fundamental misunderstanding of how citizens believed the government could build its legitimacy. Most informants with whom I spoke sought a more limited government that they could approach when they demanded its services. In this view, government could build legitimacy not by demonstrating a capacity to provide services but instead by a brave capacity to constrain itself, tying its hands and serving as a fair broker in its dealings with citizens. Legitimacy could not be gained simply by service delivery, it had to be earned through trust: trust that mediation can be provided without prejudice or that officials would not collude to plunder the public purse.

This book analyzes how Afghanistan was governed during the period from the fall of the Taliban government in 2001 until the end of the Karzai government in 2014, proceeding from the bottom-up, focusing primarily on the years when fieldwork for this project was conducted (2006–08). It begins at the village level, exploring the conditions under which individuals in villages around the country organized their affairs in the absence of an effective state. This diagnostic approach goes beyond policy panaceas and examines sources of collective action within communities to understand what they can do well without external assistance (including aid and the state), while also highlighting the areas where such collective action fails to materialize.[13] It then proceeds upward, examining the capacity and limits of self-governance and demands for state intervention at three distinct levels of analysis: within villages, in relations between villages, and in relations between villages and the state.

While the substance of this book concerns issues of local governance, it also provides insight into how to conduct research in areas of conflict. The chapters rely on interviews, focus-group discussions, as well as field observations to develop case studies about village governance. The evidence is based on more than 300 original interviews and focus-groups in thirty-two villages across six provinces of Afghanistan as well as dozens of interviews in Kabul. These field visits were done without any security accompaniment. They were facilitated by several skilled Afghan researchers who traveled and partnered with me. During the course of the research, we interviewed government officials at all levels, customary leaders, randomly selected villagers, aid workers, and diplomats.

Fieldwork proved to be illuminating in ways that I could not have imagined. Like all researchers, I had expectations before entering the field. For five years

---

[13] This work thus builds upon the path-breaking work on collective action and local governance by Elinor Ostrom who advocated for a "diagnostic" approach to understanding human behavior. See Elinor Ostrom, "A Diagnostic Approach for Going beyond Panaceas," *Proceedings of the National Academy of Sciences of the United States of America* 104, no. 39 (2007): 15181–87.

prior to entering academia, I once served as an aid worker in former Soviet Central Asia. For three years, I managed democracy and community development projects for the USAID in Uzbekistan, where I previously served for two years as a Peace Corps Volunteer (in a Tajik-speaking community). When I initially approached this research, I was very enthusiastic about the prospects for community-based state-building efforts, as I had managed and designed similar projects in the region. I expected to find what I had read in so many reports drafted by international donors and NGOs – that "community-driven development (CDD)" led by donors had radically transformed the lives of villagers for the better. It was with optimism that I began to explore the sustainability of new donor-sponsored community-based councils in rural Afghanistan.

After piloting interview and focus-group discussions in a couple of communities in one district in Kabul Province, it became clear to me that many of my assumptions about the success and "transformative" nature of the programs that I had so enthusiastically supported were unfounded. More than anything, I was surprised to see the central role customary organizations played in the lives of so many in the areas around Kabul. This stood in stark contrast to the scholarly obituaries of such authority. If aid had not been as effective and if customary governance remained resilient in these areas so close to the seat of central government authority, then what would I find in the rest of the country where the ability of outsiders to implement projects was more daunting? Thus, the pilot phase served as a wakeup call to me, to revisit my own assumptions and biases.

After the pilot phase, I completely retooled the objectives of the research. Instead of focusing on aid projects and community-development schemes, I sought to understand the scope of collective action within villages in the absence of an effective state without assuming a central role of any particular actor. More generally, it became clear the research had to be driven by how Afghan villages are actually governed and not about the perils of aid and NGOs. Plenty has been written about aid and its failures, but little has been written about village governance. Despite the glowing donor reports that were being published in the early years after 2001 or news stories of a transformed Afghanistan, the people that I talked with by and large found these efforts distant and tangential to their daily lives. While I did not find aid projects had an enduring impact, customary organizations seemed to lie at the center of local governance in rural Afghanistan.

Just as with everything else in the country, "traditional authority" had not escaped thirty years of conflict unscathed. It too had evolved. It is my hope that the account in this book provides a fair and dispassionate account of this evolution of local governance.

I

Introduction

A strong state can defend its citizens while maintaining order among various levels of government. By this standard, Afghanistan has been a very weak state throughout most of its history. The central government has never extended its reach far into the countryside. By the time NATO wrapped up nearly fifteen years of combat operations in Afghanistan in 2014, the government was neither able to defend its citizens nor extend its writ to much of the countryside. Rather, government authority stopped – as it has for most of modern history – at the district or county level.

Despite state weakness, this book shows that there is governance in rural Afghanistan, although its origins lie outside of the formal apparatus of the state. Most order in rural Afghanistan arises within the confines of customary organizations at the village level. This book seeks to understand these self-governing organizations. Empirically, it uses fieldwork to show both the capacity and limitations of these self-governing organizations in rural Afghanistan. Theoretically, this book speaks to three general questions of comparative politics and political economy: To what extent, and under what conditions, can self-governing organizations provide public goods at the village level? Under what conditions can neighboring communities work together to provide public goods that transcend the boundaries of a community without external assistance? To what extent and under what conditions are customary and formal state representatives able to govern together?

From a theoretical perspective, the goal of this book is to bring the study of self-governance into the fold of the state-building literature. In this regard, it speaks to issues confronted by European colonial powers contemplating the merits of direct rule, which replaced customary authority with new bureaucracies, to indirect rule, whereby colonial rulers relied on customary actors such as traditional chiefs and tribal organizations to extend colonial authority. As colonies in Asia and Africa gained independence, it seemed as if customary governance would wither away as the scope of the post-colonial state expanded. Yet customary order remained strong in many states. Issues of tribalism, insurgency, and state fragility in places as diverse as Iraq, Pakistan, Yemen, Somalia, and Libya serve as constant reminders of the importance of traditional authority in modern politics.

The relationship between self-governing organizations and the state was a central question for policymakers confronting the challenges of institutional reform in post-2001 Afghanistan. Although Afghanistan was never formally colonized by a European power, it has been the site of a longstanding, ongoing debate concerning the role customary authority should play in a "modern" state. Popular accounts of Afghanistan portray fiercely independent tribal elders and deeply entrenched customary law as obstacles to the extension of government capacity, modernization, and economic development. Afghan history is rife with examples of various state-backed modernization campaigns that faced substantial resistance and rebellion led by customary authority.

Rather than accept the presumption that customary and state-backed orders are irreconcilable in Afghanistan, this book explores this issue analytically, drawing on social science theory, hundreds of interviews conducted in over thirty villages, and quantitative analysis of two nationally representative surveys. It shows that village-based customary authority can serve as an effective source of governance, defined as a public organization's "ability to make and enforce rules, and to deliver services" regardless of whether such organizations are democratic or even formally part of a state.[1] The most important local public goods in rural Afghanistan are things like basic law and order, dispute resolution, and small-scale infrastructure. Despite chaos in Kabul, these goods are often provided through customary channels at the village level. Furthermore, communities governed by such organizations routinely work together to provide public goods and services that benefit an even broader audience such as inter-communal justice and systems of water management.

This book makes an empirical contribution by illustrating the continuities of self-governance across the country despite decades of conflict. Fieldwork in rural Afghanistan revealed surprising similarity in the organization of village governance across a diverse ethnic, religious, and tribal landscape. This similarity is the consequence of a common set of norms and expectations about village politics that has been shaped by history and residues of previous government intervention. I refer to this common set of expectations as the "informal constitution" of village governance whereby village authority is separated among three distinct bodies: customary leaders or representatives, deliberative bodies, and religious arbiters. Each of these organizations derives its legitimacy from a unique source in the community.

---

[1] Francis Fukuyama, "What Is Governance?" *Governance* 26, no. 3 (2013): 4.

Variation in the performance of customary organizations is explained not only by the capacity of these three organizations, but by their ability to constrain one another. In addition to separating authority, the informal constitution dictates that customary organizations should be subject to a set of checks and balances that allow them to intrude on each other's power in the case of predation or general transgression of individual or community rights. For example, elders retain enormous status, as do collective decision-making bodies, typically known as shuras or jirgas, in nearly all Afghan villages. Most villages also have community-appointed leaders (variously titled as malik, qaryadar, arbab, or wakil) that represent the interests of the community to the state. Finally, most villages have one or more religious leaders, usually a mullah, who serves as another source of order.

This constellation of organizations is present in most communities. During my fieldwork, I found them in Pashtun, Tajik, Uzbek, Turkmen, and Aimaq villages in Afghanistan. At the same time, there are important sources of variation in such factors as tribal and ethnic affiliation, as well as region and geography. Customary governance is not always and everywhere the same.[2] Ethnic and regional differences account for divergence in rules applied by these organizations across communities. For example, Pashtun villages are more likely to apply norms of Pashtunwali (Pashtun tribal code) that may differ from customary law (rawaj or adat) used in non-Pashtun areas. The structure of village governance is remarkably similar across communities despite differences in substantive norms applied in day-to-day governance.

Although this informal constitution is a source of continuity, it is not static. As a result of the enormous hardships deriving from war, mass migration, and a series of governments bent on tearing society apart in order to transform it in the name of modernization or religion, customary organizations have been forced to adapt to changing circumstances. In certain periods during the past forty years, they seemed to disappear during the fog of intense conflict, only to regenerate, albeit in somewhat different forms after fighting died down or once communities returned from exile. Customary governance in rural Afghanistan after 2001 is different than it was decades ago. Many changes are for the better, as most informants reported local leaders to be more responsive to citizen demands.

As a study of local governance, this book makes several contributions. First, it explains why customary governance in Afghanistan is generally less feudal and autocratic than "polycentric." Polycentric governance, which refers to situations in which centers of decision-making are independent yet overlapping, is a remarkably useful concept for describing political relations in Afghanistan because in most communities, there is not one individual or organization who

---

[2] Noah Coburn, *Bazaar Politics: Power and Pottery in an Afghan Market Town* (Stanford University Press, 2011); Conrad Schetter, ed., *Local Politics in Afghanistan: A Century of Intervention in Social Order* (New York: Columbia University Press, 2013).

rules authoritatively over others.[3] Instead, there are multiple power sources whose convergence significantly constrains the reach of individual customary leaders. These constraints naturally limit the authority of such leaders, while at the same time empower them by conferring upon them legitimacy and authority. When these constraints are not present in a community, customary authority does not produce public goods but instead likely yields predation.

Second, the findings clarify both the capacity and limitations of customary governance. As James Scott noted, scholars should take anarchy seriously as an organizing principle by seeking to understand how and why communities organize affairs without the state.[4] Yet Scott asseverates that there is always a role for the state, and so the analytical challenge is to explain precisely the legitimate political boundaries of the state – where it should intervene, and where it should allow for self-governance. This book explores those boundaries and in the process clarifies more precisely where citizens demand a stronger state.

Third, this book elucidates the complicated interrelationship between customary governance and the state. Some Afghan policymakers and many in the international donor community justified efforts to create new governance structures in Afghan villages immediately after 2001 on the presumption that traditional order was fundamentally incompatible with the precepts of a modern state. The reasoning echoes Max Weber, who in *Politics as a Vocation* posited an irreconcilability of "traditional" order with that of a modern state based on laws.[5] While recognizing that there are often frictions between "traditional" and "modern" orders, this book finds that the presence of customary governance actually improves support for democracy and the central government. It also explores the conditions under which customary and formal state representatives govern together even though such collaboration is facilitated entirely by informal norms.

Finally, this study departs from previous studies of non-state actors and local governance in states emerging from conflict that focus primarily on the role of warlords.[6] Understanding the dynamics of warlord governance is clearly

---

[3] For an overview of the politics of polycentricism see: Michael Dean McGinnis, ed., *Polycentric Governance and Development: Readings from the Workshop in Political Theory and Policy Analysis* (Ann Arbor, MI: University of Michigan Press, 1999); Elinor Ostrom, *Understanding Institutional Diversity* (Princeton, NJ: Princeton University Press, 2005); Michael D. McGinnis and Elinor Ostrom, "Reflections on Vincent Ostrom, Public Administration, and Polycentricity," *Public Administration Review* 72, no. 1 (2012): 15–25.

[4] *Two Cheers for Anarchism: Six Easy Pieces on Autonomy, Dignity, and Meaningful Work and Play* (Princeton, NJ: Princeton University Press, 2012).

[5] *The Vocation Lectures: Science as a Vocation, Politics as a Vocation*, ed. David S. Owen and Tracy B. Strong, trans. Rodney Livingstone (Indianapolis, IN: Hackett, 2004) [1919].

[6] Antonio Giustozzi, *Empires of Mud: War and Warlords of Afghanistan* (New York: Columbia University Press, 2009); Jackson, Paul, "Warlords as Alternative Forms of Governance," *Small Wars & Insurgencies* 14, no. 2 (2003): 131–50; Mampilly, Zachariah Cherian, *Rebel*

important in such contexts, but these are not the only players at the sub-national level. Nor should warlords be conflated with customary leaders, although as we will see, these groups often interact. I found warlord politics usually occurs at a higher level of aggregation than the village.

As a study of state-society relations, this book joins a growing literature that questions the assumption that traditional authority is necessarily a tyrannical or feudal form of governance.[7] Like others, it shows that under some conditions such authority can enhance public goods provision[8] and may even improve political participation.[9] Such findings stand in stark contrast to those who have analyzed traditional authority as village level despots whose primary interest is protecting privileges arising from ties to the state.[10]

This book also complements works that have called into question efforts by international donors to foster new democratic institutions to replace existing social institutions.[11] Although customary governance may not be an optimal solution, under conditions of state weakness creating new, donor-supported – and frequently ephemeral – village governance structures in the same communities can at best lead to wasted resources and at worst lead to unnecessary competition and rivalry at a time of enormous political fragility. Similarly, efforts to strengthen traditional leaders and support them financially can also yield substantial distortions that threaten their legitimacy. Historically, this was

Rulers: Insurgent Governance and Civilian Life during War (Ithaca, NY: Cornell University Press, 2011); Marten, Kimberly Zisk, *Warlords: Strong-Arm Brokers in Weak States* (Ithaca: Cornell University Press, 2012); Dipali Mukhopadhyay, *Warlords, Strongman Governors, and the State in Afghanistan* (New York: Cambridge University Press, 2014). Reno, William, *Warlord Politics and African States* (Boulder, CO: Lynne Rienner Publishers, 1999);

[7] Carolyn Logan, "Selected Chiefs, Elected Councillors and Hybrid Democrats: Popular Perspectives on the Co-Existence of Democracy and Traditional Authority," *The Journal of Modern African Studies* 47, no. 1 (2009): 101–28; Carolyn Logan, "The Roots of Resilience: Exploring Popular Support for African Traditional Authorities," *African Affairs* 112, no. 448 (2013): 353–76.

[8] Kate Baldwin, "Why Vote with the Chief? Political Connections and Public Goods Provision in Zambia," *American Journal of Political Science* 57, no. 4 (2013): 794–809; Patrick M. Kyamusugulwa and Dorothea Hilhorst, "Power Holders and Social Dynamics of Participatory Development and Reconstruction: Cases from the Democratic Republic of Congo," *World Development* 70 (2015): 249–59.

[9] Alberto Díaz-Cayeros, Beatriz Magaloni, and Alexander Ruiz-Euler, "Traditional Governance, Citizen Engagement, and Local Public Goods: Evidence from Mexico," *World Development* 53 (2014): 80–93.

[10] Daron Acemoglu, Tristan Reed, and James A. Robinson, "Chiefs: Economic Development and Elite Control of Civil Society in Sierra Leone," *Journal of Political Economy* 122, no. 2 (2014): 319–68; Mahmood Mamdani, *Citizen and Subject: Contemporary Africa and the Legacy of Late Colonialism* (Princeton, NJ: Princeton University Press, 1996).

[11] Humphreys, Macartan, Raul de la Sierra, and Peter Van der Windt, "Social Engineering in the Tropics: Case Study Evidence from East Congo" (Unpublished Manuscript, 2014); Ghazala Mansuri and Vijayendra Rao, "Community-Based and-Driven Development: A Critical Review," *The World Bank Research Observer* 19, no. 1 (2004); Ghazala Mansuri and Vijayendra Rao, *Localizing Development* (Washington, DC: World Bank, 2013).

the case of colonial rule and was particularly true of NATO counterinsurgency efforts in Afghanistan.

Finally, and perhaps most importantly for long-term state consolidation in Afghanistan, this book finds that customary governance in the post-2001 period served as an important bulwark against abusive behavior on the part of the state and as a source of defense against insurgents. Although self-organized communities have historically been in conflict with the state, it is also true that one of the fundamental challenges throughout Afghan history has been that the state has been just strong enough to make life very unpleasant for its citizens. Customary governance may actually improve long-term prospects for the rule of law because it serves as an obstacle for the state as it seeks to transgress citizens' rights. This political function of customary authority – defending communities from rapacious regimes – may be even more important than its role in providing public goods.

This book provides an alternative method to the study of post-conflict state building or liberal peacebuilding, which generally approaches such fragile states through theoretical prisms of international relations, international organizations, and conflict studies. Studies of places like Afghanistan most frequently analyze the effectiveness of foreign aid, humanitarian intervention, and military doctrine and strategy, viewing post-conflict states through a lens that privileges the role of external actors.[12] External actors are natural subjects of scholarly and policy inquiry in states wracked by conflict, if for no other reason than it is easier to gain access to such groups under the challenging circumstances of conflict. There are also serious drawbacks of this mode of approaching fragile states, as data sources for such endeavors tend to be expatriates who frequently have meager knowledge of how government works or how citizens cope in the context of state failure.[13] Talking to members of NGOs or international organizations (IOs) does not typically require learning local languages or require the researcher to engage citizens in their communities.[14] For this reason, government and aid agency bureaucrats, who

---

[12] Krasner and Weinstein believe that the vast majority of political science scholarship on governance focuses on domestic – not international – sources of governance. This may be true of most states in the world, but in states that are the site of international peacebuilding efforts, scholarly research focuses overwhelmingly on the success or failure of international efforts rather than on local political institutions. See Stephen D. Krasner and Jeremy M. Weinstein, "Improving Governance from the Outside In," *Annual Review of Political Science* 17, no. 1 (2014): 123–45.

[13] For example, Rajiv Chandrasekaran highlights the limited information available to expatriate policymakers in Kabul who were very rarely able to travel outside their compounds due to security considerations. He argues that poor policy choices were based on rumors and misinformation about what was really happening on the ground. The case of Afghanistan is not unique in this regard. See Rajiv Chandrasekaran, *Little America: The War within the War for Afghanistan* (New York: Knopf, 2012).

[14] Severine Autesserre, *Peaceland: Conflict Resolution and the Everyday Politics of International Intervention* (New York: Cambridge University Press, 2014).

themselves rarely leave their well-armed compounds, receive a disproportionate amount of attention. This phenomena is not unexpected – security concerns in conflict-affected areas necessarily limit the access of outsiders to communities – but its cumulative effect means that public policies developed by many outsiders in this context are not fully utilizing local knowledge.[15] It also means that scholarship may disproportionately exaggerate the importance of external efforts.

As Michael Barnett and Christoph Zurcher argue, international NGOs (INGOs) in Afghanistan and other states emerging from conflict "build barriers between themselves and the local population, discouraging first-hand contact, which, in turn [leads] to a decline in the quality of their information and a dependence on locals and information brokers for news, second-hand reports, and secondary (and recycled) data. INGO management further retreat[s] into a comforting, hermetically-sealed illusion of emails, donor reports, 'performance appraisals' and day-to-day operational activity."[16] To avoid such challenges, the conclusions of this book are based upon evidence collected during more than twenty months of fieldwork in post-2001 Afghanistan. With the assistance of a remarkable group of six Afghan researchers, we together interviewed community-identified village leaders, local government officials, and randomly selected villagers (including an equal sample of both men and women) on issues related to local governance and the role of the state. This research was conducted in thirty-two villages in seventeen districts across six provinces of the country. All told, the original data consist of more than three hundred interviews and focus-group discussions and thousands of pages of interview transcripts. The fieldwork evidence, combined with use of nationally representative surveys, hopes to place this study on a firm empirical footing.

A more extensive discussion of the research design and data collection process are found in the Appendix A at the end of the book.

This book brings local politics back into the study of the state and state building. Comparative politics long ago brought the state back in.[17] However, the state in comparative politics and especially in fragile states focuses on national political dynamics, providing little insight into how legitimacy of the state is achieved or squandered by street-level bureaucrats, systems of public

---

[15] For a very important discussion on this point, see Autesserre, *The Trouble with the Congo: Local Violence and the Failure of International Peacebuilding* (New York: Cambridge University Press, 2010).

[16] "The Peacebuilder's Contract: How External Statebuilding Reinforces Weak Statehood," in *The Dilemmas of Statebuilding: Confronting the Contradictions of Postwar Peace Operations*, ed. Roland Paris and Timothy D. Sisk (New York: Routledge, 2009), 46.

[17] Peter Evans, Dietrich Rueschemeyer, and Theda Skocpol, *Bringing the State Back In* (New York: Cambridge University Press, 1985); Charles Tilly, *Coercion, Capital, and European States, AD 990–1992* (Cambridge: Blackwell, 1992); Hendrik Spruyt, *The Sovereign State and Its Competitors* (Princeton, NJ: Princeton University Press, 1996).

management, or how informal norms shape attitudes toward the state.[18] It is now time to bring local politics back into forefront of comparative politics, complementing the now standard focus on national politics in weak states. On the other hand, a movement toward the study of international aid projects has returned scholars to villages to measure impact of external interventions. While laudable as a form or program evaluation, a focus on external intervention opens only a very narrow window into the political economy of development. Rather, improving state-building prospects requires a better understanding of local governance, not simply the impact of external projects implemented locally. Legitimacy of the state is shaped at the local level, through the ways individuals experience the exercise of state power. Politics at this level is seemingly mundane. It is where issues of administration and management shape citizens' view of the state.

The remaining parts of this chapter introduce the main questions; before doing so I define a few analytical concepts employed in the pages ahead.

FROM AREA STUDIES TO POLITICAL ECONOMY

This book considers local governance through the lens of political economy, which asks how institutions shape incentives of individuals and organizations and the consequences of institutions for key economic and political outcomes.[19] Before introducing my argument and evidence, it is important to clarify terminology that will serve as the foundation for the rest of the book.

Institutions are sets of rules or prescriptions that structure social interactions in particular ways.[20] These rules provide information about how people are expected to act in particular situations. They are recognized by members of the relevant group and so they influence the behavior of other members of the group.[21] These prescriptions, which are embodied in systems of beliefs and norms, generate regularities of social behavior.[22]

Formal institutions are those established by states, including laws and constitutions. Unlike their formal counterparts, which are codified in written laws,

---

[18] Of course, there are important exceptions to this generalization. See Lily Tsai, *Accountability Without Democracy: Solidary Groups and Public Goods Provision in Rural China* (New York: Cambridge University Press, 2007); Merilee S. Grindle, *Going Local: Decentralization and the Promise of Good Governance* (Princeton, NJ: Princeton University Press, 2007); Daniel Posner, *Institutions and Ethnic Politics in Africa* (New York: Cambridge University Press, 2005); Kathryn Firmin-Sellers, *The Transformation of Property Rights in the Gold Coast: An Empirical Study Applying Rational Choice Theory* (New York: Cambridge University Press, 1996); Lisa Wedeen, *Peripheral Visions: Publics, Power, and Performance in Yemen* (Chicago, IL: University of Chicago Press, 2008).

[19] Jeffrey S. Banks and Eric A. Hanushek, eds., *Modern Political Economy* (Cambridge: Cambridge University Press, 1995).

[20] Ostrom, *Understanding Institutional Diversity*.

[21] Jack Knight, Institutions and Social Conflict (New York: Cambridge University Press, 1992).

[22] Avner Greif, *Institutions and the Path to the Modern Economy: Lessons from Medieval Trade* (New York: Cambridge University Press, 2006), 30.

informal institutions are the "socially shared rules, usually unwritten, that are created, communicated, and enforced outside of officially sanctioned channels."[23] Informal institutions include "traditions, customs, [and] moral beliefs" that are "part of a community's culture."[24] Informal institutions are not established by any single authority, but rather exist as norms within society. In countries that have lacked functioning governments for many decades, informal institutions govern many aspects of social, political, and economic life in the absence of effective formal rules.

Organizations, on the other hand, are "groups of individuals bound by some common purpose."[25] They are "collective actors that are subject to institutional constraints."[26] In this book, I define formal organizations as those deriving at least some of their authority from the state. Informal organizations are distinct from formal or "parchment" organizations because their authority and legitimacy derives from non-state sources.[27]

Like all societies, Afghanistan has a mix of formal and informal institutions. For example, formal rules are established by the Constitution and the Criminal Code. Informal institutions, in contrast, have origins that typically predate the state (such as customary law), but in some cases they emerge to help people get around inefficiencies in formal laws (such as bribery of government officials in return for services). Some of the most important informal institutions in Afghanistan include tribal codes such as Pashtunwali. In addition to tribal norms, non-tribal and religious norms routinely play an important role in rural society. For example, norms of village governance such as the expectation that every male in a community can participate in village governance, appear to have their origins in customary mores that transcend tribal and ethnic affiliations.

Defining precisely what constitutes "custom" has been a perennial challenge for law and social science.[28] Broadly, customary institutions refer to rules associated with long-standing social practice, religion, or tradition. I define customary organizations as collective decision-making bodies with authority

[23] Gretchen Helmke and Steven Levitsky, "Informal Institutions and Comparative Politics: A Research Agenda," *Perspectives on Politics* 2, no. 4 (2004): 727.

[24] Svetozar Pejovich, "The Effects of the Interaction of Formal and Informal Institutions on Social Stability and Economic Development," in *Institutions, Globalisation and Empowerment*, ed. Kartik Chandra Roy and Jörn Sideras (Northampton, MA: Edward Elgar Publishing, 2006), 58–59.

[25] Douglass C. North, *Institutions, Institutional Change, and Economic Performance* (New York: Cambridge University Press, 1990), 5.

[26] Knight, *Institutions and Social Conflict*, 3.

[27] John M. Carey, "Parchment, Equilibria, and Institutions," *Comparative Political Studies* 33, no. 6–7 (2000): 735–61.

[28] C. M. N. White, "African Customary Law: The Problem of Concept and Definition," *Journal of African Law* 9, no. 2 (1965): 86–89.

relations defined by long-standing rules whose origins lie outside the formal authority of the state.

Although scholars describe customary organizations as falling under the Weberian rubric of traditional authority, I prefer to use the term *customary* rather than *traditional* to describe village-based informal governaning organizations common throughout much of the developing world, because the term "traditional" evokes images of extreme stasis. As Olivier Roy explained:

> By traditionalism we mean the desire to freeze society so that it conforms to the memory of what it once was; it is society as described by our grandfathers. In this vision history and tradition are merged; the historical development of society is effaced in favor of an imaginary timeless realm under attack from pernicious modernity. Traditionalism can never provide the basis for any coherent program; it is riddled with nostalgia and its politics naturally incline towards all that is conservative.[29]

Customary norms are not always "frozen." Instead, they are like the common law, a legal system based on local norms that evolved through a process of adaptation into its modern, codified form.[30] In Afghanistan, customary organizations and the institutions that govern them are similarly dynamic. As with almost everything in the country, local governance did not weather the turbulence of thirty years of war unscathed or untouched. Despite facing many challenges, these organizations have proven resilient and adaptive. Just as the confluence of both tradition and the state affected the development of common law in the United States, customary institutions and organizations in Afghanistan are not the product of "tradition" alone, but have been shaped by interactions with the state and other outside groups.

My primary concern is with three customary organizations that play very important roles in the politics of rural Afghanistan: village representatives (maliks), village councils (shuras or jirgas), and religious arbiters (mullahs).[31] Together, they constitute the fundamental political organizations in the Afghan countryside despite the fact that they have no formal status or standing with the state.

Although my primary focus is on these three customary organizations, they are not the only organizations vying for authority in the countryside. The state has some presence, especially the centrally appointed district governors (woluswal), as do formally elected members of government Provincial

---

[29] Roy, *Islam and Resistance in Afghanistan*, 3.

[30] Howard Schweber, *The Creation of American Common Law, 1850–1880: Technology, Politics, and the Construction of Citizenship* (New York: Cambridge University Press, 2004).

[31] There is linguistic diversity in how individuals throughout rural Afghanistan describe the organizations within their communities. To simplify matters, I classify the three most prominent village-based customary organization into three categories: the individuals chosen by communities to represent interests to the state generally are called maliks, village councils are called shuras (using the generic Arabic term), and village-based religious leaders are referred to generally as mullahs. See Chapter 3 for greater discussion of this point.

TABLE 1.1: *Formal and Informal Organizations and Institutions in Afghanistan*

Formal Institutions	Criminal code
	Constitution of Afghanistan
Informal Institutions	Social norms
	Pashtunwali (Pashtun tribal code)
	Adat/rawaj (customary law)
Formal Organizations	Presidency
	National Assembly, Supreme Court
	Wali (provincial governor)
	Woluswali (district government)
	Woluswal (district governor)
Informal Organizations (customary)	Malik (village representative)
	Mullah (village-based religious leader)
	Shura (village council)
Informal Organizations (non-customary)	Warlord

Councils and National Assembly. There are also donor-supported initiatives, such as Community Development Councils (CDCs) established by the Ministry of Rural Rehabilitation and Development (MRRD) with more than $2 billion in support from the World Bank and international patrons, as well as warlords and their local commanders that are active in many parts of the country. One of the main goals of this book is to sort out the strengths and weaknesses of these organizations on various dimensions to draw a more holistic picture of how village governance works in a fragile state. I provide a picture of local governance in Afghanistan told from the perspective of the individuals experiencing it.

This typology of institutions and organizations in Afghanistan are summarized in Table 1.1.

Having provided an overview of the main institutions and organizations in Afghanistan, I now introduce the central questions in greater depth.

CENTRAL QUESTIONS

This book is organized around questions that correspond to three different levels of analysis: intra-village, inter-village, and village-state.[32] Rather than measuring the performance of local governance at just one level, I analyze the provision of public goods at three distinct levels, beginning at the very bottom of political organization (the village) before working up to larger units. As there is little systematic analysis of public goods provision in rural Afghanistan,

---

[32] I use the terms village and community interchangeably.

TABLE 1.2: *Three Levels of Analysis*

Level of Analysis	Actors and Relationships	Key Questions
Intra-village	Relations between maliks, mullahs, and shuras in a single village Relations between citizens and their customary village representatives	How are villages governed? Are village leaders constrained? How does the performance of customary organizations compare to other village organizations?
Inter-village	Groups of villages, each governed by customary organizations	Under what conditions can several villages work together to provide public goods?
Village-state	Maliks and woluswals Citizens and woluswals	Does the presence of customary organizations inhibit support for the central government? Under what conditions can villages and formal government officials at the lowest level of authority engage in power-sharing?

consideration of politics at multiple levels is essential to gain a full understanding local governance. These levels and the central questions are summarized in Table 1.2.

The first question concerns the provision of public goods within a village. The question of rules governing provision of public goods by customary authority harkens back to Max Weber and Karl Marx who both viewed norms of customary governance as fundamentally incompatible with the demands of a rational-bureaucratic state. Weber defined rational-legal political institutions in stark contrast to traditional political institutions, identifying rational rules with the rule of law and traditional rules with the rule of strong men.[33] Weber posited an inherent tension, if not a zero-sum relationship, between customary order and rational-legal order. Similarly, Marx, in *The Eighteenth Brumaire of Louis Napoleon*, also conceptualized of traditional order as an impediment to economic modernization in describing peasants and their society as unorganized and helpless "sack[s] of potatoes" that required the salvation of the state.[34]

Ironically, customary order in Afghanistan tends to be far more predictable and Weberian than the rules offered by the state. In most communities,

---

[33] *Economy and Society*, ed. Guenther Roth and Claus Wittich (Berkeley, CA: University of California Press, 1978), chap. 3.
[34] Karl Marx, *The Eighteenth Brumaire of Louis Bonaparte* (Chicago, IL: C. H. Kerr, 1913), 145.

separation of authority between three distinct organizations – shuras/jirgas, mullahs, and maliks – evokes the image of governance advocated by Montesquieu.[35] Not only is authority usually separated within the constellation of customary organizations, but effective governance emerges when informal institutions promote checks and balances among these organizations that also serve to limit strong-fisted rule. For example, when a malik tries to take too much from citizens in his village, his power is often checked by the convening of a village shura or a meeting of religious leaders (or both). Likewise, when religious leaders seek to impose new rules that are out of step with local norms, the other bodies can constrain his actions.

From a methodological perspective, the evidence I employ to analyze self-governing organizations differs from anthropological perspectives, which usually analyze a single community or group to understand unique group features or practices. While some anthropologists explicitly seek to test theoretical models and by doing so use a specific case to generalize to a larger set, many hasten generalization. The comparative framework I adopt allows us to understand general principles of village governance, while simultaneously appreciating that the organizational framework and the rules meted out by organizations will vary from village to village. In this way, the framework articulates local systems of meaning and significance while at the same time provides a general framework to understand self-governing village organizations. This approach echoes that employed by the founder of contemporary Afghan Studies, anthropologist Louis Dupree who once observed, "the individual life cycle in Afghanistan varies from group to group and often within each group, but the patterns are similar enough to permit generalization."[36] Ultimately, through comparative analysis, the findings presented in subsequent chapters provide evidence that there is indeed an "Afghan" way of managing village affairs, one that seems to transcend ethnicity, region, or tribal affiliation.[37] It turns out that this Afghan way of governance is more rational than traditional.

After presenting a field-based description of village governance, I provide a conceptual framework yielding four factors that explain the conditions under which village-based organizations can facilitate the provision of public goods in the context of state weakness: political constraints that limit the influence of village representatives, local political stability (the expectation that local

---

[35] *The Spirit of the Laws*, ed. Anne M. Cohler, Basia C. Miller, and Harold S. Stone (New York: Cambridge University Press, 1989).

[36] Dupree, *Afghanistan* (Princeton, NJ: Princeton University Press, 1973), 181.

[37] Afghan journalist and historian Tamim Ansary came to similar conclusions: "But although the Pushtoons may honor this code [*Pashtunwali*] in the extreme, similar values flavor the folkways of other groups throughout Afghanistan. Tajiks, Hazaras, Uzbeks, and others all tend to revere generosity and treat guests as privileged celebrities. All tend to feel that a man's self-respect rests on the unsullied sexual modesty of the women in his family, especially the unmarried young ones," in *Games without Rules: The Often-Interrupted History of Afghanistan* (New York: Public Affairs, 2012), 14.

representatives will remain in power in the future), access to reliable sources of locally-generated revenue, and participation in local decision-making.[38] This framework facilitates comparisons of self-governing customary organizations with donor-driven development councils and even commanders in terms of public goods provision.

The main finding, arrived at from analysis of qualitative data and statistical analysis of nationally representative survey data, is that customary organizations are often effective in providing basic public goods and services. Customary organizations are especially capable of providing small-scale public goods, such as dispute resolution and local order. In contrast, citizens rarely depend on the state or even newly created donor-supported councils for such services. In interviews, the vast majority of informants did not view donor-assisted development projects as "long-run players" who they expected to be around for a long time. Rather than a source of salvation, my field data showed these new councils largely as rentier community organizations: groups entirely dependent upon aid that had few prospects for long-run viability on their own. On the other hand, although imperfect, individuals viewed customary organizations as more reliable and accountable. In their view, customary organizations were created by the community itself and therefore could be shaped to fit community needs.

These findings are relevant in light of debates within the Afghan government and the international community (who actively funded and promoted these new councils) that the new councils become official governing bodies at the village level serving to extend the writ of the state, replacing "traditional" structures. The state-building project produced a vibrant debate among scholars and donors regarding what role such development councils should have in the future of the state-building project in Afghanistan. For example, historian Christine Noelle-Karimi believed that any success one might attribute to such development councils occurs not in spite of the traditional system, but because of it: customary governance provides the institutional foundation for successful collective action in communities, thus it is an asset and not a liability for those wishing to build a democratic state.[39] She cautioned against efforts to formalize CDCs, because as agents of the state they will then assume "a life of their own" as part of the bureaucracy, operating independent of those they are designed to serve.[40] Such caution is in line with recent critiques of donor-driven blueprints that have sprung up around the world that seek to implement CDD schemes through the creation of new and

---

[38] For the purposes of this book, I define the state weakness as the inability of an external enforcer (such as a local government) to enforce its laws or rules in a systematic or predictable manner.

[39] "Jirga, Shura and Community Development Councils: Village Institutions and State Interference," in *Local Politics in Afghanistan: A Century of Intervention in Social Order*, ed. Conrad Schetter (New York: Columbia University Press, 2013), 39–58.

[40] Ibid., 58.

frequently parallel governance structures at the local level in an effort to connect communities with the state.[41] An impact evaluation using a randomized control trial examining the effectiveness of these councils showed them to significantly *worsen* governance outcomes in villages where they were implemented rather than improve them.[42]

Although customary organizations generally govern effectively within individual communities, a single community cannot provide many important public goods. In most contexts, a higher power such as the state provides those larger-scale public goods that cannot be provided by a single community. In Afghanistan, however, persistent state weakness means that communities typically cannot call upon the state to provide larger-scale public goods and services such as health care, irrigation systems, and roads. Therefore, the second general question considers the extent to which customary authorities can cooperate to provide public goods that transcend the borders of a single village.

The nature of the theoretical problem changes as we look at inter-communal cooperation. If villages are "republics," as Robert Wade described them, then the question now becomes one of attaining cooperation in the absence of a common power – that is, in the absence of a state or some other third-party enforcer.[43] In many ways, the problem of achieving inter-communal cooperation is similar to the challenge of attaining cooperation under anarchy in international relations.[44] The maliks who negotiate on behalf of their communities are like political leaders from separate republics who are unable to call upon a higher authority when they have conflicts with other communiiities, much like leaders of countries interacting in the international system.

The literature on regional governance provides a theoretical mooring to understand inter-communal governance in rural Afghanistan. Vincent Ostrom, Charles Tiebout, and Robert Warren described the central problem of regional governance as one where the "the people of a metropolitan region have no general instrumentality of government available to deal directly with the range of problems which they share in common."[45] In recent years, scholars have clarified mechanisms of self-organization in the context of regional governance, modeling the theoretical problem facing communities as one of a prisoner's

---

[41] Mansuri and Rao, "Community-Based and-Driven Development: A Critical Review"; Mansuri and Rao, *Localizing Development*; Ostrom, *Understanding Institutional Diversity*, chap. 9.

[42] Andrew Beath, Fotini Christia, and Ruben Enikolopov, "Randomized Impact Evaluation of Afghanistan's National Solidarity Programme" (Washington, DC: The World Bank, 2013).

[43] Robert Wade, *Village Republics: Economic Conditions for Collective Action in South India* (New York: Cambridge University Press, 1988).

[44] For an excellent illustration of efforts to sustained cooperation to provide public goods under conditions of anarchy in the international system see Scott Barrett, *Why Cooperate? The Incentive to Supply Global Public Goods* (New York: Oxford University Press, 2007).

[45] Ostrom, Tiebout, and Warren, "The Organization of Government in Metropolitan Areas: A Theoretical Inquiry," *The American Political Science Review* 55, no. 4 (1961): 831.

dilemma in the context of weak or nonexistent external enforcement.[46] Although this literature originated in studies of advanced industrial countries where formal rules are typically binding, the theoretical problem is similar in Afghanistan, which is to explain inter-jurisdictional cooperation under conditions of anarchy.

Drawing on theories of inter-jurisdictional cooperation, I anticipate five factors to influence the ability of communities to achieve cooperation in the absence of the state: the number of local units required to participate in provision of the public good, geographic scale of participating units, fixed costs of provision of the public good, political parameters, and social heterogeneity of participating communities. Case studies of inter-communal cooperation and conflict constructed from fieldwork data demonstrate that collaboration between communities is fairly common, especially for some kinds of public goods such as irrigation, rangeland management, dispute resolution, and smaller-scale roads. For other types of public goods, especially those requiring substantial capital investments and involving a large number of communities, such as building hospitals and schools (which includes training competent medical staff and teachers) as well as protecting communities from insurgents, self-governance often bears little fruit.

These findings also have important implications for state-building efforts in Afghanistan. The international aid community and NATO forces sought the allegiance of villagers by providing small-scale public goods at the village level. The assumption that public goods provision wins hearts and minds is an assumption common among most donors and aid organizations working in fragile states, and was especially true for those working in rural Afghanistan.[47] It is an assumption deeply embedded in the 2004 Constitution that created a long list of positive rights in the hopes of buying quick government legitimacy. The case studies suggest there is only a narrow range of aid that has the potential to help build the legitimacy of the government. In particular, aid or government projects could be especially effective if they seek to provide goods characterized by high fixed costs. Nonetheless, many donor projects in

[46] Richard C. Feiock, *Metropolitan Governance: Conflict, Competition, and Cooperation* (Washington, DC: Georgetown University Press, 2004); Richard C. Feiock, "Rational Choice and Regional Governance," *Journal of Urban Affairs* 29, no. 1 (2007): 47–63; Ronald J. Oakerson and Roger B. Parks, "The Study of Local Public Economies: Multi-Organizational, Multi-Level Institutional Analysis and Development," *Policy Studies Journal* 39, no. 1 (2011): 147–67; Elinor Ostrom, Roger B. Parks, and Gordon P. Whitaker, "Do We Really Want to Consolidate Urban Police Forces? A Reappraisal of Some Old Assertions," *Public Administration Review* 33, no. 5 (1973): 423–32; Roger B. Parks and Ronald J. Oakerson, "Metropolitan Organization and Governance," *Urban Affairs Review* 25, no. 1 (1989): 18–29.

[47] "Winning hearts and minds" through aid is implicit in most development efforts, but was a central component of the civilian and military surge in the country (2008–12). See Paul Fishstein and Andrew Wilder, "Winning Hearts and Minds? Examining the Relationship between Aid and Security in Afghanistan" (Medford, MA: Feinstein International Center, Tufts University, 2012).

Afghanistan across a wide range of sectors were fixated on community development, looking for small-scale fixes at the village level in the hopes of generating quick impact and immediate support, rather than tailoring assistance to those areas where communities persistently fail to achieve cooperation. Thus, the empirical studies of inter-communal cooperation provide insight into how to tailor international and government assistance in ways that might enhance prospects for generating state support and legitimacy.

The third question directly addresses the notion that "traditional" authority must wither away for an effective state to emerge. For Weber, traditional forms of authority frustrate social change, stymie economic growth, and promote the status quo to such an extent that "creation of new law opposite traditional norms is deemed impossible."[48] Thomas Hobbes also underscored the importance of establishing state authority at the expense of customary or other non-state sources, to ensure predictability and freedom from chaos. Life without central authority, as he famously described it, was "nasty, brutish, and short."[49] More recently, Jared Diamond suggested that "traditional" societies are bound to struggle in conflict.[50]

In Afghanistan, the presumption of irreconcilability between customary order and the state is not simply an intellectual question, but a policy one as well. The Government of the Islamic Republic of Afghanistan, together with the international community spent billions of dollars since 2001 in the hopes of not just constructing any state, but a state based on democratic principles: liberal peacebuilding. The drive to create new democratic structures at the village level was pursued out of a belief that existing social norms rooted in tradition and culture were irreconcilable with this new, modern order.

This book recasts the presumption of irreconcilability between the state and customary governance as a hypothesis, evaluating it in two ways. First, I analyze nationally representative public opinion data to understand whether the presence of customary authority in villages correlates with support for the central government as well as with norms associated with democracy. The findings from the statistical analysis contradict many of the Weberian assumptions made about customary organizations in the state-building process and question assumptions of the more recent "state and society" approach, which posit an inherent conflict between modernizing states and customary order.[51]

---

[48] Max Weber, *Essays in Economic Sociology*, ed. Richard Swedberg (Princeton, NJ: Princeton University Press, 1999), 101.

[49] Thomas Hobbes, *Leviathan*, ed. J. C. Gaskin (New York: Oxford University Press, 1998), 84.

[50] Diamond, *The World Until Yesterday: What Can We Learn from Traditional Societies?* (New York: Viking Adult, 2012).

[51] Joel S. Migdal, *State in Society: Studying How States and Societies Transform and Constitute One Another*, Cambridge Studies in Comparative Politics (New York: Cambridge University Press, 2001); Joel S. Migdal, *Strong Societies and Weak States : State-Society Relations and State Capabilities in the Third World* (Princeton, NJ: Princeton University Press, 1988).

Specifically, I find that increased access to customary organizations is correlated with higher support of the central government, as well as support for democracy, gender equality, and a belief one's vote matters.

Second, I analyze original qualitative field data to construct case studies that detail the relationship between customary representatives and the district government (the lowest level of formal government in rural Afghanistan). The case studies illustrate how political dynamics in Afghanistan are highly decentralized in practice despite the extremely centralized nature of the formal rules governing these relations. Maliks lie at the center of this informal system of power sharing. While there is no formal representation of villages to the government (as there is no formal government at the village level), maliks typically represent community interests to the state. Throughout the countryside, informants described maliks not as village leaders, but as representatives, frequently labeling them as "the bridge between the people and the government." Far from a zero-sum relationship, informal and formal officials often divide up tasks, while also working together on certain governance issues despite the fact that this division of labor is based entirely on informal rules.

These findings provide insight into how the rule of law might emerge in Afghanistan. A propitious balance of authority between the state and its citizens has long been viewed as one of the most important explanations for the emergence of the rule of law.[52] Customary organizations, by both balancing the state and partnering with it, actually represent both a safeguard against government transgressions as well as the glue linking the state together with society.

STATE BUILDING AND SELF-GOVERNANCE

Weber defined the state as a "human community that claims the monopoly of the legitimate use of physical force within a given territory."[53] Since Weber, a vast literature has emerged that underscores a wide range of mechanisms explaining successful state consolidation.

The state-formation literature is most commonly associated with successful "state building." This literature examines the process by which nascent political and social organizations attained the fiscal centralization and military capacity necessary to monopolize the use of violence allowing them to emerge as states. In this literature, states arose as unintended consequences of efforts by leaders and groups to win wars or defeat bandits.[54] For example, in Ottoman Anatolia,

---

[52] Barry R Weingast, "The Political Foundations of Democracy and the Rule of Law," *The American Political Science Review* 91, no. 2 (1997): 245–63.

[53] Owen and Strong, *The Vocation Lectures*, 33.

[54] Charles Tilly, *The Formation of National States in Western Europe* (Princeton, NJ: Princeton University Press, 1975); Charles Tilly, "War Making and State Making as Organized Crime," in *Bringing the State Back In*, ed. Peter B. Evans, Dietrich Rueschemeyer, and Theda Skocpol

sultans did not seek to create a state or an empire; they sought to bring restive bandits under control, collect rents from subjects, and protect fertile land.[55] In other contexts, rulers created bureaucratic institutions as a means to access revenue streams.[56] The creation of states was thus an instrumental means to an end – not an end unto itself. This perspective depicts tension between bandits, armed groups and warlords, as well as feudal lords, each coming into conflict with nascent states seeking to extend centralized authority in a sort of "war of elimination."[57]

A second perspective focuses on the organizational capacity of states and the rationalization of government bureaucracy as an important factor generating state strength. Here the "infrastructural" capacity of states to implement policies is just as important as coercive or "despotic" power described in the state formation literature.[58] Peter Evans and James Rauch show that a coherent and meritocratic bureaucracy not only has important consequences for the strength of a state, but also impacts economic development.[59] In the developing world, where states are typically "weak," a high-quality bureaucracy appears critical to improving public goods provision[60] and the overall quality of citizen participation.[61] Drawing heavily on Weberian models, in this view the quality of bureaucracy is a vital factor that ensures the emergence and endurance of successful states.[62]

(New York: Cambridge University Press, 1985), 169–86; Tilly, *Coercion, Capital, and European States, AD 990–1992.*

[55] Karen Barkey, *Bandits and Bureaucrats: The Ottoman Route to State Centralization* (Ithaca, NY: Cornell University Press, 1994).

[56] Thomas Ertman, *Birth of the Leviathan: Building States and Regimes in Medieval and Early Modern Europe* (Cambridge: Cambridge University Press, 1997); Mancur Olson, *Power and Prosperity: Outgrowing Communist and Capitalist Dictatorships* (New York: Basic Books, 2000).

[57] Norbert Elias, *Norbert Elias on Civilization, Power, and Knowledge: Selected Writings*, ed. Stephen Mennell and Johan Goudsblom, Heritage of Sociology (Chicago: University of Chicago Press, 1998).

[58] Michael Mann, "The Autonomous Power of the State: Its Origins, Mechanisms and Results," *European Journal of Sociology/Archives Européennes de Sociologie* 25, no. 2 (1984): 185–213.

[59] Peter Evans, *Embedded Autonomy: States and Industrial Transformation* (Princeton, NJ: Princeton University Press, 1995); Peter Evans, "Government Action, Social Capital, and Development: Reviewing the Evidence on Synergy," in *State-Society Synergy: Government and Social Capital in Development* (Berkeley, CA: University of California at Berkeley, 1997), 178–209; Peter Evans and James E. Rauch, "Bureaucracy and Growth: A Cross-National Analysis of the Effects of 'Weberian' State Structures on Economic Growth," *American Sociological Review* 64, no. 5 (1999): 748–65; James E. Rauch, "*Choosing a Dictator: Bureaucracy and Welfare in Less Developed Polities,*" Working Paper (National Bureau of Economic Research, July 1995).

[60] Judith Tendler, *Good Government in the Tropics* (Baltimore: Johns Hopkins University Press, 1997).

[61] Grindle, *Going Local.*

[62] Fukuyama, "What Is Governance?"; Bo Rothstein, *The Quality of Government: Corruption, Social Trust, and Inequality in International Perspective* (Chicago; London: University of Chicago Press, 2011).

A third perspective on state building considers the importance of representative institutions, in particular democracy, as a source of long-run state strength. Over the past several decades, state building became a conscious effort to construct political entities. International support for states seeking to consolidate is usually accompanied by expectations that improvements in capacity will also include the establishment of representative institutions. In this view, electoral mechanisms translating citizen preferences into representation are the foundation of rational legal order.[63] Douglass North, John Wallis, and Barry Weingast provide historical evidence that political institutions based on "open-access" democratic principles drive long-run prospects for both economic growth and political stability.

The "state and society" approach, constitutes a fourth perspective on the state. Joel Migdal suggests that state strength is inversely related to self-governance.[64] In order for a strong state to emerge he observed that "highly disruptive forces must first weaken existing strategies of survival."[65] When groups are self-organized, they can resist the state, leading many to assume a zero-sum relationship between the state and society, where informal forms of self-organization and traditional order "leads assuredly to massive economic inefficiency, and possibly to terminal damage at the macro-sociological level."[66] Catherine Boone takes a fine-grained approach examining how variation in the strength of rural elites resulted in differences in state strength and forms of government across Africa.[67] Patrick Chabol and Jean-Pascal Daloz argue that African states remain "vacuous" and "ineffectual" because they have not been able to govern autonomously from society and its traditional practices.[68]

While much of this literature has examined how states emerge over long historical trajectories, the study of state building took on increasing urgency at the end of the Cold War, when state weakness became an explicit challenge to peace and security around the world.[69] As Cold War subsidies came to an end, many leaders in the developing world began preying on their own people to

---

[63] Daron Acemoglu and James Robinson, *Why Nations Fail: The Origins of Power, Prosperity, and Poverty* (New York: Crown Business, 2012).

[64] Migdal, *Strong Societies and Weak States: State-Society Relations and State Capabilities in the Third World*; Migdal, *State in Society: Studying How States and Societies Transform and Constitute One Another.*

[65] Migdal, *Strong Societies and Weak States: State-Society Relations and State Capabilities in the Third World,* 276.

[66] Patrick Chabal and Jean-Pascal Daloz, *Africa Works: Disorder as Political Instrument* (Bloomington, IN: Indiana University Press, 1999), 138.

[67] Catherine Boone, *Political Topographies of the African State: Territorial Authority and Institutional Choice* (New York: Cambridge University Press, 2003).

[68] Chabal and Daloz, *Africa Works,* 14.

[69] John Lewis Gaddis, *The Long Peace: Inquiries Into the History of the Cold War* (New York: Oxford University Press, 1989).

satiate their consumptive appetites.[70] Several of these states then became vulnerable to civil wars and state failures.[71] These so-called failed states presented new challenges to policymakers.[72]

Although there are many names for such troubled states – weak, attenuated, failed, collapsed, quasi-, neo-patrimonial, fragile, crisis – each refers to a similar underlying problem, which is that the central government faces serious challenges to its monopoly on coercion.[73] Many scholars posit a connection between such conflict and crises in governance. For example, pervasiveness of colonial institutions is linked with state failure as colonial states were designed for the management of extraction but rarely for purposes of good governance.[74] State failure has also been linked to corruption and

---

[70] Robert H. Bates, *When Things Fell Apart* (New York: Cambridge University Press, 2008).

[71] Stathis N. Kalyvas and Laia Balcells, "International System and Technologies of Rebellion: How the End of the Cold War Shaped Internal Conflict," *American Political Science Review* 104, no. 3 (2010): 415–29; Jeffrey Herbst, "African Militaries and Rebellion: The Political Economy of Threat and Combat Effectiveness," *Journal of Peace Research* 41, no. 3 (2004): 357–69.

[72] Mary Kaldor, *New and Old Wars: Organized Violence in a Global Era* (Cambridge, UK: Polity Press, 1999); Robert D. Kaplan, *The Coming Anarchy: Shattering the Dreams of the Post Cold War* (New York: Vintage, 2001); Nelson Kasfir, "Domestic Anarchy, Security Dilemmas, and Violent Predation: Causes of Failure," in *When States Fail: Causes and Consequences*, ed. Robert I. Rotberg (Princeton, NJ: Princeton University Press, 2004), 53–76.

[73] The literature on "failed states" comes in many flavors. Scholars use a variety of titles to describe states that exhibit severely limited capacity: attenuated states: Daniel Bromley and Glen Anderson, *Vulnerable People, Vulnerable States: Redefining the Development Challenge* (New York: Routledge, 2012); failed states: Ashraf Ghani and Clare Lockhart, *Fixing Failed States: A Framework for Rebuilding a Fractured World* (New York: Oxford University Press, 2008); Robert I. Rotberg, *When States Fail: Causes and Consequences* (Princeton, NJ: Princeton University Press, 2004); collapsed states: John R. Heilbrunn, "Paying the Price of Failure: Reconstructing Failed and Collapsed States in Africa and Central Asia," *Perspectives on Politics* 4, no. 1 (2006): 135–50; quasi-states: Robert H. Jackson, "Quasi-States, Dual Regimes, and Neoclassical Theory: International Jurisprudence and the Third World," *International Organization* 41, no. 4 (1987): 519–49; Robert H. Jackson, *Quasi-States: Sovereignty, International Relations, and the Third World* (Cambridge: Cambridge University Press, 1990); neopatrimonial states: Shmuel Noah Eisenstadt, *Traditional Patrimonialism and Modern Neopatrimonialism* (Beverly Hills, CA: Sage Publications, 1973); Nicolas van de Walle, *African Economies and the Politics of Permanent Crisis, 1979–1999* (New York: Cambridge University Press, 2001); and fragile states: Derick W. Brinkerhoff, "Rebuilding Governance in Failed States and Post-Conflict Societies: Core Concepts and Cross-Cutting Themes," *Public Administration & Development* 25, no. 1 (2005): 3–14; *Governance in Post-Conflict Societies: Rebuilding Fragile States* (New York: Routledge, 2007); Derick W. Brinkerhoff, "State Fragility and Governance: Conflict Mitigation and Subnational Perspectives," *Development Policy Review* 29, no. 2 (2011): 131–53; and Lisa Chauvet and Paul Collier, "Development Effectiveness in Fragile States: Spillovers and Turnarounds" (Oxford: Center for the Study of African Economies, Oxford University, 2004).

[74] Daron Acemoglu, Simon Johnson, and James A. Robinson, "The Colonial Origins of Comparative Development: An Empirical Investigation," *The American Economic Review* 91, no. 5 (2001): 1369–1401; Jeffrey Herbst, *States and Power in Africa: Comparative Lessons in Authority and Control* (Princeton, NJ: Princeton University Press, 2000).

neo-patrimonial practices.[75] In some cases, democratization itself can contribute to state collapse.[76] In addition, structural factors such as ethnic fractionalization,[77] geographic factors such as environmental degradation and mountainous terrain,[78] and natural resource wealth are also linked to state failure.[79]

The apparent proliferation of failed states has also drawn attention to its devastating and tragic consequences. Under conditions of state failure, warlords, militias, and mercenaries wreak havoc on populations.[80] In fact, state failure breeds refugee flows that are also linked to conflict and failure in neighboring states.[81] Understanding sources of state failure is important because of the enormous hardship and human suffering it frequently leaves in its shadows.

Studies of state failure have been remarkably successful in identifying the various ways in which states fall apart, shedding light on the importance of violent non-state actors such as warlord or criminal groups who emerge from war-torn societies. In some cases, these violent non-state actors provide public goods such as security and protection of markets in ways that are not necessarily incompatible with well-functioning states.[82] As William Reno noted,

---

[75] Christopher Clapham, "The Challenge to the State in a Globalized World," *Development and Change* 33, no. 5 (2002): 775–95; Crawford Young, *The African Colonial State in Comparative Perspective* (New Haven, CT: Yale University Press, 1994).

[76] Edward D. Mansfield and Jack L. Snyder, *Electing to Fight: Why Emerging Democracies Go to War*, BCSIA Studies in International Security (Cambridge, MA: MIT Press, 2005); Jack L. Snyder, *From Voting to Violence: Democratization and Nationalist Conflict* (New York: Norton, 2000); Paul Collier, *Wars, Guns and Votes* (New York: Harper Collins, 2009).

[77] Joan Esteban and Debraj Ray, Conflict and Distribution, *Journal of Economic Theory* 87, no. 2 (August 1999): 379415; James D. Fearon and David D. Laitin, Explaining Interethnic Cooperation, *The American Political Science Review* 90, no. 4 (December 1996): 71535; Donald L. Horowitz, *Ethnic Groups in Conflict* (University of California Press, 2000).

[78] James D. Fearon and David D. Laitin, "Ethnicity, Insurgency, and Civil War," *American Political Science Review* 97, no. 1 (2003): 75–90; Colin H. Kahl, *States, Scarcity, and Civil Strife in the Developing World* (Princeton, NJ: Princeton University Press, 2006).

[79] Paul Collier, *The Plundered Planet: Why We Must–and How We Can–Manage Nature for Global Prosperity* (New York: Oxford University Press, 2010).

[80] Herbert M. Howe, *Ambiguous Order* (Boulder, CO: Lynne Rienner Publishers, 2001); Abdi Ismail Samatar, "Destruction of State and Society in Somalia: Beyond the Tribal Convention," *The Journal of Modern African Studies* 30, no. 4 (1992): 625–41.

[81] Idean Salehyan and Kristian Skrede Gleditsch, "Refugees and the Spread of Civil War," *International Organization* 60, no. 2 (2006): 335–66.

[82] Christopher J. Coyne, "Reconstructing Weak and Failed States: Foreign Intervention and the Nirvana Fallacy," *Foreign Policy Analysis* 2, no. 4 (2006): 343–60; Peter T. Leeson, "Better off Stateless: Somalia before and after Government Collapse," *Journal of Comparative Economics* 35, no. 4 (2007): 689–710; Zachariah Cherian Mampilly, *Rebel Rulers: Insurgent Governance and Civilian Life during War* (Ithaca, NY: Cornell University Press, 2011); William Reno, *Warlord Politics and African States* (Boulder, CO: Lynne Rienner Publishers, 1999); Stergios Skaperdas, "Warlord Competition," *Journal of Peace Research* 39, no. 4 (2002): 435–46; Stergios Skaperdas, "The Political Economy of Organized Crime: Providing Protection When the State Does Not," *Economics of Governance* 2, no. 3 (2001): 173–202.

"shadow states" led by warlords and militias emerge during what seems to be chaos of anarchy.

As policymakers struggle to fix states in real time, it has proven difficult to apply the insights of the traditional state-building literature, which examines the formation of states and political structures over the courses of decades if not centuries. As a result of widespread state failure and the threats posed by such states, the study of state building can no longer be considered "merely an academic issue."[83]

After the collapse of the Soviet Union and through the "third wave" of democratization, state building became an extremely purposive project. The end of the Cold War produced a wealth of scholarship to explain the processes of political transition and political upheaval.[84] Rather than examining the historical process through which states evolve, state building became a policy question of institutional design contemplating how to design the rules of the political game to promote economic development, democracy, or some other desired outcome.[85] Today, an entire state-building industry has emerged around the design and implementation of massive donor-supported projects with the hope of transforming authoritarian states or rebuilding territories devastated by conflict or political turmoil by establishing a rational-legal order, essentially moving countries "straight to Weber."[86] New state institutions and organizations that result from such efforts are frequently driven by "best practices" and lessons learned in other countries.[87]

The literatures considering the dynamics of state building and the causes of state failure rarely distinguish among non-state actors, which typically include customary governance, tribal authority, warlords, gangs, and militias. The literature frequently depicts all non-state sources of political and social organization as fundamental threats to the state's monopoly on coercion. Consider the following example depicting Afghanistan: "Whether in seventeenth-century France or twenty-first-century Afghanistan, a crucial prerequisite for state building is the centralization of political authority. A key challenge facing state builders, therefore, is how to deal with the local elites who stand to lose out in

[83] Herbst, *States and Power in Africa*, 257.

[84] Mark R. Beissinger, *Nationalist Mobilization and the Collapse of the Soviet State* (New York: Cambridge University Press, 2002); Valerie Bunce, *Subversive Institutions: The Design and the Destruction of Socialism and the State* (New York: Cambridge University Press, 1999); Steven L. Solnick, *Stealing the State: Control and Collapse in Soviet Institutions* (Cambridge, MA: Harvard University Press, 1999).

[85] Jon Elster, Claus Offe, and Ulrich K. Preuss, *Institutional Design in Post-Communist Societies: Rebuilding the Ship at Sea* (New York: Cambridge University Press, 1998); David Weimer, ed., *Institutional Design* (Boston, MA: Kluwer Academic Publishers, 1995).

[86] Lant Pritchett and Michael Woolcock, "Solutions When the Solution Is the Problem: Arraying the Disarray in Development," *World Development* 32, no. 2 (2004): 191–212.

[87] For an illustration of this perspective, see Dobbins et al., *The Beginner's Guide to Nation-Building* (Washington, DC: RAND Corporation, 2007).

the process. In France, this meant managing the nobility and the clergy; in Afghanistan, it means handling warlords, tribal chiefs, and the Taliban."[88] Amitai Etzioni uses similar language in depicting tribal chiefs and warlords in Afghanistan as analytical equivalents: "loyalties in the region are paramount, and 'warlords' (or tribal chiefs) are loath to subordinate themselves to a higher authority, especially one fostered by foreign powers."[89] In these views, it is the non-state actors who emerged or were strengthened during conflict – the warlords and tribal chiefs – that have the most to lose from state consolidation.

An implication from such analysis is that self-governing and other autonomous forms of political order that exist in the absence of effective states are fundamental threats to state consolidation. Typically, such self-organized groups are militia groups led by warlords or other violent non-state actors. This is not always the case.

If the issue at hand is self-governance, then the literature on self-governance may provide insight into the persistence of informal sources of political and social order. Rather than viewing self-governance as an obstacle, this literature illustrates the many ways societies cope in the absence of effective centralized authority – that is, under conditions of anarchy.[90] Although Hobbes and Weber viewed the state as a solution to the problem of disorder arising under anarchy, there is often a substantial degree of order even in the absence of the state.[91] In some contexts, the solutions provided by society may be more effective alternatives to those proffered by emerging states, which are typically weak and frequently corrupt.

In her pioneering work Elinor Ostrom demonstrated how individuals routinely organize to provide public goods without the assistance of the state.[92] In her view, efforts to build public policy should take into account forms of self-organization and institutional diversity that are particularly common below national level governing institutions.[93] As Ostrom explained, self-organization is not necessarily a threat to the state, but can serve as a complement to it. One of the main implications from this approach is that formal institutions should be designed with knowledge of how societies operate in practice because generating ties, such as those that hold together self-governing communities

---

[88] Sheri Berman, "From the Sun King to Karzai: Lessons for State Building in Afghanistan," *Foreign Affairs* 89 (2010): 6.

[89] Amitai Etzioni, "Bottom-up Nation Building," *Policy Review*, no. 158 (2009): 52.

[90] Peter T. Leeson, "An-arrgh-chy: The Law and Economics of Pirate Organization," *Journal of Political Economy* 115, no. 6 (2007): 1049–94; Peter T. Leeson, "Efficient Anarchy," *Public Choice* 130, no. 1/2 (2007): 41–53; Peter T. Leeson, *The Invisible Hook: The Hidden Economics of Pirates* (Princeton, NJ: Princeton University Press, 2011).

[91] Gary Chartier, *Anarchy and Legal Order: Law and Politics for a Stateless Society* (New York: Cambridge University Press, 2013).

[92] Elinor Ostrom, *Governing the Commons: The Evolution of Institutions for Collective Action* (New York: Cambridge University Press, 1990).

[93] Ostrom, *Understanding Institutional Diversity*.

takes a very long time. It is nearly impossible for external actors to generate such cohesion and legitimacy under their short time horizons.[94]

Frequently state efforts to eliminate or replace such ties may leave society worse-off. Although most scholarship equates non-state actors in weak states with violence, others have begun to illustrate the many ways in which non-state actors can play a positive role in failed states. In many cases, these are not armed groups (or exclusively armed groups), but instead groups that are adept at facilitating commerce and governance.[95] For example, Akbar Ahmad illustrates that in a range of Muslim-majority states, informal tribal authorities protect individuals from transgressions by the state and insurgents.[96] Peter Leeson provides a compelling argument that state failure in Somalia may have made society better off because informal governance arrangements have produced better societal outcomes than those generated by destructive, predatory regimes.[97]

In both academic and policy literatures, state consolidation means creating a uniform system of Weberian rules across disparate, frequently attenuated landscapes.[98] As we have seen, attempts to bring non-state groups and organizations under the purview of the state in the name of modernization, democracy, or state building frequently backfire by leading to increased conflict or simply rendering state policies ineffective as individuals exit the state.

The central implication of the self-governance perspective is that policymakers should anticipate that in the absence of an effective state, individuals exhibit enormous potential to solve collective dilemmas and find workable solutions to improve their situation. Although many of these solutions may seem second best or "good enough," a solution that is good enough is often quite better than what states might offer in such contexts.[99] In this regard, the self-governance perspective can be a source of optimism, as it can identify previously hidden sources of governance capacity in fragile states – potentially reducing the burden of the state.

---

[94] Elinor Ostrom, "Self-Organization and Social Capital," *Industrial and Corporate Change* 4, no. 1 (1995): 131–59; Elinor Ostrom, "Collective Action and the Evolution of Social Norms," *The Journal of Economic Perspectives* 14, no. 3 (2000): 137–58; Elinor Ostrom, "Social Capital: A Fad or Fundamental Concept?," in *Social Capital: A Multifaceted Perspective*, ed. Partha Dasgupta and Ismail Serageldin (Washington, DC: World Bank, 2000), 172–216.

[95] Ken Menkhaus, "Governance without Government in Somalia: Spoilers, State Building, and the Politics of Coping," *International Security* 31, no. 3 (2007): 74–106.

[96] Akbar S. Ahmed, *The Thistle and the Drone: How America's War on Terror Became a Global War on Tribal Islam* (Washington, DC: Brookings Institution Press, 2013).

[97] Peter T. Leeson, *Anarchy Unbound: Why Self-Governance Works Better than You Think*, (New York: Cambridge University Press, 2014).

[98] Bromley and Anderson, *Vulnerable People, Vulnerable States*; Herbst, *States and Power in Africa*.

[99] Merilee S. Grindle, "Good Enough Governance: Poverty Reduction and Reform in Developing Countries," *Governance* 17, no. 4 (2004): 525–48; Merilee S. Grindle, "Good Enough Governance Revisited," *Development Policy Review* 25, no. 5 (2007): 533–74.

An implication of this research suggests the importance of scaling back the scope of the state in Afghanistan. State builders in Afghanistan sought to heal wounds in the country by creating a state built on the notion of positive rights, asking the state to provide a mighty bundle of public goods in exchange for loyalty. Much of the state-building project in Afghanistan, embodied by the efforts to create new councils at the village level to extend the writ of the state to communities, "reflected a state-centric approach by redefining the political rules of the game and by introducing normative modes of good governance."[100]

The pages ahead will show that the failure to build the state – especially outside of Kabul – after 2001 arose from an almost complete unwillingness to understand sources of political legitimacy that exist outside the state that, in turn, led to a misdiagnosis of demands for the state and the state-building project it spawned. This is not the first study to recognize that the state-building project in Afghanistan was overly ambitious. In many ways, this study is parallel to Astre Suhrke's masterful illustration of the many follies of the international project, although this book focuses on dynamics within the Afghan government and its communities rather than on external intervention.[101]

The self-governance approach guides my empirical inquiry into the capacity and limitations of customary organizations throughout rural Afghanistan. On the one hand, as anticipated by this literature, self-governance often works quite well. At the same time, there are clear limitations to this approach. It is by examining the limitations of self-governance that this book carves out a role for the state. While informed by the self-governance approach, the central contribution of this book is to identify points of intersection in the literatures on state building, failed states, and self-governance.

CUSTOM, TRIBE, AND COUNTERINSURGENCY

One of the most challenging aspects of studying governance in Afghanistan is grappling with the concepts of customary governance and tribal governance. Did such authority persist after decades of internecine violence and government policy seeking to replace informal order with parchment rules? What toll has conflict had on customary and tribal governance? Do these structures continue to function?

Many observers writing during the past decades speculated that traditional governance had withered away due to years of warfare and migration. In fact, some of the most noteworthy scholarly accounts of Afghanistan in recent

---

[100] Conrad Schetter, "Introduction," in *Local Politics in Afghanistan: A Century of Intervention in Social Order*, ed. Conrad Schetter (New York: Columbia University Press, 2013), 7.

[101] Astri Suhrke, *When More Is Less: The International Project in Afghanistan* (New York: Columbia University Press, 2011).

decades have detailed the "fragmentation" of Afghan society, especially among tribal structures in the countryside.[102] A generation of local notables and tribal leaders were executed by the Communists, the Soviets or the Taliban.[103] In my own fieldwork, I heard dozens of accounts of the killing of village leaders since the Saur Revolution in 1978.

The perceived decline of tribal society is not just a question of socio-logical significance, but an important political question. Olivier Roy believed that the war led to the emergence of a new class of political actors who established a new political order based on religious doctrine and ideology, one which replaced an "old" political elite based on tradition and tribe.[104] According to this narrative, venerated elders were replaced by intrepid young men wielding new Islamist ideologies as the most formidable power-brokers in society. An apparent transformation of the social fabric unleashed radical religious organizations that were relatively independent of traditional structures and the forms of social control that went along with them. These new actors mobilized a generation of fighters who seemingly lacked or eschewed tribal loyalties. The conservative, Deobandi Islamist ideology of the Taliban, for instance, contrasted starkly with Hanafi-inspired Islam infused with Sufism that was traditionally practiced in Afghanistan. Ahmed Rashid argued that this radicalization occurred because the initial Taliban leadership grew up "de-tribalized" in Deobandi madrassas in Pakistan, educated in religion but not in Afghan custom.[105] The disruption caused by Afghan militias, police, and foreign troops further weakened tribal and local elders.[106]

When the U.S. military effort and accompanying state-building projects began in 2001, it appeared as if most policymakers accepted the conclusion that war had wiped out customary authority. As result, virtually no efforts

---

[102] David B. Edwards, *Before Taliban: Genealogies of the Afghan Jihad* (Berkeley, CA: University of California Press, 2002); Barnett R. Rubin, *The Fragmentation of Afghanistan: State Forma-tion and Collapse in the International System*, Second Edition (New Haven, CT: Yale University Press, 2002).

[103] Antonio Giustozzi, *Koran, Kalashnikov, and Laptop: The Neo-Taliban Insurgency in Afghani-stan* (New York: Columbia University Press, 2007); Antonio Giustozzi, *Decoding the New Taliban: Insights from the Afghan Field* (New York: Columbia University Press, 2009); Roy, *Islam and Resistance in Afghanistan*.

[104] "The New Political Elite in Afghanistan," in *The Politics of Social Transformation in Afghani-stan, Iran, and Pakistan*, ed. Myron Weiner and Ali Banuazizi (Syracuse, NY: Syracuse University Press, 1994), 72–100.

[105] *Taliban: Militant Islam, Oil and Fundamentalism in Central Asia, Second Edition* (New Haven, CT: Yale University Press, 2002). It is important to note that some Afghan mujahideen active in fighting the Soviets maintain that the Taliban existed far earlier than Rashid and most analysis acknowledges and emerged from the tribal fabric in the areas around Kandahar. See Sayyed Mohammad Akbar Agha, *I Am Akbar Agha: Memories of the Afghan Jihad and the Taliban* (Berlin: First Draft Publishing GmbH, 2014).

[106] Giustozzi, *Decoding the New Taliban*.

were made to include customary order at the village level in plans to construct a more effective state. In the hopeful moments after the seemingly quick collapse of the Taliban, foreign, and Afghan officials began an earnest and laser-like focus on the creation of formal, nationally based governance structures they hoped would trickle down to communities around the country. They assumed that in the absence of the state, individuals had descended into Hobbesian chaos.

Just a few years after 2001, some long-time scholars of the country argued that the internationally supported Afghan government efforts to promote governance and the rule of law were falling far short of expectations. This had little to do with the nature of the war effort or the amount of resources spent on Afghanistan, but instead because the model of governance Western countries, aid agencies, and many urban Afghans who had returned from exile advocated was far removed from the realities of rural life. Based on field observations, Afghan-born scholar Ali Wardak, asked the international community to take a closer look at traditional forms of justice, arguing that village-level institutions had not withered away and remained far more legitimate than state courts, which most rural Afghans perceived as corrupt.[107]

As the war effort wore on and the Taliban began to re-emerge from ashes of defeat, many U.S. soldiers based in rural Afghanistan experienced a very different country than a tabula rasa. Similarly, some soldiers argued that it was too early to pronounce the death of tribal or customary governance. Instead of seeing a vacuum of customary authority, observers interested in the conduct of U.S. counterinsurgency efforts in Afghanistan became fascinated with the notion that "tribes" might serve as allies to fight the Taliban. They believed that Pashtun tribes could mobilize villagers to fight the Taliban: an Afghan equivalent to the Anbar Sunni "awakening" of tribes in Iraq that played an important role fighting alongside the U.S. military to weaken Al Qaeda during the "surge" from 2006–09.

U.S. soldiers serving on the ground in communities began advocating and practicing this "tribal" approach. In fact, several American soldiers serving with the NATO coalition kept online journals detailing the importance of "tribes," "elders," and "jirgas" in the villages they sought to mobilize against Taliban insurgents. U.S. Army Major James Gant, argued that the international community and NATO did not have an adequate strategy to deal with traditional governance structures in rural areas. He saw how customary bodies had been brutalized by insurgent groups, including the Taliban, and how the "tribal" way of life was deeply threatened by Islamist neo-Manicheast ideology. To many soldiers on the ground, it was clear that "tribes" were alive and well and that if only foreign militaries and donors could understand this vast and

---

[107] Wardak, "Building a Post-War Justice System in Afghanistan"; John Braithwaite and Ali Wardak, "Crime and War in Afghanistan Part I: The Hobbesian Solution," *British Journal of Criminology* 53, no. 2 (March 2013): 179–96.

complicated "human terrain" then internationally-supported efforts to win hearts and mind could succeed.[108]

As this book illustrates, there is some truth to both accounts. Due to decades of conflict, the "tribal system" was thrown into upheaval. Many foreign soldiers serving in the Afghan countryside, however, proved to be more astute observers of the organizational and institutional landscape than many in the international aid community and the Afghan elites in Kabul precisely because they understood elders and customary village councils still remained the lifeblood of political decision making in rural Afghanistan. Frequently, terminology employed on such issues was imprecise. The governance systems they described had their origins in custom rather than tribe. In most instances, when military officials or policy makers referred to "tribes," they were not always referring to these broader lineage-based social structures or tribal confederations (confederations that may indeed have declined), but instead seemed to be speaking about political organization at the village level. From my observations, the term "tribe" was their shorthand for customary order.

As I will discuss in greater detail in later chapters, this distinction is important because it means that tribal affiliations or Pashtun tribal networks could weaken without necessarily undermining the role of customary institutions and organizations at the village level. When observers pointed to the breakdown of the "tribal system," they seemed to be referring to the challenges confronting tribes and clans as they engaged one another – specifically, to band together in broader networks to fight against a common foe. In Iraq, the hierarchical nature of the tribal system made it less challenging for tribes to unite against a common enemy than among Pashtun groups in rural Afghanistan, whose tribes are acephalous.[109]

In Afghanistan, there is some evidence that the tribal system no longer functions the way it once had in terms of local alliance politics. This transformation is not new, as it began with the emergence of the Afghan state itself.[110] Scholars had noted the evolution of the tribal and "traditional" system prior to the large-scale conflict in Afghanistan.[111] In fact, due to the acephalous and

---

[108] Retired General Stanley McChrystal, former commander of U.S. and NATO forces in Afghanistan during the height of the surge (2009–10) argued that a more nuanced understanding of "traditional" structures along with intelligence that was better rooted in local realties were vital for foreigners seeking to counter insurgency in Afghanistan. See McChrystal "It Takes a Network," *Army Communicator* 36, no. 2 (2011).

[109] See Lynch "Explaining the Awakening: Engagement, Publicity, and the Transformation of Iraqi Sunni Political Attitudes," *Security Studies* 20, no. 1 (2011): 36–72, for an overview of how the tribes in Iraq mobilized against al Qaeda during the course of the conflict in Iraq.

[110] Ashraf Ghani, "Islam and State-Building in a Tribal Society Afghanistan: 1880–1901," *Modern Asian Studies* 12, no. 2 (1978): 269–84.

[111] Jon W. Anderson, "There Are No Khāns Anymore: Economic Development and Social Change in Tribal Afghanistan," *Middle East Journal* 32, no. 2 (1978): 167–83.

egalitarian nature of Pashtun tribes, it is not certain that tribes were *ever* able to mobilize as effectively as a cohesive group. Yet the long decline of tribal authority should not be taken as evidence that Afghanistan is an ungoverned space. Customary governance remains an important and evolving system of governance.[112] I shall leave it to the readers to more fully draw out the implications for counterinsurgency strategy, as my main objective in this book is to understand the system of informal governance, rather than to explicitly tie this analysis into efforts to defeat an anti-state insurgency.

ORGANIZATION

This book is organized into three parts. Part I of the book, which includes Chapters 2 and 3, describes government policy toward customary organizations in historical perspective, as well as the status of these organizations in present-day Afghanistan. Chapter 2 relies on historiography as well as oral histories to describe how government policy toward customary governance and village governance has vacillated between attempts at indirect and direct rule. Chapter 3, which serves as the empirical foundation of the remainder of the book, uses fieldwork evidence to clarify the persistence of customary organization and its key features.

Part II, which includes Chapters 4 and 5, considers the political economy of public goods provision within and across villages. Chapter 4 compares customary organizations, donor-sponsored development councils, and warlords/local commanders in their effectiveness at providing public goods within villages. Chapter 5 considers the problem of inter-village cooperation to provide public goods.

Part III analyzes the relationship between customary organizations and the state. Chapter 6 uses evidence from public opinion surveys and fieldwork to see whether the presence of customary organizations is correlated with support for the central government and democratic values, finding that increased support for customary governance is associated with higher support for the state and democratic norms. Chapter 7 considers the relationship between customary and formal government authorities. Although the Afghan state is formally centralized, norms of informal power sharing between district governors and customary representatives commonly – but not always – emerges to facilitate shared governance between formal and informal representatives.

The concluding chapter discusses implications of the analysis for state-building efforts in Afghanistan and elsewhere. The central lesson is that improving prospects for state building begins with a much more thorough

---

[112] This is true of customary governance in Afghanistan as well as other contexts. See Anne M. Larson, Peter J. Cronkleton, and Juan M. Pulhin, "Formalizing Indigenous Commons: The Role of 'Authority' in the Formation of Territories in Nicaragua, Bolivia, and the Philippines," *World Development* 70 (2015): 228–38.

understanding of context, in particular the extent, capacity, and limitations of self-organized systems of governance. It requires policymakers and scholars to acknowledge the possibility that regardless of context, individuals all over the world share an ability to overcome collective dilemmas and engage in collective action – even if the landscape seems unabashedly Hobbesian. Understanding effective sources of collective action in the absence of an effective state should be the first priority of state builders as they tackle the next crises. This is how we can operationalize what we mean when we say "context matters."

PART I

THE POLITICS OF CUSTOMARY GOVERNANCE

2

The Afghan state in historical perspective

> To explain myself: I mean that I had to put in order all those hundreds of petty
> chiefs, plunderers, robbers, and cut-throats, who were the cause of everlasting
> trouble in Afghanistan. This necessitated breaking down the feudal and tribal
> system, and substituting one grand community under one law and under one rule.
> Luckily I have succeeded fully in this respect...
>
> > – Amir Abdur Rahman Khan in his autobiography,
> > *The Life of Abdur Rahman, Amir of Afghanistan.*

> We should walk slowly forever, not just run for an instance.
>
> > – Afghan proverb

The modern state is defined by mass conscription, reliable sources of revenue,
and regulation of economic activities. As states emerged, centralized rule and
eventually bureaucrats replaced "traditional" social orders characterized by
relational contracting, local allegiances, and social norms. The transformation
has rarely been peaceful. If life without the state was "short, brutish, and
nasty," efforts to build and consolidate state authority have typically been long,
violent, and coercive.

Late developers have often sought to speed up state-building processes that
unfolded over centuries in many places. This is certainly the case in Afghanistan. Since the mid-19th century most rulers of Afghanistan have relentlessly
imposed their vision of progress upon the countryside in an effort to consolidate the state. As part of a state-building strategy, Afghanistan's rulers either
attempted to eliminate customary organizations or simply disregarded them in
their quest to consolidate political power.

This chapter considers state policy toward customary organizations in the
broad sweep of history. It articulates what can be described as "customary
disregard," which refers to policies that included efforts to destroy customary

governance, co-opt it, or to simply ignore it. As we shall see, customary disregard is a pervasive feature of the history of state–society relations in Afghanistan. It was also persistent after 2001, and as well shall see in subsequent chapters, it helps to explain why the state-building process failed to live up to its potential. The historical context is also important because historical legacies continue to inform Afghans perceptions of the state: in interviews, rural informants spoke of events happening 120 years ago regarding village relations with the state as if they were yesterday.

This historical sojourn begins by considering key features of Afghanistan's period of indirect rule, which runs from the time Ahmad Shah Durrani became the leader of an empire in 1747 until Abdur Rahman ascended to power in 1880. Ahmad Shah, who derived his right to rule from a Loya Jirga ("grand council") of tribal and other notables, established a mode of governance whereby tribes and regional groups enjoyed substantial autonomy. Leaders used the Loya Jirga as a consultative mechanism to bestow authority to leaders and their policies. In some instances it had legitimacy; in others it was a rubber stamp. It served as important symbol for the people of Afghanistan as it provided a bridge between the state and its subjects. Indirect rule provided monarchs with the legitimacy necessary to consolidate authority but it also had a cost, namely, seemingly endless conflict between the king and his relatives who exercised autonomous power over the country's distant regions.

Indirect rule ended when Rahman came to power. During his rule from 1880 to 1901, the "Iron Amir" sought to ruthlessly consolidate state authority and end threats to his power coming from both his relatives in regional fiefdoms and from communities. Known for his brutality, he claimed authority to rule through divine right as an amir, rather than through consent of the tribes as a king (shah), declaring himself amir al-momenin (commander of the faithful). He viewed customary authority as a threat to his rule.

While Rahman's death in 1901 stopped the most egregious violence, it did not end the policy of customary disregard. On the contrary, direct rule and centralization of authority became the policy of choice for most of leaders who governed for most of the next century, many of whom tended to view Afghanistan as a late-developer that badly needed to get caught up with the world around it. Regardless of ideology, the late-developer mentality placed blame squarely on traditional authority as a source of Afghan underdevelopment and even moral poverty.

In addition to relating direct rule to violence and disorder, this chapter also speaks to the challenges of implementing governance styles that approximate either direct or indirect rule. The costs of indirect rule, whereby the state preserves local power relations, are usually used to justify direct rule.[1] Yet as Michael Hechter and Nika Kabiri observe, "each form of rule [direct and

---

[1] Michael Hechter, *Containing Nationalism* (New York: Oxford University Press, 2001).

indirect] has strengths and liabilities, choosing an optimal form of governance is anything but child's play. Direct rule may quell insurgent activity in some contexts, but in others it may stimulate the emergence of social groups that threaten the regime. Under indirect rule, groups may use their autonomy to challenge state authority. Evidently, there is no universally optimal choice of governance structures for the attainment of order."[2] The problem is an example of what Weingast viewed as the fundamental dilemma for emergence of rule of law: a state must be strong enough to suppress conflict between local units, but not too strong as to undermine citizen rights.[3]

Although indirect rule had its costs in Afghanistan, such social costs appear to pale in comparison to the violence imposed by direct rule. Since the fall of the monarchy in 1973, most Afghan rulers have viewed economic and political reform as something that must come at the expense of customary organizations and local autonomy. In the 1970s, the government of Daud Khan tried to co-opt customary governance structures into the state. In the 1980s, the Communist government tried to eliminate them as agents of "feudalism" and "backwardness."[4] Various warlords and political parties fighting the Soviet-backed government in Kabul in the 1980s and 1990s viewed the widespread legitimacy of these organizations as a threat to their power and sought to dominate them by populating them with their own agents.

Once we understand contemporary Afghan history as a struggle over who controls the villages, it is easier to see why many in the countryside harbor such a deep mistrust of state authority, regardless of who controls the state. One village elder shared with me the challenge of governance the historical legacy has left in Afghanistan today: "If the government is bad, people will not accept [it]; if the government is kind, people will not accept [it]."[5] Although many have interpreted Afghanistan as completely ungovernable and hostile to central government authority, this chapter illustrates why many fear the possibility of state building and a return to direct rule.

INDIRECT RULE: AHMAD SHAH DURRANI AND THE EARLY MONARCHY

The heart of what is now Afghanistan emerged when Ahmad Shah Abdali was chosen to lead the Abdali tribal confederation, a ruling dynasty that emerged from the Afsharid Empire in what is now Iran and western Afghanistan. Tribal leaders and elders from both major Pashtun tribal confederations, the Abdali

[2] "Attaining Social Order in Iraq," in *Order, Conflict, and Violence*, ed. Stathis N. Kalyvas, Ian Shapiro, and Tarek Masoud (New York: Cambridge University Press, 2008), 50.

[3] Weingast, "The Political Foundations of Democracy and the Rule of Law."

[4] Anthony Hyman, *Afghanistan under Soviet Domination, 1964–83* (New York: Palgrave Macmillan, 1984).

[5] Bamiyan-Sayghan-Village 1-#4.

and Ghilzai, from within the approximate boundaries of current-day Afghanistan met in a Loya Jirga in Kandahar and proclaimed Ahmad Shah the head of a "grand Afghan ethno-tribal confederation".[6] Ahmad Shah was a notable officer in the Afsharid army. According to lore, during his coronation ceremony he was proclaimed the Dur-e Durrani ("pearl of pearls"). The Abdalis then became known as the Durrani (a title that has stuck until today). With his accession to this position, Ahmad Shah assumed the leadership of what became known as the Durrani Empire, which eventually became Afghanistan.[7]

Ahmad Shah forged a state by establishing a broad base of authority. He counted among his supporters significant numbers of non-Pashtuns, especially the Qizilbash, who were Shia military officers from the decaying Afsharid Empire.[8] During the next twenty-five years, Ahmad Shah marshaled the rest of the Pashtun population, as well as other ethnic groups living under Afsharid Persian domination to the West and Mughal domination to the East, under an independent political unit that came to be known as Afghanistan.

Ahmad Shah relied heavily on customary authority to build his own legitimacy. Instead of pursuing direct rule, he employed the Turko-Persian model of rule in which a monarch rules indirectly through his own blood relatives. Relatives of the king or shah were dispatched to run the empire on behalf of their family in distant provinces and typically had autonomy in their regions to build up their own wealth and legitimacy. Acting according to Turko-Persian norms, Ahmad Shah Durrani sent his brothers and cousins to administer territories and their quasi-independent armed forces that protected and conquered territory on behalf of the sovereign.[9]

The Durrani Empire built by Ahmad Shah was an empire based on military governance. To provide security, the empire relied on mercenaries and tribal groups that could be mobilized through local customary leaders, who in turn expected to be rewarded for their service. As a result of this dependence on customary leaders and mercenaries, Ahmad Shah's state was not centrally strong. The early state lacked a permanent standing army, a reliable means of revenue, and a capable and competent bureaucracy. Political power was diffused among the major tribes and relatives of the monarch who enjoyed autonomy over their regions and people. Yet by employing the various ethnic groups and tribes that now comprise Afghanistan into his military force as part of his broader effort to wrest territory from the rule of neighboring empires and

[6] Amin Saikal, *Modern Afghanistan: A History of Struggle and Survival* (London: I.B.Tauris, 2004), 19.

[7] Thomas J. Barfield, "Problems in Establishing Legitimacy in Afghanistan," *Iranian Studies* 37, no. 2 (2004): 270.

[8] Christine Noelle, *State and Tribe in Nineteenth-Century Afghanistan: The Reign of Amir Dost Muhammad Khan* (New York: Routledge, 1997), 25.

[9] Thomas J. Barfield, *Afghanistan: A Cultural and Political History* (Princeton, NJ: Princeton University Press, 2010).

by relying on relatives and local leaders to govern on his behalf, Ahmad Shah was able to accommodate the patchwork of ethnic and religious groups under the umbrella of the expanding state.[10]

This system of indirect rule ensured that communities remained relatively autonomous. Ahmad Shah established what could legitimately be called an Afghan state for the first time. Richard Tapper explains that the regime was held together in a bargain whereby "tribal leaders were confirmed in their possession of lands and the main offices of state were distributed among the different tribes" and that monarchs distributed revenue to these tribal chiefs in exchange for their support.[11] In most matters not directly related to military issues, provincial governors were independent in their handling of administration, existing as virtual "mini-kingdoms."[12] According to M. Hasan Kakar, these governors were more like partners in an unequal alliance than subjects. They were able to maintain their positions as long as they kept local peace.[13] Of course, to keep tranquility these governors had to maintain their own security forces. A consequence of this system was that it was not up to the central government to maintain a monopoly on coercive authority. Nonetheless, this system of indirect rule, which provided an important role for customary governance, would remain in place for over a century and half, with communities existing "within the bounds of their traditional microsocieties."[14]

Despite holding the country together, indirect rule in Afghanistan had several notable flaws. Foremost among these weaknesses was the exacerbation of agnatic and other rivalries. Monarchs appointed their sons to important governorships, yet the central government typically lacked sufficient capacity to keep rivalries among governors and between governors and Kabul in check. It was not uncommon for brothers or cousins to wage campaigns against the monarch using the same quasi-private armies they relied upon to maintain local order in their regions. Although the system functioned well while Ahmad Shah was alive, once he died fighting broke out for control of the emergent state. These fights, which were acute among the Durrani elite, had their origins in the Turko-Persian political system that provided no way of excluding collateral heirs from the seats of power.[15]

In general, we know very little about this early period of local governance. During this period prior to state consolidation, it was the regional governors in the provinces who were the face of the state for subjects. These governors often had little to do with Kabul and were often local elites. They maintained their

[10] Saikal, *Modern Afghanistan*, 21–23.
[11] Richard Tapper, "Introduction," in *The Conflict of Tribe and State in Iran and Afghanistan*, ed. Richard Tapper (New York: St. Martin's Press, 1983), 13–14.
[12] Barfield, *Afghanistan*, 102.
[13] M. Hasan Kakar, *Government and Society in Afghanistan: The Reign of Amir Abd Al-Rahman Khan* (Austin, TX: University of Texas Press, 1979), 47.
[14] Saikal, *Modern Afghanistan*, 31.   [15] Dupree, *Afghanistan*.

own systems of taxation and military forces, rarely taking direct orders from Kabul, who struggled to control them and the people they ruled. During this early period, Afghanistan had only four main provinces. Later in the 20th century, the number of provinces expands to thirty four. It is through the creation of new provinces that Kabul is able to appoint new leaders and assert control over the countryside.[16]

Although the Afghan state under the Turko-Persian system of governance was weak, communities were allowed to govern their day-to-day affairs without much external intervention. Mountstuart Elphinstone, a British colonial administrator who detailed his expeditions to Afghanistan from British India in a voluminous ethnography, *An Account of the Kingdom of Caubul and Its Dependencies*, offers a similar conclusion, observing that, "The Afghaun government has always shown a good deal of moderation towards its own subjects, its dependence states and its enemies."[17] He noted that this moderation was facilitated through a policy of indirect rule whereby "the government endeavors to maintain quiet and prosperity among all the Afghaun tribes; but, aware of their having interests distinct from its own, it does not watch over their welfare with that solicitude which one would expect from a King towards his nation."[18] As Thomas Barfield concludes in his assessment of governance during this period:

By bringing the Durranis to power, Ahmad Shah is rightly seen as the founder of an independent Afghanistan that was no longer just a contested border region of Iran or India. But there remained a natural friction between the pretensions of the autocratic ruler who had founded an empire and a people whose politically egalitarian ethos rendered such claims to preeminence suspect. Ahmad smoothed over this problem by appointing a *majlis* (council) composed of Pashtun clan elders to advise him. Though this gave the appearance of a partnership, such clan leaders appeared to have little influence on policy. The real conflict between royal pretensions and tribal republicanism, however, would not emerge until the reigns of Ahmad's successors, who never treated the tribes as partners.[19]

The state largely maintained indirect rule for a century after the death of Ahmad Shah in 1773.[20] The instability attributed to this policy was

---

[16] I am grateful to Thomas Barfield for these points.
[17] Mountstuart Elphinstone, *An Account of the Kingdom of Caubul and Its Dependencies in Persia, Tartary and India* (London: Longman, Hurst, Rees, Orme, and Brown, 1815), 515.
[18] Ibid., 516.   [19] Dupree, *Afghanistan*, 105.
[20] Writing forty years after the death of Ahmad Shah Durrani, Elphinstone described the system of governance as follows: "There is a Dooraunee governor appointed to each, who is called a *Sirdar*. He never resides in his government; but, once a year, goes himself or sends a deputy, with or without force (according to the necessity of using intimidation), to collect the revenue. At other times, the regulation of the country is left to the heads of the tribes, subject to some control in extraordinary cases from the *Sirdar*. The *Sirdar*, in most cases, recommends the member of the head family whom he things fittest for the chiefship of each tribe under him. There are *Cauzees* [judges] appointed by the King in these divisions, but their authority, if supported at all, is

exacerbated by great power rivalries between the United Kingdom and Russia during the height of the Great Game. These foreign rivals sponsored factions within the Afghan royal family who they thought might be in a position to take over the country. During this period, the Durrani Empire transformed into the country that is now Afghanistan. The demarcation of Afghanistan was also sped up by international competition as Russia and the United Kingdom made agreements with Afghan leaders on imperial boundaries.

DIRECT RULE: ABDUR RAHMAN KHAN AND STATE CONSOLIDATION

Indirect rule struck a balance between the desire to establish an Afghan state and local power holders. This model of governance, however, bred enormous instability. Upon coming to power in 1880, Abdur Rahman perceiving the system of indirect rule as a root cause of the problems, "funneled his many talents into the creation of a nation state" through a process of "internal imperialism."[21]

Abdur Rahman eventually succeeded in centralizing political authority. He was as famous for the means with which he sought to achieve centralization as the outcome itself, monopolizing control of the state with a ruthless passion. As his brutality was accompanied by revolt and subsequent repression, his punishments became more severe such as sewing the lips shut of a person who dared to speak in public of his cruelty.[22] This was how Afghanistan's first social planner and state-builder went about the business of "modernization."

Abdur Rahman took five decisive steps to strengthen his position vis-à-vis customary authority. His first was to completely eliminate consultation with tribes as, and relying instead on religion as a means of legitimacy. He claimed a right to rule from divine authority, declaring himself amir al-momenin.[23]

Second, Abdur Rahman waged a series of brutal military campaigns against almost every tribal and ethnic group in the country. All told, he conducted seventeen major military campaigns against the population, himself estimating that he killed at least 100,000 out of a population of approximately six million. The military campaigns were not just aimed at leaders but also at whole populations, attaining a level of destruction associated with foreign invasions of Afghanistan.[24] Kakar estimates the number of citizens killed by Rahman in his efforts to consolidate his authority were higher than the number of both

---

enforced by the head of the tribe," See Elphinstone, *An Account of the Kingdom of Caubul and Its Dependencies in Persia, Tartary and India*, 522.

[21] Dupree, *Afghanistan*, 417.   [22] Kakar, *Government and Society in Afghanistan*, 38.

[23] Richard S Newell, *The Politics of Afghanistan*, South Asian Political Systems (Ithaca, NY: Cornell University Press, 1972), 44. Rahman was not the first leader to do this. For example, Dost Mohmammad (r. 1826–39, 1842–63) declared himself amir al-momenin when he waged war against the Sikhs on the periphery of what was becoming Afghanistan.

[24] Barfield, *Afghanistan*, Chapter 3.

British and Afghans killed in the two Anglo-Afghan wars combined.[25] The public reacted by wishing Abdur Rahman bad luck, even praying for the return of British forces to save them from the cruelty of the Amir.

Third, Rahman undermined customary authority through a massive repopulation campaign in which he strategically moved communities from one part of the country to another. He banished several rival Ghilzai Pashtun groups from southern Afghanistan to north of the Hindu Kush and sought to pacify Shia Hazara populations residing in the central highlands who refused to consent to central government rule. To enlist additional soldiers in his campaign against the Hazaras, he declared them infidels. This maneuver allowed him to avoid Islamic norms governing treatment of adversaries in war. Once Hazaras were declared infidels, he could promise other groups, especially his fellow Pashtuns, the land of the vanquished. By opening up new opportunities for plunder, the Amir substantially increased his military numbers.

These repopulation campaigns, as much as any of his other tactics, earned him his reputation as the "Iron Amir." Yet the displacement of the Ghilzai population from the south to the frontiers of the country served dual purposes. According to his divide and conquer logic, once these populations were moved elsewhere they would settle in areas where Pashtuns had not previously resided, thus buffering the country against outside invasion or any irredentist claims (with Pashtuns mixed among the Turkic and Tajik populations in the north and West, serving as a buffer against the Russian empire). Rahman also utilized policies of divide and rule to fuel existing rivalries between groups as well as foster new fissures. Diffusing the Pashtuns promised to weaken the political consolidation of non-Pashtun groups in specific regions that Abdur Rahman sought to weaken. This move had the effect, at least in the short term, of securing the frontier while also reducing sources of internal unrest.

Although Rahman ruled over a century ago, the divide-and-conquer strategies employed by him left an enormous legacy. These memories were particularly pronounced among the Hazara communities whose ancestors rebelled against Rahman's rule and were subjects of this repopulation campaign. Hazaras view Rahman's violence against them as genocidal.[26] In my field research, I found memories of Abdur Rahman in the north of Afghanistan to be particularly vivid. A middle-aged Hazara male farmer in Khanabad District, Kunduz province village whose family was moved from Central Afghanistan to Kunduz Province in the north recalled how Abdur Rahman took land from his family:

We have lived here all my life—only during the war [against the Soviets] did I leave for Pakistan—but during the Taliban period I came back. We faced a lot of problems with the Taliban. They took me three times and beat me because I am Hazara. They wanted a

[25] Kakar, *Government and Society in Afghanistan*.
[26] M. Hasan Kakar, "The Pacification of the Hazaras of Afghanistan" (New York: Asia Society, Afghanistan Council, 1973).

gun from me. They (Pashtuns) have always worked with us like this. Our parents came from Ghorband (a valley in the central highlands) many years ago and actually they came here because of Abdur Rahman who was very cruel and killed many of our people. He took all our land and gave it to Pashtun people. So my grandfather came here and at first it was just a forest and nothing else. They put a lot of effort into the land and so we stayed here. Today, our people don't have as much land as they used to. Subsequent Pashtun kings in Afghanistan gave our land here to other Pashtuns. So we don't have so much land here. In some cases, when we don't own land, we work for others as [tenant] farmers. This was because our land was given by Pashtun Kings to other Pashtuns.[27]

Several other Hazara informants described the violence of Abdur Rahman as if it happened yesterday. This middle-aged male qaryadar's family was resettled from the south to the northern province of Balkh:

Our Hazara people came to this district one hundred years ago when Abdur Rahman forced them to move. He killed many of my ancestors. Some of them escaped from [our native] Uruzgan and came here. A few years later Amanullah Khan gave some land to people in this area, so people named it Dawlatabad (the land of the state).[28]

A male farmer in another village in the same district bemoaned how Rahman confiscated the most productive land, giving Hazaras land of marginal economic value instead:

We came here during the reign of Abdur Rahman Khan and our people settled here. Actually, Abdur Rahman took our land and then the government gave us some land in return. At that time, the land he gave us did not have any water. Today we still don't have enough water on our land.[29]

The fourth component of his strategy was to increase domestic sources of revenue. As anticipated by Margaret Levi's theory in which revenue is the lifeblood of the state,[30] as it is an essential ingredient to building bureaucracy and promoting military capacity, Rahman took measures to drastically increase the size of the public purse. He did this in two ways. First, he radically increased taxes on trade and land holdings. Through these taxes, he laid the foundations for a harsh tax code whose ultimate purpose was to build state capacity and construct a national army.[31] Second, he increased revenue by wrangling a large increase in subsidies from the British Empire. Instead of jousting with external powers for control of his territory, he developed an agreement with the British Empire, sealed with a healthy 50 percent increase in the subsidy. Although he surrendered his country's foreign policy to the British as a result of this bargain, the subsidy allowed Abdur Rahman to focus almost exclusively on domestic

[27] Kunduz-Khanabad-Village 2-#2.   [28] Balkh-Dawlatabad-Village 2-#3.
[29] Balkh-Dawlatabad-Village 1-#5.
[30] Margaret Levi, *Of Rule and Revenue* (Berkeley, CA: University of California Press, 1989).
[31] Shah Mahmoud Hanifi, *Connecting Histories in Afghanistan: Market Relations and State Formation on a Colonial Frontier* (Palo Alto, CA: Stanford University Press, 2008).

concerns.[32] More importantly the subsidy provided him with revenue that allowed him to participate in the international arms trade and equip his soldiers.

The fifth and final element of his state-building policy was the creation of a system of formal governance through the codification and rationalization of government administration and legal codes. Under his rule, the government established formal provinces with administrative functions that came directly under the rule of Kabul. Previously, provinces were simply regions of the country (e.g., Kandahar, Herat, Turkestan) and were largely autonomous and ruled by relatives of the monarch as semi-independent fiefdoms. Creation of provincial-level administration facilitated tax collection, conscription of soldiers, and monitoring of tribal and religious leaders in a way the state had never been able or willing to do before.

In addition to establishing formal administrative divisions, Rahman sought to eliminate the customary basis of legal rules.[33] Prior to his reign, most communities primarily relied upon customary law and not on a particular vision of Islamic law; it was only during Rahman's reign that new laws emerged based almost entirely upon the state's interpretation of Islamic law.[34] The creation of state law was only permitted in cases where Islamic law did not offer a solution. In this new vision, Islamic and state law were elevated above customary law. Abdur Rahman had a strategic reason for elevating Islam over customary law, believing he could unite the people of Afghanistan under the banner of religion against outside influence.[35] In addition, by promulgating a state-backed version of shariat, Rahman elevated mullahs to the status of lawmakers in the countryside. Consequently, customary law was now challenged by mullahs, who enjoyed a position of authority not previously witnessed in the country.

As these tactics indicate, Abdur Rahman Khan engineered a frontal attack on local authority embodied in customary organizations. Although unable to eliminate it, he delivered a strong blow against it. His successors faced a choice: to continue on the path forged in blood by Abdur Rahman or to change course. While not as brutal, his successors would nevertheless engage in their own disregard of customary institutions.

Abdur Rahman died in 1901. He was succeeded by Habibullah Khan. Habibullah avoided major conflict for much of his rule, which lasted until 1919 when he was assassinated. During his two decades as king, Habibullah did undo some his father's most repressive policies while engaging in incremental reforms he believed would improve prospects for economic development.

[32] Kakar, *Government and Society in Afghanistan.*
[33] Ghani, "Islam and State-Building in a Tribal Society Afghanistan."
[34] Kakar, *Government and Society in Afghanistan,* 165–6.
[35] Asta Olesen, *Islam and Politics in Afghanistan,* 1st edition (Surrey, UK: Routledge Curzon, 1995).

In particular, he opened the door for customary leaders to participate in government affairs by allowing them to participate in governance at the provincial level when disputes arose.[36] Habibullah's small efforts paled in comparison to that of his son, Amanullah, who upon ascending to the throne in 1919 embarked upon the most ambitious royal-led reform program in the history of Afghanistan.

DIRECT RULE REDUX: AMANULLAH

Amanullah worked to institute a set of very progressive, state-centric reforms until he was forced from power in a coup d'etat in 1929. Much like Abdur Rahman, Amanullah was a modernizer, yet his vision and tactics of how to accomplish his goals differed dramatically from those of his grandfather. Instead of drawing inspiration from Genghis Khan, Amanullah drew his inspiration from the secular model of Mustafa Kemal Ataturk. He wanted Afghanistan to be a secular and modern state and sought to emulate European models of constitutional monarchy.

One of Amanullah's goals was financial independence from the British, upon whom Afghanistan had relied upon heavily for subsidies for decades. If subsidies were to be lifted, the hole in state coffers left by dried-up subsidies would have to be filled somehow. Amanallah therefore devised a plan to tax individuals directly with revenue to be used to provide large-scale infrastructure, such as education and roads. To accomplish his goals, he introduced a system of taxation that placed a heavy burden on villagers, while also disrupting the traditional systems of tax collection that both Abdur Rahman and Habibullah had come to rely upon.[37] He sought to make the tax system more efficient by mandating cash payment, substantially raising tax rates on irrigated lands that had been unchanged for more than a half-century, introducing a poll tax in Kabul and a substantial tax on education that required even the poorest provinces to pay for this public good.[38]

Only a few years into his reign, Amanullah began laying the constitutional groundwork for his ambitious reform agenda. The first major statement of his agenda came with the 1923 Constitution, which established an elaborate system of government that deemphasized the role of Islam in the political regime. Knowing full well that these reforms would be met with resistance, he immediately called a Loya Jirga to secure approval of his ambitious reform agenda from customary leaders. Instead of approving his plans, the Loya Jirga strongly opposed the new reforms. As a result of the Loya Jirga, Amanullah

---

[36] Vartan Gregorian, *The Emergence of Modern Afghanistan: Politics of Reform and Modernization* (Palo Alto, CA: Stanford University Press, 1969), 181.

[37] Leon B. Poullada, *Reform and Rebellion in Afghanistan, 1919–1929; King Amanullah's Failure to Modernize a Tribal Society* (Ithaca, NY: Cornell University Press, 1973), 151.

[38] Barfield, *Afghanistan*, 183.

was forced to amend the constitution with an appendix noting the demands of customary leaders, including their desire to reinstate shariat law and the Hanafi school (madhab) of Islamic legal interpretation as the basis of jurisprudence and the reestablishment of the traditional system of Islamic (qazi) judges rather than the state-sanctioned judges.[39] Many religious and tribal leaders from eastern Afghanistan continued to resent Amanullah's reforms, culminating in the Khost Rebellion of 1924. The rebellion never seriously challenged the government in Kabul, but took several months to put down. Rather than moderating his reform agenda, the rebellion reminded Amanullah of the importance of a centralized state that could support a more effective army to put down any future rebellions.

It was his subsequent eight month trip to Europe and Turkey in 1927–8 that cemented Amanullah's vision of his country's future. Inspired by Ataturk and the Soviets, who had engaged in major social reform north of the Amu Darya, he sought to quicken the pace of domestic reforms. Yet even his admired contemporaries cautioned him against trying to use the state to move too quickly to impose reforms that society could view as too radical. These, included Ataturk who counseled him "not to start large-scale social and political reforms until he had a strong, well-trained army."[40]

Amanullah ignored what turned out to be prescient advice from Ataturk. Rather than moderate his reforms or strengthen his army to increase his ability to withstand resistance, Amanullah went ahead with major social reforms, including compulsory secondary education of girls and boys, as well as social and cultural reforms regarding marriage (outlawing polygamy), unveiling of women, and demands that all visitors to the capital Kabul wear Western-style clothes.[41] He also proclaimed that state-controlled Islam supplant local interpretations by mandating that traditional qazis be replaced by secular government-appointed judges.[42] To this day residents of Kabul tell anecdotes of how villagers visiting the capital during this period were forced to rent suits and ties for the day at booths set up by entrepreneurs on the outskirts of town.

Shortly after declaring these reforms, a rebellion quickly formed against the king once again. A revolt among the Shinwari tribe in eastern Afghanistan was rumored to be the result not just of the Amanullah's centralizing reforms and regulation of local religious leaders, but were also sparked by pictures taken of Queen Soraya during their European trip.[43] The pictures sparked controversy because the Queen appeared in public unveiled and in a sleeveless dress. The Shinwari revolt was compounded by an uprising stirring north of Kabul, led by the Tajik Habibullah Kalakani. Despite Kalakani's humble origins, by early 1929 he had overthrown the royal family and assumed control of the country,

[39] Ibid., 186.   [40] Dupree, *Afghanistan*, 451.
[41] For more see Newel *The Politics of Afghanistan*, 56–57.   [42] Barfield, *Afghanistan*, 188.
[43] Hafizullah Emadi, *Dynamics of Political Development in Afghanistan: The British, Russian, and American Invasions* (New York: Palgrave Macmillan, 2010).

becoming the first Tajik to ever rule Afghanistan. Once in power, he immediately began to reverse these reforms.[44]

In addition to these triggers, several key policies – each reflecting Amanullah's philosophy of direct rule – stoked the flames of rebellion. First among these policies was direct taxation. The end of the British subsidy required that the king look to his own subjects to finance his elaborate reform agenda. It was through his taxation policy where we can see how Amanullah sought to implement direct rule and supplant the role of customary governance. There were two components to the taxation policy that kindled dissent. One was replacing the role of maliks and other customary leaders in tax collection efforts with government officials. Prior to this, the state ruled villages as collective units and maliks were responsible for collecting a quota of revenue from communities. Customary leaders viewed this policy change as an affront to their authority. Second, he increased the overall amount of taxes villagers paid to the state. These administrative changes, alongside an increase in the rate of taxation, provoked outrage in the countryside.

Second, Amanullah struck at customary authorities by taking away their subsidies and seeking to regulate them.[45] With the end of British subsidies, the state no longer had resources available to pay for the loyalty of customary leaders and the rural residents they represented. He also required that all village mullahs obtain a state-issued license to practice.[46] In the years since they were elevated by Abdur Rahman, mullahs played an increasingly important role in rural life. Requiring that they obtain licenses to practice created a new kind of state control over religious life, one which produced additional consternation in rural society.

Third, Amanullah eliminated the role customary authorities played in selecting conscripts for the army through plans to select soldiers through a lottery, which required all males to have a government-issued identification card, called tazkera.[47] While the issuance of identification cards certainly aroused suspicion on the part of many Afghans, eliminating the discretion villages had in the conscription process sparked mistrust of state authority because it dramatically increased decision-making authority of the state in a realm that had traditionally been subject to local discretion.

Fourth, lack of procedural legitimacy contributed to a rural backlash. Although Amanullah revived the Loya Jirga mechanism to facilitate his domestic policy agenda, he did not use it for deliberation. Instead, he sought to co-opt the process in order to rubber stamp his reforms, hand-picking members of the

---

[44] One of the few firsthand accounts of the reign of Habibullah Kalakani can be found in Muhammad and McChesney, *Kabul under Siege: Fayz Muhammad's Account of the 1929 Uprising* (Princeton, NJ: Markus Wiener Publishers, 1999).
[45] Rubin, *The Fragmentation of Afghanistan*, 56.   [46] Ibid.
[47] Poullada, *Reform and Rebellion in Afghanistan, 1919–1929; King Amanullah's Failure to Modernize a Tribal Society*, 115.

1924 Loya Jirga to facilitate his preferred outcome. Despite his best efforts, Amanullah was unable to control the outcome of the Loya Jirga, which ultimately opposed his efforts.

Despite social policies that were extremely unpopular at the time, Amanullah is fondly remembered by many because of his role in attaining independence from British influence in 1919. At the conclusion of the First World War, Amanullah declared that Afghanistan would no longer accept British subsidies, and henceforth would maintain an independent foreign policy in what unambiguously signaled an effort to cast off the yoke of British colonial influence. A visit to the mayor's office in Jalalabad City in eastern Afghanistan illustrates this point. As I interviewed the mayor of Jalalabad I could not help but notice a life-sized poster of Amanullah in his office. I asked the mayor why he was such an admirer of Amanullah. The mayor responded that it was Amanullah who gave Afghanistan its independence from foreigners. He said that Amanullah was also reform-minded and wanted Afghanistan to catch up with the rest of the world.[48]

Amanullah did not impose his vision with the same kind of violence as Abdur Rahman, but his regime bears important similarities to the Iron Amir in terms of a commitment to direct rule of the countryside. Because he was unwilling to enforce his vision with widespread and brutal force, his policies were largely aspirations since few were implemented. Rather, the mere idea of reform so expansive imposed without meaningful consultation and deliberation resulted in a backlash from a "backward" society against their "modern" king.

THE LONG PEACE: MUSAHIBAN RULE

Within months of his overthrow a distant relative and rival of Amanullah, Nadir Khan,[49] ousted Kalakani and reestablished the monarchy and the Durrani dynasty. After he assumed power Nadir said, "Since the people designate me so, I accept. I will not be the king but the servant of the tribes and the country."[50] The accession of Nadir as Shah marked the rise of a new dynasty, the Musahiban, who would rule the country until 1978.[51] Despite autocratic tendencies, they left a legacy of a half-century of peace that was largely the result of a return to de facto indirect rule and a simultaneous commitment to gradual expansion of the scope of the state.

Upon coming to power, Nadir Shah abolished most of the "modernizing" reforms of Amanullah including removing restrictions on mullahs, abolishment of compulsory education for girls, and reinstating the veil. In 1933, as he began to implement his own set of reforms, Nadir Shah was assassinated and replaced

---

[48] Nangarhar-Provincial Capital-#5.
[49] Nadir came from a different lineage than that of Amanullah.
[50] Quoted in Barfield, *Afghanistan*, 195.
[51] The Musahiban are Mohammadzai (Durrani) Pashtuns and were related to the previous dynasty.

by his son Zahir Shah for what turned out to be a forty-year reign. The apparent lesson Zahir Shah carried with him from the uprising against Amanullah and the assassination of his father was that reform must be gradual and take into consideration customary, tribal, and community loyalties. As a result, he integrated customary leaders such as maliks, urban merchants, and other notables into the government and appointed many of them as army officers or local administrators while also bringing prominent religious figures into the judiciary and state bureaucracy in an attempt to fuse customary leadership with that of the state.[52] Zahir Shah brought the state closer to customary leadership in an effort to win their favor, harkening back to a mode of governance similar to indirect rule. Although he favored Western-style modernization, he realized that embarking on dramatic reforms without a social contract would yield disorder.

Zahir Shah was only 19 when he came to power. For the first decades of his rule the country was led by his uncles who served as prime ministers. The guiding principle of the government during these first two decades was "limited guided modernization," with education promoted as a way to inform those in the countryside of the compatibility between Islam and democracy.[53] During these early years, the state remained weak.

In the mid-1950s, Zahir Shah's older cousin, Daud, served as prime minister. Believing Afghanistan was falling behind a newly independent Pakistan and a modernizing Iran, Daud wanted to use the authority of the state to rapidly transform the country, focusing on developing military strength and economic development.

Modernization schemes such as this require resources, yet Daud had a very limited ability to tax citizens. Understanding the backlash that direct taxation would generate, Daud looked to the outside to finance his plans. As he turned to foreign donors for support, Afghanistan once again became a rentier state, although this time Afghanistan was the object of desire for the United States and the Soviet Union.[54] This competition for influence fueled the modernization dreams of Daud as new flows of foreign aid poured in from both sides. External support enabled the regime to slowly strengthen the state without having to rely on domestic taxation. As Dupree observed, the price of tranquility was no taxation: Zahir Shah could have peace, or centralized taxation, but not both.[55] The price of no taxation was a weak state. Since rulers did not have

---

[52] M. Nazif Shahrani, "Marxist 'Revolution' and Islamic Resistance in Afghanistan," in *Revolutions and Rebellions in Afghanistan: Anthropological Perspectives* (Berkeley, CA: University of California at Berkeley, 1984), 52.

[53] M. Nazif Shahrani, "State Building and Social Fragmentation in Afghanistan: A Historical Perspective," in *The State, Religion, and Ethnic Politics: Afghanistan, Iran, and Pakistan*, ed. Ali Banauazizi and Myron Weiner (Syracuse, NY: Syracuse University Press, 1986), 54.

[54] See Peter G. Franck, *Afghanistan Between East and West* (Washington, DC: The National Planning Association, 1960).

[55] Dupree, *Afghanistan*, 536.

to rely on citizens for support, no clear social compact emerged between the state and its citizens.

Despite Daud's efforts to jumpstart the economy, Zahir Shah confronted slow economic growth, as well as growing dissatisfaction among political elites in the capital in the early 1960s. The state had almost no ability to tax and had weak abilities to provide public goods. In the face of increasing social and political discontent, Zahir Shah convened a national Loya Jirga in 1964 where he called for the establishment of elections under the framework of a constitutional monarchy. He also mandated that the cabinet be free of members of the royal family, thus creating a professional government (also intending to reduce the influence of his cousin Daud). He proposed a constitution that maintained the monarchy but included elements of democracy. Among other things it called for an elected national assembly as well as elected provincial, district, and municipal councils.

During the long reign of Zahir Shah, the rural equilibrium whereby the government respected the autonomy of communities and customary governance and communities in turn agreed to tacitly support the state remained largely unchallenged. Rural rebellions, which had confronted previous monarchs, were not common during this period. Zahir Shah's gradualism and flexibility in dealing with customary leaders and restraint on state-building efforts help explain his long and relatively peaceful tenure. Indeed, during fieldwork many informants across ethnic and age groups reflected favorably on his policies. One Tajik district governor in Sayghan District, Bamiyan Province praised the restraint he exhibited as a ruler. He said that Zahir Shah was a model for him as a political leader:

We have to do our work slowly. We must move slowly forward. Last night I saw a program about Zahir Shah on TV. In one of his speeches he said that we should move Afghanistan forward very slowly. There is an Afghan proverb, "We should walk slowly forever, not just run for an instance." Amir Amanullah was Afghan, but when he travelled overseas to European countries and saw the progress in these countries he returned to Afghanistan and wanted to change our country to be like them in one day. When he returned back to the country and tried to impose such a system in one day, he failed and was thrown out of office less than a year later.[56]

An elderly Pashtun large landowner in Pashtun Zarghun District, Herat Province also commented on the stability during Zahir Shah's reign:

My father (a former malik) said that [under Zahir Shah] he was coming and going and talking to farmers and poor people about whether they are happy with the government or not. During the time of Zahir Shah, security was very good and people could go anywhere they wanted to go. Now we can't even visit this mountain where my father spoke with these farmers ... At those times ... security was very good.[57]

---

[56] Bamiyan-Sayghan-District Center-#1.   [57] Herat-Pashtun Zarghun-Village 2-#6.

A Pashtun woman in the same district also compared her current situation to what she perceived as better days under Zahir Shah. She recalled how her grandfather served as a member of parliament, a wakil, during the period of constitutional monarchy:

In the past we had God's blessing and good people were living here. The agriculture and crops were flourishing and we also had influential arbabs. People in our village were not afraid of arbabs in the past, but they respected them very much. People knew who the important and respected people were and they knew who was less reliable. But now, everyone says that they are the most important people in the village. Even if they don't know anything, people are willing to say they know everything. For example, my grandfather was called Haji Baba. During the evening he would walk through the village and he would ask neighbors if they were hungry and or if they had food for dinner. He would always send things to poor families. He was wakil (member of the National Assembly in Kabul) during the time of Zahir Shah. For two years he served as a representative of Herat to the parliament in Kabul.[58]

In remote Panjab District in Bamiyan Province, I came to a village named after a man who was also a wakil in the 1960s parliament. Upon entering the village, I located the grandchildren of the wakil who, like the informants mentioned earlier, recalled peace and tranquility under Zahir Shah, despite ethnic and religious differences with the leader. Hanging prominently on the wall of the home was a portrait of the wakil, who was dressed in a suit and tie with carefully groomed hair and a moustache. The portrait was in stark contrast to the poverty of the family who now seemed to eke out a subsistence living. They recalled with pride this family heritage. They told me that one of their cousins now represents Bamiyan Province in the new Parliament. Their grandfather was once a large landholder, but today most of his land has been sold off to other families in the district.[59]

This brief period of constitutional reform came to a halt in 1973 when Daud overthrew his cousin and the monarchy in a palace coup. Once again frustrated with the slow pace of reform, Daud reemerged convinced that without rapid economic reform and social progress, the country would not be able to compete with its neighbors, especially Pakistan. To signify a break with the policies of his cousin and his belief in state-generated progress, he formed a close alliance with the Parchami ("Flag") faction within the People's Democratic Party of Afghanistan (PDPA), the Soviet-backed communist party. Upon seizing power he abolished the monarchy and declared the country the Republic of Afghanistan. He announced a modernization program based on "centralization of power, increased state regulation of the economy and a whole cluster of social reforms, including equal rights for men, women and national minorities, expansion of education, better welfare services ... [and] comprehensive land reform."[60]

---

[58] Herat-Pashtun Zarghun-Village 2-#1.   [59] Bamiyan-Panjab-Village 2-#3.
[60] Saikal, *Modern Afghanistan*, 176.

To accomplish these goals, Daud began to implement an autocratic system of government. In the process, his relations with customary authority at the village level became much more confrontational. Reflecting on fieldwork he conducted during Daud's rule, Thomas Barfield observed that "Its organization was autocratic in form, with power spreading from the top of the hierarchy downward ... The national governmental structure and the tribal and peasant peoples it ruled had little in common ...The [national and local] systems were discontinuous, and relations between the national representatives and local residents were fraught with difficulties because, with some justification, both sides looked upon the relationship as an adversarial one ... the very word government was synonymous with trouble to local residents.[61] From my own fieldwork, I heard similar descriptions of Daud's policies. Thirty five years later, a Pashtun laborer in Dawlatabad, Balkh Province had a hard time forgetting the back-breaking tax increases experienced under Daud:

> In the past during Daud Khan's time, there was a tax called maliya-ye mutaraqi that was very difficult because as a result, taxes increased a lot on people. The people were poor. Some people left their land because they couldn't afford to pay these heavy taxes. After Daud Khan's time the Communist regime came and at that time they abolished this tax.[62]

When Daud came up in conversations, informants in rural areas described his centralization policies. In particular, taxes during the time of Daud were extremely burdensome. Such taxation was in clear contrast to the reign of Zahir Shah who mandated few taxes on those in rural Afghanistan.

Daud also sought to eliminate the norm of indirect rule that had been largely stable until his reign. Informants who spoke about his regime were very clear on the changes they saw as a result of his ascent to power. For example, a Tajik namayenda in Sayghan District in Bamiyan Province described the challenges posed by Daud and why they viewed him with suspicion:

> QUESTION: How did people in the village solve their problems before the war?
> NAMAYENDA: There was a shura-ye mu-ye safidan (lit. 'council of white hairs'). About four people were considering and resolving problems in the village. But the formal government did not pay attention to or accept their decisions. I remember that during the time of Daud, a respected mawlawi had a gun and the gun fired on someone and accidentally killed one person. Some of the elders in the village gathered and they advised the mawlawi on how he could rectify his crime to the victim's family. We also talked with the government soldiers [in the area]. We told them that we would resolve the issue in our village. But the soldiers reported the issue to the alaqadari (sub-district

---

[61] Thomas J. Barfield, *The Central Asian Arabs of Afghanistan: Pastoral Nomadism in Transition* (Austin, TX: University of Texas Press, 1982), 155–56.

[62] Balkh-Dawlatabad-Village 1-#6. Dorronosso says the tax rate imposed by Daud during this period was 18 percent Gilles Dorronsoro, *Revolution Unending: Afghanistan, 1979 to the Present* (New York: Columbia University Press, 2005), 80.

government official) and the alaqadari would not accept our decision. They said that this was murder and they would not accept our judgment. The government would also not accept our judgment.[63]

Daud was determined to establish a centralized regime that maintained not just a monopoly on violence but also sought to replace customary norms with parchment legal rules. His imposition served to isolate the government from residents in rural areas.[64] He also moved away from the PDPA and Parchami allies upon whose shoulders he climbed to power. The latter decision would prove to be his undoing.

COMMUNIST RULE AND THE SOVIET INVASION

In 1978, the short-lived Republic of Afghanistan came to an end when a faction within the PDPA assassinated Daud, members of the royal family, and his administration in what became known as the Saur Revolution.[65] The revolt, led by a Ghilzai Pashtun, Noor Muhammad Taraki, ended the Musahiban Durrani dynasty. Once Taraki assumed control of the country, his administration was plagued by infighting among the dueling Parcham and Khalq factions. This inter-party conflict was compounded by revolts in the countryside against communist policy. The growing instability in the country – and especially infighting among the communist factions – provided the Soviet government in Moscow with a rationale to invade Afghanistan, which it did in 1979.

The Soviet-backed PDPA ruled Afghanistan from 1978 until 1992. Upon assuming power in 1978, the PDPA promoted a "revolutionary" strategy in Afghanistan. A rhetoric of revolt against feudalism informed their policies, as they attributed the poverty of the country to "the economic and political hegemony of the feudal class, which had to be broken before any progress could be made."[66] In typical fashion of such uprisings, the workers, peasants, artisans, and progressive elite were called upon to overthrow the "compradores, hoarders, big businessmen, corrupt bureaucrats, monopolists, and international imperialists" who dominated Afghan society.[67]

In 1978, the PDPA embarked on a two-pronged reform effort, which was announced in a series of decrees. The first component was large-scale economic reform. Because the PDPA diagnosed the problem in Afghanistan as "feudal" in nature, they sought to eliminate the system of tenant farmers and sharecroppers. To solve this perceived problem, they issued Decree #7, which cancelled all debts owed by farmers to other landowners and eliminated all mortgages

---

[63] Bamiyan-Sayghan-Village 1-#4.   [64] Dorronsoro, *Revolution Unending*, 80.
[65] Saur is the name of the month in the Afghan Persian calendar when the revolution took place.
[66] Beverley Male, *Revolutionary Afghanistan* (London: Croom Helm, 1982), 108.   [67] Ibid.

and interest. In addition to this, Decree #10 sought to limit the size of Afghan farms to ensure that every farmer owned a plot of land. The reform sought to break up large and medium-sized farms via a massive land redistribution scheme.

Although there may have been some large landholdings in rural areas, most observers have noted that land in rural Afghanistan has always been far more equally distributed than in neighboring countries, such as Iran and Pakistan.[68] Thus, PDPA diagnosis of inequality did not seem to reflect the actual state of affairs in the countryside. Furthermore, overzealous government officials used land reform as pretext to target customary governance structures they viewed as obstacles to political consolidation.

The PDPA did not stop with economic reform. The second component of the PDPA strategy was social reform reminiscent of Amanullah's efforts fifty years before.[69] For instance, further decrees abolished customary practices of bride price and set a minimum age for marriage of sixteen for girls and eighteen for boys. Through decree, the government also prohibited the use of customary leaders, such as arbabs and maliks, to handle issues of local administration. The process in which the PDPA imposed reforms also bore a close resemblance to the time of Amanullah. There was no attempt to consult citizens as to the nature of the reforms; instead, policies were imposed by decree. If there was a difference, it was in the extent to which the regime relied on the sword to implement reform. Unlike Amanullah, whose efforts to limit influence of religious and customary orders lacked teeth, the PDPA government was ruthless in its persecution of perceived opponents.

Communist leaders in Afghanistan eventually accepted that there was no industrial working class – no proletariat – to support their efforts. They also realized that members of rural society did not support them in large numbers. They were "obsessed" by the precedent of Amanullah and thought it was important to move forward quickly and "ruthlessly" before a counter-revolution (a la Habibullah Kalakani) could take shape.[70] Unsurprisingly, these "reform" efforts met resistance. After several months, it became clear to the revolving leadership of the PDPA in Kabul that its hold on power would remain precarious as long as it pursued such grandiose policies. Upon seizing control of Kabul, the Soviets insisted that the PDPA mellow its ambition.

The PDPA came to power seeking to redefine rural society. They believed that a harsh credit system – with interest rates they said were between 20 and

---

[68] For more information on pre-war patterns of land distribution in rural Afghanistan compared to other countries in the region, see Rubin *The Fragmentation of Afghanistan*, 34–36.

[69] Hugh Beattie, "Effects of the Saur Revolution in the Nahrin Area of Northern Afghanistan," in *Revolutions & Rebellions in Afghanistan: Anthropological Perspectives*, ed. M. Nazif Shahrani and Robert L Canfield (Berkeley, CA: Institute of International Studies, University of California, Berkeley, 1984), 184–208.

[70] Roy, *Islam and Resistance in Afghanistan*, 84.

50 percent – and landholding inequality contributed to persistent underdevelopment. Although there were certainly acute problems and poverty in the countryside, the reforms were imposed without consultation of citizens or their customary representatives and largely without regard to actual conditions on the ground. Rather, the communist government opted for top-down, revolutionary change, which they justified precisely because the country lacked the experience with capitalism that would have created a deeper class consciousness necessary to support a "worker's revolution." Since the Marxist preconditions for revolution in terms of the existence of an industrial working class were not present, Afghan communist party leaders sought to spark the revolution from above as Lenin did sixty years earlier during the Bolshevik revolution.

At first blush, the reforms appeared to be an effort to alter the economic structure of society, but they actually had much a much more ambitious goal of fundamentally transforming rural society. Basic functions of rural life, which were typically under the purview of communities, were "now explicitly the sole preserve of a state which was totally incapable of matching up to the task ... Both the malik and the khan ... function[ed] as intermediaries in relations with the state ... [b]ut it was the intention of the regime to get rid of them. It is thus clear that the aim of the reform was to destroy the whole socioeconomic framework of the Afghan countryside."[71] As a male informant in Bamiyan Center, Bamiyan Province explained, the PDPA replaced customary authority with its own organizations and new nomenclature:

The arbab system was removed during the communist government ... After the arbab system was demolished, the communist regime also imposed their own system. The communists appointed village leaders [rais] ... Also they established a new government organization and administration. At that time, the communist regime captured all the arbabs. They did not return back to their villages. They have disappeared. We don't have any information about what happened to our arbab.[72]

This was not simply replacement of customary authority; customary governance was under assault in order to "liberate the masses." Many elders simply disappeared. A middle-aged shopkeeper recalled events during the brief reign of Hafizullah Amin, a Ghilzai Pashtun who overthrew Taraki in September 1979:

During the time of Hafizullah Khan, 70 elders and other respected people were taken from here. We didn't see their faces ever again. During the war with the Russians we were under bombardment of Russians, but the Russian convoys which were crossing from this area did not torture or kill the people... So we passed through two very difficult times: once during Hafizullah Khan and again during the Taliban. But during the civil war (1992–6) we didn't pass through such a difficult time, though we lost our economic livelihood because of war in this period. During the civil war different troops from different parties were deployed in our area and we had to feed them. They would

---

[71] Ibid., 89.   [72] Bamiyan-Bamiyan Center-Village 2-#8.

order us to slaughter sheep, goats, and provide other food for them and we had to do it otherwise they would torture us by a different pretext.[73]

Communist rule represented a return to direct rule and modernization. Before the revolution, state-society relations were mediated almost entirely by community-selected maliks. During PDPA times, the state treated villages not as collective units, but as something the state had to impose order upon directly.[74] Predictably, the result of the state's effort to rule directly was more violence.

ANARCHY AND CIVIL WAR

Armed with a jihadi ideology, Islamist political parties that had begun to mobilize against the monarchy and Daud in the 1970s were able to further mobilize communities against a common Soviet enemy. As the Soviets represented atheism, an opposition was able to unify around the banner of religion offered by these Islamist parties. As these groups began attacking Soviet positions, they became known collectively as the mujahideen. Their dual purpose was to first eliminate "infidel" Soviet rule, and second, to bring a government based on religious principles to the country.

Many of the mujahideen parties first emerged in the 1960s and 1970s. Leaders of some of the most important factions studied together at Kabul University in the 1970s. For example, Burhanuddin Rabbani, later head of what became known as the Northern Alliance was the chair of the Department of Shariat and Islamic Law at Kabul University. Ahmad Shah Masoud, who later became a famous Northern Alliance commander, studied engineering at the university, along with Gulbuddin Hekmatyar, head of Hezb-e Islami, in the early 1970s. During his time there, Hekmatyar formed a political movement for young Muslims. His group was allegedly responsible for throwing acid on the faces of female students.

The emergence of the jihadi parties in Afghanistan marked the beginning of the rise of political Islam in the country: a new adversary to customary and traditional authority. Olivier Roy points out the contrast between traditional authority and the new Islamist movements in Afghanistan: "Far from having emerged from the clergy or traditional circles, they are to be found within the modern institutions of society (colleges, faculties of science, and in general in the urban environment)....[T]he Islamists speak of Islamist ideology rather than of religion in the strict sense of the term.... In the forefront of their thinking is the problem of the state (the 'Islamic republic')."[75] The Islam that inspired this new generation of leaders was not the folk-Islam of the mullahs of rural Afghanistan, but instead was a notion of progress. Several of these jihadi

---

[73] Bamiyan-Shibar-Village 2-#3.   [74] Roy, *Islam and Resistance in Afghanistan*, 23.
[75] Ibid., 7.

leaders sought to emulate the Muslim Brotherhood in Egypt, espousing a desire to turn away from traditional religious practices and focus on how religion can lead to social and economic progress. They had little time to actually implement a political vision, as they served as commanders rather than religious leaders, fighting a bloody insurgency against Soviet-occupation.

By the 1980s, the mujahideen gained political and financial support in their efforts to defeat the Soviets in Afghanistan from a host of foreign patrons including the United States, Saudi Arabia, and Pakistan. During the war with the Soviets, that became known as the "jihad," some of the largest anti-Soviet parties set up shop in neighboring Peshawar, Pakistan. Assistance to these parties was distributed by the Pakistani government, who focused their support on seven key religious parties known as the seven tanzims.[76] The Pakistani government made it clear to the United States and others who wished to support the anti-Soviet Afghan insurgency that they would only permit foreign support to be channeled to Islamist groups they selected, namely the seven tanzim.

Many informants spoke of the hardships faced during the anti-Soviet jihad. A middle-aged man, a Hazara shaykh in Balkh Province, who was conscripted to serve in the PDPA army, recalled violence from that era:

I was [a conscripted] soldier during the Khalq and Parcham governments. At that time the people in our village rioted against the government. We began to build relations with the mujahideen because the communists were killing so many of our people. One guy in our village said that we should fight against the communists; I said we should wait until we had some kind of organization to lead us. ...We had 15 people in our village die during that war. There are 20 families from our area that migrated away that have still not come back. I remember that one day twelve airplanes descended upon our village and they fired 500 rockets on our village. We all went inside wells to hide. When we came out of the wells we saw that many houses had been destroyed.[77]

After a decade of fighting, the insurgency forced the retreat of Soviet forces from Afghanistan in 1989. The PDPA was surprisingly able to hold onto power in Kabul without Soviet military backing until 1992.

Upon defeating the communist government and seizing Kabul in 1992, mujahideen groups from Northern and Western Afghanistan, known as the Northern Alliance (Shura-ye Nazar or the United Front), and Hezb e Islami crafted a power sharing agreement, complete with a rotating prime minister-ship. Yet after winning power, they were unable to honor their agreements and fought ferociously for control of Kabul and the country, thus dragging the

[76] The history of the United States and other foreign involvement in support of the mujahideen is chronicled in Steve Coll, *Ghost Wars: The Secret History of the CIA, Afghanistan, and Bin Laden* (New York: Penguin, 2004); and George Crile, *Charlie Wilson's War* (New York: Grove Press, 2004).
[77] Balkh-Dawlatabad-Village1-#5.

country through a bloody civil war that lasted until 1996. A district governor spoke of how the campaign to oust the Russians emboldened insurgent groups who eventually spent most of their time fighting each other:

> During the war with the Russians, there were so many factions fighting: Jamiat-e Islami, Hezb-e Islami, Harakat, and [Shura-ye] Nazar. There was not a problem between Sunni and Shia people at that time. During the Taliban time, the Taliban did a lot of bad things to the (Shia) Hazara people. During the mujahideen times the Sunni parties were fighting with each other. Jamiat was fighting Hezb-e Islami and the Shia parties were fighting each other. Harakat was fighting Wahdat.[78]

Villages were caught up in a Hobbesian war of all against all. Many described horrific dynamics as "political parties" fought for control of rural areas.

Customary governance also faced challenges during this period, as many mujahideen groups had little patience for such authority. As Barnett Rubin explains, groups such as Hezb-e Islami, under the "totalitarian" thumb of Gulbuddin Hekmatyar, did not consult with customary authorities and only recognized religious leaders who were party members. On the other hand, commanders allied with Northern Alliance leader Ahmad Shah Masoud were more sympathetic to customary authority and incorporated representatives of these groups into their decision-making circles. They regularly consulted with elders as well as local religious leaders. Rubin believes Masoud understood the importance of gaining support from customary authority from his experiences in the 1970s when he led a revolt against Daud without their approval that ultimately failed.[79]

The mujahideen groups that sought to replace customary authority with their own representatives at the village level would ultimately preside over major changes in local governance during this period. Several informants recounted these changes at the local level, which often involved the replacement of customary leaders by military commanders from these political parties. Consider this account by a Pashtun day laborer in Balkh (approximately 65 years old):

> [After the Saur Revolution] commanders were solving the problems of the people. If someone had a problem they would refer this to the commander. If the commander said something, or issued a statement, then we would accept this. People would accept what the commander said.... [Before the war] we had spinzheri (lit. 'white beards'). We had this system [of governance] before the revolution. When there would be a problem in a family or in the village they would come together and discuss the problem. And they would find a good way for people to settle issues. Also, at that time the people had good unity in the village. They were able to work together. People would call this meeting a jirga.[80]

[78] Bamiyan-Sayghan-District Center-#1.   [79] Rubin, *The Fragmentation of Afghanistan*, 233.
[80] Balkh-Dawlatabad-Village1-#6.

The following account, provided by a malik in Herat, encapsulates the political goal of mujahideen, which was weakening consultation of villagers in local governance:

During the period of mujahideen rule, the arbabs had no power and position in the community, because every commander declared himself to be the arbab in the community and they would do the job of arbabs. The party of the commander ruling the village would play the role of arbab and would do whatever he wanted. Every village had a commander and they would rule in this village and try to solve the problems of the people. Yet these commanders could not interfere in affairs in other villages because others would not allow him into their territory.[81]

A Pashtun farmer in Dawlatabad District, Balkh Province offered similar sentiments, explaining how commanders in many areas replaced customary authorities: "[D]uring the Taliban and mujahideen periods, all the problems in our village were solved by desert commanders (qumandan-e sahrayi)."[82] A Tajik farmer from Pashtun Zarghun District, Herat Province, offered the following account of the changes during the anti-Soviet insurgency:

Before the Saur Revolution, all of these issues such as disputes and other issues were handled by the arbab. When the mujahideen came to our community, the arbabs left the area. The mujahideen decided to resolve these issues themselves. Before the revolution, the arbabs resolved disputes. When the mujahideen came, every mujahideen leader became like their own president to the community. Everyone had their own weapon. We had a commander in the village that was named Muhammad. He had more power than any president could ever have. He was a very cruel man. Once a man took a letter (an invitation) to another village. When the commander found out about this, the commander brought this man to his home and asked him, "Why would you visit another village without my permission?" The man responded and said that this was his personal work and that his personal work wasn't the business of the commander. The commander then asked, "This is your personal work?" And then he took out his Kalashnikov and killed the man.[83]

A Pashtun elder in a neighboring village in the same district in Herat believed the country was most secure under the Musahiban. As he explained, "We have faced many changes after Daud Khan and my beard became white because of war and it had a very bad effect on people's lives here ... People were happy under Zahir Shah because we had good security at that time."[84] Many informants recalled the horrors they experienced during war or hardships they suffered during migration to neighboring countries. Unfortunately, for many people in the country, the horror experienced during civil war would be eclipsed by life under Taliban rule.

---

[81] Herat-Karokh-District Center-#1.   [82] Balkh-Dawlatabad-Village1-#3.
[83] Herat-Pashtun Zarghun-Village 1-#5.   [84] Herat-Pashtun Zarghun-Village 2-#6.

THE TALIBAN ERA

Most accounts suggest the Taliban began as a localized insurgent group centered on Kandahar in the early 1990s, with dual goals of bringing Islamic justice and fighting the predatory mujahideen parties.[85] Although the mujahideen were able to steward an insurgency, they proved incapable of governing. The informant recollections in the previous section provide just a small taste of the incredible brutality and corruption by which the mujahideen factions used to control the country. Emerging as an alternative, the core Taliban leadership emerged from a group Afghan Pashtuns who were raised primarily in Pakistani madrassas as war refugees and orphans. By 1996 they had emerged as a formidable military faction and had spread out from their base in Kandahar, gradually gaining control of most of the country. As they rose from the chaos of the civil war in 1996, they sought to impose a new kind of order on the people of Afghanistan. As with previous efforts to reform Afghan politics and society, initiatives emanating from above were imposed upon a public without any semblance of deliberation or consultation.

Initially, the Taliban had some appeal in their promise to end the disorder and carnage that characterized the years of mujahideen rule. Indeed, in the early days after they took power, they demonstrated an ability to govern effectively in the areas around Kandahar. They were able to co-opt local leaders by directly appealing to local populations, especially in Pashtun areas.[86]

As the Taliban emerged as a national movement, they also began to implement governance policies based on their ideological vision – one that went beyond the imposition of social order to include a utopian view of the world based on Wahhabi-infused Deobandi Islamic principles. Among the defining feature of their brand of Islam was loyalty to religion before the state and purification of religion to rid it of customary practices. Their ruling philosophy declared the Shia Hazara population as infidels providing an opportunity to persecute them and then allowing the Taliban to levy the jizya tax designated for non-Muslims upon them. They sought to impose a rigid political and social order on the country, where men were to grow beards and women were not allowed to leave their homes without a mahram (male relative). The Taliban built a centralized government based in their capital, which they had moved to the southern city of Kandahar. At the same time, they disbanded the provision of many social services, including health care for women. The force and rapidity with which the Taliban imposed these rules was only perhaps matched by the ruthlessness by which the Iron Amir imposed reform. Seizing power on a

---

[85] The definitive account of the rise of the Taliban is Rashid, *Taliban*.

[86] Abdulkader H. Sinno, "Explaining the Taliban's Ability to Mobilize the Pashtuns," in *The Taliban and the Crisis of Afghanistan*, ed. Robert D. Crews and Amin Tarzi (Cambridge, MA: Harvard University Press, 2008), 59–89.

basis of "good governance" principles, the Taliban quickly became corrupted by their own desire to acquire and maintain power.

The content of Taliban reforms was substantively different from those of Amanullah or the PDPA. However, the Taliban similarly alienated the population by imposing a set of cultural values on a reluctant public. Several informants recounted vividly the horrors of Taliban rule. For example, a middle-aged Hazara man in Dawlatabad District, Balkh Province recalled:

The Taliban were far worse than even the mujahideen or the communists. The Taliban took our land and they were so oppressive to our people. During the reign of Najibullah and the mujahideen we were at least free to visit other areas. But the Taliban government prohibited us from going anywhere. We could not even go to Kabul at that time. The Taliban kept coming to our homes and demanding things from us but we could never speak up to them.[87]

Nor did the Taliban simply take from the population. They taxed and killed to ensure restive communities feared them. For example, a Tajik qaryadar in Nahri Shahi District, Balkh Province depicted violence under the Taliban:

We faced so many problems during the Taliban government. They were beating people. They just wanted guns from people but our people did not have weapons at that time. They even killed some people for this.[88]

A Pashtun widow in Pashtun Zarghun District, Herat Province recalled the hardships as well:

We stayed in our village during the time of the Taliban. At that time the Taliban had did not have good relations with the people. The Taliban destroyed a lot of houses in the area. The Taliban soldiers took a lot of crops and wheat from the people by force.[89]

A Hazara woman, who lived on a small rain-fed farm in remote Panjab District in Bamiyan Province recounted similar destruction to their meager sources of economic livelihood:

Our house was not destroyed [but a lot of other houses in the village were burned]; just some of our animals were taken by the Taliban. Therefore, we faced a lot of difficulties rebuilding our lives when we came back because the main sources of our income were no longer there.[90]

While many recounted violence during the past thirty years, the most horrific accounts of deliberate violence seemed to occur during the period of the Taliban. Among these, the Hazara in Bamiyan Province, experienced the most extreme violence during Taliban rule. A Hazara widow in Bamiyan Center, Bamiyan Province provided a detailed account of life under the Taliban:

---

[87] Balkh-Dawlatabad-Village2-#3.   [88] Balkh-Nahri Shahi-Village 1-#3.
[89] Herat-Pashtun Zarghun-Village 2-#1.   [90] Bamiyan-Panjab-Village 2-#5.

WIDOW: I am a widow. I have three daughters and one son. I lost my husband during the Taliban time.

QUESTION: How did you lose your husband?

WIDOW: (She started crying). This is a very long story. When the Taliban came to the village and occupied our village, we went to the mountains. For two or three days we stayed there. During the night time women would return back to the village so that we could take things to eat. One day, the Taliban announced from the mosque that the people living in the mountains should return to their houses. The Taliban said that if the families did not come, they would burn our houses. The Taliban said that if we came, they would not bother or disturb us at all.

We were deceived by the Taliban. We came from the mountain to our house. After one night of being home in the village, the people woke up and were preparing breakfast. Women were cooking bread. At that time, the Taliban came to our house and they arrested my husband and two other male family members (her sister's husband and her husband's uncle). They beat them a lot in our house after arresting them. They told the people that our men left our young boys in the mountains (allegedly to fight) and that we just came back ourselves. I told the Taliban that I don't have any other sons, just the one small son who is here with me.

The Taliban left the house with these three men. We walked behind the Taliban for a long time. We were weeping, following them on the street. We asked them to give our men back, but they would not. That day nine people from the village were arrested. We went to the head of the Taliban [in the district]. When we went to the Taliban, they told us they themselves are good boys and are just doing their jobs. They said that they were just following the regulations.

After one week we were able to retrieve my husband's dead body from the Taliban. They killed him. None of the men were in the village at the time (they fled after that incident), so the women in the village were forced to make the coffins for their loved ones. After that, we left our village for Mazar-e Sharif.[91]

An elderly haji and veteran from a neighboring village in Bamiyan Center shared a similar story of devastation:

During the war with the Russians, life here was continuing as it was before. Some people in our area were working for the government. Other people were working in the fields. But when the mujahideen came, there was fighting between different mujahideen groups during the day. We just stayed in our homes. Most of our people were working at night - because the mujahideen couldn't fight then. So believe it or not, we had to do all of our work in the fields at night. It was very difficult.

Our people were very affected by the Taliban. There were some Tajik people living here during Taliban times. Those Tajik people assisted the Taliban and they helped them. We were really upset with the Tajik people for doing this because these people were our neighbors.

When Shia people pray, they put their heads on a special stone. When the Taliban was here, the Tajik people would tell the Taliban that we Hazara Shia people were praying

---

[91] Bamiyan-Bamiyan Center-Village 1-#1.

on the stones that were taken from the Buddhas.[92] We lost 120 people from the village during the war with the Taliban. During the Taliban time we were oppressed. The Taliban took all four of my trucks. I lost everything. When I came back to my home, I saw that I didn't have anything except for my life.[93]

Finally, a Tajik woman in Anjil District, Herat province, explained the nature of violence and how it continued in other parts of Afghanistan:

The Taliban captured those people in the village who had weapons. They did not bother the other people in the village who did not have weapons. But sometimes they beat the people and were constantly asking people for weapons. With my own eyes, I saw the Taliban behead eight people with a machete. The Taliban didn't bother the women very much. The Taliban would only bother women who weren't wearing complete hijab. Also, the young men who did not have long beards would also have problems from the Taliban. They would also beat the boys who had longer hair.

I heard that a few days ago two young men were killed by the Taliban. These two people were killed because they had long hair. They were beaten to death. They were beaten to death on the road from Herat to Kandahar.[94]

Like the communists before them, the Taliban also sought to fundamentally transform rural life and eliminate customary governance, which they viewed as a threat to their control. In this way the Taliban implemented a form of direct rule by appointing their own network of mullahs to be the heads of village governance. For example, they mandated that the Pashto word jirga be replaced with the Arabic term shura and then appointed their own mullahs as the head if these councils in every village. These mullahs became government employees and were paid salaries by the Ministry of Pilgrimage and Endowment (Wazarat-e Haj wa Awqaf). Instead of forming by consensus, it was the mullah who selected four to five adult males to work under him, who together formed the jirga. Village governance was linked up to the district as one member of the village jirga represented the village at the shura-ye ulama (council of clergy) at the district level.[95]

The Taliban had little time to govern. By September 11, 2001, they had ruled the country for five years and had gained control of almost the entire country, with the exception of parts of Badakhshan province in the far Northeastern part of the country. As they were so busy fighting to maintain control of conquered territory, they were not able to fully implement their vision of direct rule.

---

[92] These are the ancient Buddhas in Bamiyan that were blown up by the Taliban in 2001. The Taliban were thus inferring that the Shia was praying to Buddha. Praying to anyone but God is prohibited by the Koran.
[93] Bamiyan-Bamiyan Center-Village 2-#7.   [94] Herat-Anjil-Village 2-#1.
[95] Neamatollah Nojumi, Dyan Mazurana, and Elizabeth Stites, *After the Taliban: Life and Security in Rural Afghanistan* (New York: Rowman and Littlefield, 2008), 252–53.

CONCLUSION

In the years since Afghanistan emerged as a state, the country has fluctuated between periods of direct and indirect rule. The most common theme is one of efforts to impose direct rule. It is also fairly clear that Afghan rulers who aspired to direct rule rarely exercised moderation in their effort to extend rule to the countryside. As a general rule, political reformists, either conservative or modernizing, viewed the customary system of village governance as one of the primary obstacles to their rule. As one Pashtun woman said, "Both the mujahideen and Taliban were bad to us. We have a proverb in Dari "sag-e zard, baradar-e shaghal," which translates roughly as "six of one, half dozen the other."[96] For many people, there is no real difference between these armed factions and other leaders that have sought to rule the country despite their differences in ideology.[97]

With the exception of governance during the period of Zahir Shah, Afghan governments had little respect for governance in rural areas, viewing autonomous forms of social organization as something that must be controlled or eliminated in order for the state to grow. These efforts have not only been in vein but have extracted an enormous human toll.

The next chapter will turn our attention to the status of customary governance after 2001. When the smoke cleared and the fighting in most of the country ended (at least for a brief period), millions of families returned to their communities from internal or external displacement and began rebuild their villages after decades of war without much external interference. Surprisingly, customary governance was not wiped away during the war. Rather, it was transformed. Despite the resilience of customary organizations, foreign state builders and those in the Karzai government did not anticipate any role for customary order in the state-building process, especially during the crucial period of government formation in the early days after 2001. The chapter that follows contrasts the resilience of customary organizations alongside the persistence of customary disregard that characterized much of the post-2001 period.

[96] Herat-Pashtun Zarghun-Village 2-#1.
[97] Literally, this means "The dog is yellow, and your brother is a yellow jackal."

3

The architecture of village governance

There has not been village governance in Afghanistan for more than 200 years.
– Afghan Advisor, Ministry of Rural Rehabilitation of Development in a presentation to the international donor community.[1]

The Afghan peasant has labored for the feudal lord for centuries, and the concept, 'the landowner is my lord,' is deeply rooted in his consciousness. We have to break the psychological barrier of fear and educate and organize the peasantry politically so that it can take an active part ... People in remote settlements have a poor understanding of current events. Their class enemies exploit this ... Party activists will be sent to all 25,000 settlements in Afghanistan and village committees will be established. The government will also be helped by various mass organizations—workers, youth, and women's organizations.
– Soviet news report from Afghanistan, June 1978[2]

This chapter considers the extent to which customary governance survived and even adapted, against the backdrop of decades of conflict and more than a century of systematic, state-backed efforts to extend the reach of the state. Rather than disappearing, customary organizations continued to govern, but conflict, poverty, and migration since 1978 transformed them. The story of customary governance in rural Afghanistan is one of evolution amidst turmoil.

This chapter illustrates how customary governance in most villages exists as a shared responsibility between three distinct informal organizations: village councils (shuras/jirgas), religious judicial authority (mullahs), and community representatives (maliks). As I found, each of these organizations plays a similar

[1] Observation by author, Kabul, 2007.
[2] A. Akhmedzyanov and V. Baykov, "Afghanistan Begins a New Life," *Moskva Za Rubezhom*, June 1, 1978, FBIS Daily Report, FBIS-SOV-78–111 edition, 2.

role in communities regardless of ethnicity, region, or religious affiliation. For example, village councils are typically governed by norms of deliberation and accountability to the people within the community regardless whether the village is Pashtun, Tajik, and so forth. Norms governing the behavior of maliks tend to be quite consistent across communities. For example, nearly every malik was described by villagers as "a bridge between the people and the government." Religious leaders are also governed by a common set of community expectations.

The confluence of these three organizations forms what I describe as an "informal constitution" of village governance. Before proceeding, it is important to recognize that the substantive norms implemented by these organizations differ substantially from village to village and group to group. For example, in Pashtun-majority areas, Pashtuns usually use their version of Pashtunwali to resolve disputes. There is enormous variation in what constitutes norms of Pashtunwali across the Pashtuns in Afghanistan.[3] Non-Pashtun areas will not apply Pashtunwali, but instead may appeal to rules of shariat or unwritten customary norms (adat/rawaj), for instance. Substantive norms embody different notions of "justice," and so they will differ across communities. As this book is interested in understanding governance *of* villages – that is, general features of village governance that transcend individual communities, this analysis requires comparing villages to understand whether function or form (or both) generalizes.

The analytic description of customary governance as one based in consensus departs from other work offering a more feudal interpretation of traditional authority as the purview of "village headmen" who are described monolithically as large landowners.[4]

This study is not the first to depict similarities in self-governing organizations across ethnic groups in Afghanistan. Louis Dupree recognized that groups in rural Afghanistan share common norms.[5] Yet his foundational work on Afghanistan was published in 1973, before the massive upheaval documented in the previous chapter. This chapter suggests that the architecture of customary village governance continues to generalize across groups and regions but that it had evolved over decades of war.

The informal constitution is a framework that implies that the rules of the game affect outcomes, but it does not imply that all communities are governed

---

[3] International Legal Foundation, "The Customary Laws of Afghanistan" (New York: International Legal Foundation, 2004).

[4] For example, see Beath, Christia, and Enikolopov, "Empowering Women through Development Aid." In other parts of South Asia, it was colonial empowerment of local notables that exacerbated inequalities leading to extreme inequalities. See Abhijit Banerjee, Lakshmi Iyer, and Rohini Somanathan, "History, Social Divisions, and Public Goods in Rural India," *Journal of the European Economic Association* 3, no. 2–3 (2005): 639–47. Afghanistan neither had pervasive feudalism nor was in characterized by direct, internal European colonialization.

[5] Dupree, *Afghanistan*, 181.

in the same way. Most communities have all three organizations, but not all communities have organizations that are governed by the informal constitution. The descriptive inferences presented here therefore suggest a set of testable hypotheses and variation in the quality of customary governance across communities. By identifying the institutional characteristics that contribute to better governance, I am able to leverage a set of factors that help explain why some communities have more effective and responsive customary organizations than do others.

Many policymakers assumed that traditional, informal order was "gravely damaged" as a result of conflict and violence.[6] Yet there is another narrative that offers a more nuanced perspective. Olivier Roy, writing during the height of the anti-Soviet jihad, described how the power of village-based maliks "has been less diminished than that of the khan. . . . Appointed by vote, they continue to represent their village, but this time in the context of the resistance; when the resistance movement established a system of elected representatives (the namayenda), the malik were frequently chosen to fulfill that function. Their power has not really diminished."[7] Similarly, Neamatollah Nojumi, Dyan Mazurana, and Elizabeth Stites, while acknowledging that customary governance lost some authority due to the war because they were often co-opted by jihadi parties and commanders, found that customary order reconstituted itself.[8] The reason, they argue, is because villagers believe local solutions are superior to those supported by the Afghan government, warlords, or coalition troops.[9] As a result, after 2001 villagers were "pushing for the institution of jirga as a superior form for making decisions, managing conflict, and maintaining group identity."[10]

The description here provides a micro-level perspective on state-society relations in Afghanistan, which complements macro-historical studies by offering an account of continuity and change in local governance drawing on fieldwork evidence from diverse communities. The analysis in this chapter, taken alone, has important implications for the state-building enterprise in Afghanistan and elsewhere. Widespread presence of legitimate customary order at the village level throughout Afghanistan call into question assumptions of an institutional and organizational tabula rasa – an important assumption that drove initial institutional choices by the international community and some groups within the Afghan government after 2001. At the same time, this account is a first step, as is serves as the foundation for the inquiry in the rest of the book. Subsequent chapters will explore the consequences of the informal constitution for public goods provision and public policy.

---

[6] William A. Byrd, "Lessons from Afghanistan's History for the Current Transition and Beyond" (Washington, DC: United States Institute of Peace, 2012), 1, www.usip.org/sites/default/files/SR314.pdf.
[7] Roy, *Islam and Resistance in Afghanistan*, 150–51.
[8] Nojumi, Mazurana, and Stites, *After the Taliban*. [9] Ibid., 256–57. [10] Ibid., 257.

THE INFORMAL CONSTITUTION

The informal constitution of villages in Afghanistan refers to norms governing authority relations between shuras, mullahs, and maliks. Rather than feudal rigidity and exploitation, anthropologists writing before the Saur Revolution found village decision-making to be characterized by cooperation and consensus. Anthropologist Fredrik Barth, for example, described the Pashtuns as an egalitarian group, featuring decentralized leadership.[11] Akbar Ahmed refined Barth's argument by maintaining that there are several kinds Pashtun tribes, not all of which are egalitarian in nature.[12] He differentiated between egalitarian and *nang* ("honor-bound") Pashtuns of the rugged mountains and the more hierarchically organized *qalang* ("tax paying") Pashtuns in irrigated valleys maintained far more contact with government. As discussed in the previous section, many of these insights apply not only to Pashtuns, but to other ethnic communities in the country.

The most comprehensive descriptions were based on research done before 1978, mainly because conducting ethnographic research in villages during the war was not possible.[13] The analysis that follows takes the perspectives of these anthropologists as a starting point – perhaps more precisely, as a working hypothesis – to understand the nature of customary authority after 2001. After describing the organization of customary governance, the chapter proceeds to consider how the state has dealt with customary governance since 2001.

Shura: Village Council

Shuras, defined not by fixed membership but instead by a deliberative process, are the center of village governance because they usually derive their authority directly from the will of community members. A village may have a malik and a mullah, but without consultative bodies, people in rural areas generally do not have a mechanism for collective decision-making.

It is important to recognize the diverse nomenclature attached to such shuras or village councils. During fieldwork, informants commonly referred to their

---

[11] Fredrik Barth, *Political Leadership among Swat Pathans* (London: Athlone Press, 1959).

[12] Akbar S. Ahmed, *Pukhtun Economy and Society* (New York: Routledge, 1980). Both Ahmed and Barth conducted their analysis of Pashtuns living in Pakistan. Anthropologists working on Afghanistan came to similar conclusions.

[13] Among the most notable ethnographies from this period include: G. Whitney Azoy, *Buzkashi: Game and Power in Afghanistan*, 3rd edition (Long Grove, IL: Waveland, 2011); Barfield, *The Central Asian Arabs of Afghanistan*; M. Nazif Shahrani, *The Kirghiz and Wakhi of Afghanistan: Adaptation to Closed Frontiers and War* (Seattle, WA: University of Washington Press, 2002); M. Nazif Shahrani and Robert L. Canfield, eds., *Revolutions & Rebellions in Afghanistan: Anthropological Perspectives* (Berkeley, CA: University of California Press, 1984); Audrey Shalinsky, *Long Years of Exile: Central Asian Refugees in Afghanistan and Pakistan* (Lanham, MD: University Press of America, 1994); Nancy N. Tapper, *Bartered Brides: Politics, Gender and Marriage in an Afghan Tribal Society* (New York: Cambridge University Press, 1991).

village-based deliberative bodies as "elders" or as jirgas. The term shura, an Arabic word that translates literally as "council," is used by many non-Pashtun villages to indicate a village council. Jirga is a Pashto term that also means "council," although it translates literally as "circle," reflecting the seating arrangements participants assume when they assemble. There are differences between different kinds of councils, but these differences are typically exemplified in the norms applied to the dispute in question, not typically in the process itself. Although Pashtuns informants often told me that a jirga process is distinct from how disputes are resolved in non-Pashtun communities, I found sufficient similarities in the nature of these bodies and decision-making processes to generalize among them especially when considering how outcomes were achieved. The terms that communities use to describe to their councils are not necessarily fixed by ethnicity. To illustrate, in Kunduz Province, an Uzbek village used the Pashto term, jirga to describe its village council.

Quite often villages did not have a specific name for their council, but instead referred to the deliberative process as spinzheri, mashran, or rish safidan, the Pashto and Dari terms, respectively, for elders, the individuals who physically engage in deliberation. In fact, the term "elders" or "white beards" were employed more frequently than the term shura or jirga. I found the title "elders" or "white beards" to be misleading, for I found that younger men were frequently participating in such councils or processes. Some villages simply said they had meetings (jalasa or maraka) to resolve issues of collective concern.

To illustrate the diversity of names for similar processes, consider the description by a middle-aged man in rural Khanabad District, Kunduz Province when asked how his community resolved disputes prior to the war:

The rish safidan were solving our problems. At that time people did not use the term shura, instead they were just calling them rish safidan.[14]

A Hazara woman in Panjab District, Bamiyan Province made a similar observation. Although she said that after the war they used the term shura to describe the way they resolve disputes, the body was simply referred to as "elders" (rish safidan) in an earlier time:

We didn't have any kind of specific shura in name, but all village issues were solved by the rish safidan.[15]

The diversity of names encountered during fieldwork, which is by no means exhaustive, is presented in Table 3.1. In order to avoid confusion, the narrative that follows will use the generic term shura to refer to the primary collective decision-making body present in most communities, although in direct quotations I use the term used by informants. I prefer the Arabic term because it is

---

[14] Kunduz-Khanabad-Village 1-#8.   [15] Bamiyan-Panjab-Village 2-#1.

TABLE 3.1: *Names of Village-Based Deliberative Bodies*

Name	Meaning
Qawmi Shura	Tribal Council
Jirga	Pashtun name for local council
(Shura-ye) Rish Safidan	Elders Council (Dari) (lit. council of white beards, Dari)
Spingeri, Spinzheri	Elders (lit. white bears, Pashto)
Meshrano Jirga	Council of Elders (Pashto)
Mashran	Elders (Pashto)
Oq Soqol	Elders (Uzbek)
Mu-ye Safidan	Elders Council(lit. white hairs, Dari)
Majlis/Jalasa	Meeting (Dari)
Maraka	Meeting

generic is an acceptable term for use among all Muslims in Afghanistan. At the same time, by grouping these organizations together under the same title – shura – I am making a point of descriptive inference, which is that these bodies perform the same general tasks despite the diversity of their titles.

The essential political function of a shura is deliberation. Theoretically, every male can aspire to participation in these bodies, as the jirga or shura is based on the concept of communal authority.[16] Richard Newell offered one of the most comprehensive pre-war accounts of this process:

> The structure and authority of the council varies with local traditions and experience. Its most basic feature is the acceptance of the principle that all family interests within the group concerned may be represented in deliberations of justice, war, labor, and land. The spirit and procedure are usually democratic. Theoretically, a consensus of the whole group in question is necessary, if it is to act. The jirga therefore encourages a considerable degree of individual initiative, although in many instances it may be dominated by powerful chiefs. It is also a convenient device for accommodation among competing interests. ... There is no traditional limit to the size of the group to which the jirga principle may be applied ... a jirga might consist of tribal chiefs (khans) or clan leaders (maliks) representing their communities.[17]

In most villages, I found that shuras were not formal, fixed-membership organizations. They meet frequently, but meetings are not predictable as they gather to discuss issues or resolve disputes that arise within the village or with neighboring areas on an ad hoc basis. Although they were ad hoc, there were respected members of the community who were expected to attend such meetings when they arose. In smaller communities, these shuras tended to have more of a fixed membership. A Pashtun shopkeeper in Nahri Shahi district in Balkh Province described how his jirga works: "We call [our village council] a jirga.

---

[16] Gregorian, *The Emergence of Modern Afghanistan*, 40–41.
[17] Newell, *The Politics of Afghanistan*, 26.

The members of the jirga are the spingeri. The jirga listens to both sides of a conflict [when issues arise]."[18] A Pashtun elder in Behsod District, Nangarhar Province, provided a more extensive explanation of the deliberative process:

The people of Afghanistan are quite traditional and they have various customs that govern their daily lives. People usually resolve their problems through discussion in the village. The rish safidan act as judges and resolve most of the disputes in villages. The people usually refer their conflicts to the elders then they try to resolve all the problems. Elders talk with both sides and then they talk with each other. If both sides accept the authority of the elders to resolve their conflict, they will make a decision that both sides are bound to accept. The elders try to make their decision in accordance with shariat as well as with Pashtunwali. Another important thing is taking a signature or a fingerprint [from each party] before a decision is made to make sure they abide by the decision after it has been decided. This is called *wak* (oath). This is the structure of our village shura and the people have selected these members.[19]

A Pashtun male informant in a community that has Uzbeks, Tajiks, Pashtuns, and Hazaras among its residents used the term jirga to describe his community council. Despite being young and the leader of the community's newly established CDC, he believed these customary councils serve as an important alternative to a government he perceived as ineffective and corrupt:

We have a jirga in our community. I remember the last time it met was at Habib's house. All the elders of the village came. We had a jirga. There was a conflict between two families that we wanted to resolve. We solved it through the jirga. The qaryadar also helped us solve that problem ... [The jirga] only meets when a problem arises. People are happy with this system. They don't like to go to the woluswali (district administration) because the courts will try to take lots of our money.[20]

Although these organizations are pervasive they had to overcome assaults from governments as well as insurgent groups such as the Taliban or the mujahideen, who sought to replace them. Much to my surprise, after 2001, villages began reconstituting these collective decision-making processes. A male elder from a Pashtun community in Balkh Province described how jirgas in his community come to decisions:

The jirga has some formula or a decision rule that is applied to both parties. Both sides sit in the jirga and both sides have a representative to speak on their behalf. One representative tells the other, "If my side doesn't accept the decision, they should pay some money or receive some other kind of punishment." That way you know ahead of time that the decision of the jirga will be respected by all members of the community.[21]

Several varieties of councils can co-exist in villages. For example, there are shuras that deal with specific issues, such as water or land. In some multi-ethnic

[18] Balkh-Nahri Shahi-Village 1-#7.   [19] Nangarhar-Behsod-Village 1-#7.
[20] Balkh-Nahri Shahi-Village 1-#4.   [21] Balkh-Dawlatabad-Village 1-#6.

communities, I found that there was a qawmi shura that was devoted to resolving issues specific to individual ethnic or tribal groups. I also found religious shuras that dealt with matters pertaining to religious jurisprudence.[22] As these councils confront with issues as they arise, they are flexible not just in membership but also in scope.

The legitimacy of the shura system did not escape government officials at the district level. In fact, government officials often used the term shura or jirga to describe government-created councils in an effort to gain support for policies that required citizen input or participation. Frequently this included efforts to use the legitimacy of village shuras as a stepping stone to establish informal district- or provincial-level shuras. In Anjil District, Herat Province, the district governor organized a district-level shura of teachers and elders to help put a stop to anti-government forces that were burning down schools and threatening girls who wanted to go to school. The district governor tried to build upon the legitimacy of village shuras as a means to protect educational investments, but more importantly, to shield students from violence.[23] The district governor also established an "environmental shura" at the district level so that villagers could discuss issues like solid waste removal and how to deal with pollution from local brick factories. By relying on shura models of decision-making, these formal state organizations tried to ensure local buy-in to their efforts.

Although the origins of deliberative councils in Afghanistan go back a long time, governments, militias, and NGOs have tried to build on the shura concept in efforts to gain legitimacy for their activities. In the post-2001 period, international donor projects created countless types of "shuras," such as educational, agriculture, and health shuras, at the district and village level.

Many informants said they did not use the term shura prior to the Saur Revolution. They said it was employed by NGOs and warlords who sought to create councils in support of their activities after fighting began. For example, during the jihad against the Soviets in the 1980s, mujahideen factions created their own "shuras." Beginning in the 1980s, international NGOs providing assistance to Afghanistan channeled their aid to communities through "development shuras."[24] In village after village, informants detailed decades of donor "shuras." For example, several informants in both Balkh and Bamiyan provinces mentioned "mujtame" shuras that were implemented by a UN agency during the Taliban period:

---

[22] The term *qawm* is a flexible term representing social identity in Afghanistan. Depending on the context it can mean ethnic group, tribe, sub-tribe, clan, or even region. See Torsten Jochem, Ilia Murtazashvili, and Jennifer Murtazashvili, "Social Identity and Voting in Afghanistan: Evidence from a Survey Experiment," *Journal of Experimental Political Science* 2, no. 1 (2015): 47–62.

[23] Herat-Anjil-District Center -#2.

[24] Lynn Carter and Kerry Connor, "A Preliminary Investigation of Contemporary Afghan Councils" (Peshawar, Pakistan: Agency Coordinating Body for Afghan Relief [ACBAR], 1989).

MALE ELDER: We have suffered from a lack of water and drought. We have suggested and proposed that NGOs and the government do some work for us, but no one has listened to us. In the past, our mujtame shura built a culvert here.
QUESTION: What is a mujtame shura?
MALE ELDER: It was the same as a CDC. It was organized the same way. It had a head, a deputy, and other members. It was created before the CDC came to our village. It was created by NGOs who would come and implement their projects through the mujtame.
QUESTION: When was the mujtame created?
MALE ELDER: It was created before the coming of Taliban and it continued up to the time of the creation of the CDC in the area. When the CDC was created, the mujtame finished.
QUESTION: What work was done by the mujtame?
MALE ELDER: NGOs would give them money and they would implement development projects in the village. They would work the same as CDCs except they were not supported by the government.[25]

In fact, in some villages the term shura was strictly associated with development projects. Thus, when the Afghan government began implementing "CDCs" (shura-ye enkeshafi-ye mahali [qaria], in Dari), the concept resonated with many villagers because it reminded them of very similar efforts launched by donors during the past several decades. Informants also described how Daud and the Communist government also tried to create their own village-level shuras in an effort to extend state rule to communities.

People in rural areas uniformly differentiated between the externally imposed "development" shuras created with external donor-funding from customary shuras. In many cases, people did not have a specific name for their customary deliberative body, but instead refer to it as a council of "elders," reserving the term shura to refer to donor-supported efforts. For these reasons, asking individuals whether they have a shura never told the full picture of community decision-making. In interviews and focus groups I tried to avoid asking directly about the presence or absence of a village shura, but instead asked broader questions about dispute resolution and small scale public goods provision to understand whether a deliberative body played an important role in such efforts (see Appendix A for more information on interview techniques). To surmise whether communities maintained functioning deliberative bodies it became necessary to understand the meaning and context of terms used by residents.

Although shuras are the most deliberative bodies villages in rural Afghanistan, they are by no means a fully democratic body. Women and young adults rarely participate in these bodies. According to female informants, their interests are typically represented by their male relatives. Despite such weighty

[25] Bamiyan-Bamiyan Center-Village 2-#9.

drawbacks, the shura process remains the foundation of deliberative governance in rural Afghanistan.

Mullah: Religious leader

Mullahs represent the lowest level of religious organization in Afghanistan.
They are distinct from other religious leaders and organizations, including
formally trained priests (imam), judges (qazi), scholars (mawlawi), and those
who have gone on religious pilgrimages (haji/karbalayi). In Afghanistan, imam
is a title given to someone who has had official training to lead prayers.[26] In
contrast, a mullah is someone who carries out this function "regularly and pro-
fessionally," despite a lack of formal training.[27] Indeed, in rural Afghanistan,
there tends to be a significant divide between the educated clergy of the ulama,
who often seek to implement shariat as the basis for lawmaking and dispute
resolution, and village mullahs, who typically lack sophisticated religious training but are still able to apply fundamental principles.[28] Their lack of training
tends to make them "traditionalists, and not fundamentalists."[29] Although
the influx of Deobandi-influenced mullahs has injected more purist forms of
religious teaching that forbids the use of customary law.

Nearly all communities have a mullah. Villages may have several depending
on their size as well as religious diversity. For example, Shia and Sunni populations coexisting in one community maintain separate mosques as well as separate
spiritual leaders. In fact, informants often described the size of their community
by its number of mosques (e.g., "our village is big, we have six mosques").

Mullahs are a fundamental pillar of village governance because they frequently represent community interests, as opposed to clerical interests. Mullahs
are not typically tied in any direct way to a larger organization or the clerical
hierarchy; nor are they appointed by outsiders. Instead, a mullah enjoys status
in a community based on his legitimacy in that community, which is derived
from their personal reputation for piety and wisdom.[30] As Dupree explained,
mullahs are "at the bottom of the hierarchy [who] function as part time
religious leaders. Technically, Islam has no organized clergy, and every man
can be a mullah. Anyone can lead in prayer."[31]

Similar to village councils, I encountered a range of titles informants used to
describe village-based religious leaders. These findings are summarized in

---

[26] In most of the Middle East, rural religious leaders are imams. In Afghanistan an imam usually
has a higher status than a village mullah.

[27] Dorronsoro, *Revolution Unending*, 48.

[28] M. Nazif Shahrani, "Local Knowledge of Islam and Social Discourse in Afghanistan and
Turkistan in the Modern Period," in *Turko-Persia in Historical Perspective*, ed. Robert L.
Canfield (New York: Cambridge University Press, 2002), 161–88.

[29] Roy, *Islam and Resistance in Afghanistan*, 4.   [30] Ibid., 32.

[31] Dupree, *Afghanistan*, 107–8.

TABLE 3.2: *Names of Religious Leaders*

Name	Meaning
Mullah	Community selected religious leader that usually has no formal training
Imam	Formally trained religious leader
Ulama	Group of religious scholars
Mawlawi	Religious teacher
Pir	Sufi religious leaders
Sayyed/Sadat/ Eshan	Notable or "holy" families who are believed to be descendants of the Prophet Muhammad
Qazi	Islamic judge (also a government judge)
Haji (Bibi Haji)	Pilgrim (Bibi Haji is a female equivalent)
Karbalayi	Shia who made pilgrimage to Karbala in Iraq
Shaykh	Man respected for religious training or knowledge, sometimes a Sufi leader

Table 3.2. Imams are the most formal religious leaders and tend to have the lowest level of local legitimacy (although this is highly context dependent) because they represent doctrinal interests rather than those of the community. In some communities, formally trained religious leaders such as mawlawis play an important role alongside, or instead of, mullahs in mediating village life. Typically, the mawlawi has more formal religious education than do village mullahs. It is often the mawlawi who are left to bridge religious doctrine with community realties. Pirs (Sufi masters) and those that have made important religious pilgrimages (either to Mecca or the Shia shrine in Karbala, Iraq) also constitute part of the matrix of religious leadership, and in some instances, they too play an important role in mediating spiritual life in communities.[32]

Mosques are the center of religious and community life in rural communities. They also play a central role in organizing community politics, serving as a deliberative center for (usually male) villagers. For instance, many interviews and focus groups for this book were conducted in mosques because they are open to community members and outsiders. Despite being a woman and non-Muslim, I was often permitted to enter mosques to conduct interviews.

Religious leaders have a range of responsibilities. They perform religious rites and services. They are also sought out to help resolve disputes, especially regarding family or other personal issues, but also disputes that arise within the community and sometimes between communities as well. Although individuals

[32] The only important and ubiquitous religious figure missing from this list are *malangs* or wandering mystical preachers. *Malangs* remain prevalent in the countryside where they provide advice and faith-healing. They are not fixed to one community, but instead roam the countryside living off of alms. I do not include *malangs* in this list because typically do not have the legitimacy at the local level to serve as effective arbiters.

are more likely to take personal and spiritual matters to a mullah for resolution than other bodies, the governance domain of mullahs is not limited to family or religious affairs. In fact, the significance of mullahs in village life is why the government has often targeted them for cooptation. The expansion of the state into religious affairs began almost immediately after the founding of the Durrani Empire, but became much more aggressive during the period of Abdur Rahman Khan. Religious leaders were also heavily persecuted under the reign of the PDPA.

The fortunes of mullahs were reversed as the Taliban vigorously sought to displace shuras and maliks with mullahs as the center of village politics. During the period of the Taliban government, the roles of mullahs were redefined, as they were responsible for implementing Taliban legal codes as well as collecting taxes. This presented challenges because in many cases, the mullahs the Taliban government promoted were illiterate. In principle, the Taliban as a movement sought to eliminate Pashtun customary law, which contradicts some aspects and interpretations of Islamic jurisprudence, by elevating the role of mullahs.

The Taliban's efforts to elevate mullahs to leadership roles in communities during the period they controlled the government were largely unsuccessful because the mullahs had little governing capacity. In post-2001, mullahs still play an important, though less prominent, role in village life. They worked in concert with, or are checked by, the authority of other organizations in the community. Their power is also checked through competition among mullahs. It is not unusual for villagers to "venue shop" to find a mullah who might be more inclined to rule in their favor. I found occasions when maliks or shuras were called upon to decide which mullah was most "just" in situations when the parties to a dispute approached separate mullahs who came to different conclusions. The following example, from a Pashtun woman in Behsod District, Nangarhar Province, provides insight into the process of venue shopping:

We have a few mullahs in our village. When there are difficulties or disputes then they will come together with the malik to solve problems. For example, two sides in our family were having a land dispute that we were unable to solve internally. We decided to call the mullah to our home to help us solve it. After the mullah came my aunt was upset [because the mullah denied her claim]. She continued to claim this land despite the instructions of the mullah. She said that the mullah gave our side a lot of land and didn't give her as much. So she called another mullah and he divided the land a second time. They took six jeribs from us.[33] My father went to the first mullah and asked him why he divided the land unequally and he said that he didn't know.[34]

---

[33] *Jerib* is a customary measure of land used in Afghanistan and other parts of the Muslim world. It is approximately one half acre.

[34] Nangarhar-Behsod-Village 2-#2.

Of course, people sometimes disagree with or disregard mullahs. In another village in Behsod District, a Kuchi (Pashtun nomad) woman commented that nomadic groups do not use the village mosque. As a result, they do not believe the decisions of the village mullah should apply to Kuchi families:[35]

The village mullah is not from our side. He is from another group and usually makes decisions that favor them. My father-in-law doesn't have good relations with them. For Eid prayers, for example, he won't go to the village mosque but instead will do all his prayers at home as there is no other mosque in this area [that serves our people].[36]

It should come as no surprise that people sometimes disagree with the decisions or authority of mullahs. After all, they wear many hats, serving as both spiritual advisors but also as community arbiters. People often dislike their decisions, but found it difficult to completely disregard them.

Despite the veneration of religion and religious practice, informants shared a wealth of jokes about mullahs. Although rural Afghans regularly consult religious leaders and respect their decisions, they often make light of their lack of education and relative poverty.[37] Individuals seemed to select maliks (see next section) based on educational credentials; being able to read was often a minimum criterion as the malik is responsible for interfacing with the government and dealing with government documents. In contrast, mullahs are often illiterate and not respected for their intellectual prowess. Throughout my fieldwork, I heard this joke repeated in various incarnations across the country:

In the past, some people asked a mullah to come to their house because they had an issue that needed to be resolved. At the same time, another family asked the mullah to come to their house because they needed some advice. The first family told the mullah that they would prepare some soup for him. The second family said that they would prepare the some palow for him.[38] The mullah could not decide between the two invitations and did not show up to either home. He would walk toward one house and smell the palow, but remembered the soup and would walk toward the other house only to change his mind again. He ended up missing food at both houses due to his indecision. He then asked God to kill him because he missed all of the food.

So now, a lot of mullahs have left the village and their numbers have decreased. There used to be a lot of them but now there are fewer of them because they are not trained. There was a dispute in the village between a son and his mother about the son's wedding party. The elders solved the problem together ... Afterwards, the elders ... went to the

---

[35] The community mosque here was a Sunni mosque and the worshippers were primarily Pashtun Sunni Muslims. In this case, the Kuchis (who are also Pashtuns and Sunni) saw themselves as a separate and distinct group from the sedentary, Sunni Muslims in the community.

[36] Nangarhar-Behsod-Village 1-#4.

[37] See Thomas J. Barfield, "An Islamic State Is a State Run by Good Muslims: Religion as a Way of Life and Not an Ideology in Afghanistan," in *Remaking Muslim Politics: Pluralism, Contestation, Democratization*, ed. Robert W. Hefner (Princeton, NJ: Princeton University Press, 2004), 213–39.

[38] Palow is a rice and mutton dish.

mullahs and asked for their blessing of the decision. The mullah agreed with the decision and he said their decision was correct. After getting the blessing of the mullah, the woman and her son accepted the decision of the shura.[39]

As the joke indicates, mullahs are often remunerated for their services resolving disputes with a meal. In addition to this small payment, mullahs collect zakat (portion of income required of all landowners; a pillar of Islam) and sadaqa (charitable giving) from villagers on a regular basis for needy families in the community. Mullahs may also collect revenue locally from families for upkeep and preservation of village mosques. Finally, mullahs rely upon the community for their income. They survive on fees for "ceremonial and advisory services on behalf of their clients and often receive endowments of land or agricultural income from the villages or tribes who engage them."[40] I found that while people often trusted their religious leaders, their services were very rarely rendered free of charge. In other words, people may have joked about them and disagreed with them, at the end of the day they largely respected them and paid them for their services.

Mullahs are an integral part of village governance precisely because of their religious legitimacy and that they provide so many services. An Aimaq woman in Karokh District, Herat Province described the role of mullahs in her community:

We have a mullah in our village. He is Pashtun and came from somewhere else. When people gather their harvests, every family gives him some wheat as sadaqa. He teaches the children the Quran. He is a poor man."[41]

Mullahs also serve communities by maintaining good relations with local government officials. The district governor of Sayghan District in Bamiyan province, a mixed Tajik Sunni and Hazara Shia district, described the strong influence of mullahs in his district:

If the woluswal [district governor] tells people to do something a hundred times, they might not listen. But if the mullah tells them once they will always listen. Afghanistan is a very traditional country and mullahs are the leaders of the community. So these mullahs still have a lot of power in the community...We need to consider the customs of the people. If we don't consider these facts in society then we are like a car which has two tires going in opposite directions. We should know the culture of our people.[42]

Malik: Primus Inter Pares

There is a high degree of consensus regarding the role of shuras and mullahs in village governance. In contrast, the role of maliks – village executives or village representatives – is more complex. Most informants regarded the malik to be

---

[39] Bamiyan-Bamiyan Center-Village 1-#3.   [40] Newell, *The Politics of Afghanistan*, 26–27.
[41] Herat-Karokh-Village 2-#1.   [42] Bamiyan-Shibar-District Center-#3.

the first among equals and not a village chief, although the title is often translated as such. Rather, he is usually selected by the people. In his autobiography Abdur Rahman described the process of selecting maliks: "In every village or town there is one man elected by the citizens of that town who must have certain qualifications which I need not give here in detail. He is elected by the inhabitants of that village or town, and is called malik or arbab."[43]

Of the most important functions of a malik in contemporary times is their ability to represent community interests to formal state officials. In this sense, the malik serves as the "bridge between the people and the government," but is very much an agent of the community and not of the state. In some instances, he also had authority to make some executive decisions because villagers have bestowed upon him this discretion. In this sense, they are village representatives but can also serve as village executives. The extent of such executive authority varied from village to village.

For the sake of clarity, I refer to the individual villagers pointed to who represented community interests to the outside world, including to the state and the international donor community, as maliks even though individuals who fulfill this role were variously referred to as arbab, qaryadar, khan, kalantar, namayenda, wakil, rais, mir, or by another title. As M. Hasan Kakar explains, "broadly speaking, the term *arbab* was used in western Afghanistan and the term malik in eastern Afghanistan."[44] Sometimes the term malik is synonymous with that of a Pashtun sub-tribe or clan leader, but tribal status often had little to do with selection of village representatives in many of the villages I studied. Thus, a malik is not necessarily a clan leader, or necessarily Pashtun, even though journalists and analysts of Afghanistan commonly refer to a malik simply as a "tribal leader."

The authority of maliks was most often limited jurisdictionally to cover a single community, although in some cases several small villages were represented by a single malik. In this regard, maliks are analytically distinct from the khans described in the anthropological literature – large landowners or tribal leaders presiding over dozens of village-based maliks. I did not find that khans generally continued to function in this manner. In some villages, people used the title khan in reference to their self-appointed village leader, although this notion of khan was more akin to a malik since it was an individual who represented an area, rather than an individual who represented a tribe or sub-tribe. In this way, the power of khans did seem to diminish from the status they had in earlier eras.[45] From interviews and observations, I did not

---

[43] 'Abd al-Raḥmān Khan, *The Life of Abdur Rahman, Amir of Afghanistan*, ed. Mir Munshi Sultan Mahomed Khan, vol. 2 (London: J. Murray, 1900), 188.

[44] Kakar, *Government and Society in Afghanistan*, 58.

[45] This is consistent with the trends emerging in rural Afghanistan prior to 1978. See Anderson, "There Are No Khāns Anymore: Economic Development and Social Change in Tribal Afghanistan."

TABLE 3.3: *Titles of Village Representatives*

Name	Meaning
Malik	Representative; general term taken here to mean village representative
Qaryadar	Executive
Khan	Executive, tribal leader, can also signify landowner
Qalantar	Leader
Wakil	Representative
Namayenda	Representative
Arbab	Leader
Mir	Leader
Rais	Leader/Head

gather that the post-2001 khans had as much regional governing authority as they had in previous eras.

The deputy governor of Nangarhar province compared the situation in Nangarhar to that of Kandahar, where he previously served, although his family originally came from Helmand (he considered himself Helmandi). He said that in Kandahar, people in rural areas used the term khan, but in Nangarhar, they had maliks:

[In Nangarhar] we have formal maliks which register in the district government offices. The situation here in Nangarhar is different from other areas like Kandahar. In Kanda-har we don't have maliks. . . . There the khan is very important and the people respect the khan and the people resolve their problems through the khan [like people use the malik in Nangarhar]. . .Here in Nangarhar there are many tribes in Spingar district each with their own malik. Sometimes there is some competition between maliks. Some of them are weak and some of them are powerful. . ... Here the malik system is strong. To become a malik, you have to get votes from your tribe.[46]

Thus, the names of village leaders varied substantially across regions and even within villages in a single district. The various titles are summarized in Table 3.3.

Although community members viewed maliks as leaders who derive their legitimacy to lead from custom, their history is deeply entwined with the state. Throughout most of modern Afghan history, governments attempted to utilize maliks as agents through which they could implement indirect rule. During Daud's autocratic rule of the 1970s, the government administration at the local level tried to establish its own maliks to collect a land tax in rural areas. A few years later in the 1980s, the Communist PDPA government tried to appoint their own parallel "maliks" to villages as representatives of the Party. Despite several attempts to coopt or replace maliks, these efforts were largely

---

[46] Nangarhar-Provincial Capital-#4.

unsuccessful. Due to past efforts to formalize the position, the title "malik" has a different meaning than it does elsewhere in Central and South Asia.[47] As we saw in the previous chapter, the state tried to rely on maliks because it did not have the capacity to govern the country directly. Consequently, they were enlisted to deal with issues such as tax collection, registration of peoples, and in basic administrative tasks as a form of indirect rule.[48] They are Afghanistan's street-level bureaucrats. Nonetheless, today as in the past, maliks have no formal role in the government and their legitimacy derives from custom.

In districts across the country I found communities used similar processes to select their maliks. Male community members, usually through a shura process, select a single person to represent them, bestowing upon them authority. The malik is then presented by community members to the district governor. In some instances, the district governor sends a designation letter appointing the malik to the local district court, who in turn provides the malik with an "entitlement seal" that recognizes him as the representative of his village.[49] In many districts, I found that maliks did indeed have stamps or seals, although in many communities their stamp was not issued by the woluswal. Instead, maliks used a homemade seal consisting of their thumbprint on paper with their name signed on top of it in lieu of a stamp. In every district where maliks used seemingly official processes such as fingerprints or stamps, the government recognized the authority of the malik to do so.

Despite their fairly clear functions, this role as liaison between villagers and the state is not mentioned in any official law or in the constitution. I could find no such law in Afghanistan that required or enabled local government officials to bestow government authority upon or even recognize maliks.[50] The practice of issuing stamps or seals to maliks appears to be a policy inherited from previous regimes. Alternatively, it could be an institutional innovation devised by local government officials. Several district governors told me that the policy of issuing stamps was a practice that was expected of them by the community and for that reason they issued stamps to maliks. Some said that this was a practice initiated by the monarchy and continued by Daud and the PDPA.

At first glance, it may appear that the stamp bestowed upon the malik the authority of the state. Yet none of the communities I studied interpreted the stamp this way. Rather, they viewed the use of the stamp as an important signal to the government. If a villager approaches a local government official

---

[47] In neighboring Pakistan, for example, the title malik appears to signify a feudal lord who has a tight grip on local authority. The notion of a malik in Afghanistan is far more egalitarian than the Pakistani malik.

[48] Roy, *Islam and Resistance in Afghanistan*, 18.

[49] Nojumi, Mazurana, and Stites, *After the Taliban*, 260.

[50] During the course of field research I consulted with an Afghan constitutional lawyer who could also find no legal provision giving maliks such authority or that gave woluswals the ability to recognize maliks.

with a document stamped by the malik, it means that the document is legitimate because it was recognized by the community. In other words, a stamp or thumbprint signified village approval, rather than government approval, and so it was an integral feature of an informal system that allowed the village to communicate in a systematic way to the formal government at its lowest level.

In several villages, I found that when villagers became dissatisfied with their malik, they could dismiss the malik from his duties and select another one. In Herat province, for example, maliks in several communities were elected through the use of ballot boxes. In the past, it was more frequent for the position to be inherited from generation to generation. Although I could not measure this precisely, it was my sense that this hereditary practice of transmission continues in some communities but is increasingly an exception rather than the rule. This is because of the mass migration experienced in recent decades along with the fact that many maliks were targets of regime and insurgent violence. More generally, I found that they were selected using consensus procedures typically found in shuras as described by a Pashtun mardikar (day laborer) in Balkh Province:

We respect the qaryadar because he assists people who face problems in our community. He goes everywhere on our behalf. He has good contacts with the woluswal. If we need a tazkera or something else or face some other problems he can go to the woluswal for us. The qaryadar is like the ceiling of the room. If the room doesn't have a ceiling, the village is vulnerable.[51]

Despite the respect they elicit in most areas, there are also maliks who abuse their authority. In some cases, maliks engage in predatory behavior, as a mullah in Behsod District in Nangarhar Province recalled:

You know that maliks are very strange people and they want to make war between people instead of resolving the conflicts, the people do not have good memories from maliks and they are always trying to make war between people. . . .The malik is just one person and he can decide by himself and he does whatever he wants. They are maliks just because their father or maybe their relatives were also maliks. The malik never serves the people and always facilitates bribes and corruption together with the woluswal.[52]

Sentiments like this typically reflected historical efforts to coopt maliks. Just as the Taliban elevated the status of mullahs during their rule, Daud and the Communists elevated the status of maliks in an effort to rule the countryside directly through them.[53] In oral histories, informants were more likely to be

---

[51] Balkh-Dawlatabad-Village1-#6.   [52] Nangarhar-Behsod-Village 2-#5.

[53] During this period, Daud used the title *qaryadar* to signify the state appointed representative to communities. I believe that the title *qaryadar* emerged in many communities during this period. Many communities continued to use the title but it did not signify a state representative to a community, but community representation to the state.

critical of maliks during periods of history when they were co-opted by the state and made formal instruments of state power thus damaging malik legitimacy. Just as some maliks were rewarded by the state in some periods, there were almost endless accounts of the harsh treatment of maliks by the state. Informants commonly described how the maliks were among the first to be executed or jailed by communist authorities during their assault on villages in 1970s and 1980s.

People across communities also described how they reconstituted the malik system after returning to their communities after the collapse of the Taliban government. After returning to their communities after 2001, it was not unusual for villagers to call their maliks by new titles. For example, in an Ismaili village in Shibar District, Bamiyan Province, the namayenda described how the previous qaryadar system under Daud and the Communists fell apart. Villagers, realizing the vital role such individuals played in linking communities with the government, reconstituted the system using different titles (in this case, calling them namayenda):

Many people from our village left to Iran, Pakistan, Pul-e Khumri, Mazar, Kabul and other places [during the war]. A lot of the old system disappeared because so many people left. When the Taliban were in charge, they would take people from our village into minefields and use them to clear the mines. Many people from our village died this way. ... We used to have qaryadars and we trusted them. The qaryadar was the bridge between the people and the woluswal. The woluswal wouldn't do any work without the qaryadar. ... Now we have a namayenda .... The names are different. During the war we had a namayenda as well. Different commanders had namayenda. If they If they needed something they would gather the namayenda. The namayenda consults with the people.[54]

The title "namayenda" in this community was a residual of mujahideen rule. Rather than revert to the pre-war term, arbab, the community continued to use the name utilized by the commanders. Although the title was the same, the authority behind the name after 2001 signified a representative of the people rather than a representative of one of the political factions.

One of the recurrent themes from fieldwork was that the malik system was more responsive and under control of citizens than it had been at any other time in the past, especially during periods when central government tried to co-opt the malik system. A Tajik arbab in Karokh District, Herat Province contrasted his current role with those that preceded him:

In the past, the government was not good. In that time the government relied solely on its own power and might. Any person who had strength or who was powerful ruled and these people used their power over villagers. In every village there was an arbab – he ruled the village like a king (padshah). Now arbabs don't have as much strength. The people are choosing the arbabs themselves as representatives to the woluswal.

---

[54] Bamiyan-Shibar-Village 1-#5.

If the arbab does not work on behalf of the people, the people will send him back and take away his power. Now the people are not afraid of the arbabs, but in the past the people were afraid of them.[55]

In Khanabad District, Kunduz Province, informants referred to their village representative as an arbab. They depicted contemporary arbabs as having a very different structure of accountability than those in the past.[56] They said that there used to be just a few big arbabs (akin to past khans) in the district but now each village has one and they consult with community members far more than they had before. I found that after 2001 they represent the people's interests to the state. A relatively young malik, just 28 years old, in Qarabgh District, Kabul Province explained the current role of the malik in his community, as well as the challenges he faces as a young leader in the community dealing with elders:

The malik system has very deep roots in the community. ... Maliks in our district are registered with the Ministry of Interior. We have stamp. If the people have some work with the government, the people will ask us to help them with the woluswal. During some periods of our history, some maliks could abuse their authority. But this is not the case now. As I've learned, a malik should be a very tolerant person and should be willing to help people. I work as a volunteer and do not have a salary. I was selected through an election in our village. After the election people went to the woluswal and told him of my election. The woluswal accepted the suggestion of the people. That is how I was selected...As the malik in my community, I am just a symbol which links the village to the government.[57]

Although the selection process of maliks and their titles varies across provinces and districts, I found them in almost every community I visited. The deputy governor of Herat Province, a former commander for the notorious jihadi leader Ismail Khan, explained that the maliks are the only legitimate organization representing the interests of villages to the government:

The people of the village come together and try to choose a smart and educated person to lead them. This person is introduced to the woluswal and is registered in the court as an official representative of the people to the government. The arbab then works as the representative for the village. Every village has an arbab and he is the representative of the people to the government. ... The arbab is responsible for the activities of the government in that area. He is responsible for government activities in the community.[58]

Although each village I visited had a malik, there was not a single type of procedure used to select them. In some cases, the position passed down a hereditary chain. In other cases, the position rotated after a term of several years. In other situations, the incumbent would retire from the position asking the elders to select a new leader. Finally, in some villages there were elections

---

[55] Herat-Karokh-District Center-#1.   [56] Kunduz-Khanabad-Village 1-#7.
[57] Kabul-Qarabagh-Village 2-#4.   [58] Herat-Provincial Capital - #1.

with ballot boxes. For example an Aimaq woman in her thirties in Anjil District, Herat Province said, "The people of the village selected the arbab themselves. The people of the village cast their votes in a ballot box and cast vote for their arbab. ... Now the arbab takes all of our problems to the district government and gets our issues resolved there."[59]

BACK TO THE FUTURE: SUBNATIONAL GOVERNANCE AFTER 2001

Despite the dynamism of community self-governance, the post-2001 period featured a great deal of continuity with the past as the formal government continued to pursue a governing strategy that had no room for communities in the political system. Despite enormous opportunities to be more inclusive of local interests, the design of the post-2001 government represented path dependent continuities with previous regimes, instituting the old centralized formal bureaucratic system designed for authoritarian rule with all decision-makers at the subnational level appointed by and accountable to Kabul. Although the 2004 Constitution introduced some democratically elected bodies, it served as a continuation viewing "informal systems of justice and dispute resolution in local communities...as an unfortunate (if understandable) by-product of state collapse that would wither away as the formal legal system expanded."[60]

Policies toward subnational and village governance were bound up in post-Taliban efforts to redefine the Afghan state. In the aftermath of terrorist attacks on the U.S. on September 11, 2001, U.S. and other military forces from around the world joined to oust the Taliban from power. In December of that year, a range of political factions who opposed Taliban rule came together in Bonn, Germany, in a forum sponsored by the United Nations, to form an interim government. Hamid Karzai, a Popalzai Durrani Pashtun, assumed leadership of a transitional administration. The interim period came to an end in the early days of 2004 with the ratification of a new democratic constitution based on democratic and some Islamic principles. Later that year, Hamid Karzai won the country's first-ever presidential election.

In the early days after the fall of the Taliban, the infrastructure necessary to conduct national elections was inadequate to support a national referendum on the new constitution. In place of a constitutional referendum, political leaders at the 2001 Bonn Conference, which established the Transitional Government of the Islamic Republic of Afghanistan, proposed a national Loya Jirga as the mechanism that would approve the new constitution. Just as customary governance had evolved over the years, so too had individual perceptions of the

---

[59] Herat-Anjil-Village 2-#1.
[60] Thomas J. Barfield, "Culture and Custom in Nation-Building: Law in Afghanistan," *Maine Law Review* 60, no. 2 (2008): 350.

Loya Jirga process.[61] To attain legitimacy, the gathering included not only customary leaders and men, but also civil society activists, women, as well as the warlord class that had emerged in the preceding 25 years. At the same time, the entire procedure itself – a jirga – was premised on continued legitimacy of customary authority. In early 2004, the Loya Jirga ratified a constitution that established the Islamic Republic of Afghanistan and defined the scope of the central government.

The new constitution did not change the way government was organized. Instead of instituting a new form of government that was willing to accommodate citizen preferences into local government policy, the country maintained the heavily centralized political system derived from Soviet models that created a strong executive branch at both the national and subnational levels. Specifically, it created a powerful presidency despite proposals from some participants calling for a prime minister to counter the powerful executive. Several factions argued that the creation of a prime minister would lead to same kind of tensions that led to the civil war in the early 1990s that resulted in the destruction of Kabul and the rise of the Taliban.[62] A decentralized system was rejected in favor of the previous, highly centralized system that reflected many aspects of the 1964 Constitution, with the notable exception that the monarchy was now abolished and there would be democratic elections for the president, national assembly, and local councils. Specific executive powers included the authority to appoint members to the Supreme Court, ministers, diplomats, as well as one-third of the members of the upper house of the bicameral national assembly, the Meshrano Jirga (House of Elders).[63]

The Constitution created a fairly weak bicameral national assembly consisting of an upper house, the Meshrano Jirga, and a lower house, the Wolesi Jirga (House of the People).[64] According to the Constitution, members of the Wolesi Jirga should be elected popularly with seats allocated in proportion to the population of each province. Seats in the Meshrano Jirga were to be both elected and appointed: a third should be elected by members of the provincial council, another third should be selected by members of the district councils, and the final third were to be appointed by the President "from among experts and experienced personalities."[65] In contrast with the broad institutional

---

[61] M. Jamil Hanifi, "Editing the Past: Colonial Production of Hegemony through the 'Loya Jerga' in Afghanistan," *Iranian Studies* 37, no. 2 (2004): 295–322.

[62] Larry P. Goodson, "Afghanistan in 2003: The Taliban Resurface and a New Constitution Is Born," *Asian Survey* 44, no. 1 (2004): 20.

[63] Most of the important aspects of executive authority are detailed in Article 64 of the 2004 Constitution.

[64] Article 82, Constitution of the Islamic Republic of Afghanistan, 2004.

[65] Article 84, Constitution of the Islamic Republic of Afghanistan, 2004. Because elections for district councils had yet to take place by the seating of the first Parliamentary session in 2005, the executive branch appointed the seats apportioned for district council members. Thus, the executive branch appointed two-thirds of the upper house of Parliament during its first and

powers granted to the president, neither house wielded substantial power. Legislative authority in the upper house was limited to modification of laws or decrees, approval of the state budget, ratification of treaties, and creation and modification of administrative units, while the lower house has the authority to confirm ministers and Supreme Court nominees, hold votes of no-confidence against ministers, and initiate bills.[66]

Courts also stood in the shadow of a strong executive. Although the judiciary had authority to interpret the Constitution, laws, and other decrees, it could only do so at the request of the government or other courts.[67] The executive was to appoint members of the Supreme Court, who in turn appoint members of the provincial and district courts. The Constitution included a repugnancy clause, whereby no law may contravene the principles of Islam. However, Islamic law is not the source of most laws as the Constitution also makes room for civil law. Nonetheless, by relying on Islamic law as a source of law, Islamic jurisprudence can in principle be invoked by the state in particular cases (if it so wishes). If a case involves personal matters, then the Supreme Court and all lower courts are bound to observe specific Sunni or Shia jurisprudence, depending on beliefs of the plaintiffs.[68]

The strong presidency is one of two defining features of the Afghan constitution. The other is bureaucratic centralization of authority vis-à-vis local governments. The province (wilayat) is the largest unit of subnational governance, each of which is led by a provincial governor (wali) who is appointed by the president. Within each province there are several districts, woluswali, led by district governors (woluswal) who are also appointed by the president. Provincial governors are the official representatives of the executive branch in their provinces. They have very weak official capacity, limited to overseeing implementation of national-level ministry policies in each province and providing direction to police forces. District governors also represent the executive branch at the district level and have very limited formal authority.

The Constitution declared that "principles of centralism" shall govern relations with subnational units with no discussion of decentralized decision-making processes. On paper, formal subnational governments have little autonomy or authority. They serve as representatives of the national government to the local level.[69] It is difficult to label the post-2001 subnational government

subsequent sessions. By the end of the Karzai administration, district council elections had not taken place. It is unclear when or if district council elections will take place due to exorbitant costs of holding such elections, deteriorating security situation around the country, as well as difficulties involved in physically delimiting district boundaries.

[66] Articles 93 and 95, Constitution of the Islamic Republic of Afghanistan, 2004.

[67] Article 121, Constitution of the Islamic Republic of Afghanistan, 2004.

[68] Article 131, Constitution of the Islamic Republic of Afghanistan, 2004. According to the Constitution, shariat courts in Afghanistan can apply Hanafi jurisprudence to Sunnis and Jafari jurisprudence to Shia populations.

[69] Article 42, Constitution of the Government of the Islamic Republic of Afghanistan, 2004.

units as true "local governments," as these local bodies have no ability to create or oversee meaningful local policies. Instead, policy direction comes directly from Kabul. They are best seen as administrative subunits of the national government. Most importantly, there is no room for citizens at the subnational level to have input into the policies and programs implemented in their districts and provinces.

Subnational units do not have the right to collect or retain revenue. All taxes generated locally are collected by representatives of various line ministries (representatives of national-level government ministries working at the provincial or district levels) and sent back up to Kabul.[70] Kabul then formulates a national budget and should (in principle) send resources back down to the provinces, while the provinces are then expected to disperse resources to the district level. Subnational governments have essentially no formal authority to tax or make spending decisions. Those crucial decisions – the foundation of government activity – are made in Kabul.

The example of the provincial councils illustrates the challenges of slapping weak democratic institutions on a government structure designed for authoritarian rule. The only subnational elections held in the 2001–2014 period were for provincial councils. Although established by the Constitution, the mandate of provincial councils was nebulously defined as to "participate in the attainment of the development objectives of the state and improvement of the affairs of the province in the manner prescribed by laws."[71] Three cycles of provincial council elections have been held (in 2006, 2010, and 2014). Elected members of these councils have been frustrated due to the fact that their mandate remained unclear.[72] Similarly, public opinion data indicate that these councils, despite the fact that they are democratically elected, have very little popular support.[73] With the support of the international donor community, the provincial councils have carved out a niche in supporting development planning of donor funds at the provincial level that, in principle, should feed into a national process. The highly centralized nature of government means that

---

[70] The one exception to this is municipalities, which are allowed to collect and retain locally generated revenue.

[71] Article 139, Constitution of the Government of Islamic Republic of Afghanistan, 2004

[72] "Afghan Provincial Councils Complain of Low Salaries, Poor Coordination" (Kabul, Afghanistan, May 22, 2008) Tolo TV, BBC Monitoring South Asia Service. In 2012, I interviewed Provincial Council members in Balkh and Nangarhar Provinces and they continued to express outrage over the lack of a clear mandate. On the other hand, the vast majority of village-level informants continued to believe that Provincial Council members simply used their positions to access international donor assistance for their own benefit. In 2015 Provincial council members protested their lack of oversight over provincial government officials.

[73] For a comprehensive look at public attitudes toward the state, formal and informal political organizations, and elections in Afghanistan see Jennifer Brick Murtazashvili, "Survey on Political Institutions, Elections, and Democracy in Afghanistan" (Washington, DC: Democracy International and United States Agency for International Development, 2012).

plans from the local level have almost no influence on actual policy outcomes.[74] As there is no requirement that provincial or district governors should be elected, it is unclear what role provincial or district councils might play, if any, in checking the authority of these governors. For example, these councils have no oversight in local budgetary matters or over formal public policy. Most informants at the village level had little information about the activities of provincial council members – despite the fact that they are the only formally elected local representatives in the country. They simply did not come up during the course of interviews as having any immediate consequence for local governance outcomes in rural Afghanistan.

The status of the constitutionally-mandated district and village councils was equally vague. According to the Constitution, they shall, "organize activities as well as attain active participation of the people in the provincial administrations in districts and villages, in accordance with the provisions of the law."[75] Despite the discussion of village councils in the Constitution, there is no mention of village executives. Each village is to have an elected council – that has no clear mandate – but no elected or appointed executive. While all constitutions are vague (and even intentionally so) on some issues, over a decade after the ratification of the Constitution, the roles and responsibilities of these bodies remained inchoate.

Districts had little formal authority in the 2004 Constitution and in practice had almost no funds to support their goals. They had very small operating budgets relative to the line ministry officials operating in each district. Between 2001 and 2014, district and provincial governors had been variously supported by the budgets of NATO-supported Provincial Reconstruction Teams (PRTs), as well as several ad hoc donor-supported local government projects. A routine complaint from district governors whom I interviewed is that they had meager operating budgets, no discretion to select staff working in their offices, and little say over donor-controlled resources spent in their district. By 2015, all of the PRTs set up by NATO to support local governance closed in anticipation of the withdrawal of most U.S. and NATO-led troops. International funds from the PRTs that had been used to support initiatives of district and provincial governors dried up alongside with the PRTs themselves.

The centralized system of governance meant that policy decisions affecting subnational units were made in line ministry offices in Kabul, with line ministry

---

[74] An NGO representative, who participated in provincial development planning meetings in Balkh Province, said that the plans created in that province had no effect in policy at the national level. He warned that the further creation of what he believed to be "faux" participatory bodies at the local level would at worst lead to a backlash by participants, and at best a weariness of individuals to participate in such planning processes in the future. He said that the donors had created myriad participatory bodies at the provincial and district levels that had no influence on actual policy outcomes. Balkh-Provincial Capital-#10.

[75] Article 140, Constitution of the Government of the Islamic Republic of Afghanistan, 2004.

directorates at the provincial and district level responsible for implementing these policies. The capacity of these line ministries varied greatly. For example, although the Ministry of Rural Reconstruction and Development claimed to have enormous capacity as a result of donor support and said they had representatives in most districts, upon visiting the districts I could not locate most of these officials. In many districts, the Ministry could not identify qualified personnel willing or able to take these government positions.[76] A great deal of this Ministry's work was contracted out to foreign NGOs.

After almost fifteen years of international assistance to extend the state to the countryside throughout Afghanistan, very little had changed in the way Afghans experienced the state from previous regimes. The organization of government at the subnational level was essentially a continuation of the principles of centralization that was found in the 1964 Constitution, which also created elected councils at the subnational level that had purely advisory or symbolic roles.[77] Government officials as the subnational level had limited discretion and authority, existing primarily to implement directives of Kabul. Provincial and district governors continued to be appointed by the central government with no local input. The Constitution stated that villages are a formal level of subnational administration, but makes no clear statement about the authority of subnational officials. As a result, factions in the Afghan government clashed over who should control and create village government after 2001.

WHO CONTROLS THE VILLAGES?

The constitutional ambiguities surrounding subnational governance and village governance in particular, created opportunities for political factions within the new Afghan government – each vying for billions of dollars in international donor support – to jockey for political control of rural Afghanistan. Turf fighting between ministries in Kabul to control the "village portfolio" had negative effects on the stability of village governance as policy debates in Kabul played out in communities around the country leaving district governors and citizens as seemingly hapless bystanders. This section recounts one of the major policy debates that played out between ministries in Kabul over the question of who should control the villages. This battle reflects a deeper struggle over what influence, if any, customary governance should have in Afghan politics.

---

[76] Officials I spoke with at the Ministry in 2007 said they were to have at least two officials representing the Ministry at the district level, but in many instances I could not find these representatives. Moreover, district governors were often uniformed about the personnel selected by the range of line ministries who were to fill these positions and thus, they had very little information about whether positions in his office had been created or who had filled them.

[77] Esther Meininghaus, "Legal Pluralism in Afghanistan," Working Paper, Amu Darya Series Paper No. 8 (Bonn, Germany: University of Bonn, Center for Development Research, 2007).

It illustrates that bureaucratic battles in Kabul contributed to the broader inability of the state to govern the provinces. In addition, this discussion provides an opportunity to introduce CDCs in greater depth. Most importantly, the section illustrates the perils of donor assistance when international donors treat something like the extension of the state into rural communities for the first time as a mere technical issue rather than a fundamental issue that is naturally wrought with conflict and politics.[78]

When I began fieldwork in 2005, the Ministry of Interior (MoI) had the most legitimate claim to ownership of village governance issues. Since the establishment of the post-Taliban government, both provincial and district governors were appointed by and reported to MoI, a responsibility this Ministry had dating back to the days of the monarchy. Although provincial and district governors were often vetted and selected by the president, they were officially appointed by MoI.

Subnational governance at that time was a very small part of MoI activity, as the Ministry mainly functioned to supervise and reorganize the beleaguered Afghan National Police. As a result, most informants I spoke with in communities believed the district governor was only responsible for security and policing issues. Furthermore, because the district governors were appointed by and reported to a single ministry, representatives of other line ministries at the district and provincial level viewed governors as competitors. From a purely institutional perspective, district governors faced the seemingly impossible task of governing effectively but had almost no oversight authority over officials employed by other ministries working in their districts.

MoI policy towards customary governance then was reminiscent of Daud-era policies of direct rule, although many of their activities were not based in any formal policy that I could identify. There was also a strong PDPA legacy in this ministry that might also explain this perspective: many bureaucrats I met in MoI had studied in Moscow during the 1980s with Soviet support. MoI officials in Kabul appeared to believe that customary governance fell under its policy portfolio. As a result of the often close ties between district governors and maliks found in most districts some MoI officials in Kabul regarded maliks as MoI employees or, at the very least, representatives of MoI at the village level despite the fact that maliks were selected by communities. The attitude among MoI officials in Kabul was very different than among district governors, who were also MoI employees, but who viewed maliks as partners in governance, rather than agents of the state.[79]

Although MoI believed it was the only ministry responsible for subnational governance, as it was responsible for appointing mayors and provincial and

---

[78] On this point see Ferguson, *The Anti-Politics Machine*.
[79] Kabul-Kabul City-#24. In some cases, district governors did believe that maliks were agents of the state, but these governors clearly understood that maliks were selected by communities and not the state.

district governors, it was not the only ministry vying for control of this portfolio. In the early days after 2001, The MRRD challenged MoI dominance of subnational governance, by creating a program in 2002 called the National Solidarity Program (NSP). This program, based on CDD models developed by the World Bank in Indonesia, East Timor, and elsewhere, was to develop local, democratic government through the provision of infrastructure projects. It was championed by Ashraf Ghani, an anthropologist who worked for the World Bank and who by 2014 had become president of Afghanistan. Formally, the NSP had two main goals: (1) to deliver project-based, community-based development; and (2) to improve community governance.[80]

To facilitate these goals, MRRD contracted out for the creation of more than 30,000 CDCs in villages across all 34 provinces.[81] In principal, CDCs were created to provide project funds of up to $60,000 per community, calculated at $200 per family, to undertake infrastructure and human capital development programs. By 2015, the NSP had received more than $2.2 billion in funding from international sources.

According to its own set of regulations, a CDC should comprise between 50 and 300 households and should receive $200 per household in block grant funds that support community development projects selected by the community (between $10,000 and $60,000 per community).[82] Communities were required to provide a 10 percent "contribution" to each project, which could be done through in-kind contributions, such as provision of labor in project construction or direct financial contributions. From field interviews and observations, individuals usually contributed in-kind labor during the construction phase of project implementation to satisfy these requirements.

The CDCs were not created or implemented by the government itself. Instead, MRRD subcontracted out its work to create these councils to more than thirty – mostly international – NGOs.[83] In most cases, MRRD contracted the NGOs to cover entire districts. The NGOs then took ownership of implementation of local governance projects in entire districts, determining the size of CDCs and demarcating borders between communities. In most districts

---

[80] Ministry of Rural Rehabilitation and Development, "National Solidarity Programme (NSP)" (Islamic Republic of Afghanistan, April 2008), http://nspafghanistan.org/media/downloads/NSP_Brochure_April_2008.pdf.

[81] MRRD, "NSP-3rd Quarterly Report- 01st Mizan to 30th Qaws 1393 (23rd September to 21st December 2014)," NSP Quarterly Report (Kabul: Ministry of Rural Rehabilitation and Development, 2015).

[82] Ministry of Rural Rehabilitation and Development and World Bank, "National Solidarity Program Operations Manual" (Kabul, October 2004).

[83] MRRD called the organizations who implemented the NSP on behalf of the government "Facilitating Partners." To simplify terminology and use of acronyms, I refer to the Facilitating Partners as simply NGOs. In 2015, all the organizations implementing the NSP were NGOs (mostly foreign but a few Afghan) and one UN Agency (UN-Habitat).

I visited, the NSP office was far better staffed and equipped than the district government office as a result of the abundant sources of funding it had received from foreign donors.

The number of CDCs in a community was not based on the actual number of villages but on the size of the population in the district.[84] Thus, the boundaries of a CDC often conflicted with self-identified community boundaries. For example, in one district the implementing NGO received a contract from MRRD to create 40 CDCs in a district, yet according to local government officials there were only 15 villages in the district. This implementation strategy was itself a source of confusion in many villages. During fieldwork, most informants did not recognize that the CDCs arose from a government program. Because the NSP was heavily reliant on foreign NGOs for the creation of CDCs, many people believed they were just another in a long litany of development shuras. The NSP even used the term "shura" to describe the CDCs.[85]

In addition, each CDC was supposed to have elections for members of an executive board consisting of a head, deputy, secretary, and treasurer. There were also provisions for female participation. A major objective in the creation of CDCs was to increase female participation in decisions involving distribution of funds due to the fact that customary and other local organizations do not usually include women in public deliberations. According to the initial NSP directives CDCs should be equally representative of men and women and both sexes should meet jointly.[86] Funds were to be distributed to the community only after these village elections had been held. These elections were not implemented by the government, but instead presided over by the mostly foreign NGOs that were contracted to create the CDCs. NGOs assisted in project selection, approved budgets, helped the CDCs set up bank accounts where they would receive their funds after project approval, and monitor project implementation.

Before going further, it is important to note that I found very little evidence that elections as mandated by official guidelines occurred in most villages. CDC members were not selected as specified in the NSP governing regulations, which required the use of formal ballot boxes where all men and women in the community openly participate, in any of the 34 villages I visited. In fact, many villagers were not aware of any elections for the CDC, or how positions in the council were allocated. Very few of the informants I spoke with associated the project with democracy or elections, but instead said either the NGO selected the participants because they were young, literate and had time to engage with NGOs, or that they simply asked the malik to run the CDC. Furthermore, female participation was more symbolic than representative. In the few

---

[84] Kabul-Kabul City-#3.
[85] Literally, *shura-ye enkeshafi mahali (qarya) (dehot)* ("Local Development Council" in Dari)
[86] See Ministry of Rural Rehabilitation and Development and World Bank "National Solidarity Program Operations Manual."

instances where women actively participated, they did so separately from the men in their community (NSP later changed its regulations to make accommodations for these political realities, allowing men and women to serve on separate councils). In some areas, the NGOs established separate female CDCs that had their own executive boards. Female CDCs may exist in name for accounting purposes, but I found only a few instances of them operating in practice.[87]

Weaknesses in perceptions of the program were due to "shura fatigue" that seemed to result from the fact that "development shuras" have been the primary conduit of humanitarian and development aid to communities since the early 1980s. For example, a report written by the Agency Coordinating Body for Afghan Relief detailed the creation of extensive development shuras by foreign NGOs during the 1980s.[88] Almost every aid project – whether it be for education, health, or agriculture – that came to communities during the past four decades employed a shura model. In this model, an NGO or donor tasked to implement a specific project, arrived in a community, identified a key group of community stakeholders, and then asked them to deliberate on how project funds should be used. This group of key community stakeholders is then identified as a shura. Donors have been explicit in their use of the term shura because they seek to build on the legitimacy of customary practices as they build their own councils. To many donors, applying the term "shura" seemed to guarantee participation and a way to channel traditional forms of legitimacy into a new endeavor. Informants generally appeared happy to comply with the requests of donors to receive aid, providing a generous veneer of democratic and participatory decision-making to satisfy donor reporting.

While I found the program excelled the most in terms of providing infrastructure to communities, it had other more ambitious political goals. This became very clear from conversations with government and donor officials in Kabul. In stark contrast to the goal of service delivery, which was stressed by MRRD at the local level to communities, the primary rationale communicated

---

[87] A randomized impact evaluation of the NSP that was finalized after I had finished my fieldwork had mixed results regarding gender impacts. On the one hand, it found that that in villages where it was implemented, the NSP increased the acceptance of female participation in local governance, but found no evidence that the program changed attitudes towards the economic or social participation of women, attitudes towards the education of girls, or increased female participation in economic activity or household-decision making. See Beath, Christia, and Enikolopov, "Randomized Impact Evaluation of Afghanistan's National Solidarity Programme." It is also important to note that this field experiment sought to examine the impact of different ways of organizing CDC elections in a sample of communities. Thus, NGO implementing partners were instructed to hold elections in specific ways with an understanding that the elections would be evaluated. It is therefore difficult to compare my sample of randomly selected communities where I found that elections had not been held to those communities participating in the randomized impact evaluation where variation in election methods was specified to implementing partners. Because NGO implementers understood the importance of holding elections for the evaluation, it is highly unlikely they did not hold them.

[88] Carter and Connor, "A Preliminary Investigation of Contemporary Afghan Councils."

to the international community in Kabul for the NSP was the introduction of new democratic structures – and with them, transformation of political institutions at the village level. In fact, MRRD, the World Bank, and other donors and NGOs suggested the CDCs serve as the de jure village governance bodies in rural Afghanistan in lieu of elected village councils shortly after their creation.[89] They believed that formal elections administered by the Independent Elections Commission (IEC) were not necessary, as the NGOs had already administered successful elections in villages that created the NSP. In their view, the CDCs not only filled a developmental deficit in communities, but were successful because they had generated enormous "social capital" that was somehow missing prior to the implementation of the program.[90]

The buzzword of "social capital" creation in Afghan villages was one that was quite popular among MRRD officials. In many donor meetings I witnessed and in interviews with Ministry officials, the impression the Ministry sought to cultivate to the international community was that prior to the creation of the CDCs, villagers in rural Afghanistan did not know how to cooperate and were not able to deliberate to identify issues of common interest and concern. In their view, the CDCs filled this important vacuum. Indeed, the CDCs were created through the National *Solidarity* Program. In Dari, the term solidarity (hambastagi) literally means "to tie together." The name of the program reflects the assumption that before it, villagers were not bound together in a positive way. In this view, building infrastructure through project grants was just the conduit through which more meaningful social capital could be constructed. This assumption is central to other CDD programs (of which NSP is one) funded by the World Bank.[91]

MRRD, the NGOs implementing the project, and donors active in funding and creating CDCs I spoke with truly believed that the CDCs had a transformative effect on the lives of villagers. In fact, some of the NGOs implementing the NSP claimed that the program remained vital to Afghans not because of its potential to provide basic infrastructure, but because it could generate political participation in the countryside. According to the director of a foreign organization implementing the NSP, "If the CDCs just provide infrastructure, then all of our work has been a massive failure. Our goal is to transform the way decisions are made in villages in Afghanistan."[92] Indeed, according a book co-authored by President Ashraf Ghani the program was a substitute, not a complement to existing local norms:

---

[89] Kabul-Kabul City-#5
[90] Presentation, MRRD official, Workshop on Investigating the Sustainability of Community Development Councils, Kabul Afghanistan. March 6, 2007.
[91] Mansuri and Rao, "Community-Based and-Driven Development: A Critical Review."
[92] Statement by manager of an International Organization implementing NSP, January 21, 2008. Workshop: Toward Sustainable Community Development Councils. Ministry of Foreign Affairs, Kabul, Afghanistan. Sponsored by the Afghanistan Research and Evaluation Unit (AREU).

The intent of the National Solidarity Program was to address the process of democratization from the group level up, in parallel to the process of constitution making and rule writing at the center...Villages that were once the sites of neglect or predatory behavior by lower-level government functionaries were turned into the building blocks of a democratic process...Having gathered the necessary institutional and social capital and demonstrated its usefulness in the creation of infrastructure and services, the program is now ready to become the platform for a more ambitious series of undertakings at the village level. It could...become a mechanism for the registration and formalization of property rights and dispute resolution at the village level.[93]

This expansion of the mission of NSP reflects a deeper theme in the political economy of development. Although development interventions are designed with good intentions to address needs, they are also inherently political. In Afghanistan, the designers of the NSP viewed its introduction as an important first step towards political modernization of rural Afghanistan facilitated by the creation of new community bodies that would displace, what seemed to be in their view, unfortunate customary residues.

The massive influx of aid after 2001 spurred a turf war over resources between ministries who shared very different visions of realities in rural Afghanistan. From the earliest days of the program, it became clear that MRRD wanted to take control of the local government portfolio that was initially in the hands of MoI. Tensions between the two ministries emerged very quickly over the question of local governance and the role the CDCs would play in local governance.

Given the lack of clarity about the village councils mandated in the Constitution, less than two years after they first were created MRRD advocated that the CDCs should become the formal government village councils. In 2005, MRRD brought together some of the CDC heads from around the country for a national "jirga." As a result of this meeting, some CDC members, with the urging of MRRD called for the formalization of the CDCs as governmental entities. With more support from the World Bank, MRRD subsequently promoted the idea of crafting legislation that would formalize the CDCs as village councils. In November 2006, President Karzai signed a bylaw that gave some formal administrative authority to the CDCs, but stopped well short of recognizing them as the formal village councils that were called for in the Constitution. According to an Afghan legal scholar, a bylaw in this context was merely an administrative regulation that only applies to MRRD itself, not to other ministries within the government.[94] As such, the bylaw gave MRRD a document stating CDCs were legal entities giving them the ability to open bank accounts and other activities, but other ministries including MoI, refused to recognize them as such. No doubt, the vast sums of money poured into communities by the international community through the NSP alleviated the

---

[93] Ghani and Lockhart, *Fixing Failed States*, 206–8.   [94] Kabul-Kabul City-#26.

need – at least temporarily – for the government to consider how it might finance rural development and local government in the long term.

In 2007 the Ministry began educating villagers on a new draft MRRD regulation stating that the CDCs should become formal government village councils. While this regulation had not been signed by members of the National Assembly, the intention to undermine not only MoI but customary authority at the village level was apparent.

On the face of it, the ambitions of the NSP to bring democratically elected local governance and public goods to rural Afghanistan were admirable. Peering closer into MRRD documents and interviewing MRRD officials at the national and local level, it became clear that the objectives of the NSP were not simply to create village democracy, but to transform rural society, in many ways reminiscent of the policies of Amanullah and the PDPA. The NSP could finally bring modernization to villages by displacing customary authority, which in the view of many in the Ministry and the international NGO community was the source of Afghanistan's rural underdevelopment. On its English language website MRRD touted its most important achievement – the displacement of customary authority:

The single most important achievement to date is the creation of mechanisms for local governance and decision making. The community empowerment that has taken place manifests itself through the rapid absorption of NSP funding and the mobilization of additional resources. The broad-based introduction of an alternative decision making process at the lowest community level represents a form of government at its most basic form; one that the central government and the international community have envisioned for Afghanistan. The introduction of democratically elected community decision-making bodies as a viable alternative to the traditional local governance structure has provided a vehicle to re-build the social fabric and relationships at grassroots level.[95]

MRRD officials I interviewed – both expatriate and Afghan – expressed deep dismay over the fact that MoI would not recognize or cooperate with the CDCs at the village level.[96] A foreign advisor in MRRD stated that the malik system needed to be replaced with a new democratic one because the maliks simply exploited peasants.[97] During a presentation to the World Bank and other donors during an evaluation mission, a western-educated MRRD official proclaimed in a PowerPoint presentation that the formalization of the CDCs was so pressing because, "there has not been village governance in Afghanistan for more than 200 years."[98] The speaker went on to say that customary structures had withered away and villages were in dire need of effective leadership and democracy. Despite the confusing empirical basis of such claims, such

---

[95] Ministry of Rural Rehabilitation and Development (MRRD), "The Most Important Achievement of the NSP to Date," May 27, 2010, www.nspafghanistan.org/Default.aspx?Sel=103.
[96] Kabul-Kabul City-#2. [97] Kabul-Kabul City-#3.
[98] MRRD Presentation, August 2007, Kabul.

comments guided public policy in the donor bubble of Kabul and by extension Washington, London, and elsewhere.

By contracting over two billion dollars to the largest and most vocal international NGOs (and one United Nations agency), MRRD, through its English-speaking expatriate advisors, ensured strong international support for their efforts. These NGOs had moral authority that for-profit contractors (both foreign and domestic) used by other Afghan government ministries simply lacked while also providing a foundation to advocate on behalf of MRRD. While the Washington Post or the New York Times were running seemingly monthly exposes on corruption with for-profit aid projects-gone-bad, the NSP appeared to have a halo hanging over its head.[99] Based on no systematic empirical evidence, it was heralded by many of the foreign NGOs implementing the project and subsequently the Western media as Afghanistan's only success story. The editorial board of the Washington Post claimed in 2010 that the program was an unabashed success.[100] One foreign correspondent claimed the Taliban respected the program so much, it would not burn schools built by the program.[101] The sad truth was that between 2004 and 2015, the Taliban had claimed responsibility for many of the 357 people – mostly Afghan – killed working on the project.[102]

There was little concern from foreign supporters – including the World Bank – that formalizing new government bodies at the village level might have political consequences or could be a source of tension at the village or district level. Many Afghan officials I spoke with in MRRD were aware of these political challenges, but seemed assured that the international community was on "their" side in this political battle. Most donors were stridently optimistic believing that the NSP and had contributed to major social change and progress in rural Afghanistan by fostering democracy, liberating women, providing new infrastructure, and serving as the basis for renewed economic growth because it relied on innovative programmatic implementation.

Most importantly, Ministry information was so easily digestible in English by members of the aid and diplomatic community who rarely traveled out of Kabul. This community had little idea of what life was like for most Afghans in the countryside. When they did visit, many visited communities hand selected by their staff implementing NSP projects. During my visits to district centers and interviews with NSP implementing partners in district centers, they too

---

[99] Ben Arnoldy, "Afghanistan War: Successful Foreign Assistance Lets Afghans Pick Their Project," *Christian Science Monitor*, July 28, 2010; Sabrina Tavernise, "Afghan Enclave Seen as Model for Development," *The New York Times*, November 13, 2009; Robert B. Zoellick, "The Key to Rebuilding Afghanistan," *The Washington Post*, August 22, 2008, sec. Opinions.

[100] "Afghanistan's Nation Building," *The Washington Post*, July 20, 2010, sec. Opinions.

[101] Gregory Warner, "The Schools the Taliban Won't Torch," *Washington Monthly*, December 2007, www.washingtonmonthly.com/features/2007/0712.warner.html.

[102] Mujib Mashal and Jawad Sukhanyar, "Gunmen in Northern Afghanistan Kill 9 Local Aid Workers," *The New York Times*, June 2, 2015.

were eager to show me the model village in their district that had been host to the visiting donor or supervisor from Kabul. Seemingly, all the donors seemed to imagine was a tabula rasa whose contours would be shaped by the state-building process embodied by the NSP.

The project moved full speed ahead with great urgency. Ministry officials spoke of the need to facilitate democratic participation or to liberate women in the countryside, giving donors the feeling that they were the first ones ever to reach out to Afghan villages. Ironically, many of the NGOs were selected because they had a long history in certain districts. For example, CARE International was selected to implement the NSP in Logar Province because it had a long history of working there. Likewise the French NGO ACTED was chosen to work in several northern provinces due to its decades-long legacy implementing community development projects using participatory methods on behalf of international donors. Of course, donor-driven community development was not new in the Afghan countryside.

Most of the informants I spoke with in the international donor community understood that MRRD wanted to formalize the CDCs as the formal government-sponsored village councils at the village level. They also viewed the CDCs as important conduits for development assistance. Very few expatriates in Kabul had any sense that a proposal to build formal governance at the village level on the basis of CDCs could be considered controversial – or even political: it was all technical assistance.

MRRD presented the contradictory message that customary structures had disappeared and thus new structures were needed to replace them, but also argued that customary structures were an impediment to democratization and modernization. In contrast to the English-speaking, foreign-trained technocrats in MRRD, MoI officials appeared to be Soviet-era lumbering stalwarts, focused on the needs of policing the countryside, while adamantly opposing formalization of the CDCs. Unlike the numerous MRRD officials who seemed to speak perfect English and hold foreign degrees in development studies, many MoI officials received their training in the Soviet Union.

A provincial-level MRRD official in Nangarhar Province commented on the political tensions with other Afghan government ministries:

> Our relationship with other ministries is very good but MRRD needs to coordinate more effectively with other ministries, especially with the Interior Ministry. ...I think some believe that the CDCs are just the responsibility of MRRD...I've told the NSP people about this problem. They told us that they want to discuss this problem with the Ministry of Interior, but they think Interior does not want the CDC system to replace the role of maliks in communities.[103]

These inter-ministerial conflicts were not confined to Kabul. Rather, they spilled over into local politics in the countryside. As MRRD accelerated its plan to

---

[103] Nangarhar-Provincial Capital-#3.

formalize the CDCs, they appeared to violate the implicit social contract through which villagers had allowed the mostly foreign NGOs and CDCs to begin operating in their communities. In many communities, informants remarked that they liked projects they received from CDCs but did not see the new councils as governing structures. When "social organizers" initially came to communities to ask permission of villagers to create the CDCs, they said the councils were needed to implement projects and were not for political purposes. In fact, MRRD officials and implementing partners recalled some challenges they faced when they began implementing the first CDCs as community members thought the new councils would be used for political purposes and to advance specific social causes. More fundamentally, citizens had given NGOs license to operate in their communities not to extend the state, but to provide large NGO block grants that could help improve rural livelihoods. An employee of an NGO implementing the NSP in Qarabagh District, Kabul Province spoke of the growing tension between the CDCs and the maliks.

I have not read the entire bylaw [signed by Karzai] yet, but it is a very important document for the future of the CDCs because under it the CDCs get a lot of privileges. Two weeks ago maliks from the district went to the woluswal to complain to him about the bylaw. One day, the woluswal came to me and said that the maliks were complaining about the CDC bylaw and as a result of this bylaw they feared they will be replaced. They thought that now we will have the CDCs instead of maliks. I told the woluswal that the bylaw was not done by my orders, but MRRD is responsible for the bylaw. It is just our responsibility to educate people about the bylaw. I told the woluswal that if he wanted more information he should talk to the Ministry of Interior and MRRD.[104]

If the purpose of the CDCs was to extend formal governance to the village level, then this guidance certainly did not reach the district government. Indeed, many district governors I interviewed expressed that the CDCs and the political maneuverings of MRRD undermined their authority. There was little cooperation between the CDCs and the district governors, as the district governors preferred to deal with customary authority. In the view of most district governors, cooperation with maliks was not the result of a policy position but out of recognition that communities expected political interactions with the state to be mediated by maliks and other customary bodies. More often than not, however, district governors said that they simply were not aware of CDC activities in their district because the mostly-foreign NGOs working in the district would not share information about projects or because they were too busy with other more pressing matters.

The tension between the CDCs, the implementing NGOs, and local governments was very visible in some regions. It was palpable in an interview with the woluswal of one district in Bamiyan Province. During my interview with the woluswal, a man entered the room without knocking, hastily sitting on an adjacent sofa. He appeared very impatient by constantly pointing to his watch

---

[104] Kabul-Qarabagh-District Center-#1.

urging me to leave. Without exchanging words, I wrapped up the interview, assuming the well-dressed man in a Western suit was a deputy to the woluswal or an important official. I thanked the woluswal for his time and began to leave assuming governor had important business to attend. As I stood up, the woluswal told me not to hurry and asked me to take my seat. He said the man who so "rudely" interrupted us could wait.

As it turns out, this visitor was not a government employee, but the Afghan head of a UN agency implementing the NSP. In fact, the woluswal had summoned him to his office to talk long before I had requested an interview. Apparently, one week prior, this international agency implementing the NSP in the district selected several villagers to represent the district in a national government conference discussing the future of local governance. The local NSP office had done this without consulting the woluswal. The woluswal was very upset that this agency was acting "as if it was the government" and reminded its head that he was not a government employee. Matters dealing with the government, the woluswal suggested, should be vetted with the government. The NSP/UN representative was very dismissive of the woluswal, both in his verbal and physical demeanor, but promised better communication in the future. The woluswal reiterated that the work of the government should go through the government, not through foreign aid agencies.

Resource inequality also created conflict. The NGOs had more cars, computers, and better trained staff (usually from Kabul or other provinces) than did the local government. Furthermore, these outside NGOs as contractors for MRRD were distributing money through grants to villages – something the cash-strapped government could not do itself. Several woluswals complained that when MRRD established these NGO offices in the district, it undermined the authority of the government. In many instances, woluswals said that the MRRD-funded NGOs would fund projects without informing them. These projects often involved complex infrastructure, which should have the approval of the local government if not other ministries who might have jurisdiction over the construction of such infrastructure. MRRD and the local NSP office implied that they were simply delivering public goods directly to citizens.

Despite vast funds, these organizations and the legacy left by them were in many ways illusory. The NGO capacity did fill a vacuum in the districts, but it was rarely sustainable. When the contract for NSP implementation would come to an end, the NGO closed its office, and with its demise, MRRD presence in the district also ceased. In the years after their creation, NSP presence in communities would rise and fall with the tempo of donor support. CDCs that stopped functioning when donor support dried up would have to be "remobilized" in subsequent years. This was largely due to the fact that the work of the CDCs centered on project implementation contracted to foreign NGOs. When the contract to an NGO concluded the program finished. I visited several districts where the NSP had ceased operation, or where operation was winding down, and staff and been let go or sent to other districts. Several informants expressed exasperation with the waste they associated with projects fueled by foreign aid. This was from a focus group discussion among CDC participants in Bamiyan Province:

The system of our government is just wrong. The government gets a lot of money, but they don't use this money properly. For example, if you go to the MRRD (NSP) office, you will see many advisors sitting there. Every advisor earns more than five thousand dollars salary a month. Look at Afghanistan. We have a lot of professional people who are jobless now. (Pointing) You see that man over there? He is an engineer and he is unemployed. He is a very good advisor. I hope that you will pass on our suggestion to MRRD.[105]

Inter-ministerial rivalry introduced an added amount of uncertainty into local politics and governance. According to one NGO official implementing the NSP in Kabul Province, discussion of the bylaw created uncertainty, as MRRD encouraged NGOs to educate villagers on the bylaw as if it were a new law on local governance, creating a sense of inevitability of the project.[106] A former commander in Qarabagh District, Kabul Province described such conflict:

The [development] shura system is not new for Afghan communities. We had similar programs during the time of Daud Khan. When the NSP process came to our village it was very strong. But now many villages which had NSP do not have meetings any more. Our Ministry of Interior does not support the NSP shuras, it supports the malik system. ...The woluswal doesn't recognize the CDCs as formal bodies in the community. They don't have regular meetings with the woluswal. He just sees the CDCs as a big development project...[107]

A Pashtun malik in Sorkhrod District, Nangarhar Province recounted growing tensions in the village that resulted from CDC bylaw awareness education undertaken in the villages by the foreign NGO implementing NSP in the district. He believed that the CDCs were created as an instrument for foreigners to exert greater control over Afghan villages and represented a new kind of meddling:

It is not clear who has what role and what responsibility. We need just one council here in our village not all of these development councils. We have one qawmi shura that meets with the woluswal. But a problem with these CDCs is that the woluswal can't ask about their work in the villages. There has been a lot of money spent but people have not received what was promised to them. He has no authority over them. And there are all these foreigners working in our villages trying to replace our village system. If the government or villagers ask these musaseh [NGOs] how the money is being spent, they'll tell you it's none of your business and that we have no right to interfere. I think this is a policy from other countries that want to remove our maliks from the villages. If the

---

[105] Bamiyan-Bamiyan Center-Village 2-#8.
[106] Kabul-Qarabagh-District Center-#1. The NGO responsible for administering the NSP in Qarabagh district did not have an office in that district, but instead was located in the neighboring district of Kalakan. Both districts are very small and close to one another.
[107] Kabul-Qarabagh-Village 1-#5.

people don't like their malik they have the right to remove them and they can select another malik. If they cannot trust a malik, they can select another one.[108]

It appeared that the tension between MoI and MRRD over local governance issues was going to end in September 2007 when President Karzai removed the local governance responsibilities from MoI and transferred them to a new body: the Independent Directorate for Local Governance (IDLG). Afghan and foreign officials hoped that the creation of IDLG would result in better policies related to local government issues as authority to appoint provincial and district governors, along with all other issues related to subnational governance, was moved to IDLG.

Animosity that existed between MRRD and MoI was quickly redirected to IDLG and vice versa. From its onset, IDLG was not supportive of MRRD efforts to formalize the CDCs. One reason was that most of the initial IDLG staff came from the local governance division formerly housed at MoI. In some of its first projects, IDLG began directly funding the customary organizations that NSP had been designed to challenge.[109] As a separate entity, however, it also competed with MRRD for donor attention and resources. This competition for resources was further fueled by the onset of the civilian and military "surge" to Afghanistan that began not long after the creation of IDLG.

The policy conflict between the government agencies was on broad display in the first months after the president established IDLG. In November of 2007 MRRD planned to hold a second national "Loya Jirga" of CDC members in Kabul (following up on the first jirga they organized in 2005, which called for the creation of the CDC bylaw). The results of this jirga were known to MRRD staff long before the meeting. As they were preparing for the jirga, several members MRRD officials told me in preparation for the meeting that CDC members would issue a declaration calling for the formalization of the CDCs as the village councils called for by the Constitution. As elections for village councils had yet to be held, MRRD seemed largely successful in convincing the NGOs implementing the NSP as well as the donors funding it that formalizing their authority would be a logical next step.

After catching wind of these plans, IDLG told MRRD that they were not to use the term "jirga" to describe the meeting, as holding a national Loya Jirga had a very specific meaning in the Afghan Constitution and in modern history (primarily referring to a constitutional Loya Jirga).[110] MRRD clearly wanted to use the imagery and legitimacy of a Loya Jirga in bringing CDC members together, and even planned to hold the event in the same tent in Kabul where the Constitutional Loya Jirga was held four years before. IDLG insisted that MRRD change the name of the meeting to a national "consultation." MRRD

---

[108] Nangarhar-Sorkhrod-Village 1-#3.
[109] Adam Pain and Sayed Mohammad Shah, "Policymaking in Agriculture and Rural Development in Afghanistan," Case Studies Series (Kabul, Afghanistan: Afghanistan Research and Evaluation Unit, 2009), 29.
[110] Kabul-Kabul City-#23.

obliged IDLG in formal written documents, but nonetheless MRRD used the term jirga throughout the meeting itself.

My research team and I were able to observe several days of the national consultation. In our interviews with CDC members and observation of small group break-out discussions, there was no call for formalization of the CDC members themselves. Many CDC members complained about being asked to work on CDC activities without receiving a salary for this work, but none that we spoke to sought formal state recognition of their positions.[111] During the opening plenary session, several CDC members interrupted the speeches of MRRD officials demanding salaries for their work.

Several members of my research team were asked by MRRD, at the last minute, to facilitate a break-out discussion of CDC members. It appeared as if the purpose of the discussion was to find out whether CDC members desired formal government authority. During this discussion, CDC members did not express strong interest to formalize the CDCs because they did not believe their work could continue without the foreign funding and NGO facilitation. After nearly an hour and a half of discussion, an MRRD official came running to the session as he heard that CDC members themselves were not pressing for formalization in their discussion. He immediately ordered that the discussion topic change to: "If the CDCs were formalized, what would they look like and what authority should they have?"

As a result of the "national consultation," CDC members "drafted" a resolution calling for the formalization of the CDCs, although neither my colleagues nor I ever saw these specific points discussed by CDC members during the four-day meeting. Ironically, the resolution used specific language that the CDCs be recognized as "the official structure linking the government to the people," language that villagers in rural Afghanistan routinely use to describe the malik system (the full text of this resolution can be found in the Appendix at the conclusion of this chapter). The resolution said that all government functions at the village level should operate under the control of CDCs and that one CDC representative from each village should sit on the constitutionally-mandated district council. In this way, the CDCs would emerge not only as political bodies at the village level, but would populate

---

[111] Lack of salaries was a very common complaint of those working with CDCs in villages. Villagers believed that people would give more effort to CDC work if they were paid. For example a Hazara man in Balkh Province said: "I think it is better if CDC members have salary. [As of now] they have worked without any payment. This work has become boring for them. If they don't have a salary then they also become corrupt. Also many people already think that CDC members must be stealing because they think if CDC members don't have a salary how can they work without payment? Salaries would help us work better. But if they want us to spend more time on their activities, then what should we eat? . . .I think everyone will get tired of this. . .Actually we told Hanif Atmar (former MRRD Minister) about this in a meeting of CDCs in Kabul (the first national consultation of CDC members held in Kabul in 2005). . . .. But after three years they haven't paid us anything." Balkh-Dawlatabad-Village2-#3.

the district councils as well. In the process, MRRD would expand its bureaucratic turf at the expense of IDLG.

In 2010, MRRD held another "national consultation" of CDC leaders once again pushing the formalization of the CDCs. Unlike the 2007 meeting, President Karzai did not attend the meeting. Instead, he met with CDC representatives across all 34 provinces of Afghanistan. According to a MRRD press release, the consultation ended with another resolution proposing formalization of the CDCs. This time, a resolution was not distributed but was "read publicly to the participants."[112] In 2015, President Ghani - an important initial supporter of the NSP - convened a national meeting of CDC members and announced the program would expand to urban areas as well. He also asked international donors for stimulus funds to help CDCs implement a Kabul-directed job-creation program.

IDLG was not been alone in its objection to the formalization of the CDCs as government bodies several years later. A high-ranking member of the Independent Elections Commission said that the CDCs are development bodies and MRRD should limit their activities to supporting the implementation of development projects. According to this official, they could not be formal government entities that represented the will of the people at the village level. He believed that formalization of the CDCs as formal government bodies would be a violation of the Constitution as Afghan elections must be held to international standards and be certified as free and fair. According to this official, there has been no oversight of CDC elections by other government entities, and the fact that they have been managed by mostly international NGOs for the purposes of implementing development projects suggests such elections are not legitimate.[113]

CONCLUSION

Customary governance survived and adapted to decades of civil war. Although the khan system may have declined in significance, a unique and largely effective system of self-governance remained. To be sure, customary governance is not a perfect system. It does not generally facilitate female participation and in some cases these bodies favor elites. Yet for all its imperfections, customary authority is largely defined by norms of deliberation and representation, as well as separated authority at the village level. The bodies are sustainable and will endure regardless of levels of donor funding coming into Afghanistan.

---

[112] Press release, Islamic Republic of Afghanistan, Ministry of Rural Rehabilitation and Development, National Solidarity Program, "The Third CDC National Consultation Conference," Kabul, October 21, 2010.

[113] Kabul-Kabul City-#37.

Despite the presence and apparent effectiveness of customary governance, policymakers in the post-Taliban period struggled to find a place for customary governance. The customary disregard in the post-2001 period was not nearly as cruel as it was during the reign of the Iron Amir. Consequently, government ministries exploited ambiguity related to customary authority to promote a new system of village governance, one that bears a great deal of resemblance to the direct rule embarked by past modernizers. Many of the international donors in Afghanistan who supported such efforts believed they were providing technical assistance to create village councils for public goods provision and the facilitation of social capital. Efforts to extend the state in such a manner was not interpreted by many rural residents as simply technical assistance: it was political and targeted the soul of Afghan politics.

The findings of this chapter suggest that customary organizations are an effective source of governance. They also indicate that customary governance is both neglected in in the political system and highly politicized. Yet it remains to be seen how well these organizations govern in comparison to the new development shuras: the CDCs. The following chapters consider in the capacity and limitations of self-governing village organizations.

Appendix to Chapter 3

The text of the resolution adopted by the national consultation of CDC members, Kabul, November 2007:

1. The CDC bylaw be ratified by Parliament as soon as possible and transformed into a proper law;
2. CDCs are recognized as the official structure linking the government and the people;
3. All other existing structures at the village level be merged under the authority of the CDCs and operate according to the CDC rules and regulations;
4. A member from each CDC, preferably the chairperson, be made a member of their district council;
5. Local authorities and sectoral development authorities resolve their development social, and cultural issues through CDCs representatives on the district council;
6. CDCs have the responsibility to implement all their activities in a proficient, transparent, and accountable manner in accordance with existing laws and regulations;
7. Local security personnel must cooperate with CDCs in order to ensure the implementation of development projects at the village level;
8. Local security authorities must cease to interfere in CDC activities;

If CDC rules are violated by a CDC members, he or she should be questioned and by peers in the CDC and, if necessary, be handed over to the relevant police and judicial authorities.

PART II

CUSTOMARY GOVERNANCE AND PUBLIC
GOODS PROVISION

4

The political economy of village governance

No one is rich here. All the villages are poor. Like you, a thousand people have come here to ask about our lives, but they have gone. Nothing has been done. Some people came about a credit program, but this did not happen yet. So these NGOs and NGO workers keep their jobs but they don't do anything for the people. These workers support themselves and make their work strong, but they don't do anything for the poor people. They don't pay attention to the widows and the poor people. These people are not useful. The people from the NGOs came in the past, but they did not do anything. They just take their salaries, that's all.

– Female Homemaker, Sorkhrod District, Nangarhar Province[1]

There was a king and he had a horse. He loved this horse a lot, but it was getting sick and thin. So he asked another man to help him take care of this horse. After a while, he noticed that the horse was getting thinner and thinner. Then he asked some more people to help take care of his horse. After a while, he figured out that the people who were supposed to be helping were actually stealing the horse's food. When one person was helping him, the horse was losing just a little weight. When many people were helping him take care of the horse, it was losing a lot of weight because more people feeding the horse meant more people were stealing from him. So we can say the same thing about maliks and CDCs. If you have one malik, he can steal just a little as he is just one person. When the CDC is corrupt, they will take a lot.

– Malik, Sorkhrod District, Nangarhar Province[2]

Customary organizations are persistent, adaptive, and largely deliberative, but can they govern effectively? This chapter considers how well customary organizations govern in comparison to several different organizations vying to

[1] Nangarhar-Sorkhrod-Village 1-#6.   [2] Nangarhar-Sorkhrod-Village 1-#3.

provide public goods in rural parts of the country, in particular CDCs and "warlords" and their associated networks of commanders.

These organizations are ideal for comparison because each has played a role in village governance in rural communities. Furthermore, policy proposals have recommended that these organizations be responsible for elements of village governance. For example, as we saw in the previous chapter, representatives of some government ministries and many in the international donor community have argued that CDCs fill a governance gap and should become formal, government organizations. Some Afghan government officials – especially those in local government offices – and many informants in rural areas maintained that customary authorities played the most prominent role in government and should be given formal authority. Finally, the United States established programs to support a range of local commanders and militias, many ostensibly based on "traditional" models, to supplement the Afghan Army and Police.[3]

The goal of this chapter is not simply to describe which organizations are more effective in providing public goods, but also to explain why. Answering the "why" question requires a conceptual framework. To this end, the chapter begins by providing a conceptual framework that suggests a number of conditions that should be satisfied for a local, self-governing organization to provide public goods. These conditions include constraints on local leaders, time horizons of leaders (the expectation that they will be in power in the future), ability of leaders to collect local revenue, and the extent to which organizational rules encourage participation in decision-making. In a broad sense, local governing organizations – customary organizations, CDC, or warlords/network of commanders – should govern more effectively when they attain success on more of these dimensions. The framework outlines a set of variables that contribute to better governance outcomes, thus allowing us explain variation among these organizations in communities across the country.

The analysis, developed from field-based case studies as well as econometric analysis of household livelihood and public opinion survey data, show the relative effectiveness of customary organizations in providing public goods at the local level. This finding may not surprise those who have spent time in rural Afghanistan or rural areas in the developing world more generally. Yet there have been no systematic studies of the extent to which customary organizations provide public goods in post-Taliban Afghanistan. Existing studies of governance in Afghanistan have not considered systematically the mechanisms that explain the organizational effectiveness of different organizations in rural Afghanistan in an increasingly crowded rural landscape. This chapter, through in-depth comparative analysis of different organizations vying for authority in

[3] For a comprehensive overview of these efforts see Jonathan Goodhand and Aziz Hakimi, "Counterinsurgency, Local Militias, and Statebuilding in Afghanistan," Peaceworks (Washington, DC: United States Institute of Peace, 2014).

rural Afghanistan, seeks to do undertake this comparison. While there have been several important evaluations – both statistical and qualitative – of the National Solidarity Program and the CDCs, such studies tell us little about alternative governing bodies. Furthermore, impact evaluations can show us the effect programs have on outcomes without telling us why they work (or do not). Similarly, there have been numerous studies of warlord governance in Afghanistan, but these studies have not examined alternatives in a systematic manner.

In addition to shedding light on the competencies of different local governing organizations in rural Afghanistan, this chapter hopes to open the black box of local governance in Afghanistan to help explain why certain organizations perform better or worse on key dimensions. It also speaks to important policy questions. The findings show that well-funded programs seeking to build local governance in the presence of existing customary political organizations at best misallocate resources. At the very worst, development programs that create parallel organizations that fuel conflict over local authority can destabilize village governance and public goods provision in a highly charged and fragile political environment. There are important costs when outsiders or local governments fail to consider the existing institutional context when building new organizations. In this case understanding context means understanding and appreciating existing sources of collective action. This chapter is organized as follows. The first section presents a conceptual framework to analyze public goods provision by local organizations. The second section applies the framework to the three most common local governing organizations in rural Afghanistan and derives hypotheses about their organizational performance. The third section examines these hypotheses using evidence from fieldwork to gain deeper insight into processes of local governance. Section four relies upon nationally-representative household livelihood and public opinion surveys to examine whether the findings from analysis of qualitative data generalize.

THE POLITICAL ECONOMY OF LOCAL PUBLIC GOODS PROVISION: A THEORY OF LOCAL SELF-GOVERNING ORGANIZATIONS

One perspective on public goods provision considers the conditions when individuals voluntarily contribute to public goods even though there is no requirement to do so.[4] This literature seeks to understand when individuals are able to overcome incentives to "free ride" on the contributions of others, whereby an individual expects others to contribute and they themselves

---

[4] Mancur Olson, *The Logic of Collective Action: Public Goods and the Theory of Groups* (Cambridge: Harvard University Press, 1971); Ostrom, *Governing the Commons*.

contribute nothing. Although one obvious solution to the problem of generating voluntary provision is to establish a state, there is a large literature seeking to explain how individuals can overcome collective-action problems without the state through voluntary contributions.[5]

There are several general mechanisms explaining how individuals can overcome incentives to free ride on the contributions of others. One answer is through social norms, which can be effective to the extent people care about their reputation or standing within a community.[6] For example, Lily Tsai found that norms of morality increase provision of public goods among local government officials in China.[7] Reputational mechanisms of this sort can be effective provided a community has a strong sense of identity that allows people to observe actions, as well as penalize people for behavior that is inconsistent with these norms.[8] Another mechanism that influences public goods provision is identity.[9] Ethnic heterogeneity is the dimension of identity that receives the most attention in the social sciences. Edward Miguel and Mary Kay Gugerty, for example, find that ethnic diversity in Kenyan communities reduces provision of education services.[10] A third factor, resource inequality, is also thought to influence public goods provision. For example, when landholding is unequally distributed, many people who would benefit from provision of a public good may not have the means to voluntarily contribute even if they so desire. Empirical studies have shown that highly unequal landholding or inequities in access to land reduces public goods provision.[11]

[5] James Andreoni, "Why Free Ride? Strategies and Learning in Public Goods Experiments," *Journal of Public Economics* 37, no. 3 (1988): 291–304; Thomas R. Palfrey and Howard Rosenthal, "Participation and the Provision of Discrete Public Goods: A Strategic Analysis," *Journal of Public Economics* 24, no. 2 (1984): 171–93.

[6] There are many studies empirically assessing the role of reputations in public goods provision, typically from an experimental perspective. These studies consider reputation and "prosocial behavior" James Andreoni and Rachel Croson, "Partners versus Strangers: Random Rematching in Public Goods Experiments," in *Handbook of Experimental Economics Results*, ed. Vernon L. Smith and Charles R. Plott, vol. 1 (New York: Elsevier, 2008), 776–83.

[7] Tsai, *Accountability without Democracy.*

[8] Avner Greif, Paul Milgrom, and Barry R. Weingast, "Coordination, Commitment, and Enforcement: The Case of the Merchant Guild," *Journal of Political Economy* 102, no. 4 (1994): 745–76; Michihiro Kandori, "Social Norms and Community Enforcement," *Review of Economic Studies* 59, no. 198 (1992): 63–80.

[9] Alberto Alesina, Reza Baqir, and William Easterly, "Public Goods and Ethnic Divisions," *Quarterly Journal of Economics* 114, no. 4 (1999): 1243–84.

[10] Edward Miguel and Mary Kay Gugerty, "Ethnic Diversity, Social Sanctions, and Public Goods in Kenya," *Journal of Public Economics* 89, no. 11–12 (2005): 2325–68.

[11] Jean-Marie Baland and Jean-Philippe Platteau, "The Ambiguous Impact of Inequality on Local Resource Management," *World Development* 27, no. 5 (1999): 773–88; Pranab Bardhan and Jeff Dayton-Johnson, "Unequal Irrigators: Heterogeneity and Commons Management in Large-Scale Multivariate Research," in *Drama of the Commons* (Washington, DC: National Academies Press, 2001).

These perspectives on public goods provision are each highly decentralized in the sense they have a very limited role for organizations that might compel contributions. Nonetheless, these decentralized perspectives provide insight into certain aspects of rural governance in Afghanistan. In particular, social norms and reputations should be important in rural communities that are relatively small and where qawm or tribal affiliations remain an important organizing aspect of social life. For example, hashar is a norm throughout both Afghanistan and Central Asia in which every able-bodied community member contributes labor or even money to some collective good in the village.[12] Often elders or religious leaders will call for hashar, summoning people to build or refurbish a mosque or school, clean streets, or irrigation canals. A Hazara farmer in Bamiyan Province described the importance of hashar work in his community:

[M]ost of the work we have done in our village is done through hashar. For example, we worked to clean our canals in our village through hashar. We have also built our mosque through hashar. We have also worked to build a shrine through hashar. During the years of the government of Karzai, the Karzai government has not put one brick in our village. We do all of the work in our village by use of hashar.[13]

Participation in hashar activities is voluntary, yet social norms incentivize people to participate. In particular, those who do not participate are typically shamed by other villagers who understand quite well who has participated and who has shirked. Although some have argued that norms of hashar declined with the war,[14] I found that after relative peace was restored to communities, communities reconstituted these practices and that they were fairly common and came up quite a lot during the course of field work.

Decentralized perspectives on public goods provision have a certain appeal in a persistently weak state such as Afghanistan because in such environments there is a general assumption is that there are often few organizations capable of providing public goods. Reputational perspectives of this sort, however, cannot explain why some organizations are better at providing public goods than others. For example, the ubiquity of hashar cannot explain in a direct sense why customary organizations may perform better (or worse) than alternatives in terms of public goods. Explaining public goods provision in rural Afghanistan requires a more political perspective, one which recognizes how variation in the institutional features of different organizations translates into differences in terms of governance outcomes.

---

[12] Madeleine Reeves, "The Ashar-State: Communal Commitment and State Elicitation in Rural Kyrgyzstan" unpublished manuscript.
[13] Bamiyan-Bamiyan Center-Village 2-#7
[14] Jonathan Goodhand, "Aiding Violence or Building Peace? The Role of International Aid in Afghanistan," *Third World Quarterly* 23, no. 5 (2002): 837–59.

Among the first studies to consider how variation in political features of organizations explain local public goods provision were by economists interested in the consequences of decentralized governance for matching public spending with voters' demand for government spending.[15] These economic studies showed how political decentralization allowed voters more voice in fiscaldecision making and promoted inter-jurisdictional competition. When citizens can "vote with their feet" there are increased incentives for policymakers to choose "efficient" levels of government expenditures in the sense that the bundle of public goods provided is more likely to be preferred by the average voter in a community.[16]

These models of organizational performance and inter-jurisdictional competition were subsequently extended to help explain the political consequences of decentralized governance and federalism. In addition to improving effectiveness of public goods provision, decentralization is thought to be desirable in countries that have a history of extractive central governments because democratically elected local units can serve as a layer of protection against a predatory central government.[17] Thus, decentralization of political authority in the best case promises to limit the reach of the central government thereby strengthening the rule of law as well as potentially preserving market institutions.[18] The constraining effect of decentralization of governance is an important yet oftentimes overlooked virtue of political decentralization in countries where state failure can be attributed to predatory behavior on the part of the state.

There are several factors that can be discerned from the literature that should influence the extent of public goods provision among local governing organizations. The factors that follow are not all necessary for provision of public good. Rather, when an organization attains success on more of these dimensions, it should be more likely to provide public goods.

First, constraints within an organization are expected to influence public goods provision. Rulers cannot necessarily be trusted to work on behalf of the citizens they govern. An important insight of political economy, one that goes

---

[15] See, for example, Charles M. Tiebout, "A Pure Theory of Local Expenditures," *The Journal of Political Economy* 64, no. 5 (1956): 416–24.

[16] Mohammad Arzaghi and J. Vernon Henderson, "Why Countries Are Fiscally Decentralizing," *Journal of Public Economics* 89, no. 7 (2005): 1157–89; Jonathan A. Rodden, *Hamilton's Paradox: The Promise and Peril of Fiscal Federalism* (New York: Cambridge University Press, 2005).

[17] Roger Myerson, "Constitutional Structures for a Strong Democracy: Considerations on the Government of Pakistan," *World Development, Decentralization and Governance* 53 (2014): 46–54.

[18] Yingyi Qian and Barry R. Weingast, "Federalism as a Commitment to Preserving Market Incentives," *The Journal of Economic Perspectives* 11, no. 4 (1997): 83–92; Barry R. Weingast, "The Economic Role of Political Institutions: Market-Preserving Federalism and Economic Development," *Journal of Law, Economics and Organization*, Journal of Law, Economics and Organization, 11, no. 1 (1995): 1–31; Weingast, "The Political Foundations of Democracy and the Rule of Law."

back to Alexander Hamilton, is that political constraints are necessary for leaders to have incentives to provide public goods honestly, as opposed to engaging in various forms of predation.

One of the most basic political constraints on leaders is separation of powers, which refers to situations in which institutionally-defined political actors have autonomy within a specific policy-making domain. Separation of powers among formal government organizations influences economic and political outcomes, such as size of government and protection of citizen rights.[19] In addition, organizations characterized by separated political authority should be associated with increased levels of public goods provision, including the rule of law and property protection.[20]

Checks and balances are another important kind of political constraint on leaders. Although checks and balance presuppose separation of power, they are an additional constraint on government in a separated system. By allowing actors in one sphere to intrude into the sphere of another actor to prevent abuse of power, checks and balances further restrain the strength of any one actor or group of actors in a political organization. Accordingly, they are hypothesized to increase incentives of leaders to provide public goods and forgo predation.

Institutional constraints play an important role in explaining public goods provision at the national level[21] as well as at the community level.[22] In addition, constraints on rulers can exist in non-democratic or partially democratic settings, as well as settings in which state rule is virtually absent.[23] These perspectives suggest that constraints on leaders, including informal authorities, are important to understanding the extent of public goods provision.[24]

[19] Jean-Jacques Laffont and Mathieu Meleu, "Separation of Powers and Development," *Journal of Development Economics* 64, no. 1 (2001): 129–45; Torsten Persson, Gerard Roland, and Guido Tabellini, "Separation of Powers and Political Accountability," *Quarterly Journal of Economics* 112, no. 4 (1997): 1163–1202; George Tsebelis, *Veto Players: How Political Institutions Work* (Princeton, NJ: Princeton University Press, 2002).

[20] David Weimer and William Riker, "The Political Economy of Transformation: Liberalization and Property Rights," in *Modern Political Economy*, ed. Jeffrey S. Banks and Eric A. Hanushek (New York: Cambridge University Press, 1995), 80–107.

[21] Daron Acemoglu and James A. Robinson, *Economic Origins of Dictatorship and Democracy* (New York: Cambridge University Press, 2006).

[22] Arun Agrawal and Clark C. Gibson, "Enchantment and Disenchantment: The Role of Community in Natural Resource Conservation," *World Development* 27, no. 4 (1999): 629–49.

[23] Jean Ensminger, *Making a Market: The Institutional Transformation of an African Society* (New York: Cambridge University Press, 1992); Kathryn Firmin-Sellers, "The Politics of Property Rights," *The American Political Science Review* 89, no. 4 (1995): 867–81; Barbara Geddes, *Politician's Dilemma* (Berkeley, CA: University of California Press, 1996); Stephen Haber, Noel Maurer, and Armando Razo, *The Politics of Property Rights Political Instability, Credible Commitments, and Economic Growth in Mexico, 1876–1929* (New York: Cambridge University Press, 2003).

[24] Daron Acemoglu, "Why Not a Political Coase Theorem? Social Conflict, Commitment, and Politics," *Journal of Comparative Economics* 31, no. 4 (2003): 620–52; James A. Robinson and

A second broad factor identified in the literature is the time horizons of decision-makers. Once leaders come to power, either in the formal or informal context, they are confronted with a choice of doing what is in the interest of society or acting in their personal benefit. This choice inevitably arises because leadership creates opportunities to use political power to benefit elites vis-à-vis less powerful members of society. Those leaders that have longer time horizons – who value the future more than the present – are more likely to do what is in the best interest of their constituents.[25]

There are several factors that affect time horizons of local leaders. Institutions, such as longer term limits for office holders and tenure for good behavior are expected to translate into stronger incentives to provide public goods. In addition, political stability is expected to increase time horizons of leaders within an organization. In contrast, organizations in which leaders expect to be out of power shortly or those with high degrees of political instability, perhaps arising due to political violence or civil war, should create stronger incentives for political leaders to choose public policies that benefit themselves at the expense of their community[26]

An organization cannot simply rely on constraints, but also requires capacity to execute and implement policies.[27] Therefore, a third factor that is expected to influence the ability of an organization to provide public goods is a reliable revenue stream. Political constraints and time horizons impact the incentives of leaders; however, governing will be a challenge when constrained leaders lack capacity or revenue. The key to this dimension is that a revenue source is reliable in the sense that it is derived locally. In thinking about sustainable revenue at the national level, this means that a central government's budget is not solely, or mainly, dependent upon external or foreign sources. Locally derived sources of revenue are important for states, because of rentier effects.[28] The requirement of reliable revenue is also important for local organizations. In most weak states, local organizations cannot depend on resources from outside sources, as they are rarely available. The central government might be a potential long-term source of transfers to lower levels of government in developed states, yet in the most fragile

Q. Neil Parsons, "State Formation and Governance in Botswana," *Journal of African Economies* 15, no. S1 (2006): 100–40.

[25] Mancur Olson, "Dictatorship, Democracy, and Development," *The American Political Science Review* 87, no. 3 (1993): 567–76; Olson, *Power and Prosperity*.

[26] Bates, *When Things Fell Apart*.

[27] Francis Fukuyama argues that in some contexts state capacity is more important than constraints on political power, as excessive constraints hamstring the ability of governments to make effective policy by forging gridlock. See *Political Order and Political Decay: From the Industrial Revolution to the Globalization of Democracy* (New York: Farrar, Straus and Giroux, 2014).

[28] Michael Ross, "The Political Economy of the Resource Curse," *World Politics* 51, no. 2 (1999): 297–322; Michael Ross, "Does Taxation Lead to Representation?" *British Journal of Political Science* 34 (2004): 229–49; Kurt Weyland, "The Rise of Latin America's Two Lefts: Insights from Rentier State Theory," *Comparative Politics* 41, no. 2 (2009): 145–64.

states, such dependence on the central government or external agencies is typically a recipe for disaster. For example, one-time transfers of funds from third parties may actually increase incentives for local leaders to engage in predation as they are aware that access to resources is not dependent on their behavior, either today or in the future. Individuals are keenly aware that aid will come to their community regardless of the behavior of local organizations and leaders.

States become rentier states when their income is generated largely from nonproductive sources of revenue, such as natural resource extraction or aid, thus undermining their incentives to govern well. Local organizations can end up in a similar predicament, becoming what I call "rentier community organizations," the defining feature of which is excessive dependence on outside sources of funds to deliver basic public goods and services. The problem caused by the rentier effect at the local level is similar to that at the national level: it harms accountability mechanisms by which citizens can hold their government officials accountable.[29] Citizens who are not paying for the services of the state have fewer reasons to demand specific policies. When revenue is generated locally, citizens have increased incentives to hold local officials accountable as taxpayers will want to know how their funds are being utilized. For these reasons, the extent to which local self-governing organizations attain self-sufficiency in revenue is a potentially very important in explaining the extent to which the organization is able to provide public goods.

Finally, participatory institutions are expected to influence the ability of organizations to provide public goods, in particular the extent to which community members participate in decision making. Institutions that aggregate citizen interests are expected to increase incentives to provide public goods and services.[30] At the local level, a number of studies how show participatory institutions increase the effectiveness of public goods provision.[31] For example, referendums increase satisfaction and legitimacy of public good provision.[32] The well-known risks of decentralization to local political organizations, such as capture by local elites, can be ameliorated when mechanisms exist to ensure public participation.[33]

---

[29] Deborah A. Brautigam, Mick Moore, and Odd-Helge Fjeldstad, *Taxation and State-Building in Developing Countries: Capacity and Consent* (New York: Cambridge University Press, 2008), Mick Moore, "Between Coercion and Contract: Competing Narratives on Taxation and Governance," in *Taxation and State-Building in Developing Countries: Capacity and Consent*, ed. Deborah Brautigam, Odd-Helge Fjeldstad, and Mick Moore (Cambridge University Press, 2008), 34–63.

[30] Acemoglu and Robinson, *Economic Origins of Dictatorship and Democracy*.

[31] T. Besley, R. Pande, and V. Rao, "Just Rewards? Local Politics and Public Resource Allocation in South India," *The World Bank Economic Review* 26, no. 2 (2011): 191–216.

[32] Benjamin A. Olken, "Direct Democracy and Local Public Goods: Evidence from a Field Experiment in Indonesia," *American Political Science Review* 104, no. 2 (2010): 243–67.

[33] Pranab Bardhan, "Decentralization of Governance and Development," *The Journal of Economic Perspectives* 16, no. 4 (2002): 185–205.

The centrality of participation in local decision-making now permeates most donor-funded interventions at the community level.[34] Today, it is almost inconceivable that a village-level development program would be implemented without a participatory component that seeks to elicit input of community members. The driving force behind CDD programs is to bring citizens into the decision-making process to enhance accountability of donors and to ensure projects selected meet local demands.[35] Therefore, increased levels of participation in local governing organizations should be associated with higher levels of public goods provision.

This literature suggests community development organizations are an important fix to autocratic and unresponsive forms of village governance. Of course, it is important that the new organizations are participatory in practice, not just in name. Many programs may promise to increase participation, yet fail to deliver on meaningful improvements.[36] For this reason, it should not be surprising that there is mixed evidence regarding the effectiveness of such CDD schemes.[37] Nonetheless, the extent to which an organization facilitates participation is expected to translate into improvements in the provision of public goods.

Broadly speaking, customary organizations are hypothesized to provide public goods more effectively than competing organizations because they attain more success on each of these dimensions. While the qualitative case studies in the next section cannot necessarily specify which of these factors matters most, when organizations attain higher levels of each of these dimensions they will be more likely to provide public goods and services. With this caveat in mind, I turn to the empirical studies of village self-governance.

CASE STUDIES OF PUBLIC GOODS PROVISION

The case studies that follow provide insight into ability of local governing organizations to provide public goods and are constructed from semi-structured

---

[34] The origins of this movement are rooted in the participatory development agenda. See Robert Chambers, "The Origins and Practice of Participatory Rural Appraisal," *World Development* 22, no. 7 (1994): 953–69.

[35] William Easterly, *The White Man's Burden: Why the West's Efforts to Aid the Rest Have Done So Much Ill and so Little Good* (New York: Penguin Press, 2006); Albert O. Hirschman, *Getting Ahead Collectively: Grassroots Experiences in Latin America* (New York: Pergamon Press, 1984).

[36] Jean-Philippe Platteau, "Information Distortion, Elite Capture, and Task Complexity in Decentralised Development," in *Does Decentralization Enhance Poverty Reduction and Service Delivery?* ed. Ehtisham Ahmad and Giorgio Brosio (Cheltenham: Edward Elgar Publishing, 2009), 23–72.

[37] Elisabeth King, "A Critical Review of Community-Driven Development Programmes in Conflict-Affected Contexts" (International Rescue Committee and Department for International Development, 2013); Mansuri and Rao, *Localizing Development*; Mansuri and Rao, "Community-Based and-Driven Development: A Critical Review."

interviews, focus groups, and participant observations. Among other things, one of the main purposes of the fieldwork was to better understand the extent to which various local organizations provide public goods in villages throughout rural Afghanistan. The illustrative cases that follow are constructed from 6 to 12 interviews and focus group discussions (of equal numbers of men and women) along with participant observation in communities and in the district center where each village was located.

The outcomes of interest in each case study are different measures of local order, which is a public good in the sense that it benefits all in a community once it is provided. In developed economies, there is typically a highly institutionalized system to resolve disputes without conflict. Afghans cannot typically call on the state to resolve conflicts, and so the extent to which local self-governing organizations provide the public good of dispute resolution serves as a key indicator of local order.

The cases were selected because they capture variation in geography and ethnicity. The security situation in each community at the time research was conducted was fairly similar: they were safe for outsiders to visit without much concern and were not the site of intense conflict. Security conditions may have led to selection bias at the time of research, but it is important to note that many of the communities where I conducted research for this project later fell under insurgent control or were hotly contested making them unsafe for such research at subsequent dates.

While case selection issues are always important in drawing inferences, they are less important for comparative purposes in this particular situation, as the central conclusion from the cases – that villagers rely more on customary governance than CDCs for public goods provision – is the general conclusion from the majority of villages in each of the districts where I conducted research. In this regard, the broad conclusions regarding the comparative performance of customary organizations and CDCs would be unchanged by a different selection of cases from the sample of districts and villages visited. Given these similarities in the broad outcomes, one of the cases was selected because it involved the return of a commander, a trend observed in other cases but increasingly problematic in rural Afghanistan. As we saw in Chapter 1, much of the literature on failed states frequently conflates the relationship between customary authorities and local commanders, so this case allows me to explore this relationship, while at the same time understanding how informal rules affect outcomes at the community level.

Finally, there is a temporal aspect to each case that enables me to identify how changes in informal institutions affect public goods outcomes during periods in history. As most interviews involved elements of oral histories, informants discussed variation in village governance over time. Not only is there variation in cases across the country, each case presents opportunities to exploit within-case variation and obtain variation on the dependent variable.

The theoretical framework provides a set of factors whose presence help us understand when local governing organizations should be able to govern well and when they should not. Not all customary organizations are characterized by the factors described earlier. The case studies that follow are mainly used to illustrate the theory rather than test it. The econometric analysis that follows provides a more traditional test of comparative organizational performance.

Hazrati Imam Sahib District, Kunduz Province

The first case study, which recounts the experience of people living in a desert village in the northern part of Kunduz Province in northeastern Afghanistan, illustrates the effectiveness of customary organizations in resolving disputes as well as the comparative ineffectiveness of CDCs. In addition, events in this village show how large infusions of cash can encourage "roving bandits," such as commanders to return to communities. In this instance, a commander who had previously left returned upon hearing the news of the arrival of large amounts of development assistance. He hoped to secure a share of these funds for himself.

One of the key informants from this village was the commander in question. As he explained, he had left the community but returned to position of authority by seizing control of the CDC, although the fairness of the election that brought him to power was questioned by community members. Nonetheless, the formal election process allowed the commander to claim legitimacy to govern.

The village itself has about 3,000 people and is mostly Uzbek, although there are a few Turkmen and Pashtun families in the area. It is located about 15 kilometers from the district center. Most residents migrated to Pakistan, Iran, Kunduz City (the provincial capital), as well as Kabul, during the war. Many homes in the village were destroyed during two rounds of fighting: in the 1980s when villagers fought the Russians, and during the late 1990s, when Northern Alliance forces fought the Taliban. Due to geography and lack of an advanced irrigation system, water in the village was scarce. Men in the village were employed harvesting wheat and corn, while women sometimes wove carpets. Some men worked as daily laborers (mardikar).

Residents described their respect for the malik. Several informants remarked that he came from a pious family, which seemed to confer upon him with a sense of legitimacy.[38] The village has a "tribal" shura (qawmi shura) that, despite the name, actually transcended the ethnic and tribal groups in the community. In this shura, elders made decisions and resolved disputes. Both men and women said that if they had a dispute in the village, they would

---

[38] In this province, *maliks* were referred to by the title *arbab*.

normally take their problems to the elders and the malik, although recent events (which are described later) disrupted their ability to call on elders in such a fashion. Yet prior to these disruptions, customary representatives actively worked to resolve disputes. For example, a female Uzbek homemaker in her mid-30s recalled the following example illustrating customary methods of conflict resolution:

There was a wedding party organized between two villages and a large bride price was paid to the family of the bride. After the wedding the bride was not happy with the groom and wanted to separate from her husband. The elders and the religious leaders sat together and resolved the issue so that the couple could peacefully separate.[39]

In this case, the elders extracted a fine and transferred it from one family to another in order to keep peace. Such opportunities are especially important in light of the few options citizens have to resolve conflicts through formal channels, such as state courts, which in this case were too far away for most residents to consider engaging.

Although there was already a fairly effective system of governance in place in this village, it received a CDC along with its associated funds to promote development and good governance. When the CDC first began its work, the people selected their malik to be the head of the organization. The election procedure was consensus voting in an open forum rather than a formal ballot-box election with secret voting as mandated by the NSP. Although technically not in line with procedures, consensual elections in most areas were preferable to most citizens and considered just as legitimate (if not more so) than formal ballot boxes.[40]

The launch of the CDC did not go well in the community. Although they had initially selected their customary leader to head the CDC, he did not seem to play an important role. Instead the NGO implementing the project seemed to make most of the important decisions. Members of the community did not mention having an active role in selection of projects. None of the informants were aware of anyone making contributions to CDC activities. On the contrary, they were promised salaries for work building small scale projects in the community. For example, one metal worker said he installed many of the hand pumps built by NGOs in the village, but he was never paid for his labor or materials as he was promised.[41] This was a common complaint in the community.

---

[39] Kunduz-Imam Sahib-Village 1-#1.

[40] This common (and surprising) sentiment seemed to result from corruption associated with formal government elections. In other words, as early as the first Presidential (2004) and National Assembly/Provincial Council (2005) elections voters experienced corruption. For this reason, many people interviewed had a very cynical view of "formal" elections using ballot boxes.

[41] Kunduz-Imam Sahib-Village 1-#7.

Most problematically, as the amount of money flowing into the village increased, residents complained that local commanders took greater interest in village activities. In the first years after the fall of the Taliban, informants said the commanders had left the community. Yet when development projects and their associated funds appeared, one commander in particular, suddenly reappeared to take over management of these projects.

People feared this commander, as he was part of Junbesh-e Melli political party, a faction led by Abdul Rashid Dostum, a prominent Uzbek warlord from northern Afghanistan and later Vice President under President Ghani. Upon taking charge of village development activities, the commander forced the malik to resign his position in the CDC. The commander, however, expressed little interest in taking the customary position of malik, as actual responsibilities came with this position, but he took it anyway. When asked about how he came to head the CDC, the commander said that he had done such a good job managing a German NGO project (another "development shura") that the villagers "voluntarily" decided to have reelections. He said the incumbent malik "decided not to run against me."[42] Authority of the CDC eventually came to be fully concentrated in the hands of the commander, although on paper he was "elected" through common consent. People in the village, including the deputy director of the CDC (moween), did not seem to have information about CDC meetings or any other activities since the commander wrestled control of the organization from the community.[43] Things appeared to go from bad to worse; at first, the CDC was just ineffective; now it was captured by a commander who was nonetheless able to claim legitimacy of having been elected.

This commander had access to a larger network of commanders allowing him to mobilize individuals outside of the community – something customary leaders were unable to do. He even bragged openly about how he brought order to the village with his iron fist (although informants did not speak of any particular disorder before his arrival). Although he had access to power, the commander said he was not really interested in governing, but that he accepted the position because the people wanted him there. As he explained, "Actually, I'm not really interested in being the arbab in this village and solving all these disputes. I have wanted to resign many times but my people say, 'what will we do if you resign?'"[44] But despite his claims of maintaining order, there were an increasing number of conflicts in the village, ranging from unresolved land disputes to arguments over unpaid CDC work.[45]

Most shockingly, he even admitted that he had been accused of sexual abuse of two boys in the village (and claimed his innocence). There were also complaints about corruption. According to other residents, the commander bought two cars for himself since the CDC started its work. Residents also speculated

[42] Kunduz-Imam Sahib-Village 1-#4.   [43] Kunduz-Imam Sahib-Village 1-#5.
[44] Kunduz-Imam Sahib-Village 1-#4.   [45] Kunduz-Imam Sahib-Village 1-#7.

that the CDC treasurer, a close ally of the commander, bought two cows with CDC money.[46] When villagers were asked why they did not try to put a stop to this corruption, they said that because the aid money was not theirs they did not feel they had a right to protest the activity.[47]

Although I could identify some women in the community who had some involvement with the CDC, the women in this community were not active participants. Female informants said that the foreign NGO that set up the CDC first came to the village and selected the female participants for the CDC themselves. Other women in the village believed that the women chosen to be CDC members received enormous funds from this NGO for their work and that they kept the money for themselves rather than putting it into community efforts. When asked about this, the women who were ostensible CDC members suggested that they had not received funds and that the funds allocated for the community were taken by the commander. It was impossible to find out what happened to these funds, but regardless of what transpired, most women in the village believed the female CDC members were responsible for taking it.

None of the residents, aside from the commander, were aware that the CDC was a government project. They believed it was just an NGO project, like so many that had come before it.

Residents did say they saw positive results from several donor projects, such as water wells, culverts, as well as a newly graveled road. Yet they were not sure what project had brought these improvements to the community, as many had come and gone during the course of the years since 2001. They speculated that more could have been done with the vast amount of funds the commander had received. People feared the commander.

Nonetheless, customary organizations proved resilient. Since the commander came back to this village, local decision making through customary organizations had continued informally but not publicly, as the previous malik became increasingly afraid of the power of the commander. To be sure, many conflicts remained unresolved, as villagers were afraid to bring them to the attention of the commander. However, the secret meetings mitigated several issues. The instability brought into the community by the commander, however, illustrates how expectations about the future – time horizons – affect individual behavior. As individuals were unsure of the status of customary governance vis-à-vis the commander, they were not sure rulings by customary authorities would be binding in the future. Hence, many disputes remained unresolved and a sense of instability emerged in a previously stable community. Although customary governance once was characterized by constraints on local authority and checks and balances (among the qawmi shura, the malik, and local mullahs). This broke down over time with the infusion of donor resources into the community.

---

[46] Kunduz-Imam Sahib-Village 1-#7.   [47] Kunduz-Imam Sahib-Village 1-#6.

Customary organizations were once able to resolve disputes but they were no longer able to function as well as they had in the recent past due to interference from outsiders. During the period of interference, they appeared to weaken (this was true during the war and also during this period of reconstruction). CDCs were unable to fulfill their promise because there was insufficient accountability of CDC activity to community members, due to the lack of constraints on CDC activity as well as an absence of checks and balances on leaders. As revenue used for this project did not come from the community, members of the village had little incentive to get information about the amount of funds coming to the community or what the funds should be used for. Furthermore, due to the numerous NGO projects operating in the community, residents did not expect CDCs to operate in the future, mainly because they believed all NGO projects in their community would eventually come to an end. Finally, village commanders were ineffective in providing public goods for a number of reasons, but most apparently due to the fact that they were unconstrained and were not subject to participatory or local oversight.

This case also illustrates how the creation of organizations that compete with existing governance arrangements, in this case customary organizations, may destabilize the provision of local order. Prior to the arrival of a new shuras, villagers were broadly satisfied with customary governance. The new CDC was not simply an ineffective alternative, but its infusion of funds attracted roving bandits to the community who came to plunder its resources until they were exhausted. The previous system of customary governance dissimulated during the presence of the commander continuing to operate underground.

This case seems to be illustrative of trends in Afghanistan that emerged after the period of my field research. As insecurity gripped much of rural Afghanistan after 2008, with insecurity came many of these local commanders. As aid skyrocketed, so too did insecurity. As my fieldwork was at the very beginning of the surge period, I did not see first hand in communities how these dynamics played out. The limited ability of donors to monitor their projects created enormous opportunities for predation and abuse. This either forced customary authority to dissimulate during periods of conflict (as it had in the past) or be co-opted by these commanders.

Sayghan District, Bamiyan Province

The second case study of village governance is from Bamiyan Province in the central Hazarajat highlands. The village itself is average-sized for rural Afghanistan. According to residents, there are approximately 60 households in the village or about 450 people.[48] The community is about 2 kilometers from

---

[48] The village is not listed in official population numbers issued by the Central Statistics Office. All population data, where available, comes from official government statistics provided by this Office. Data is available for download at www.cso.gov.af.

the district center, giving it easy access to government offices. The entire district of Sayghan is quite small, with a population of only 17,000. Prior to the Taliban, Sayghan was a sub-district of neighboring Kamard District.[49] According to the district governor, two-thirds of the population is Tajik, while the remaining one-third is Hazara. This case differs from the previous case in that it illustrates continuity and change in village governance in historical perspective, but also the relationship between civil war and customary governance.

As was the case in most villages, customary organizations came under fire during the war. In this particular community, the village changed the names of their customary organizations as well as their leadership structures when the fighting ceased after 2001. The reliability of customary governance also varied, with customary leaders exhibiting more accountability in some historical periods than in others. Many of the informants in this region had bad memories of the customary system as it existed before the civil war. Specifically, they recalled highly extractive arbabs, who taxed them excessively at the behest of the government beginning during the time of Daud. According to the villagers, the PDPA was responsible for dissolving the arbab system. They said the property of the arbabs had been divided by Communist party factions when the arbabs were driven away in the 1970s and the 1980s.

Even though residents had bad memories of the prewar system of governance, during that period their arbab played an important governing role as a broker between the community and the government. For this reason, villagers reconstituted the arbab system, but in a more representative form. In the place of the arbab system, villagers created, seemingly spontaneously, a namayenda ("representative") system that had many of the same responsibilities of the previous arbab. It was unclear when the term namayenda first emerged in the community. It seems to have emerged sometime during the late 1980s or early 1990s – it was likely the title mujahedeen factions used in selecting village representatives during the anti-Soviet jihad. This new system proved to be an integral part of village governance in the following years.

Unlike the government-controlled arbab system, villagers spoke favorably of the customary system that replaced it. The serving namayenda and other residents with whom I spoke in the district asserted that the namayenda represented the will of the people to the government, a function identical to that of the malik in other areas. I found the title namayenda to be used in parts Bamiyan Province to indicate a village representative. I could not differentiate how the authority of the namayenda differed from maliks found in other provinces.

The namayenda system was not insulated from political violence. Indeed, external conflict continued to be a major threat to customary order. One threat

---

[49] In Dari a sub-district is alaqadari. The Taliban eliminated the sub-district system, thus it is no longer used. This was a unit of public administration that existed prior to 1996. There are no sub-districts remaining in Afghanistan; all alaqadari have become full districts (woluswali).

was from the Soviets, who stepped in shortly after the PDPA communist government had begun to reorganize village governance. According to the namayenda of the village (who was also a mullah), most homes in the district were almost completely destroyed by the Soviets during the 1980s. As he explained, "During the war with the Russians, people would go to Pakistan and they would bring guns back to fight the Russians. People were united then, but when the Russians left, civil war began."[50] This long period of political instability undermined the work of customary organizations, as many fled their homes. Customary leaders were executed by various militias or governments. During the civil war between mujahideen groups in the 1990s, there was heavy fighting between Tajik groups associated with the Northern Alliance and Hazara militias in the district. Many Tajiks emigrated out of the district as a result, but most had since returned. Despite a very violent history, according to informants, good relations had emerged between the groups.

During Taliban times, government officials harassed customary representatives. The Sunni Taliban brutalized Shia Hazara communities in Afghanistan because they considered Shia to be infidels, often focusing their violence first upon community leaders. The Tajik namayenda said that the cruelty of the Taliban brought both communities closer together:

I was the namayenda for two or three years during the regime of the Taliban. During that period some Hazara people came to me and asked that I represent them because they needed someone to help them. They were afraid of the Taliban at that time. I accepted their namayendagi (call to represent them). I accepted their suggestion that I be their representative. When they had some business in the district, first they would come to me. I would try to resolve their problems alone. During that time I was very busy. Every day, every moment, the Taliban police were coming to me and they were asking me to do things for them in the community. They would always take me to different villages to help them resolve issues.[51]

The jihadi commanders active in the area who fought the Soviets largely fled, and many of the Taliban were killed during the war, so the area returned to relative peace after 2001.[52] Prospects for peace at that time were good, as the village was in an area that was fairly remote and did not have substantial land or other resource endowments that could draw the attention of commanders.

Relations between local maliks, religious men, and the shura appeared cordial. Religious leaders regularly interacted with members of the shura. Although the namayenda was also a mullah, the community had an ulama shura, which is a council of religious scholars. Despite the fact that the namayenda was a religious leader, he had frequent disputes over interpretation of Islamic Law with the ulama. The namayenda told of an NGO that came to the village to teach children how to play musical instruments. He said the ulama

[50] Bamiyan-Sayghan-Village 2-#1.   [51] Bamiyan-Sayghan-Village 2-#1.
[52] Bamiyan-Sayghan-Village 2-#4.

complained about the organization, believing that music lessons would bring social problems to the community. The organization then left the area because it did not want to be a source of conflict in the community. The namayenda said, "I told the ulama shura they should have stayed out of this... They should have left this organization alone, but they did not accept my wish."[53] He said the ulama learned from its mistake and said it would allow music lessons in the future.

Informants overwhelmingly spoke of reverence for the woluswal in this area. Unlike woluswals in most other districts, this woluswal was from the district and had served in the position since the fall of the Taliban government. Several informants repeated the story of how the father of the woluswal was shot and killed on his son's wedding day by a Northern Alliance jihadi group fighting the Soviets more than twenty years prior. Apparently, the commanders heard rumors that the father of the woluswal was going to side with the Khalqi government.

When asked about how they resolve conflicts, everyone interviewed in the community described the same procedure: they first try to solve the dispute internally, between parties; if the dispute cannot be solved internally, they then go to the shura for counsel; if the shura experiences difficulty, then they send the dispute to the woluswal (which villagers have the opportunity to do because the woluswali office was close by); and because the woluswal "respects" the authority of the elders, he often sends the dispute back to the village for adjudication. The namayenda offered an example, which illustrates the procedure:

A few days ago, there was a problem between two people. One side had a donkey. Their donkey was running around in the neighbor's field and eating their wheat. The person went to the district security commander (police chief) and then to the woluswal. The woluswal sent the dispute back to me. And I sat between them. I told them that this is not such a big problem. If the donkey eats a lot of wheat, then your neighbor will simply pay you some money. I told them that I didn't want to hear any more about this donkey.[54]

According to residents, the customary system resolved most disputes. Not long after the fall of the Taliban government, the NGO implementing the NSP in the area came to the community. Residents first appointed the mullah to be the head of the CDC, but then realized this work should be given to a younger person who had more time to do paperwork and attend NGO trainings. There were no complaints of corruption about CDC members in the village, but villagers were quite distraught by corruption in the NGO implementing the project. Informants did not view the CDC as anything more than an organization set up by an NGO for the purposes of implementing a reconstruction project. They did not perceive it as a governance project, but rather, as a service delivery project. Informants reported that the NGO forced them to contract out

---

[53] Bamiyan-Sayghan-Village 2-#1.   [54] Bamiyan-Sayghan-Village 2-#1.

their construction projects to engineers who they believed to be relatives of the NGO workers. They believed that the NGO employees, in turn, had taken a cut from these contracts. The result of this, residents said, was a collapsed retaining wall they pointed to that was built with CDC funds. It was built just one year before my visit, but lay in ruins on a river bed. Villagers said that engineers working for the NGO in the district were corrupt and skimped on construction materials.

Part of the reason customary organizations governed effectively in this area was because power was not concentrated in the hands of a single individual. Not only was power separated between organizations, it was characterized by checks and balances between them. For example, when one organization over-stepped community norms of acceptability – in this case, village mullahs – it was corrected by other village organizations. In addition, the customary organizations in the community – despite challenges to their existence during the war – had been around for a long time and citizens expected them to endure.

In contrast to customary governance, residents did not view the CDC as a solution to a governance concern. One of the main reasons why the CDC did not perform well is that it was not a venue for broad participation. Additionally, the revenue used in the projects was not from reliable local sources. As a result, villagers did not trust it to provide public goods, either today or in the future.

Through recollections of recent history, the informants in this village provided insight into the extent to which commanders govern, or fail to govern, effectively. Although commanders were not present in this village when I visited, it was clear from their accounts of the past that neither the mujahideen commanders nor the Taliban were effective in governing, mainly because they were not subject to any constraints on their behavior. During periods of war, they behaved only briefly as stationary bandits and provided some public goods. As threats to security increased, they took on more predatory roles.

Finally, this case also illustrates the way customary organizations are able to recreate and regenerate themselves not just after conflict but during the turmoil of fighting. Villagers were able to resurrect a system of customary governance, based on the previous system but one that was seemingly more representative.

Behsod District, Nangarhar Province

The final case study comes from Nangarhar Province, which lies on Afghanistan's eastern border with Pakistan. This case considers a special category of dispute resolution: conflict over land, which is one of the most important issues in Afghanistan. As an Afghan political scientist remarked in a conversation in Kabul, land conflict is the single most important security issue affecting the country.[55] Substantively, the case illustrates that customary officials are often

---

[55] Kabul-Kabul City-#35.

effective in resolving land disputes. For example, the malik in this case was able to resolve a large land dispute and manage a contentious transfer of wealth from one party to another. In addition, it illustrates how communities deal with corruption in customary institutions through local checks and balances. Although customary leaders may have opportunities to expropriate wealth, they may be limited in their ability to do so for very long in the face of constraints. In addition, the events in this community illustrate that wealthy individuals are not always above the law when it comes to land disputes.

The village, which has about 800 people, is located about 10 kilometers from Jalalabad, one of the largest cities in Afghanistan. The population of the community is a mix of settled Pashtun Kuchi nomads and Khogiani Pashtun tribes who in recent decades emigrated from neighboring Kunar Province.[56] There is also a small Shia Hazara population in the community. According to residents, there were 22 farms in the village, allowing for small, fairly equally distributed landholdings. Unlike many other areas of the country, most residents felt that there was adequate irrigated land in the community, but said they never had sufficient inputs such as seeds to produce abundant and profitable harvests.[57]

The village had an active shura, as well as a several mullahs and a malik. The community had recently replaced its malik, as several residents complained about his corruption. They described how the previous malik expropriated external assistance, including food aid and cows, provided through NGO animal husbandry projects. Even worse, he was allowing his greed to influence shura decision making: "The malik was not a good man. He would sit in the marakas and jirgas and made decisions on behalf of those who could give him the biggest bribe."[58] Out of frustration the villagers, using a mixed-ethnicity maraka, appealed to a young man whose father was a malik before the war to serve in place of the corrupt malik. Residents appealed to the young man several times, but he was not interested in serving because he had other interests and work. He also did not want to cause conflict with the incumbent malik. After some cajoling he took the position. The newly selected malik was only 30 years old and was from a Kuchi family. People in this village did not hold a formal election for this position; they selected him during a shura meeting called for this purpose. He was chosen not only because of his personal attributes, but also because of his family's reputation for "honesty" in village

---

[56] The two main Pashtun tribal confederations in Afghanistan are the Ghilzai and Durrani. Khogiani are a subtribe of the Durrani while most Kuchis are Ghilzai. Most Afghan monarchs and leaders, including Hamid Karzai, have been from the Durrani tribe while most of the most of the leadership of the Afghan Taliban movement have been Ghilzai. Ashraf Ghani is a Ghilzai from the Ahmadzai subtribe. The Khogiani here often referred to themselves as Khogiani or Kunari. They maintain links with relatives in Kunar through marriage. During periods of fighting and instability this group migrated to Kunar and back.
[57] Nangarhar-Behsod-Village 1-#2.   [58] Nangarhar-Behsod-Village 1-#4.

decision making. According to informants, he was one the more educated people in the community.

As is the case throughout Afghanistan, the cessation of large scale violent conflict after 2001 resulted in the return of millions of refugees to the country. In this village, return prompted conflict over land as returning families claimed ownership of the same parcel. Successive governments handed out their own titles to the same plot of land, making definitive land ownership uncertain. Some families remained during the war and others fled. Inevitably, there were conflicts between returnees, those who never left, and new migrants to the area.

The village shura handled most of these land disputes, doing so without too much difficulty.[59] However, a powerful former commander (now disarmed) had recently returned to the village after nearly thirty years. Upon his return, the commander claimed a large parcel of land, to which he had a deed issued by a previous government, that others had lived on and cultivated in his absence. This raised an important question: did customary bodies have the legitimacy and authority to tell a powerful commander who owned the land? As the following account indicates, the will of the community exerted through customary organizations proved surprisingly sufficient to constrain powerful individuals:

> Some Hazara people from our village had land and one commander came and took this land. The Hazara man tried to take his land back from the commander but he could not. The commander said that the land was his, but he hadn't lived in our village for 28 years! The jirga divided the land. They gave one-half to the Hazara and one-half to the commander. In the end, the Hazara agreed to the settlement that the jirga negotiated. Instead of taking the land from the commander, the Hazara man received 2 million Afghani ($40,000) for the land.[60]

Despite the power and wealth of this commander, he was not above customary law in this community. He had to use the shura (or in this case a jirga) process to resolve his dispute with the much less wealthy Hazara farmer, which required that the commander pay the poorer Hazara for the land regardless of his possession of a land title. The fact that a commander was accountable to the shura and accepted its decisions as legitimate speaks to the power of customary organizations to make decisions and govern. In this case, the shura protected the rights of a minority community in an overwhelmingly Pashtun community. Although taking half the land may not be considered fair to some, the alternative – one which we might expect had there been no deliberative council – was that the poor farmer would receive nothing allowing the commander to simply expropriate land holdings.

---

[59] Customary authorities play an important role in resolving land disputes throughout Afghanistan. See Ilia Murtazashvili and Jennifer Murtazashvili, "Anarchy, Self-Governance, and Legal Titling," *Public Choice* 162, no. 3–4 (2014): 287–305.
[60] Nangarhar-Behsod-Village 1-#6.

Another interpretation of this situation was that the commander was able to return to the community and use the shura to extract land from the Hazara farmer without adequate cause. The Hazara farmer had been living on the land for almost thirty years. Community members, however, recognized that the commander did have some right to the land and they believed the settlement was "fair." I was unable to get the Hazara farmer's side of the story because he had left the community several years before.

The community also provided insight into varieties of local councils. There was a community shura and a larger inter-communal shura. Each ethnic and religious group had its own group of elders that formed the basis of a smaller, sub-shura. According to the malik:

We have a shura with 13 people and they usually resolve conflicts. This shura is composed of elders who find who is guilty and not guilty in our village. We have another larger shura called a meshrano jirga [council of elders] that has about 21 members that includes our settlement as well as neighboring villages. . . .There are several ethnic groups here so they are all represented there.[61]

The malik indicated that responsibility for resolving conflicts lies with the shura (or jirga as the malik used both terms to describe a single organization), not the malik. An elderly man described the process of dispute resolution, as applied to recent land conflicts:

Afghan people are very traditional and they live by different customs. People usually resolve their problems by discussion in the village and elders resolve most village disputes. The people usually refer their conflicts to elders and they try to resolve all the problems. Elders talk with both sides and then they talk with each other; finally. . .they will make a decision and both sides have to accept it.[62]

He said that the role of the malik in the village was to communicate individual needs to the government and then help the government implement policies in the village. For example, "the woluswal [district governor] wants us to stop growing poppies and he uses the elders of the community to communicate this to the villagers. He says that if we plant any poppies we will not receive any assistance from the government."[63]

It is hard to overstate the importance community members across the country attached to having an effective forum to resolve disputes – including disputes over land. Land was one of the most contentious issues in the community. In particular, there was tension in the community between settled Pashtun Kuchi nomads who were given deeds by the communist regime during the 1980s and the Khogiani population who claimed original owner- ship. The mullah of the community was aware of these tensions, and although he himself was a Khogiani, he tried to integrate the Kuchi population into the

---

[61] Nangarhar-Behsod-Village 1-#5.   [62] Nangarhar-Behsod-Village 1-#7.
[63] Nangarhar-Behsod-Village 1-#5.

community. According to an elderly woman in the community, "the mullah in the village teaches Islamic books to the children. Some Kuchis are coming into our mosque because our mullah is kind to them [despite tensions in the community]."[64]

Despite ethnic and communal differences and a fairly important conflict between two residents over land, informants did not report widespread conflict over other issues. Although residents were surprised that the commander had returned to the village to claim this land, they did not believe his claim was completely illegitimate because he had lived there before and possessed legal title. Yet they also had available a well-defined customary system that served to police his behavior. When community members thought it was unfair to evict someone off of this land who had lived there for many years – who had never fathomed the former commander returning to the community – they were able to do something about it.

As in the other cases, customary organizations proved capable of resolving conflict. In contrast, none of the informants in this area were engaged with CDCs. The new malik said that there was a CDC that covered one part of the community but the NGO implementing the NSP joined it with a CDC in another neighboring village. The community itself had no role in determining the boundaries of the CDC. The informants desired a CDC because they had heard advertisements for the program on the radio and had heard of project funds and infrastructure that neighboring villages received. Yet they sought project funds and infrastructure, not a new way of organizing their political life.

The case illustrates the capacity of customary organizations to resolve disputes, including land disputes. In this case, the customary organizations in the community had the legitimacy to counterbalance the will of powerful individuals in the community. The reasons for these outcomes can be attributed, at least in part, to the ability of the village to remove a malik from power after a series of abuses through the collective process of the shura (illustrating checks and balances as well as separated power). The shura processes were also sufficiently powerful to collect revenue and redistribute wealth. By relying exclusively on local resources to resolve issues, they eschewed the dependence on outsiders to fund their activities. Finally, the shura ensured broad participation by most families in local political life. Despite decades of war and chaos, the customary system had remained a source of continuity in the community and citizens expected it to be around in the future.

A QUANTITATIVE STUDY OF PUBLIC GOODS PROVISION

The case studies above provide insight into the processes of village governance. To see whether these findings generalize, this section analyzes nationally

---

[64] Nangarhar-Behsod-Village 1-#1.

representative survey data from rural Afghanistan. As with the case studies, the outcome of interest is local order and basic public good provision, in particular three measures of local public order: local perceptions of safety, dispute resolution, and resolution of land disputes.

The key independent variables in the statistical models measure the presence of local governaning organizations in a given community. Specifically, comparative organizational performance can be analyzed by indicating whether a shura or CDC (or both) is present in a community. Inclusion of variables for presence of customary organizations or CDC facilitates assessment of whether the presence of these organizations corresponds, in a statistical sense, to higher levels of public goods provision. Since the shura represents the heart of local deliberation, the central check on local authority and the main conduit of democratic decision making, the presence of customary organizations is measured by whether or not the village has a shura.[65]

The data on public goods provision and community organizations are taken from two surveys. The first survey, an annual survey of the Afghan people, was conducted by the Asia Foundation with support from the USAID. This nationally-representative survey interviewed more than 6,200 people in over 570 communities from every province in the country.[66] The purpose of the survey was to gauge individual attitudes on a range of governance issues at the national and subnational levels. I use the Asia Foundation survey for 2007 because it was fielded at the same time that I was conducting qualitative fieldwork. The second survey analyzed is the 2005 National Rural Vulnerability Assessment (NRVA) that was administered and designed by MRRD with support from the World Bank.[67] The purpose of the NRVA was to provide vital information about rural livelihoods in a country where there is no census or general population data. It was conducted across all 34 provinces in the country and interviewed more than 30,000 households in more than 2,500 communities. Analysis of both surveys is limited to the rural subpopulation.[68]

---

[65] Unfortunately, neither survey inquires as to the presence of warlord or commanders within communities. As a result, the analysis later cannot systematically evaluate public goods provision in the presence of commanders.

[66] Asia Foundation, "Afghanistan in 2007: A Survey of the Afghan People" (Kabul, Afghanistan: The Asia Foundation, 2007).

[67] Information about the NRVA survey is available through government's Central Statistics Office. www.cso.af.

[68] There was a round of the NRVA survey conducted in 2007–8, during the same period as my fieldwork. Unfortunately, this round of NRVA data did not include questions on customary governance structures (perhaps assuming they were no longer important in rural life). For that reason, the analysis relies on 2005 data (which includes questions about customary governance as well as CDCs). The NRVA survey included three population strata: urban, rural, and the nomadic Kuchi population. The Asia Foundation survey did not stratify for the migratory Kuchi population and included them under the larger Pashtun subpopulation (as Kuchis are Pashtun). I do not include urban or Kuchi populations in the analysis of NRVA data, although in the Asia Foundation survey the Kuchi are included in the rural population strata.

Summary statistics for variables used in all of the models are found in Appendix B at the end of the book.

Although the CDCs had only been around for less than five years in these communities, we would anticipate the effect of these organizations to be weak (as institutional change is a slow process). Despite this, by the time these surveys were fielded, many policymakers in Kabul and the international community were already certain that the CDCs had already transformed rural life, so much so that they had already advocated entrenching them as formal government structures. These claims became stronger in subsequent years. These data allow us to examine these important claims to see whether these new organizations are associated with improved governance outcomes.

Safety and security

The first set of statistical tests, which are presented in Table 4.1, assess the relationship between community organizations and security, which is perhaps the most important public good that can be provided by any organization in a village. The survey captures two measures of safety and security. The first measure is whether an individual fears for the personal safety or security of their family ("Do you fear for your personal safety?"). The descriptive statistics reveal substantial variation in fear for personal safety and security: 30 percent of the rural population stated that they never fear for their safety, 22 percent said they rarely experience such fear, 38 percent sometimes feel fear, while 11 percent of the population fears often for their safety. As the dependent variable is an ordinal variable, measuring fear on a scale of one to four, an ordered logit model is used to estimate how various factors influence fear of safety (see Table 4.1: model 1 and model 2).

In contrast to the first dependent variable, which is a subjective measure of safety, the second measure of local safety is an objective measure, asking whether a person has been a victim of crime, such as a physical attack or beating, burglary, or pick-pocketing in the past year ("Have you or a member of your family been a victim of violence in the past year?"). Seventeen percent of the rural population indicated that they or someone in their family had been the victim of violence in the past year. The dependent variable in this case is binary, thus logit models are used to estimate how other factors influence whether an individuals has been a victim of violence (see Table 4.1: model 3).

In model 1, the presence of a customary organization is measured by accessibility of a village shura or jirga, which is an ordinal variable measured on a scale from one to four.[69] According to the theoretical framework above,

---

[69] This measure is imperfect, as access to a community organization is not equivalent to measuring its presence. However, the survey asks a battery of subjective questions about the performance of customary institutions (e.g., are they fair, do they represent local norms and values, etc.).

TABLE 4.1: *Estimated Relationship between Village Organizations and Disputes, Security, and Safety*

	Dependent Variables				
	Do you fear for your personal safety?		Victim of violence in the past year	Individual requires help resolving dispute	Community involved in formal dispute
Independent Variables	Model 1	Model 2	Model 3	Model 4	Model 5
CDC in community	0.209** [0.100]		0.582*** [0.099]	0.794*** [0.114]	0.543*** [0.118]
Shura/jirga accessible	0.075 [0.062]		−0.116* [0.063]	0.031 [0.076]	0.026 [0.076]
Shura/jirga fair or trusted		−0.216** [0.096]			
CDC satisfaction		−0.019 [0.089]			
Trust other people	−0.176** [0.078]	−0.257** [0.120]			
Income	−0.05 [0.031]	−0.085* [0.049]	0.060* [0.034]	−0.019 [0.043]	−0.014 [0.040]
Education	0.014 [0.019]	0.018 [0.025]	0.070*** [0.023]	0.066*** [0.025]	0.025 [0.025]
Female	0.184 [0.113]	0.144 [0.165]	−0.074 [0.111]	−0.171 [0.137]	−0.616*** [0.135]
Age	−0.184 [0.237]	−0.833** [0.350]	0.755** [0.320]	0.153 [0.343]	0.391 [0.340]

(continued)

137

TABLE 4.1 (*continued*)

Independent Variables	Dependent Variables				
	Do you fear for your personal safety?		Victim of violence in the past year	Individual requires help resolving dispute	Community involved in formal dispute
	Model 1	Model 2	Model 3	Model 4	Model 5
Listen to radio	-0.12 [0.080]	-0.568*** [0.135]	-0.212** [0.104]	0.001 [0.121]	-0.188 [0.121]
τ_1	-1.436*** [0.283]	-3.336*** [0.480]			
τ_2	-0.436 [0.284]	-2.478*** [0.486]			
τ_3	1.753*** [0.282]	-0.213 [0.466]			
Constant			-1.861*** [0.310]	-1.767*** [0.393]	-1.726*** [0.414]
Observations	4540	1621	4625	4561	4643
prob >F	0	0	0	0	0
PSUs	564	404	566	564	565

Models 1,2: Ordered Logit Coefficients; Models 3,4,5: Logit Coefficients. Heteroskedasticty robust standard errors that correct for correlation of error terms within PSUs in brackets. Estimation also controls for region, survey design including household weights and population sampling units. The baseline response in each model is a negative response to the specific question.
* Significant at 10%; ** significant at 5%; *** significant at 1%

presence of a shura is expected to reduce fear of safety. Presence of a CDC is measured by whether a respondent was aware of a CDC working in his or her village, which is coded one if they said they were aware of a CDC in their village, and zero otherwise. In general, I expected residents to be aware of whether or not a CDC is present in their community since villages in Afghanistan are small and the CDC often represented a large influx of funds to a community. From my field experience, informants were aware when a CDC was established in their communities. According to the survey, 37 percent of those respondents are aware of a CDC in their village. According to the hypotheses generated from the theoretical framework, presence of a CDC should have little effect on whether individuals fear for their safety as these organizations have little consequence for public goods provision.

Model 2 includes somewhat different measures of the main independent variables. The measure of customary organization is a somewhat more subjective measure: whether people believe their shura is fair or trusted. The measure of CDC is also more subjective in that it measures satisfaction with the CDC. Analysis of this alternative specification allows us to test whether attitudes towards various organizations are related to perceptions of security.

Aside from the organizational variables of interest, models 1 and 2 include the same control variables, including income, education, gender (whether the respondent was a female), age, and region. The analysis also indicates whether the family listens to the radio, capturing two important aspects of rural life. First, listening to a radio indicates whether families have access to outside information. Access to knowledge of other parts of the country may affect perceptions of fear. Second, this variable captures the proximity of a community to a population center. Due to difficult terrain AM radio signals are not easily heard in many parts of rural Afghanistan.[70] Hence, the radio variable is a measure of how close one is to a city, which is expected to influence governance, although there is no clear theoretical expectation regarding the direction of influence. Both models estimating fear for personal safety include an additional variable measuring the extent to which a person trusts other people. A person who is less likely to trust others might be more inclined to fear for their safety. Unlike the other statistical models analyzed in this chapter, the dependent variable – perception of fear – is subjective. For that reason I explore

---

I measured the presence of customary institutions using this variable as it is the least subjective of all the questions on the topic. Other questions inquired as to whether shuras are "fair and trusted," "follow local norms and values of the people," "are effective at delivering justice," and "resolve cases timely and promptly."

[70] It is important to note that Afghans have had access to radio broadcasts for several decades, but access to AM radio in more remote, mountainous areas is challenging. During fieldwork I was unable to listen to radio broadcasts from provincial capitals in many research sites. Of course, people are able to access shortwave radio signals, but I expect access to radio to be significantly higher when individuals can access AM radio signals.

not only the presence of organizations (model 1) in affecting perceptions of personal safety (as I do for the other public goods explored here), but also measure the degree to which perceptions of organizational performance (model 2) affect perceptions of safety. Finally, all models include variables to control for geographic variation.

This question about personal safety was framed as a community issue to include such issues as burglary, murder, and other localized forms of crime – that is, it is not violence as a result of insurgent activity. The survey asked a separate battery of questions about security related to terrorism and insurgent attacks. Personal safety here is a measure of community governance. These variables are described in greater detail in the Appendix B.

Models 1 and 2 estimate those factors correlated with perceptions of public safety. In model 1, the presence of a CDC, as measured by an individual reporting that a CDC is present in their community, is associated with increased fear for personal safety. This finding is consistent with evidence from the case studies, which suggested that introducing a CDC led to instability as it promotes rent seeking. Presence of a shura was not statistically significant, which suggests that customary governance is not related to improvements in security along this dimension. Nonetheless, the finding that customary governance performs better relative to CDCs is broadly consistent with the expectations regarding comparative organizational performance.

In model 2, which explores subjective evaluations of organizational performance, the variable for customary organizations has the expected effect: trust in a shura reduces fear for safety. The measure for satisfaction with CDCs, by contrast, is not statistically significant. Thus, even if individuals are more satisfied with their CDC, such satisfaction is unrelated to perceptions of personal safety. This finding has important implications for proponents of CDD schemes who believe they will improve community governance. Since security is an important measure of governance in fragile states, increased satisfaction with a CDC should reduce fear for safety, but as the results illustrate, there is no correlation in these models. In terms of comparing customary organizations with CDC performance, these findings are also consistent with the theoretical framework suggesting that customary organizations will be associated with higher levels of public goods than CDCs.[71]

Model 3 explores local order using an objective measure of safety: whether a family member has experienced violence in the past year, measured dichotomously (respondents answered "yes" or "no"). In this model, the key independent variables – presence of shura and CDC – are identical to those used in model 1. In addition, the control variables (with the exception of interpersonal

---

[71] Of the control variables, trust in other people is statistically significant in both models 1 and 2. Thus, when people have more trust in others, they are less likely to fear for their own personal safety.

trust, which is not included in this and subsequent models) are the same as in the previous models.[72]

In model 3, presence of a shura is negatively correlated (although only at the 10 percent significance level) with whether an individual had been the victim of violence in the past year. In contrast, the presence of a CDC is positively correlated (significant at the 1 percent level) to whether an individual was a victim of violence. Substantively, the presence of a CDC is associated with an increased probability that an individual was a victim of violent crime from 13 to 23 percent, a 56 percent increase. On the other hand accessibility to shuras is associated with a reduced likelihood that an individual is a crime victim: 19 percent in communities where a shura is not accessible to 15 percent in communities where a shura is very accessible – a 21 percent decrease.

These results are consistent with the case study evidence. The case studies also provide insight into the causal mechanisms explaining the statistical correlations. One of the reasons CDCs may be associated with increased perceptions of insecurity is because they lead to competition over resources, for example, luring dormant commanders to return in the hopes of accessing funds and resources, or by instigating conflict among groups vying for local authority. That the shura is correlated with a reduction of crime is expected since these collective bodies provide source of collective punishment that deters localized forms of crime.

It is important not to overstate the findings here. One of the potential criticisms of this research design is failure to control explicitly for selection bias, which arise because the selection of communities for CDCs is not random. However, selection bias is unlikely to be a problem for these results. The results regarding public safety and perceptions of security are surprising because there is no reason to expect that CDCs are placed in areas that had *less* security. If anything, donors appeared to place the CDCs in areas that had *more* security in the early stages of the program – as those that were easiest to access – to increase their chances for success, which would allow them to serve as model for other communities.[73] If there was selection bias in the placement of CDCs, we would have anticipated this relationship to go in the opposite direction than the results in the models. For example, selection bias would be a plausible explanation for a finding that CDCs are associated with lower levels of crime – the opposite of what the analysis actually found. Since selection bias would work in favor of CDCs, and since the findings produce the opposite results, we can be confident that these statistical results reinforce findings from the case studies that CDCs may actually disrupt rather than assist local dispute

---

[72] Interpersonal trust was only used as a control variable in models 1 and 2 because the dependent variable measured perceptions. I expect trust to be correlated with perceptions. Trust should not be correlated to objective measures of other public goods, so it is not included in other models.

[73] Beginning project implementation in safer and easier to access districts was an explicit reason shared with me by senior advisors at MRRD.

resolution and local ordering mechanisms. Rather than being merely ineffective, CDCs may actually be detrimental to local order because they undermine customary organizations – which is exactly the scenario suggested by the case study from the village in Kunduz Province as well as many other communities where I heard similar stories of aid funds inviting conflict.

It may be the case the CDC variable measures not only the presence of a CDC but the availability of donor funds to communities. At the time when this survey was conducted, the CDCs were created in the most easily accessible communities where other aid programs may have been located. It may be the case that provision of aid is what undermines governance outcomes, rather than the CDC itself. I explore this specific question in greater depth in Chapter 6.

More generally, while the cross-sectional data here are imperfect and do not allow us to test causal relationships, causal relations can be elicited from the case studies and field observations. The case studies revealed that individuals who experienced the introduction of CDCs found that they often performed well providing infrastructure, but were largely ineffective as local governing organizations. Frequently, they undermined customary governance and enduring forms of local collective action. They also revealed that the introduction of CDCs contributed, in some cases, to perceptions of insecurity. The qualitative findings provide insight into causal relations behind the associations found in the quantitative analysis of the local order.

Dispute resolution

Dispute resolution is a second measure of local order. The data capture two aspects of dispute resolution: whether individuals required outside assistance in resolving a dispute and whether the community itself has been involved in a dispute. The first measure depicts the degree to which individuals are party to disputes, asking respondents whether they have had a dispute in the past two years that they could not solve with the other party and had to go to an outside party, such as a state court or village council to resolve ("Did you require help resolving a dispute?"). The second outcome, prevalence of community disputes, is measured by inquiring as to whether or not a community has had a problem in the past five years such that outside help was needed to resolve the issue ("Has your community required help in resolving a dispute?"). As both measures are dichotomous, the relationships are estimated with a logit model.

The central hypotheses are similar to the analysis of safety and security: the presence of a shura will be associated with increased public goods provision, while the presence of the CDC will have no effect on this outcome. Here we should expect the presence of a shura to be negatively associated with individuals requiring help to resolve disputes and whether the community is involved in formal disputes. The design of the statistical models – with the exception of the dependent variables – is almost identical to those in model 3.

The results of the analysis are also shown in Table 4.1, which shows that the presence of a shura has no association with the emergence of individual disputes (model 4) or community disputes (model 5). Although the results are not as strong as the case studies would suggest, customary organizations are not associated with a detrimental outcome – and so at a minimum, the findings reject the hypothesis that customary organizations are a source of conflict. The finding of no strong relationship between customary organizations and disputes serves to refute the notion that presence of customary organizations is correlated with conflict or that they somehow breed instability due to unequal treatment of disputants or other factors.

The findings for CDCs are perhaps more surprising. While the theoretical framework predicted the CDCs would have a no correlation with public goods provision, the findings in both models 4 and 5 indicated that the presence of CDCs is actually negatively correlated with public good provision: presence of a CDC increases the number of individuals requiring help to resolve dispute and is positively correlated with whether communities are involved in disputes in general. Thus, the presence of CDCs in communities appears to exacerbate conflict: when there is no CDC in a community, the predicted probability of individual conflict is 13 percent, while prospects for conflict increase to 26 percent – a 100 percent increase – when there is a CDC in a community. Moreover, 12 percent of individuals reported a community conflict when no CDC was present, while 22 percent reported a conflict in the presence of a CDC, or an increase of 83 percent. While the case studies suggested that CDCs are sometimes associated with conflict, the statistical results seem to indicate an even stronger relationship.

Land disputes and resolution

The provision of the public good of local order can also be understood by examining the frequency with which land disputes arise and whether such disputes are resolved. Conflict over land is a highly contentious issue in rural Afghanistan, as the system of land ownership is highly fragmented.[74] In the past thirty years, various governments have issued their own titles resulting in multiple claims to the same plot of land. Since the fall of the Taliban, issues of land ownership have sparked intense debate, even escalating into physical violence in many communities.[75] Understanding how well alternative

---

[74] For a reporting on the issue of land and conflict see Peter, Tom A. "What May Be a Bigger Threat to Afghanistan than Insurgency? Land Disputes." *Christian Science Monitor*, August 11, 2011.

[75] Allan Roe and Colin Deschamps, "Land Conflict in Afghanistan Building Capacity to Address Vulnerability," Issues Paper Series (Kabul, Afghanistan: Afghanistan Research and Evaluation

organizations resolve disputes over land is particularly important from a policy perspective. To the extent customary organizations resolve land disputes effectively, they can become an integral part of the land-reform and state-building process, in particular because land management is an important function of most states.

The source of data on land disputes comes from the NRVA survey described earlier. Land relations are measured in two ways. The first measure is whether a household reported having a dispute over land. The second measure is whether the land disputes were resolved once they emerged. Local governing organizations that are effective in providing local order are expected to be associated with a lower likelihood that a dispute over land might arise as well as an increased likelihood that the disputes will be resolved should they arise. Only 3 percent of the rural population reported having a conflict over land.[76] Of the 3 percent of households that reported having land conflicts, half indicated that their dispute was resolved. According to the theoretical framework described earlier, the presence of a shura is hypothesized to be associated with fewer disputes as well as an increased ability of communities to resolve these disputes. On the other hand, presence of a CDC is not expected to have a significant relationship with either outcome.

To measure the presence of customary organizations using NRVA data, it was necessary to construct a variable to measure the presence of a shura in a community. The variable for presence of a shura was constructed using a composite of responses by male focus groups as to whether a community had at least one of the following customary institutions: jirga, elder shura, mixed gender shura, tribal shura, female shura, and male shura.[77] Approximately

Unit, 2009); J. David Stanfield et al., "Rangeland Administration in (Post) Conflict Conditions: The Case of Afghanistan," in *Innovations in Land Rights Recognition, Administration, and Governance*, ed. Klaus Deininger et al. (Washington, DC: The World Bank, 2010), 225–41; Liz Alden Wily, "Land Rights in Crisis: Restoring Tenure Security in Afghanistan," Issues Paper Series (Kabul: Afghanistan Research and Evaluation Unit, 2003).

[76] According to the NRVA survey, 54 percent of the rural population own agricultural land, while 5 percent manage land for others, and 42 percent own no garden or agricultural land. Out of those that own land, only 3 percent reported having a dispute over their land. This number is surprisingly small given other qualitative reports on the escalation of land disputes in Afghanistan. One explanation for this could be that disputes do occur, but they occur between family members who may rarely seek recourse outside the family to resolve it. Another explanation is that individuals may in fact be involved in a dispute but do not report it because they are aware they do not have legal or any formal recourse as they are not entitled to use of the land in the first place. For example, most rangeland in Afghanistan is owned by the government, not by private individuals. In any event, we want to describe what determines the probability of disputes.

[77] The NRVA dataset includes both household survey responses as well as one focus group in each community (population sampling unit).

75 percent of the rural population claimed to have one type of customary political organization. Similarly, I coded whether a village had a CDC if the male focus group reported the presence of a male CDC, female CDC, or a mixed gender CDC in their community. Communities could have more than one kind of CDC or customary political organization.[78]

The NRVA household survey exhibits a nested or hierarchical structure, as it consists of household-level information collected in household interviews, and village-level characteristics collected in focus group discussions in each village. The presence of a village governance organization, specifically a CDC or a shura, is measured at the village level. The survey responses measure land disputes and their resolution at the household level. As such, estimation of the effect of village-based governing organizations using this data on household level outcomes was conducted using a hierarchical mixed-effects model.[79]

A hierarchical mixed-effects model is a mixed-effects model in that it includes both fixed and random effects. Standard linear models are inadequate to analyze these data for several reasons. First, they do not take account of the hierarchical structure of the data and pool household level information in the error term, inflating standard errors. Second, because households that are part the same group, such as a shura, will exhibit similar characteristics resulting in correlated (or, equivalently, "clustered") errors, violating a basic assumption of linear models. Finally, by ignoring the effect of the village, the models assume that estimated coefficients have the same effect in all contexts. A hierarchical mixed-effects model corrects for these potential errors and avoids confounding village and household level effects. In particular, mixed-effects models can correct for these issues by estimating household characteristics together with the inclusion of a random village level effect in the model as a means for accounting for clustering of errors across villages.[80]

As the dependent variables for both models are dichotomous, I estimated results using logit techniques. Estimations using logit were unable to converge, likely due to the fact that the mean of the dependent variable in the first model is

---

[78] I rely on results from the male rather than the female focus groups interviews as female responses were not enumerated in all districts. In many southern regions of the country involved in ongoing conflict, NRVA did not interview female household members or conduct focus group discussions with women. To capture a more comprehensive sample, I used responses from the male focus group discussions.

[79] Andrew Gelman and Jennifer Hill, *Data Analysis Using Regression and Multilevel/Hierarchical Models* (New York: Cambridge University Press, 2006).

[80] The basic models used to estimate both household land disputes and their resolution is below, where i represents the individual level and j represents village level effects: $P(y_{ij} = 1) = x'_{ij}\beta_1 + x'_j\beta_2 + x'_j\varepsilon_j + \varepsilon_{ij}$. In this model $x'_{ij}\beta_1$ captures household level effects and $x'_j\beta_2 + x'_j\varepsilon_j$ is the random component that takes into account village-level heteroskedasticity. This component of the equation also incorporates this heteroskedasticity through shrinking the estimated average effect of village organizations (shuras and CDC), while taking account of village-to-village heterogeneity

very close to zero (recalling that only 3 percent of families are involved in land disputes). To overcome this difficulty, I estimated the model using General Least Squares (GLS). While this is an imperfect substitute, the GLS estimates are still best linear unbiased estimates. Furthermore, only 6 percent of predicted values fall outside zero or one – one of the primary reasons generally given for preferring a logistic or probit model over least squares in this scenario.[81] Finally, by using GLS, interpretations of coefficients are straightforward as a linear probability model, i.e., each coefficient can be interpreted naturally on a probability scale.

Estimation included several other variables in addition to those related directly to village governance, namely variables that control for household characteristics including household income, the number of years a family has lived in a village (expecting that newcomers will be more likely to be involved in disputes), and whether the head of the household is literate.[82] The models also include a variable indicating whether the household owns a deed to the land. Finally, the models include provincial fixed effects. Estimation of models using both datasets account for the unique design of each survey by including household weight. Estimation also identifies each primary sampling unit (PSU) to correct for unobserved differences between members of different units that may affect standard error estimates.[83]

The results of the land dispute models are presented in Table 4.2. The findings for each of the dependent variables and across various specifications support the hypotheses that the presence of customary organization should be negatively correlated with the emergence of conflict and positively associated with their resolution. Customary organizations, measured through the presence of a shura, have the expected influence on both the emergence of disputes (models 6 and 7 in Table 4.2). The χ^2 statistic comparing alternative specification (with no random effects for shura or CDCs at the village level) indicates the importance of including the random effects in the estimation. The results in model 7 indicate that the presence of a shura is negatively correlated with the emergence of land conflicts in communities. Substantively, the presence of a shura in a community reduces the probability by 66 percent that a household will be party to a land dispute. On the other hand, the presence of a CDC actually appears to increase the probability that a household will be party to such a dispute, although the substantive increase is only three percent.

The final set of models estimate whether local organizations are associated with the resolution of land disputes (models 8 and 9 in Table 4.3). The models vary in the inclusion of random effects (the second model includes random

[81] Most of these are below one and are very close to zero.
[82] I use the natural log of income. In these data, income and education are not correlated.
[83] See Angus Deaton, *The Analysis of Household Surveys* (Washington, DC: World Bank Publications, 1997).

TABLE 4.2: *Estimated Relationship between Village Organizations and Emergence of Household Land Disputes*

Dependent Variable: Have you been party to a land dispute in your village?

Independent Variables	Model 6			Model 7		
Fixed Effects	Coefficient	S.E.	t value	Coefficient	SE	t value
Shura	-0.0205	0.0006	-37.2	-0.0175	0.0006	-29.84
CDC	0.0001	0.0005	0.09	0.0013	0.0005	2.59
Deed	-0.0123	0.0004	-33.17	-0.0125	0.0004	-33.69
Income (ln)	-0.0018	0.0002	-8.89	-0.0021	0.0002	-10.51
Years in Village	-0.0004	0.0001	-51.26	-0.0005	0.0001	-52.59
Household Head Literate	-0.0045	0.0004	-11.69	-0.0039	0.0004	-10.13
Intercept	0.0650	0.0024	27.07	0.0655	0.0024	27.27

Random Effects	Model 6		Model 7	
	Std. Dev.	Variance	Std. Dev.	Variance
Village Intercept	0.005	0.0001	0.0001	0.0085
Shura			0.0001	0.0096
CDC			0.0001	0.0047
Residual	0.161	0.026	0.0258	0.1606

Model Fit	Log Likelihood -21631		Log Likelihood -21619	
	Individuals 10377	Villages 1532	Individuals 10377	Villages 1532

Anova Results Comparing Models 6 and 7

Chi sq.	DF	Pr(<Chi Sq.)
26.1	5	.00001

Mixed-Effects Models, GLS Coefficients. Heteroskedasticty robust standard errors that correct for correlation of error terms within communities in brackets. Estimation accounts for survey design including household weights and population sampling units. The baseline response in each model is a negative response to the specific question. Estimation includes provincial fixed effects.

effect). However, χ^2 post-estimation comparison of the specification does not provide sufficient evidence that the inclusion of random effects statistic is justified.[84] The results of the two models, however, are fairly consistent.

[84] This is most likely due to the relatively small number of households involved in land disputes. Although the NRVA survey exhibits a relatively large household sample, the number of

TABLE 4.3: *Estimated Impact of Village Organizations on Resolution of Household Land Disputes*

Dependent Variable: If your household was party to a land dispute, did you solve it?

Independent Variables	Model 8			Model 9		
Fixed Effects	Coefficient	S.E.	t value	Coefficient	SE	t value
Shura	0.1944	0.0006	22.40	0.1795	0.0078	23.01
CDC	0.0131	0.0087	1.55	−0.0257	0.0080	−3.21
Deed to Land	0.1873	0.0068	27.47	0.1693	0.0066	25.6
Annual income (ln)	0.0398	0.0030	13.3	0.0356	0.0028	12.83
Household Head Literate	−0.0062	0.0002	−31.96	−0.0059	0.0002	−31.47
Years in Village	0.0198	0.0072	2.76	−0.0026	0.0070	−0.38
Intercept	1.4180	0.0369	25.49	1.5466	0.0349	25.49

	Model 8		Model 9	
Random Effects	Std. Dev.	Variance	Std. Dev.	Variance
Village Intercept	0.0228	0.0005	0.008	0.0001
CDC			0.005	0.0000
Shura			0.013	0.0002
Residual	0.3511	0.1233	0.170	0.0259
Model Fit	Log Likelihood −617.4		Log Likelihood −615.1	
	Individuals 202	Villages 139	Individuals 202	Villages 139
			Chi. Sq. 7.10	DF 5	Pr(<Chi Sq.) .2133

Mixed-Effects Models, GLS Coefficients. Heteroskedasticty robust standard errors that correct for correlation of error terms within communities in brackets. Estimation accounts for survey design including household weights and population sampling units. The baseline response in each model is a negative response to the specific question. Estimation includes provincial fixed effects.

Each specification provides evidence that the presence of shura is correlated with the resolution of land disputes, increasing the probability disputes are resolved by between 36 and 39 percent depending on the specification (models 8 and 9, respectively). The substantive impact of a CDC on the resolution of these disputes is slightly positive in model 8, associated with a slight increase in

households actually reporting disputes is quite small – approximately 3 percent. The number of observations in these two models is 202 distributed across 139 villages.

dispute resolution of 2.4 percent. If we interpret the mixed-effects of model 9, the presence of a CDC is correlated with a decrease in the probability that a household can solve disputes by 6.5 percent.

The analysis of land disputes indicates that the presence of a shura is associated with a reduced probability that disputes over land emerge, as well as associated with an increased likelihood that disputes will be resolved. These findings hold across various specifications. In contrast, CDCs either have no impact or are associated with increased frequency of disputes.

OTHER RESEARCH

The observational econometric data utilized for this analysis is subject to the inferential shortcomings discussed earlier. Despite these challenges, the results here are strikingly similar to those found from a randomized control trial impact evaluation of the NSP funded by the World Bank. In the evaluation's final report, the authors found that while the NSP might improve provision of infrastructure during project duration, the project actually had a statistically significant negative impact on governance outcomes, including the ability of communities to solve disputes, in communities where it was implemented.[85] Together, the results of both studies show the ways CDD activities can actually harm the ability of communities in contexts where policymakers are spending enormous funds to create social capital. The evaluation found that many of the gains in infrastructure dissipate after project completion. Synthesizing evidence from CDD projects in conflict-affected areas, Elisabeth King and Cyrus Samii found similar results: that CDD activities (such as the NSP) "failed to increase the capacity for collective action in a way that is durable and transferable beyond the CDD interventions."[86] They find that such "fast track institution building" is not a panacea. Jesse Ribot explains the failure of these organizations is a result of what he terms "participation without representation."[87]

The results here similarly shed light into why CDD endeavors frequently fail to live up to their promise: because the introduction of new governing bodies that intentionally or unintentionally undermine existing authority may generate competition or conflict and weaken existing mechanisms of collective action by generating competition or by introducing rentier effects. This is in line with other research from other contexts that the creation of new community-based

---

[85] Beath, Christia, and Enikolopov, "Randomized Impact Evaluation of Afghanistan's National Solidarity Programme."

[86] Elisabeth King and Cyrus Samii, "Fast-Track Institution Building in Conflict-Affected Countries? Insights from Recent Field Experiments," *World Development* 64 (2014): 740.

[87] Jesse C. Ribot, "Decentralisation, Participation and Accountability in Sahelian Forestry: Legal Instruments of Political-Administrative Control," *Africa: Journal of the International African Institute* 69, no. 1 (1999): 23–65; Jesse C. Ribot, "Authority over Forests: Empowerment and Subordination in Senegal's Democratic Decentralization," *Development and Change* 40, no. 1 (2009): 105–29.

governing institutions in the presence of enduring customary organizations may subvert existing governance systems.[88]

CONCLUSION

The theoretical framework outlined in this chapter helps us understand why customary organizations continue to provide public goods. One is the presence of constraints on village leaders. Norms of separation of power ensure a competitive balance prevails in most villages. In addition, there are substantial checks that that allow different actors in customary to intrude upon the authority of another one if one body acts against community interests. The stability and resilience of customary organizations also increases their ability to provide public goods, as does their ability to fund projects. Participatory norms further contribute to their effectiveness.

The findings in this chapter, along with other research, should give great pause to those hoping that many foreign-funded and implemented community development programs like CDD programs can provide a basis of effective governance in fragile or other developing countries. In the case of Afghanistan, the CDCs imposed few de facto constraints on the representatives of these newly established councils. CDCs do not have any formal responsibility to discuss their activities with district government officials; their only requirement was report to the NGO implementing the program in the district, which as mentioned earlier, are usually foreign NGOs.[89] This lack of vertical accountability among donor-created local councils is an obstacle facing CDD activities worldwide.[90] Informants generally viewed CDCs as transitory organizations.

Compounding these issues, the CDCs do not have an effective means of generating local revenue, and so they behave like rentier governing organizations. When asked whether they felt they could continue the work of the CDC after the donors had left, most of those interviewed were overwhelmingly pessimistic – not because sustaining a small organization was impossible, but in the minds of villagers, the raison d'etre of the CDC was to distribute donor funds. Across the board, informants said that the CDCs were unsustainable because they would not be able raise the level of funds donors provided to their villages. There were also issues with corruption and lack of opportunities for

---

[88] Pranab Bardhan and Dilip Mookherjee, "Decentralizing Antipoverty Program Delivery in Developing Countries," *Journal of Public Economics* 89, no. 4 (2005): 675–704.

[89] NGO staff at provincial levels recognized problems of corruption at lower levels, but did not want to report such problems to supervisors at the national level as employees feared such corruption below them would reflect poorly on their managerial capacity.

[90] Jean-Philippe Platteau and Frederic Gaspart, "The Risk of Resource Misappropriation in Community-Driven Development," *World Development* 31, no. 10 (2003): 1687–1703; Platteau, "Information Distortion, Elite Capture, and Task Complexity in Decentralised Development."

participation. In several cases, informants alleged that NGO staff selected certain projects because they were receiving kickbacks from suppliers provided material for projects such construction materials,[91] generators,[92] and solar panels.[93] Finally, while CDCs encourage participation and deliberation, I found little evidence of CDC elections actually taking place in many of the research villages.

Warlords and commanders are the final group under consideration. Warlords and their accompanying web of commanders, militias, and political parties have long sought to dominate the countryside in Afghanistan, especially during periods of fighting or ambiguous political transition. In Afghanistan, there are several cases where large and powerful former warlords engaged successfully in politics. For example, several important former warlords are well regarded among their populations for bringing economic development and prosperity to the areas they govern or exert influence. Two former Northern Alliance leaders, Atta Mohammad Noor and Ismail Khan, in Balkh and Herat Provinces respectively, developed reputations as developing infrastructure and other public goods in their regions with minimal assistance of Kabul.

In the countryside, a commander, in contrast, is an individual "attached to a party, who fulfilled at the local level the functions of military and political leadership."[94] Mobilization of these networks has been well documented.[95] While they may impose order regionally, commanders are less effective at the village level, for several reasons. Because they usually rule by force, they face few constraints. They also seem to resemble what Olson called "roving bandits,"[96] which are organizations that extract as much from subjects as possible. Local commanders secure resources in the form of tributes directly from individuals, mainly by extorting local producers and intermediaries. The Taliban, for example, which has always made its living on heroin, made enormous profits smuggling and and taxing trucks. They imposed a tax of 20 percent on poppy and also proved capable of securing rents from international aid

---

[91] Bamiyan-Sayghan-Village 1-#6   [92] Kabul-Paghman-Village 2-#5

[93] Bamiyan-Panjab-Village 2-#6. The corruption in the NSP been reported elsewhere. Given high levels of corruption associated with the aid enterprise in Afghanistan, it should not be surprising that this program exhibited similar characteristics. See "Corruption Hampers Development in Afghan Districts," *Institute for War and Peace Reporting*, November 14, 2104, https://iwpr.net/global-voices/corruption-hampers-development-afghan-districts; "Afghans Question Reconstruction Scheme," *Institute for War and Peace Reporting*, June 23, 2015, www.iwpr.net/global-voices/afghans-question-reconstruction-scheme; Safi Maiwand, "Afghanistan: Local Reconstruction Effort Goes Awry," *Institute for War and Peace Reporting*, May 17, 2011, https://iwpr.net/global-voices/afghanistan-local-reconstruction-effort-goes-awry.

[94] Dorronsoro, *Revolution Unending*, 108.

[95] Antonio Giustozzi, *War, Politics and Society in Afghanistan, 1978–1992* (Washington, DC: Georgetown University Press, 2000); Giustozzi, *Empires of Mud*; Rashid, *Taliban*; Abdulkader H. Sinno, *Organizations at War in Afghanistan and Beyond* (Ithaca, NY: Cornell University Press, 2008).

[96] Olson, "Dictatorship, Democracy, and Development"; Olson, *Power and Prosperity*.

projects.[97] In fact, these profits have been proposed as an alternative to ideology as the motivation for Taliban organization.[98] Yet when combined with their vertical features, lack of constraints, and few opportunities for participatory governance, commanders provided a poor framework for achieving enduring local governance outcomes in the Afghan context.

At a minimum, this chapter has shown that customary organizations in rural areas are more than just an artifact of the past or an obstacle to modernization. Rather, they are an important source of governance in a very challenging environment. This chapter has opened up the "black box" of tradition and provided an institutional explanation for the performance of customary organizations in rural Afghanistan. While these organizations have some virtues, as the next chapter illustrates, they also have limitations.

---

[97] Jennifer Murtazashvili, "Gaming the State: Consequences of Contracting out State Building in Afghanistan," *Central Asian Survey* 34, no. 1 (2015): 78–92; Rashid, *Taliban*.

[98] Gretchen Peters, *Seeds of Terror: How Drugs, Thugs, and Crime Are Reshaping the Afghan War* (New York: Picador, 2010).

5

Cooperation among communities

The previous chapter showed that under certain conditions customary organizations can provide small-scale goods in the absence of an effective state. Yet many public goods cannot be provided by citizens within the contours of a single village. For example, it is virtually impossible for single communities to produce public goods most vital for economic development such as irrigation and public health systems. More generally, economic development is not driven by small-scale public goods, but by groups coming together into larger organizations to take advantage of economies of scale in the production of larger scale public goods.[1]

This chapter focuses on the problem of cooperation between villages to provide these sorts of larger-scale public goods that are critical to economic development. On one hand, the findings presented in this chapter may be a reason for guarded optimism, as groups of communities regularly come together to provide a range of public goods. On the other hand, while cooperation is not uncommon, there are several types of public goods that are typically underprovided by communities despite efforts at self-provision. By highlighting the capacity and limitations of local governing organizations in communities to provide public goods in the absence of effective external intervention by the state, this chapter demarcates areas where government intervention is most pressing.

In order to explain when cooperation between communities might occur, the chapter begins by providing a conceptual framework which outlines several

---

[1] Greif, *Institutions and the Path to the Modern Economy*; Timur Kuran, *The Long Divergence: How Islamic Law Held Back the Middle East* (Princeton, NJ: Princeton University Press, 2010); Douglass C. North, John Joseph Wallis, and Barry R. Weingast, *Violence and Social Orders: A Conceptual Framework for Interpreting Recorded Human History* (New York: Cambridge University Press, 2009).

factors that should contribute to inter-communal cooperation in the pursuit of public goods. The conceptual framework presumes villages function like their own "republics" due to their high degrees of autonomy, evidenced by myriad social organizations within them, as well as a very limited presence of the state in regulating relations between villages.[2] This description fits Afghanistan, where there is no clearly agreed-upon system of rules governing relations between villages seeking to work together to provide public goods and where these collections of communities can rarely call upon the state to facilitate such public goods provision. Several factors are proposed to explain cooperation among villages, including the number of participating villages, geographic scale, fixed costs required to provide the good, political stability in a region, and social homogeneity.

The conceptual framework is used to explore the provision of several categories of public goods: irrigation, local order and security, and public infrastructure. The findings, which are presented as case studies, reveal that while communities are generally able to deal with issues involving water and even law and order, they typically are unable to provide public goods involving larger-scale capital investments. The main implication for state building is that the state should have a much more active role funding those activities, such as public infrastructure, that require significant capital investments at the inter-communal level.

The broader policy implications are to identify where rural communities demand a larger role for the state. Although accounts of Afghanistan certainly conjure up images of communities hell-bent against outside intervention, this chapter tells a different story. It helps us understand where outside intervention may be most welcome and where the state is actually demanded by citizens to fill gaps in self-governance. As this chapter explains, state building from the "bottom-up" should not mean governing from the village up. Rather, it should mean identifying where self-governance ends and understanding where demands for the state services and intervention should begin.

This chapter begins by considering perspectives on inter-communal cooperation, drawing on insights from the literature on regional governance. The chapter then presents several case studies of successful and unsuccessful cooperation to provide public goods across communal boundaries.

REGIONAL GOVERNANCE AND PUBLIC GOODS PROVISION

Regardless of how well individual communities govern themselves or how passionately citizens in a community may desire a particular good or service, many public goods cannot be provided by a single community. In developed

---

[2] Robert Wade coined the term "village republics" in rural India to depict such semi-autonomous villages. See Wade, *Village Republics*.

countries and even in many developing countries, individuals can typically call upon the government to provide goods and services they demand. In contrast, in countries recovering from conflict or those that are persistently fragile, individuals rarely can call on the state to fill these needs. Impatient citizens find, more often than not, that there is no external authority to help them organize for the provision or production of these goods and services. It is the absence of these larger scale goods that keep countries, such as Afghanistan that maintain well-functioning systems of self-governance through informal institutions, poor because a wealth of community governance does not automatically translate into economies of scale. Yet we also know that anarchy often does not translate into chaos. When can communities cooperate to provide public goods in the absence of an external enforcer?

The underlying theoretical problem here is cooperation under what is essentially an anarchic situation. The notion that cooperation is possible under anarchy is not new in the social sciences. There is a large theoretical literature in economics explaining how rational individuals can cooperate when there is no external enforcer to compel them to do what is in their collective interest.[3] Political scientists have also long considered how states in the international system can achieve cooperation without relying on external enforcement.[4] These frameworks, which are mainly based on theories of repeated interactions from game theory, have subsequently been applied to topics such as international economic relations, emergence of international organizations, as well as provision of other kinds of public goods at the global level.[5]

Economic theories of cooperation have also been applied to regional governance, which refers to cooperation between institutionally independent yet geographically adjacent communities.[6] The foundational studies of regional governance, which focused on the United States, showed how independent jurisdictions can achieve cooperation when mutual benefits are at stake.[7] These jurisdictions are the site of a "very rich and intricate 'framework' for negotiation, adjudicating, and design questions that affect their diverse public interests."[8]

The concept of polycentric governance emerged from these studies to help scholars and policymakers look at governance at multiple levels.[9] Most governments are polycentric in that they have multiple, overlapping levels. The scale of production is not the same for all public goods and services.

[3] David M. Kreps et al., "Rational Cooperation in the Finitely Repeated Prisoners' Dilemma," *Journal of Economic Theory* 27, no. 2 (1982): 245–52.
[4] Robert Axelrod, *The Evolution of Cooperation* (New York: Basic Books, 1984).
[5] Barrett, *Why Cooperate?*; Helen V. Milner, *Interests, Institutions, and Information* (Princeton, NJ: Princeton University Press, 1997).
[6] McGinnis, *Polycentric Governance and Development.*
[7] Ostrom, Parks, and Whitaker, "Do We Really Want to Consolidate Urban Police Forces?"
[8] Ostrom, Tiebout, and Warren, "The Organization of Government in Metropolitan Areas."
[9] Ostrom, *Understanding Institutional Diversity.*

In addition, not all relationships between various levels of government are clearly specified, which leaves space for various levels of government to craft their own rules governing cooperation. The regional governance literature underscores the importance of looking beyond the formal rules to see how different levels of government actually interact, as well as to consider carefully the relationship between governing bodies.

One of the central findings in the vast literature on polycentric regional governance is that voluntary, self-enforcing regional governance arrangements are quite common.[10] Even when there is no formal framework for governance in an issue area, norms and practices typically emerge to improve the ability of communities to collectively respond to issues and needs that simultaneously affect several of communities. Subsequent studies of regional governance explained the factors that contribute to cooperation, such as such as collective benefits, transaction costs, and community characteristics.[11] These studies illustrate that municipalities often establish robust systems of informal governance to provide public goods and services, even in contexts where the formal state is relatively strong.[12]

There are several reasons why the notion of polycentric governance is appropriate for understanding inter-village relations in rural Afghanistan. First, the challenge of attaining inter-jurisdictional cooperation is not peculiar to developed economies in which the scale of economic activities is much greater in the developing world. In Afghanistan, communities often strive together to provide public goods. Sometimes they succeed and sometimes they fail. Studies of polycentric governance can help explain these divergent outcomes.

Second, analyzing formal institutional relationships alone tells us very little about how governance occurs in practice, in particular in persistently weak states such as Afghanistan. As a result of the veritable vacuum of effective formal authority at the inter-jurisdictional level, a risk is that a nearly Hobbesian condition prevails between communities when issues of common interest or conflict arise. Yet governance occurs informally, even though it has no

---

[10] Roger B. Parks and Ronald J. Oakerson, "Local Government Constitutions: A Different View of Metropolitan Governance," *The American Review of Public Administration* 19, no. 4 (1989): 279–94; Oakerson and Parks, "The Study of Local Public Economies"; Parks and Oakerson, "Metropolitan Organization and Governance."

[11] Feiock, *Metropolitan Governance*; Richard C. Feiock, "Metropolitan Governance and Institutional Collective Action," *Urban Affairs Review* 44, no. 3 (2009): 356–77; David Lowery, "A Transactions Costs Model of Metropolitan Governance: Allocation Versus Redistribution in Urban America," *Journal of Public Administration Research and Theory* 10, no. 1 (2000): 49–78; Mark Lubell et al., "Watershed Partnerships and the Emergence of Collective Action Institutions," *American Journal of Political Science* 46, no. 1 (2002): 148–63.

[12] For examples of such cooperation see Richard C. Feiock and John T. Scholz, eds., *Self-Organizing Federalism: Collaborative Mechanisms to Mitigate Institutional Collective Action Dilemmas* (New York: Cambridge University Press, 2009).

formal mandate. We would miss these oftentimes robust political relations if we simply focused on formal parchment institutions, on the one hand, and community self-governance, on the other.

Third, there is a substantial amount of variation in the ability of villages to cooperate with one another. Sometimes self-organized regional arrangements are successful and other times they are not. Communities can strike deals with the villages next door facilitating public goods provision and generate enduring cooperation. In other cases, communities will fester in conflict. Despite the importance of inter-communal cooperation in rural Afghanistan, there is very little known about the factors explaining why it emerges and why it fails or breaks down.

Fourth, explaining the capacity and limits of customary organizations to cooperate across jurisdictions sheds light in the areas where communities most demand state intervention. One of the central themes in the polycentric approach to governance is that community interactions are an action arena that are nested within a larger action arena. In this case, the larger arena is the state. The ability of decision-makers in the state arena to improve the lives of members at the inter-communal level depends on the extent to which they recognize and act upon the needs and demands of communities. In Afghanistan, however, the state arena and community arenas are poorly linked to the actual interactions between communities. Rather, the state-building effort in Afghanistan was an enormous, encompassing project emphasizing the role of the government as a public goods provider from the national level all the way down to the lowest level of government across almost every sector and jurisdiction. A more precise understanding of the conditions under which communities can cooperate and when such cooperation breaks down can help isolate a more appropriate and tailored role for the state and state-building efforts that is more likely to be sustainable in the long run.

Although there is tremendous diversity in approaches to understanding inter-communal and inter-jurisdictional cooperation, several factors from extant perspectives are particularly salient in the Afghan context. Although the factors that follow are each important to understanding the provision of public goods across communities, the framework and analysis that follows does not view them as necessary or sufficient conditions. Rather, cooperation is more likely in situations when each of the variables are present. When more of these variables are present, we are more likely to observe the emergence of inter-communal cooperation.

The first factor is the number of villages. Theoretical and empirical studies of collective action show that as the size of a group increases the ability to achieve cooperation decreases.[13] One of the reasons why the number of participants

---

[13] Olson, *The Logic of Collective Action: Public Goods and the Theory of Groups.*

influences cooperation is due to monitoring costs. As monitoring costs increase, the ability to cooperate in provision declines.[14]

This is an important variable in rural communities. For some categories of public goods, the number of communities needed to participate to successfully provide a public good is quite small. For example, resolving a dispute between two communities involves only a small number of communities, but managing an irrigation system may require cooperation of three or more communities. When the numbers of communities required to provide a public good is small, it is easier for those communities to work together to find a solution without external intervention.

Second, geographic scale, which refers to the distance separating various political units who have to participate for successful public goods provision, is expected to influence prospects for intercommunal cooperation. The number of communities required to cooperate in some cases may be small, but when they are separated by large distances they face higher transaction costs in their struggle to achieve cooperation, such as costs of monitoring participation. When a public good requires political units cooperate to over larger distances, they may be less likely to cooperate.[15]

Geographic scale is expected to affect the ability of communities to cooperate and as a result, provide some public goods. For example, successful self-regulation of pasture land often requires the cooperation of a large number of communities spread out over great distances. This is one of the reasons why communities often face challenges managing conflict over pasture in Afghanistan.

Third, overcoming fixed costs is one of the main rationales for government. In economics, the inability of firms to overcome fixed costs is one of the main rationales for government to coordinate investment to achieve development.[16]

---

[14] Arun Agrawal and Sanjeev Goyal, "Group Size and Collective Action Third-Party Monitoring in Common-Pool Resources," *Comparative Political Studies* 34, no. 1 (2001): 63–93.

[15] The growing literature on the size of nations has several implications for public good provision in communities Alberto Alesina, William Easterly, and Janina Matuszeski, "Artificial States," *National Bureau of Economic Research Working Paper Series* No. 12328 (June 2006); Alberto Alesina and Enrico Spolaore, "On the Number and Size of Nations," *Quarterly Journal of Economics* 112, no. 4 (1997): 1027–56; Alberto Alesina and Enrico Spolaore, *The Size of Nations* (Cambridge, MA: MIT Press, 2005); Alberto Alesina and Romain Wacziarg, "Openness, Country Size and Government," *Journal of Public Economics* 69, no. 3 (1998): 305–21; Alberto Alesina, "Joseph Schumpeter Lecture: The Size of Countries: Does It Matter?" *Journal of the European Economic Association* 1, no. 2–3 (2003): 301–16; David Friedman, "A Theory of the Size and Shape of Nations," *The Journal of Political Economy* 85, no. 1 (February 1977): 59–77. These studies investigate whether there is an "optimal" size of nations, finding that there is a trade-off between economies of scale and heterogeneity. Those studies are not directly relevant here since I am explaining voluntary cooperation in provision of public goods, rather than provision by a state.

[16] William Brian Arthur, *Path Dependence* (Ann Arbor, MI: University of Michigan Press, 1994); Kevin M. Murphy, Andrei Shleifer, and Robert W. Vishny, "Industrialization and the Big Push,"

Just as firms face fixed costs, village governing organziations face fixed costs in providing public goods. Higher fixed costs require that each community must increase the size of its contribution in order for public goods to be successfully self-provided. As such, public goods that exhibit significant fixed costs will be more challenging for communities to self-produce. Indeed, the economic theory of the state rationalizes state formation largely in terms of fixed costs and economies of scale.[17]

Most categories of public goods also vary on this dimension as well. Management of common property resources, for example, generally involves low fixed costs. One of the reasons why cooperation is common in management of common property resources is because the fixed costs of managing these resources tend to be low. In particular, the cost to most communities in these settings is ensuring adequate contributions of labor, such as time and effort expended to monitor and enforce the behavior of neighbors.[18] However, when villages have to provide public goods that are more capital intensive, such as building a school that benefits several villages in a region, they will likely face larger obstacles providing it due to the capital intensity of such infrastructure relative to other types of public goods.

Fourth, political parameters may also influence the ability of communities to cooperate across jurisdictions. The main political parameters I am interested in are those that affect the time horizons of the participants. In a repeated prisoner's dilemma, cooperation is expected to breakdown when players become impatient. When there is a government in place, patience of the actors depends at least in part, on political institutions. For example, political institutions that constrain leaders increase their incentives to provide public goods and forgo predation.

The main implication of such theories is that leaders will be more likely to act in their own interest when confronted with political instability. When communities are seeking to cooperate to achieve an outcome of mutual interest, political instability may influence the expectation that a malik, for example, decides to shirk in his dealings with the malik of another community. Such a situation could occur when maliks anticipate that they will no longer be

Working Paper (National Bureau of Economic Research, 1988); Charles Wolf Jr., "Market and Non-Market Failures: Comparison and Assessment," *Journal of Public Policy* 7, no. 1 (1987): 43–70.

[17] Yoram Barzel, *A Theory of the State: Economic Rights, Legal Rights, and the Scope of the State* (New York: Cambridge University Press, 2001); Douglass C. North and Robert Paul Thomas, *The Rise of the Western World: A New Economic History* (New York: Cambridge University Press, 1973).

[18] Krister Andersson and Elinor Ostrom, "Analyzing Decentralized Resource Regimes from a Polycentric Perspective," *Policy Sciences* 41, no. 1 (2008): 71–93; Karthik Panchanathan and Robert Boyd, "Indirect Reciprocity Can Stabilize Cooperation without the Second-Order Free Rider Problem," *Nature* 432, no. 7016 (2004): 499–502.

interacting with each other in the future. When they believe there is an endpoint to the game, they have incentives to shirk because they do not expect to be around to reap the gains from future cooperation.[19]

Political instability is a common threat to achieving cooperation in a country such as Afghanistan. As the political environment becomes less stable, due to some exogenous factor such as a growing insurgency, coup d'état, financial crisis, or foreign invasion, villagers and their leaders face fewer incentives cooperate with other communities. The reason is that under such circumstances, leaders have less reason to believe that their partners from other villages will be around to deal with in the future (as they may migrate, for example), or they have a good reason to believe that the incentives they or their partners face will change in ways that undermine prospects for cooperation.

It was not possible for me to conduct research in areas experiencing extremely high levels of political instability, which makes it difficult to provide examples of how current instability damaged inter-communal cooperation. During fieldwork, however, informants frequently provided historical examples of how conflict interrupted cooperation between villages or village representatives. When recalling the past, residents discussed how successful self-governing water management schemes such as the mirab system did not function during periods of fighting. In one of the cases discussed later, villagers in Bamiyan Center, Bamiyan Province, recounted how they were unable to manage irrigation systems during Taliban rule because they were not allowed to leave their homes to grow crops or tend the water issues. Similarly, a case from Paghman District, Kabul Province illustrates how conflict created new political fissures that destabilized intra-communal cooperation over irrigation systems.

A final factor influencing inter-communal cooperation is social heterogeneity. When heterogeneity increases, individuals have fewer incentives to trust their partners in exchange. When groups are more homogeneous in preferences, measured by economic, racial, ethnic, and religious differences, individuals are more likely to cooperate with one another and provide public goods.[20] Most field-based research has found that heterogeneity decreases cooperation.[21] Thus, when parties seeking to provide a public good are more diverse, they

---

[19] This is similar to the International Relations literature in political science that discusses how domestic audience costs can influence war and other outcomes between states James D. Fearon, "Domestic Political Audiences and the Escalation of International Disputes," *The American Political Science Review* 88, no. 3 (1994): 577–92; Kenneth A. Schultz, "Looking for Audience Costs," *Journal of Conflict Resolution* 45, no. 1 (2001): 32–60. In the context earlier, the domestic politics of the village (the "audience") may well influence the propensity to cooperate.

[20] Alesina, Baqir, and Easterly, "Public Goods and Ethnic Divisions"; Alberto Alesina and Eliana La Ferrara, "Who Trusts Others?" *Journal of Public Economics* 85, no. 2 (2002): 207–34.

[21] Bardhan and Dayton-Johnson, "Unequal Irrigators: Heterogeneity and Commons Management in Large-Scale Multivariate Research."

are hypothesized to be less likely to come together to achieve this even though they have common interest in doing so.

Before delving into the cases, I should explain some of the methodological challenges in studying this question. Identifying examples of successful cooperation among communities was surprisingly difficult to establish through semi-structured interviews, group interviews, and focus group discussions. This is because when informants were asked about relations or joint activities with neighboring villages, they were more quickly able to identify and detail problems and complaints they had with their neighbors. Many people had long lists of complaints about the community next door, while at the same time they appeared to take collaborations for granted. When looking at a broader array of evidence, it was clear that there was significant cooperation taking place between communities. In fact, from the context of discussions, cooperation between communities often appeared to have been ongoing for decades. As some of this cooperation is routinized or simply second nature in many areas, villages often did not think of it when asked. It was often through answers to other questions, observations, or general discussion that led informants to talk about how they cooperate with other villages.

One of the most significant changes I made in the interview protocol after piloting it in several villages was to completely rework questions that explored the issue of intra-communal cooperation because informants tended to be so negative in their attitudes about neighboring communities. It is unlikely that such animosity is unique to Afghanistan. In the United States, people frequently comment that "good fences make good neighbors." Instead of asking directly about such cooperation, information about such cooperation was elicited indirectly. In some cases, this involved asking questions about specific public goods that could be identified either from the physical environment, observations, or from other interviews in the community. In areas where irrigation systems were visible, for example, it seemed logical to ask about how such systems functioned. When discussing irrigation systems, informants were probed about dynamics of cooperation with other communities. Anytime an informant brought up a neighboring community during the course of discussion, they were probed on the nature of the relationship.

The analysis that follows is organized according to categories of public goods whose production typically requires inter-communal cooperation. These include irrigation; law and order; and public infrastructure (roads, hydro dams, electricity, health services, and mosques). The reason for selecting these categories of public goods is that they were those most commonly discussed by informants during the course of interviews and focus group discussions. Due to the limitations in the data collection strategy, questions about inter-communal cooperation were usually only asked from one of the communities involved in production rather than all of them requiring me to make inferences about inter-communal cooperation from studying only one group of participants. Studying all communities who participated in the provision of public goods would have required visiting a potentially large cluster of villages in every research site, which would have dramatically increased the number of communities visited and vastly increased the costs of research.

For each category of public good, several cases of inter-communal cooperation (both successes and failures) are discussed. Examples, which exhibit variation on both the dependent and independent variables, were selected so that they were representative of the fieldwork more generally.[22] For example, most villages discussed water issues, but most explained that they were able to cooperate across communities, with a few exceptions. The cases of irrigation management include mostly examples of cooperation, with one example where cooperation broke down, which is representative of the findings from fieldwork more generally and likely representative of the country.

IRRIGATION MANAGEMENT

Water is scarce in rural Afghanistan due to the country's climate and terrain. For this reason, irrigation infrastructure is among the most important public goods in rural Afghanistan, because the rural population is mostly engaged in agricultural activity. Thus, effective management of irrigation water is vital to the livelihoods of most Afghans.

Effective management of irrigation systems was also one of the most common examples of inter-communal cooperation I found during the course of fieldwork. This should not be surprising, as rural Afghans have a widely accepted customary mechanism used to manage irrigation schemes: the mirab system. Mirab, which translates as the one who governs (mir) water (ab), is the individual appointed by members of several communities tasked to monitor water irrigation systems over span of several villagers. It is an old system tracing its roots back to the Persian Empire.[23] As with many customary organizations, it may have its origins as a formal organization centuries ago, but over time as governments and empires changed, it has evolved into a de facto system of governance throughout the countryside.

In order to ensure that water was fairly managed, communities developed a set of norms to limit capture of the mirab. For example, I found that it was unusual for the mirab to come from the wealthiest family in a community. Furthermore, it was not uncommon for communities to insist that the mirab come from the tail-end of the irrigation scheme.[24] These norms ensure that his

[22] Gary King, Robert Keohane, and Sidney Verba, *Designing Social Inquiry: Scientific Inference in Qualitative Research* (Princeton, NJ: Princeton University Press, 1994).

[23] Ann S. K. Lambton, *Landlord and Peasant in Persia: A Study of Land Tenure and Land Revenue Administration* (New York: I.B.Tauris, 1991).

[24] Katja Mielke, Iskandar Abdullayev, and Usman Shah, "The Illusion of Establishing Control by Legal Definition: Water Rights, Principles and Power in Canal Irrigation Systems of the Kunduz

livelihood depended on how well he managed resources, as his own livelihood would depend on his performance.

The cases later, which are from three villages across three different provinces, shed light into self-managed irrigation systems. Perhaps due to the long history of the mirab system, individual communities were likely to cede authority over management of water resources within their community to control of this individual. In most instances, cooperation required only a few villages and a small capital investment. However, as the accounts below indicate, cooperation was sometimes difficult to maintain and in some areas it broke down.

Bamiyan Center, Bamiyan Province

This community is close to Bamiyan City, the capital of Bamiyan Province. Bamiyan City is a very small provincial capital that has only about 40,000 people, though it can hardly be described as an urban area as its center consists of a small main thoroughfare with a bazaar and a few shops, as well as several NGO and government buildings. The geography of the city consists largely of fields, where most families grow potatoes. The villages that constitute the "city" are almost exclusively Hazara. From an economic perspective, residents did not describe any pressing inequalities of concern in their community.

The villages around the capital, including this one, had seen enormous fighting during the past thirty years. They recalled with emotion the hardship they endured during Taliban rule, but also during the jihad in the 1980s. Many informants said they were unable to grow any crops at all during Taliban rule, as the Taliban forbid them from leaving their homes. More than 80 homes in the village were destroyed during the past decades of war. Several people said that after the Taliban government fell in Kabul they began to repair their homes. In fact, families were so poor that they had to share shovels and building supplies with people in neighboring villages because no one could afford their own. Such sharing of shovels is symbolic of the good relations between communities.

Cooperation between communities appeared common and routine. According to a haji who lived in the community, "[Our communities] have joint benefits. [We] are close to one another. We have relations from a long time ago."[25] A female CDC member said that relations between communities are so good, that, "when one village has a celebration, they always invite neighboring villages to participate."[26]

The overall conditions in this area suggested that cooperation should be common between communities, as each of the factors that facilitate cooperation

River Basin, Afghanistan," in *Negotiating Local Governance: Natural Resources Management at the Interface of Communities and the State*, ed. Irit Eguavoen and Wolfram Laube (New Brunswick, NJ: Transaction Publishers, 2010), 181–210.
[25] Bamiyan-Bamiyan Center-Village 2-#8.   [26] Bamiyan-Bamiyan Center-Village 2-#1.

were present: a small number of physically close villages that reduced monitoring costs; public goods in demand that were not especially costly to provide; political stability (these villages were in one of the safest provinces in the country); and ethnic and economic homogeneity. These features enabled the communities in this district to provide several public goods without external intervention (the next section discusses dispute resolution in this region). These everyday examples of cooperation were the ones that were often more difficult to identify because, for reasons discussed earlier, informants tended to talk about contentious issues or challenges more than behavior that had become more routine.

People in this community mentioned that the only prickly issue between communities in their area involved the management of irrigation water. Nonetheless, communities overcame obstacles to cooperation by appointing a credible and reliable mirab. According to a female literacy instructor:

We don't really have any problems with neighboring villages. We share water resources and an irrigation canal with the village next door. Our villages came together to select a mirab that can resolve issues of water between villages. At the end of every year when we collect our harvest, we give some wheat and potatoes to this man. He knows that he will get paid well by us if he does his work well. If every village has enough water and is given water equitably, then each family will have more wheat and food to give him at the end of the year. So he distributes the water to us equally and people are pretty happy with this system. It has been around for a long time.[27]

Because mirabs frequently receive a share of each farmer's harvest as remuneration for their work, mirabs have incentives to distribute water equitably and mediate disputes when they arise. The more prosperous the harvest for all, the more the mirab can collect. Villages selected a mirab who had technical knowledge in water resource management, but most importantly, they picked someone who could negotiate with and maintain the respect of individuals across communities in the region.

Close proximity of communities in the area facilitated cooperation. As the villages were close together, residents worked with the mirab to monitor work being done in each community participating in shared governance of water. According to one middle-aged man in the community:

Our village is close to five other villages. We don't have any problems with these neighboring villages. Sometimes we have small issues with [one of the neighboring] villages because our water comes from that side of the mountain (*pointing to mountain*). During a recent drought, we had some problems with that village because the people there were taking all the water. We have some problems with that village that have yet to be resolved because we don't have a government that is in firm control that can be relied on to resolve these issues.

---

[27] Bamiyan-Bamiyan Center-Village 2-#1.

A man from [the neighboring village] named Aziz came to our village during the drought. He told us that the water belonged to his village. He said that they need the water and that we wouldn't be allowed to use the water. He didn't want us to use it... A man (Pashtun elder) came to our community and said that both of our communities are Hazara [and we should be able to solve the dispute ourselves]. He said that it would be bad if only one side used the water because we are both Hazara brothers. He said that the people in [the neighboring village] should share the water with us because we don't have a regular government that can resolve these issues. He said that we should accept each other. At that time, the people in the other village accepted this proposal and gave us some water. Nevertheless, we complain about the government all the time to anyone who will listen.[28]

Cooperation between communities is not always easy to maintain. In situations of stress, such as the drought discussed earlier, normally good relations suffer from strain. These kinds of external shocks place enormous burdens on local stability. This haji spoke of how a recent flood threatened collective action between communities over the irrigation system:

A village upstream had a problem with another village. When a flood came from the mountain we wanted to build a protection wall, but the neighboring village did not allow us to come into the village to build this wall. They told us that if we built the wall, they would suffer more than us. They said the protection wall would cause flooding to be more intense on their land. They said that their area would get a lot of stones that would come with the water from the flood. That was a very big problem. So as a result, both villages joined together and built a [common] protection wall. This was a good solution to the problem. During this process, we got a lot of advice from the elders.[29]

Although informants reported effective self-management of the irrigation system, during periods of drought, uncertainty associated with management over water resources put enormous pressure on their system of governance and generated instability. Yet for the most part, people in this village were able to manage their irrigation system without incurring significant costs. The features mentioned earlier, such as ethnic and social homogeneity, as well as low fixed costs of managing water, in addition to political stability, provided a fertile context for inter-communal cooperation.

Khanabad District, Kunduz Province

Villagers offered a similar account of water governance in a village in Khanabad District, Kunduz Province. The district itself is ethnically diverse, with significant numbers of Pashtuns, Tajiks, Hazaras, and Uzbeks. Pashtuns in this area settled in Kunduz during the reign of Abdur Rahman Khan several generations ago. The population around this particular village was predominately Tajik.

---

[28] Bamiyan-Bamiyan Center-Village 2-#7.   [29] Bamiyan-Bamiyan Center-Village 2-#8.

Management of water resources was the most contentious issue in village life as the area is extremely arid, water is extremely scarce, and irrigation systems had been largely destroyed as a result of the war. Compared to other villages in the district, the water resources in the community appeared to be particularly well managed. This community was growing rice, a crop that is very intensive in its use of water. Unlike many other villages, the people tending the fields appeared to be very well organized. The mirab worked with four other villages to manage water resources in the area. He also met with government officials and other mirabs in the area when issues over water arose.[30] In this community, the mirab also served as the arbab as well as the head of the CDC. He had a long history of being able to work well with the government. The mirab and most other residents in this community spent most of their time complaining about CDC activity in the community rather than discussing irrigation issues, which led me to conclude that irrigation was relatively well managed.

Water resources were so important in this area that they selected the mirab to be the arbab. This also seemed to be the result of his administrative competence. Despite his demonstrated ability to work with others, conflicts still arose from time to time with neighboring villages over irrigation water. An unemployed man in the village described how the respected elders of the village would accompany the mirab when he visited neighboring villages to negotiate equitable use of irrigation water.[31] According to residents, they had to renegotiate water usage rights with neighboring villagers every year as the amount of water available annually was highly variable.

According to the mirab, he spent most of his time working on other issues in the community (as he is also the arbab). In fact, his effectiveness in managing water relations allowed him to spend more time solving other problems.

The community was able to manage its resources for a number of reasons. The number of communities required to manage water resources was small and confined to a small geographic area. The irrigation system had been in place for many decades, according to the villagers, so there were very few costs associated with its maintenance. Community members made regular contributions to the mirab for his service. During the time of field research, the area was fairly stable from a political perspective (although several years later this was no longer the case). Finally, the communities in this particular area were fairly homogenous. The mirab said that of the communities he answered to, all were Tajik, with the exception of one Pashtun family who lived in the area.[32] As a consequence of these favorable conditions, the community was able to work well with surrounding ones to manage water resources.

[30] Kunduz-Khanabad-Village 1-#5.   [31] Kunduz-Khanabad-Village 1-#7.
[32] Kunduz-Khanabad-Village 1-#5.

Paghman District, Kabul Province

Cooperation over irrigation is common, but certainly not inevitable. Decades of conflict polarized some communities and with such schisms came new kinds of political cleavages among groups that had not existed before. This heterogeneity of political views sometimes managed to disrupt cooperation where it had existed earlier.

Paghman District, Kabul Province provides such an example. It is home to the notorious commander Abdul Rasul Sayyaf, one of the most conservative jihadi leaders who emerged during the anti-Soviet insurgency. In the 1970s he was a professor of Islamic Law at Kabul University. He spent much of the 1980s in Saudi Arabia where he was able to leverage support for other mujahideen.[33] He is also well known for his cruelty in battle.[34] In 2005, Sayyaf was elected to the lower house of the Afghan National Assembly, the Wolesi Jirga, and later ran for president in 2014.

In interviews and focus groups in the district, it became clear that many families in the district remained closely allied with him and were still heavily dependent upon his patronage. Residents in the area appeared to support Sayyaf and many families said that they provided their sons to serve as soldiers under his command both during the war after 2001. When informants were asked what they do for a living (or in the case of female informants, what their husbands or sons do for a living), more than half said they, or their relatives, "work for Sayyaf." When probed about what kind of work they do for him, they said that they were "bodyguards" for him. From observations, it did not seem as if being a bodyguard for Sayyaf involved much work, but instead was a source of income for the family in exchange for loyalty.

In one village in Paghman people described the breakdown of their karez, which is a traditional system of underground canals and wells found in Afghanistan and parts of the Middle East. A 51-year-old male farmer described how political factions created during the war created tension between communities, resulting in a breakdown of cooperation:

> We had a karez. The wells are in the neighboring village, but we have always used them. We fought a lot with this village during the war as they supported another faction. After the fighting ended and we all came back to our villages the people in the neighboring village said that it was their fathers that granted us permission to access the wells in their village, but now they won't allow us to use them. So this has led to a huge conflict between our villages. But we keep taking the water as it was our right. Some villagers in the neighboring village even tried to go to the state court to ensure that we couldn't use this karez, our karez.[35]

---

[33] Coll, *Ghost Wars*.
[34] Kathy Gannon, "Afghanistan Unbound," *Foreign Affairs* 83 (2004): 35.
[35] Kabul-Paghman-Village 1-#3.

In the absence of effective external support from the state, villagers desperately appealed to outside forces that could help them manage their water resources. A male elder who worked as a mason in the community recalled the situation faced by community members:

We had one problem with [the neighboring village]: we have a karez that has wells that are on their land. This karez is from ages ago, but recently they told us that they won't allow us to use these wells anymore. So we are having a lot of problems with them. A person from that village works in Supreme Court and he is a very proud person. He says that all the water from the karez is only the right of the people in that village. So my family became fed up. We went to Sayyaf's house and the people there solved it. Sayyaf said that it is our right to use the water as well. So he was able to solve the dispute for us. But we are having problems again.[36]

The geographic area around this karez was ethnically homogenous (largely Pashtun). Maintenance of the system did not present any fixed costs. Due to its proximity to Kabul and good access to water and land, it was far more economically viable than most other districts in the country. The number of communities involved in joint management of this particular karez was quite small, as only two villages were involved. Political instability served as a shock to the area and as a result, cooperation over water resources broke down. Political fighting introduced a new kind of heterogeneity and destroyed successful intra-communal management of water resources. Even pressure from a strongman such as Sayyaf was unable to contribute to the resolution of the conflict.

These cases suggest that communities can effectively manage water resources, although it is by no means guaranteed. The framework above provides insights into the factors that contribute to cooperative outcomes. In each of these cases, irrigation involved a small number of communities interacting over a fairly small geographic area and low fixed costs, which mainly consisted of local labor as none of the communities were constructing new irrigation systems, but instead were working to maintain existing systems. In the two cases where cooperation was successful other factors enabled cooperation, including local security and homogeneity of communities. Cooperation between communities broke down in one of the cases due to exogenous shocks to key political parameters that led to political instability. Conflict during the past thirty years fed insecurity and mistrust and also involved interventions by commanders.

It is also important to clarify what these findings do not say. A common complaint among communities (not those discussed here) was that irrigation was the most important issue among groups of communities and that they were looking for outside money to help them build or reconstruct systems that were destroyed during the war. Thus, the high fixed cost of providing a new system

[36] Kabul-Paghman-Village 1-#4.

or resurrecting an old one prevents intra-communal cooperation on this issue. The issue of constructing a new irrigation system, rather than managing an existing system fits more appropriately under the discussion of public infrastructure later.

LOCAL ORDER AND SECURITY

Provision of basic law and order is perhaps the most important public good in any society. As discussed in the previous chapter, managing dispute resolution within a single community is typically facilitated by customary organizations. Yet the some of the most challenging disputes in rural Afghanistan involve more than one community. When such disputes arise, communities must work together to find solutions to issues on their own because there are usually no third parties available to resolve disputes and enforce decisions. The case studies in this section consider the strengths and limitations of communities seeking to improve prospects for local order when the underlying conflicts transcend the boundaries of a village.

Dawlatabad District, Balkh Province

An example of a conflict over marriage from Dawlatabad District, Balkh Province illustrates the capacity of communities to resolve disputes and provide public order. In rural Afghanistan, unresolved family and marriage disputes have potential to spill over into larger scale conflicts when they involve families and their kin across several communities.[37] Sometimes conflict arose between families, while at other times, conflict followed qawm divides. Conflicts of these sort were a major concern among women who frequently discussed how marital problems between and bride and bridegroom from different villages could escalate into inter-communal strife. A Pashtun mother in her 20s recalled trouble that arose from a marriage across qawm lines in this community:

For example, we had a problem with our neighboring village. Someone in our village married a girl from that village next door. They took her from the neighboring village and brought her here. You should know that her father took a lot of money for that girl. After the wedding her husband refused to give the bride permission to visit her family in her native village. He didn't give her permission to go to her father's house. The father of the bride [from the neighboring village] came to our family and went to the elders. At that point elders from both villages came together and discussed the problem. They resolved the problem and now the bride can go freely to her father's family in the

---

[37] For a beautiful illustration of how seemingly simple conflicts over marriage or inheritance, if left unresolved, can turn into violent feuds between communities, see David Edwards, *Heroes of the Age: Moral Fault Lines on the Afghan Frontier* (Berkeley, CA: University of California Press, 1996).

neighboring village. In our village every qawm has an elder on this council. They have their own representative. So if something happens they always come together to discuss the issue and make a decision together.[38]

In Dawlatabad, communities collectively resolved this conflict without fighting, for reasons anticipated by the theoretical framework. In this case, the neighboring family was also Pashtun. The dispute also involved only one other party, although it crossed community lines. Dispute resolution such as this does not involve high fixed costs.

Although this case is brief, it was not the only one of its sort that I came across. Such disputes over marriage issues often took an inter-communal rather than simply familial nature. When such disputes arose between communities under such conditions, they seemed fairly easy to resolve. When they involved parties of different qawms, for instance, they were more challenging to resolve, yet when the informal constitution governing customary authority functions, such authority frequently facilitates solutions that are acceptable to parties across communities.

Bamiyan Center, Bamiyan Province

We have already seen evidence of the central importance of deliberative bodies in rural communities, such as shuras, jirgas, or village meetings. Yet the concept of a shura is not exclusive to deliberative processes that occur within a community. In addition to having local management of irrigation systems as discussed in the section earlier, residents in Bamiyan Center reported that they created a new council to resolve intra-communal disputes.

Community members said they created this council to help resolve these kinds of issues because there was nobody outside their villages they could turn to for assistance. Several informants said that over the course of the past several years they had visited government offices seeking assistance in resolving disputes that confronted their communities, but the government was "corrupt" or "too lazy" to help out. The inability of the government to provide larger scale public goods drove them to action to create a new governing council. This council, called mardomi shura (a "people's shura"), brought together interested parties from each community to discuss festering issues that involve more than one community. The elected head of the shura said that participants contribute 200 Afghani a month from their community (about $4) to ensure the organization can finance its basic activities. They even maintain a room where members come together and meet. According to a male haji in the community:

The mardomi shura cooperates and coordinates with government [officials]. It solves the people's problem. When governmental officials don't do their work well, the shura even reports [these issues] to Kabul or can complain about them to higher officials. Last year

[38] Balkh-Dawlatabad-Village1-#2.

the shura resolved a murder case which was [unsolved] from long ago. This shura solved it by taking a sheep from one side [the defendant] and inviting both disputants to the accuser's house. [They had a dinner which served as a reconciliation ceremony]. Lots of disputes and other cases were resolved by this shura.[39]

Community resolution of this dispute is evident by the punishment: exchange of livestock and a dinner ceremony where families from both sides come together and agree to reconcile. Surely, this is not the punishment for murder mandated by the state criminal code. Rather, it is a local norm of restorative justice that emerged among these and most other communities.[40] Community members also set up a neighborhood watch system that tried to track down cars that regularly hit pedestrians on a busy thoroughfare. For example, the head of the shura said there has been an uptick in traffic deaths on a highway that connects Bamiyan to the rest of Afghanistan.[41] When someone is hit, community members call others down the road to alert them to the accident. They try to stop and catch the assailant without state assistance. These are some of the ways community members, acting through their inter-communal shura, provide order on a regular basis.

The head of the mardomi shura said the council was established in response to government inaction. They saw it as a self-organized alternative to the government. As the head of the mardomi shura explained:

From the beginning, when our shura was established we tried to collaborate with the government. Also, our shura had a good effect on the government departments because in the government departments there is a lot of corruption. Many times we criticized them. We had meetings with the government about the problem of corruption in this area. We told the Wali (governor) about these issues, but the wali does not pay attention to us.[42] Finally, we complained to the President's office. We sent our complaint to their office directly. It has been nearly two months and we have not received a response. Two months ago, the Governor got mad at us for complaining. She asked us why we complained and went directly to the President. Now we have been talking to the Governor since we made this complaint.[43]

---

[39] Bamiyan-Bamiyan Center-Village 2-#9.
[40] It is important here to differentiate between punitive and restorative systems of justice. Under a perspective of restorative justice, crimes are seen as offenses against victims and the community tries to restore both loss to the victim and heal the social damages between the offender and the community so that community life and return to normal. Under a perspective of punitive justice, crimes are viewed as offenses against state law and the state punishes offenders. Customary law and organizations remain popular in part because they practice restorative justice, while states are simply punitive. Of course, it also helps that customary organizations are perceived by most Afghans to be more fair and honest than punitive systems of the state.
[41] Bamiyan-Provincial Capital-#3.
[42] Bamiyan Province had the first, and for many years the only, female provincial governor in post-Taliban Afghanistan.
[43] Bamiyan-Provincial Capital-#3.

One of the older men in the village said that the mardomi shura had effectively replaced the role of the government. This veteran lost a leg during the war; he was still very upset by the toll that violence had on his community during the civil war, as well as during Taliban times. He expressed his dissatisfaction with the work of the government and the corrupt bureaucrats:

> The government does not have a namayenda [representative] in the village. . . . But we have a mardomi shura. Once municipal official came and told us that they should come to our village and see everything here. They told us that they wanted to collect taxes from the shops in our village. I told him, "No, I will never let you come to our village because during these past three or four years you have never been to our village. You have never been here once. You don't care about our problems. Now you want to collect taxes from our people? When you build something for the people in our village, then I will invite you so that you can collect taxes from our people." Then the municipal official got angry. He turned around and went back to his office. I told him that I know my rights but the government does not. If the government respects the rights of the people, then I will respect the rights of the government. If the government wants to take something from the people, then the people should have some rights as well. If you don't work for our village, I won't even recognize the municipality. He got angry with me. But I didn't care about his anger. I was not afraid because it is not my sole wish alone. It is the desire of the people. The people in the village share my feelings. It is my duty to tell the government and inform them.[44]

In addition to the mardomi shura, residents could call on local third-party mediators (muslehin) to resolve intra-communal disputes. These mediators are typically elders from other villages who work with several communities when issues arise. As one informant described the situation, under normal circumstances, such a role would be filled by a government official, but the government is simply incapable of performing this basic duty. For example, in the irrigation dispute discussed earlier in this same district, the muslehin was a Pashtun who traced his origins to Paktia. He has lived with his family for several generations in Bamiyan – a rare Pashtun in the Province. Due to his ethnic status as an outsider and reputation for being an honest broker, informants trusted him as a reliable third-party mediator. He was not tied by blood to disputants. Disputants, however, were typically of the same ethnic group (Hazaras). As the following account indicates, these mediators had the strong support of the people:

> Some matters are solvable. We have mediators (muslehin) because some people just hate the government. Also the muslehin are rish safidan and elders from outside villages [third party mediators]. Our elders are much more honest than the government. We saw corruption in the government, but the rish safidan are never corrupt.[45]

These communities seemed adept at managing disputes that arose between several communities. This success reflected the factors hypothesized to

---

[44] Bamiyan-Bamiyan Center-Village 2-#7.   [45] Bamiyan-Bamiyan Center-Village 2-#8.

contribute to cooperation, such as a small number of communities involved in a common dispute, close geographic proximity, low fixed costs, and political stability. Geographic proximity, for example, facilitated the emergence of a low-cost system to handle hit-and-run accidents on the roads. In addition, the area was one of the most politically stable in all of post-2001 Afghanistan. It is also one of the most homogenous from an ethnic perspective, making many disputes that emerged across communities easier to resolve.

Panjab District, Bamiyan Province

Petty criminal activity is an important threat to local law and order. In one remote district of Afghanistan, Panjab District in Bamiyan Province, bands of thieves posed a serious challenge to communities in this district which was among the poorest and most remote of those I visited. Informants from this area recounted how several villages in the area had been the victim of looting. This was not political or insurgent activity; rather, it was a criminal issue. Although they desperately tried to resolve this issue on their own, they were unable to do so with much success.

It was unclear to the villagers who the thieves were or where they came from, as neighboring villages were quite distant. Rough mountainous terrain surrounding their villages, together with the physical spread between them, made monitoring trespassers difficult. Initially villagers tried to come together and find a community solution to the issue on their own. The few villages in the area had come together to try to track down the thieves but to no avail. As a a young Hazara farmer in the village recounted:

Last year there some criminal gangs who came to our village from Yakawalang (a neighboring district, at least one hour away by car). Over the period of several months, we noticed things missing from our homes. This happened here in our village as well as in neighboring villages. We tried for a long time to find these criminals. We got together with our neighbors to find them, but we could not [track them down].[46]

Initially, the community felt that it could handle the situation of looting on its own. Once they tracked down the criminal or criminals, the community was certain they could collectively adjudicate punishment. When the community proved unable to find the thieves, the residents trekked several hours by foot to the district center to call upon the government for help. The farmer continued:

After several months, we went to the woluswal and asked him for help. After a few weeks, he sent some soldiers to our village. The soldiers were walking around the mountains and found some candy wrappers on the ground. They followed these candy wrappers up to an abandoned house in a very remote area. The wrappers led right to the door of the house. When the soldiers opened the door, they found two thieves. The two

---

[46] Bamiyan-Panjab-Village 1-#8.

thieves were caught. One of the thieves paid a bribe to the government. He was released from jail. The other one who couldn't pay is still in jail.[47]

Although these communities attempted to respond collectively to a common threat, they could not overcome the challenge posed by the criminals because of the geographic scale associated with providing security. In situations such as this, the state can play an important role in intervening in community affairs when security threats come from external sources, trusting, of course, that the state can behave as an honest broker.

PUBLIC INFRASTRUCTURE

In addition to dealing with issues arising from irrigation management and local disputes, communities frequently discussed their attempts to organize neighboring communities to provide public infrastructure that benefitted villages in their area. In most other countries in the world, citizens can turn to the government to provide such infrastructure. In Afghanistan, the government is unable to fulfill these desires for two reasons.

First, local government authorities had little capacity to implement many projects. There were resources at the local level, but they were largely channeled to international NGOs or contracting organizations charged with implementing projects on behalf of the government funded by international donor aid.[48] Although most aid projects emphasize participatory project planning, communities and local governments often had no say regarding who implemented the projects or even what projects were chosen. For example, when a water project comes to a community, community members often participate in the project planning project. While people liked being consulted on the water project, they much would have preferred another project, such as a program that brought a clinic to their community instead. These were decisions that were made elsewhere, typically by donor agencies who have their own geographic areas of concentration or line ministries who work with donors to determine the nature of projects (in most cases). A common complaint about the CDCs was that they were focused on communities, but communities often did not want projects that focused on their community alone: their most pressing needs involved several communities.

Second, local government authorities in Afghanistan had virtually no discretion over what kind of infrastructure projects were implemented in their communities. The heavily centralized budgetary system did not facilitate much local input into the formal budget process, giving communities little input into the small amounts of government infrastructure.[49] Although many aid projects (which may have been government programs) stressed "participatory"

---

[47] Bamiyan-Panjab-Village 1-#8.   [48] Kabul-Kabul City-#38.
[49] Nangarhar-Sorkhrod-District Center-#2.

development and included local voices in project selection, the menu of projects from which community members could select was confined to what donors choose to implement. As a result, much of what was provided by outsiders was not always the top of the list in terms of local demand, which frequently left it up to communities to try to provide these public goods. I was often astonished at the degree to which communities sought to self-provide and produce infrastructure projects without external assistance.

Panjab District, Bamiyan Province

In the section on local order, we saw how one community in Panjab District, Bamiyan Province faced challenges in securing local order due to the vast distances between communities. Another group of villages in the same district discussed similar problems they faced when trying to build a road to connect two villages. In more densely populated areas, it is not uncommon for several communities to join together to level and pave with gravel a road that joins them. Yet when the physical space separating communities becomes quite large, paying for such a road becomes prohibitively costly. This distance turned a good that might be more intensive in labor in more densely populated areas to one that exhibited capital intensiveness in this remote region. The remoteness of these villages not only left them without a significant road that connected them to the rest of the district, but also without schools, educational facilities, and health clinics. According to a middle-aged Hazara female homemaker:

We have so many problems in our area. First, we can't seem to build a road. When we have to go to Bamiyan (the provincial capital) or somewhere else, we face so many obstacles. We have to pay 4000 Afghani (80 dollars) to get there. So if someone gets sick or needs to be taken to Bamiyan by one if his relatives that family must spent 8000 Afghani (160 dollars) to get there. Second, our village has no electricity. We want to be in the light like the others. There is a proverb: graves are places of darkness. So now we live in a place that is like a grave. It's so dark! We could never afford a generator nor could we afford fuel to run it. All the men and women in this village want the village to be a developed place. Us women want to have educational courses, like carpet weaving courses, tailoring courses, and even have a bakery for women who lack the facilities to bake bread in their own homes. We want to have a clinic and schools close to our village. In our manteqa (cluster of villages), all of us have tried to fix these issues, but it has been impossible. We want the government to pay attention to our village.[50]

It was clear when speaking to residents in this area that they had tried to work with neighboring villages to provide some of the goods described by the young woman earlier. This is because villagers frequently used the term manteqa, a Dari term which loosely translates into "area," or cluster, of villages, to

[50] Bamiyan-Panjab-Village 1-#4.

describe their collective dilemma.[51] With regard to some issues, informants spoke of problems within their village, but when describing larger scale issues they talked about the hopelessness of manteqa action. The manteqa in this case refers to a set of villages nestled in a very narrow and mountainous river valley.

Another woman in the community also complained about the about the lack of a road. She said she that everyone in the village has to go to the center of the district several kilometers away by foot. She says that she gets very tired from this long walk and what their village needed most is a small gravel road that connects the village to the outside world.[52] They have tried to organize this construction, but cannot do it because it is so expensive.

Other villagers said they had received some outside assistance for infrastructure projects including the construction of a school. From the NSP, the community received more than 40 solar panels to provide the village with electricity, but the residents were supposed to provide the battery cells to collect the solar energy themselves. A male elder in the community said that none of the communities in the village could afford these batteries, so the solar panels remained unused.[53] Upon visiting homes of informants, they proudly showed off their solar panels, which in all but a few cases remained boxed up. They brought them out to illustrate the assistance they had received from the international community, although they really had no use for them without the batteries.[54]

Villagers said that at least three development shuras were created in their community past five years: the CDC, a shura created by Oxfam (a British development NGO), and a shura created by the Food and Agriculture Organization of the United Nations (FAO).[55] The Oxfam shura distributed wheat and fertilizer to the village a few years ago. The FAO shura was established to implement a bee-keeping project in the village. Two boxes of bees were distributed by the FAO to the women in some families. An mullah said the project was good as they were able to "taste some honey from the bees."[56] But the bees died

---

[51] N. J. R. Allan, "Defining Place and People in Afghanistan," *Post Soviet Geography and Economics* 42, no. 8 (2001): 545–60; N. J. R. Allan, "Rethinking Governance in Afghanistan," *Journal of International Affairs* 56, no. 2 (2003): 193–203.

[52] Bamiyan-Panjab-Village 2-#2.   [53] Bamiyan-Panjab-Village 2-#8.

[54] The deputy governor of the Province, assuming I was an aid worker who had come to implement a project, berated me as a result of the proliferating solar panels in his province. He said that while it seemed fashionable among donors, he said that such panels had little economic or social value in the villages in the province. Specifically, he mentioned the fact that villagers rarely had the training or education to use them properly and that most could not afford to maintain them or buy batteries for the cells to store electricity. He said that the proliferation of such panels all over his province was such a waste because even when villagers could use the panels properly, they did not generate sufficient levels of electricity to help families engage in any productive economic activity. At best, they could power a television, but he noted that due to the remote nature of most communities, villages were outside of the range of TV broadcasts. Bamiyan-Provincial Capital-#4.

[55] Bamiyan-Panjab-Village 2-#8.   [56] Bamiyan-Panjab-Village 2-#6.

because "no one showed the people or trained them how to take care of the bees so that they wouldn't die."[57]

In Panjab, the physical proximity between communities increased costs of cooperation to build a simple gravel road that joined two villages. As a result, the road designed by the villagers had not yet been constructed. This case also provides insight into what is oftentimes a mismatch between what development organizations seek to provide and community aspirations.

Qarabagh District, Kabul Province

While self-governance did not always facilitate construction of roads, groups of communities were frequently able to come together to build mosques.[58] The importance of providing mosques as a public good is hard to overstate. In Afghanistan, mosques are important meeting places where male community members discuss matters of common interest. They serve as town halls in most rural communities. They are among the most important of public buildings, and in some areas, a single mosque services several communities.

Yet the provision of a mosque, given that a trained mullah is already present, is in many ways a much easier public good to provide than other kinds of public infrastructure. To illustrate, in Qarabagh District, Kabul Province, three neighboring villages had come together the year before to build a new mosque for their communities. The villages were close together and densely populated. The construction of the mosque involved construction materials, namely mud and bricks, which were available locally. Communities organized labor through hashar. The low cost of mosque construction enabled the communities to construct this without external assistance.

Although these communities could provide a mosque, informants complained that they could not organize themselves to provide the same area with a health clinic.[59] It was not that villagers valued a mosque over a clinic, but given available resources in the community, construction of a clinic required more resources than their communities could jointly offer. Women believed lack of health care was the most pressing problem facing their community, stating that the nearest clinic was so far away that they were unable to access health care (despite the fact that Kabul is just one hour away).[60] They expressed reluctance to send their own children to clinics.[61] In the absence of medical care, the mother of the village malik was providing folk remedies and acting as a midwife to other women in the community.[62] Unfortunately, the construction

---

[57] Bamiyan-Panjab-Village 2-#6.
[58] I cannot say with absolute certainty that there were villages in my sample that attempted to build mosques and failed to do so, but none of the informants mentioned such a failure.
[59] Kabul-Qarabagh-Village 2-#1.   [60] Kabul-Qarabagh-Village 2-#2.
[61] Kabul-Qarabagh-Village 2-#2.   [62] Kabul-Qarabagh-Village 2-#3.

of a clinic required not just a building, but materials and personnel that the community did not have the ability to provide without serious outside assistance.

The homogeneity and physical proximity of communities along with political stability and the low fixed costs associated with mosque construction allowed them to build the mosque quite easily. Communities were able to meet this demand without external assistance. Construction and staffing of a health clinic (and training of health care workers), on the other hand, was a task the village was not able to do on its own due to the high fixed costs associated with the project. As a result, this intra-communal good – a clinic that would serve several villages – was not built by the community despite enormous local demand and even attempts by some in the community to organize it.

Sorkhrod District, Nangarhar Province

Cooperation is common when it comes to managing access to irrigation water, although larger-scale infrastructure is often necessary to truly harness the value of water for communities. Informants in a village in Sorkhrod District, Nangarhar Province complained that they lacked resources to build a small hydroelectric dam in their village. Although there was a clear need, the cost of the dam proved to be too much for the community to overcome.

There was no denying the importance of investing in a dam. Informants mentioned that they wanted to construct a dam on the river to harness water for their fields. They also felt that construction of such a dam would generate hydro-electric power, thus giving them access to electricity.[63] The villages in this part of the district seemed to have decent relations with one another. When asked if they had any problems or conflicts with neighboring villages, a young man in the village responded, "No, we don't have any problems with our neighbors. We are all the same qawm."[64]

Villages were eager to cooperate and build the small dam, but lacked the capital necessary to build it. Construction of even a small dam exhibits high fixed costs (higher than that of a mosque because of the technology involved). Informants in the area believed that if only they had access to resources, they could cooperate to build the dam themselves. According to one merchant:

In Sorkhrod the NGOs have spent a lot of money on small things and if they had spent all of this money for that big dam it would have been enough for all the people [in this area]. We could have good agriculture. This is just basic work. When the NSP came here for the first time so many people in our village, even my [elderly] father asked them to please build that dam. People said that if this would happen they would collect money

---

[63] Nangarhar-Sorkhrod-Village 1-#3.   [64] Nangarhar-Sorkhrod-Village 1-#7.

from their land after each harvest to pay for the dam, NSP did not accept it. They wanted us to do small projects.[65]

Despite demand for a dam, high fixed costs in terms of wealth and technical expertise prevented it from being built.

Sorkhrod District, Nangarhar Province

In another area of Sorkhrod District, just a few miles away, two villages were struggling to provide a less costly public good: building access to an existing electrical grid. Yet lower fixed costs do not guarantee success. This case of two neighboring villages in Sorkhrod District, Nangarhar Province illustrates how group tension can become polarized in the face of political instability, and stymie possibilities of inter-communal cooperation.

The two communities in question were from different Pashtun sub-tribes. Yet their group differences were not an inherent problem. Informants said that mistrust between the two groups was not an issue before the war, but the two communities supported different groups during the decades of conflict, with one community lending to support to the Taliban out of political convenience not out of ideological reverence.

Group and political differences aside, both communities shared a common interest: they wanted to connect to a state-supported electrical grid, which was close to their communities. A female elder said that disputes between two tribes had prevented groups from working together. At various times in the recent past, residents tried to collect money among the relevant nearby villages to purchase wire and build poles to connect to a nearby grid. Informants believed they had the resources among the communities to fund such a project, but persistent tension between groups prevented the collaboration from taking place. In addition, an elderly woman described persistent fighting over land as well as various other local conflicts.[66]

Conflict seemed to pervade all issues confronting these communities. For example, one woman described how there was fighting between the two villages over the construction of a retaining wall. One community built a wall along the side of the road and the neighboring community said the wall obstructed passage on the road. One resident got so mad about the retaining wall that he attacked someone in the neighboring village. Here is a description of the conflict from a female in her late 60s who was the eyes and ears of the community through her in-home work as a seamstress:

One person named Nadir [from the neighboring village] attacked a guy named Emran [from our village]. Nadir had a knife and attacked Emran. Emran was not hurt seriously, but he went to the woluswal to complain. The woluswal said the communities should find a solution to the problem themselves and he referred the issue back to the maliks

---

[65] Nangarhar-Sorkhrod-Village 1-#5.   [66] Nangarhar-Sorkhrod-Village 2-#5.

and the village elders. The maliks and elders came together and decided that the wall is there and it should not be taken down. But in the future if there are future fights, the wall might have to come down. All of them agreed to this solution.[67]

Group heterogeneity that was tied to previous conflicts – thus introducing political instability to a region – appeared to hurt prospects for intra-communal cooperation in this community in Sorkhrod.

Khanabad District, Kunduz Province

In Khanabad District, Kunduz Province, several villages decided to organize a school for girls on their own without any external assistance. They desired a school and training programs because there was only a school for boys that was accessible to children. In addition, there were no female teachers in the vicinity. Residents wanted to bring in several female teachers from Kunduz City, the provincial capital, more than 20 kilometers away. They wanted to build the school and pay for its staff themselves.

Residents had approached the woluswal several times to help them find funds so that they could construct a school, as the temporary school they devised had just a few teachers and meets in a tent. The woluswal told the villagers that he was not in charge of his own budget – as all of his local plans are made by donors and government officials in Kabul – and had no discretionary funds to build a school and staff it with qualified teachers. Members of this village decided that they would have to find the teachers and pay for them out of their own pockets.[68]

The elders of the community came together to try to fund this project but were unable to come up with the funds on their own. Despite their best efforts, the large number of villages who came together to build the school could not agree on how to manage funds for the project. Residents did not trust individuals in neighboring villages to manage funds wisely, despite the fact that all villages in the area were from the same ethnic group. Accordingly, they again appealed to the government and were persistent in their complaints. Residents even appealed to the district governor. Once again, the district governor said he was powerless to build this school. If they wanted a school, then they would have to build it and staff it themselves.[69]

---

[67] Nangarhar-Sorkhrod-Village 2-#5. Once again this is an example of the government using restorative rather than punitive justice to solve a problem. Community members seemed to be much more satisfied with the government when it relied upon restorative justice (despite the fact that it was not legally mandated to do so).

[68] This was a phenomena I saw elsewhere in rural Afghanistan where teachers were scarce. Communities would work to recruit teachers on their own and provide them with a salary, room, and board. Paying for teachers was clearly a government responsibility, but many informants were unwilling to wait for the government to act on this. Many communities took up teacher staffing on their own.

[69] Kunduz-Khanabad-Village 2-#6.

In this case, communities were unable to complete the project due to the large numbers of communities necessary to achieve cooperation and because building a school and staffing it was expensive. People in this area felt that they could afford the cost of the school and teacher salaries, but the large number of communities created obstacles to cooperation.

CONCLUSION

The case studies provide insight into why communities succeed and why they fail in their effort to govern collectively. The broad finding that communities sometimes come together affirms an insight of the literature on regional governance, which is that relatively autonomous communities can govern together even without an external enforcer. The case studies also provide some insight into the mechanisms sustaining cooperation. As the empirical studies illustrated, cooperation is more likely when there are a small number of villages, the public goods in question have limited geographic scale, they are labor intensive, participants are homogenous, and there is some degree of political stability.

In addition to contributing to our understanding of the dynamics of cooperation in a general sense, the findings presented in this chapter have important implications for the state-building process in Afghanistan. For several categories of public goods, state intervention into community affairs did not seem pressing, such as to help communities manage irrigation water in communities where a mirab exists. Villages also seemed quite capable of building mosques without external assistance. The demands for outside intervention were specific to the context of the communities in question.

This diagnostic approach to public goods provision helps us understand where the state should concentrate its efforts in order to improve the lives of residents in rural areas. Most external assistance rural residents described were community development projects, where residents could select from a menu of community development projects. Frequently the most pressing goods they desired were not community-based, but were at a larger scale. Many donors and military actors seemed to have an obsession with villages in rural Afghanistan as the site of most legitimate political action. While village governing organizations may feature extraordinary legitimacy, such a wealth of informal political institutions at this level meant that more attention was required elsewhere – not at the village level.

The lack of a match between goods provided and community demands in the face of vast resources given to community development efforts in Afghanistan suggests that community development may not be the greatest challenge facing the country. Instead, the most important challenges are at the intra-communal level. It is at this nexus where self-governing mechanisms frequently struggle to quickly and cost-effectively generate important public goods demanded by residents.

To this point, the state has been considered only in the background. The next two chapters consider explicitly the relationship between village governance and the state.

PART III

CUSTOMARY GOVERNANCE AND THE STATE

6

Customary organizations and support for the state

Does the presence of customary organizations undermine individual support for the state or values associated with democracy? There is a long tradition in social science positing that the presence of customary authority undermines prospects for consolidation of the state. Indeed, popular images of Afghanistan depict the country as one that is inherently ungovernable because of the opposition of nonstate entities to central government control. In addition, customary organizations, regardless of their attitudes toward particular governments, may undermine core values essential to promoting democracy.

The literature on state building and consolidation is rich with a litany of assumptions regarding the nature of conflict between customary order, the state, and democracy. These assumptions can be recast as hypotheses. This chapter asks whether the presence of customary organizations undermines support for the state itself, democratic values, or both. Such perceptions of irreconcilability between informal and formal orders are more than intellectual questions, but are increasingly central policy questions in many fragile states around the world.

The findings of this chapter may come as a surprise. Contrary to conventional wisdom, customary organizations do not undermine support for the state. In some instances their presence is associated with increased support for the state as well as democratic values, such as support for gender equality. The findings also indicate that awareness of only a few kinds of foreign aid programs is associated with increased support for the state, yet for most projects, the effect is negligible. All told, the findings do not support the contention that customary organizations are an obstacle to consolidation of state authority and democracy in the Afghan context. To the contrary, their presence is in some situations, associated with stronger support for the central government and democracy.

COMPETING LOYALTIES, COMPETING VALUES, AND STATE BUILDING

There are two main explanations as to why customary and traditional orders are hypothesized to undermine state-building prospects. The first is by generating loyalties that compete with those of the emerging state. This view can be attributed to Weber, who stressed the tensions between societies based on traditional or charismatic rules and bureaucracies grounded in rational rules. In the Weberian vision of political development, rational bureaucracy grounded in legal authority can only come about when individuals shed devotion to non-state organizations rooted in religion or tradition. State building, from this perspective, transforms societies rooted in tradition and tribalism to a rational form of governance where laws come primarily from the state. State consolidation requires the replacement of non-state orders with state-made rules.

More recently, scholars have suggested that strong local organizations deriving their authority from sources outside the state can hinder political and economic development. As Joel Migdal observed, "societies in which social control is vested in numerous local-level social organizations... [are] fragmented societies."[1] Where social structure is marked by resilient non-state political organizations, Migdal argues, such fragmentation limits the ability of states to govern effectively and to implement "developmental" policies. Likewise, where such organizations have been weakened, "state leaders have greater opportunities to apply a single set of rules – the state's rules – and to build channels for widespread sustained political support."[2] Similarly, Peter Evans argued that government actors will have the greatest opportunity to achieve policy success when the state can act autonomously from societal actors.[3] These perspectives suggest that competing loyalties will continually frustrate efforts of state builders in their efforts to achieve political development.

Economic approaches to state–society relations also assume an incongruity between customary organizations and the rule of law, which is necessary to coordinate society. The divide is often depicted as a conflict between relation-based systems, which bind individuals in personal exchange through their community-based reputations, and rule-based systems, which are based on formal contracts or transparent laws enforced by the state.[4] Prior to the

---

[1] Migdal, *Strong Societies and Weak States : State-Society Relations and State Capabilities in the Third World*, 428-9.

[2] Ibid. 428.

[3] Peter Evans, Embedded Autonomy: States and Industrial Transformation (Princeton, NJ: Princeton University Press, 1995).

[4] See, for example, Greif, *Institutions and the Path to the Modern Economy*; and Dixit *Lawlessness and Economics: Alternative Modes of Governance* (Princeton, NJ: Princeton University Press, 2004). One of the early works on reputational contracting is Macaulay "Non-Contractual Relations in Business: A Preliminary Study," *American Sociological Review* 28, no. 1 (1963): 55–67.

establishment of rule-based governance, organizations often rely on personal and implicit agreements, without much help from the state to enforce contracts.[5] Generally speaking, relation-based organizations can work effectively if the numbers of partners are small, whereas rule-based governance is necessary to take advantage of economic opportunities when societies grow.[6]

Both political and economic perspectives depict an inherent conflict between relation-based and rule-based institutions. The presence of relation-based organizations can lead to political instability and civil war. For example, emergence of parallel contracting systems may lead to distrust of state institutions as individuals withdraw from formal politics.[7]

Competing values inherent in customary organizations are a second obstacle to state consolidation. Contemporary state-building efforts seek not simply to build a more effective system of public administration whose tentacles extend down to the local level, but also seek to consolidate and build democratic order in the form of liberal peacebuilding. If authoritarianism and predatory rule contribute to state failure, then democracy should prove a healthy antidote to cure the ills of failing states.[8] Thus, another implicit goal of contemporary state construction activities is to engineer social norms that support democratic values.

Although there is agreement among states and international organizations promoting liberal peacebuilding efforts that state building and democracy promotion go hand-in-hand, there is also a strong presumption that customary governance is antithetical to democracy. Furthermore, important groups, such as women, are usually excluded from participation in the day-to-day activities of customary governance. For these reasons, international donors encourage local policymakers to side step customary governance structures because they consider them to be "anachronistic remnants of less enlightened epoch [not] adequate to the task of governance of a modern society.... [and] part of the problem of parochial populism or traditional fundamentalism."[9]

---

[5] Greif, *Institutions and the Path to the Modern Economy*.

[6] Dixit, *Lawlessness and Economics*; North, *Institutions, Institutional Change, and Economic Performance*.

[7] Diego Gambetta, *The Sicilian Mafia: The Business of Private Protection* (Cambridge, MA: Harvard University Press, 1996); Skaperdas, "The Political Economy of Organized Crime"; Stergios Skaperdas, "An Economic Approach to Analyzing Civil Wars," *Economics of Governance* 9, no. 1 (2008): 25–44; Federico Varese, *The Russian Mafia: Private Protection in a New Market Economy* (New York: Oxford University Press, 2005); Vadim Volkov, *Violent Entrepreneurs: The Use of Force in the Making of Russian Capitalism* (Ithaca, NY: Cornell University Press, 2002).

[8] Acemoglu and Robinson, *Why Nations Fail*.

[9] Samuel Bowles and Herbert Gintis, "Social Capital and Community Governance," *The Economic Journal* 112, no. 483 (2002): F428–F429.

These perspectives on the relationship between democracy and customary authority is likely a remnant of modernization theory, which argued that as countries experience economic growth and individuals become more mobile, dense ties to their communities will fade away.[10] Sweeping cultural change is expected to accompany economic development.[11] Daniel Lerner was one of the first scholars to apply the modernization ethos to predominantly Muslim societies.[12] In his book, aptly titled *The Passing of Traditional Society*, Lerner maintained that throughout the Muslim world there is an inherent contradiction between the forces supporting economic growth, political participation, and traditional or customary values.[13] Democracy, he argued, is the final stage in a process of modernization, one which arrives only after a system of "self-sustaining" economic growth has been achieved. Lerner gathered an impressive array of survey data from Middle Eastern countries, grouping individuals into three separate categories: traditionalists, modernists, and those in between: the transitionalists. According to his findings, those who participate in traditional society are less likely to be educated, less exposed to media, far less mobile, less supportive of a free media, and less able to express opinions on a wide range of political issues. The modernization paradigm is instructive because it predicts that "traditional" societies will not only be underdeveloped, they will be less likely to support democratic values. In this view, traditional life breeds an illiberal society.

Despite critiques of modernization, there is an almost undeniable relationship between economic development and "culture" uncovered by economists interested in long-run economic growth.[14] These studies have led to a new concern with cultural change in the effort to get the institutions "right." There is widespread agreement that institutions matter but since institutions are culturally contingent, it is important to take culture seriously to understand

---

[10] Karl Wolfgang Deutsch, *The Nerves of Government* (New York: Free Press, 1963); Seymour Martin Lipset, "Some Social Requisites of Democracy: Economic Development and Political Legitimacy," *The American Political Science Review* 53, no. 1 (1959): 69–105.

[11] Samuel Huntington, *Political Order in Changing Societies* (New Haven, CT: Yale University Press, 1968).

[12] *The Passing of Traditional Society: Modernizing the Middle East* (Glencoe, IL: Free Press, 1958).

[13] For more recent perspectives see Michael Ross "Oil, Islam, and Women," *American Political Science Review* 102, no. 1 (2008): 107–23; and Kuran, *The Long Divergence*. Ross argues that in the Middle East it is oil and not Islam that inhibits female participation, because in countries that are reliant on oil revenue, fewer women will participate in economic activity. Nonetheless, he attributes the lack of female engagement in these societies to the maintenance of traditionalism in oil rich states.

[14] Yuriy Gorodnichenko and Gerard Roland, "Culture, Institutions and the Wealth of Nations," Working Paper (Washington, DC: National Bureau of Economic Research, 2010); Yuriy Gorodnichenko and Gerard Roland, "Which Dimensions of Culture Matter for Long-Run Growth?," *American Economic Review* 101, no. 3 (2011): 492–98; Avner Greif and Guido Tabellini, "Cultural and Institutional Bifurcation: China and Europe Compared," *The American Economic Review* 100, no. 2 (2010): 135–40.

prospects for economic development. A key purpose of post-conflict reconstruction efforts, for example, is "to change the preferences and opportunities
of the members of the country... to foster preference for freedom, democracy,
the rule of law, markets, and tolerance".[15] Christopher Coyne suggests that
most reconstruction efforts fail because the norms "imposed" by foreigners and
state builders are not grounded in the "informal everyday practices of a
society."[16] In other words, one of the reasons why reconstruction efforts fail
is because "modern" norms clash with "traditional" values.

STATE BUILDING IN AFGHANISTAN

These debates are more than an intellectual concern, as they have informed
policies in Afghanistan. The seemingly quick collapse of the Taliban led to a
two-pronged approach to state-building: a bottom-up effort to strengthen
citizen support of the state at the local level through massive public goods
provision accompanied by top-down institutional building at the national
level.[17] The idea behind the strategy was to overcome or co-opt nonstate
sources of authority and bring them under the umbrella of the state. These
non-state sources included not just former warlords and their associated political parties, but customary authority as well. The institutional strengthening
component focused overwhelmingly on national-level political organizations
including a full slate of national-level elections along with strengthening of
myriad line ministries in Kabul. New formal bodies at the local level would
be joined to the strengthened ministries in Kabul. The "bottom-up" part of the
strategy involving linking the central government to communities through new
donor and government supported bodies, the CDCs. There was no effort to
engage, at least through formal channels, with customary authority.

Proponents of this two-pronged strategy believed that the people of Afghanistan would associate the enormous amount of aid they received at the local level
with a renewed sense of state legitimacy. The plan was for the state to improve
its legitimacy as citizens witnessed the provision of vast amounts of public
goods and services.[18] Foreign aid promised to enhance the legitimacy of the

---

[15] Christopher Coyne, *After War: The Political Economy of Exporting Democracy* (Palo Alto, CA:
Stanford Economics and Finance, 2007), 28.
[16] Ibid.
[17] This strategy was formally articulated in the Afghanistan National Development Strategy in
2007, but was previously articulated in the Interim Afghanistan national Development Strategy
(I-ANDS) as well as the London Compact (2006), an international agreement that affirmed
international donor support for state building efforts in Afghanistan – both at the national and
subnational levels as well as the initial Bonn Agreement in 2001. These development strategies
were also heavily tied to the Millennium Development Goals (MDGs) of the United Nations.
[18] On the logic and evidence regarding whether winning hearts and minds works see Berman et al.,
"Can Hearts and Minds Be Bought? The Economics of Counterinsurgency in Iraq," *Journal of
Political Economy* 119, no. 4 (2011): 766–819.

state provided it was properly channeled and implemented.[19] In particular, the visibility of a few projects could have an important impact, convincing individuals that the new government is one for which it is worth taking risks or making sacrifices. The logic behind these ideas is that aid could somehow break a vicious cycle of mistrust between individuals and the state: if individuals see the government providing public goods and services (subsidized by aid), then they will be more likely to support the state by playing by the rules of the state and swearing allegiance to it. States thus win hearts and minds through service delivery. Eventually, citizens would become more willing to pay taxes because they experienced a government that was worthy of citizen support because it could deliver public goods and services. Donor funding, in this view, is a short-term phenomenon intended to help jumpstart governance and improve trust in the government. According to this perspective, public goods provision, subsidized by the international community, helps citizens in states wracked by prolonged conflict break vicious cycles of bad governance.

In this strategy, new governments can gain legitimacy not only by providing public goods, but by promoting the appearance that things are moving forward. This can be done through small but visible projects that may not dramatically improve public goods provision yet instill in confidence among community members. Some even argue that the state "can only be legitimized through its provision of public goods to its populations; without these goods, it degenerates into a mere conspiracy for oppression and distortion."[20]

Public goods provision – especially the provision of infrastructure – also promises to reduce incentives to participate in socially costly activities. In rational choice theories of rebellion, incentives to rebel depend on opportunity costs. When public goods provision is high, people have to forgo more in order to wage war against the state under the assumption that open conflict will lead to a reduction in public goods provision.[21] A complementary implication relating public goods and state support can be derived from sociological approaches to state consolidation that emphasize dense networks between citizens and the government. Efforts to gain citizen support through public goods provision can be viewed as a kind of patronage or neo-patrimonialism that permeates state-society relations.[22] Neo-patrimonialism arises from governments seeking to gain "vertical legitimacy" and stability through redistribution and patronage.[23] From this perspective, public goods

[19] Ghani and Lockhart, *Fixing Failed States*; Stephen D. Krasner and Carlos Pascual, "Addressing State Failure," *Foreign Affairs* 84, no. 4 (2005): 153–63.

[20] Clapham, "The Challenge to the State in a Globalized World," 779.

[21] Paul Collier and Anke Hoeffler, "Greed and Grievance in Civil War," *Oxford Economic Papers* 56, no. 4 (2004): 563–95; Collier, *Wars, Guns and Votes*; Fearon and Laitin, "Ethnicity, Insurgency, and Civil War."

[22] Eisenstadt, *Traditional Patrimonialism and Modern Neopatrimonialism*; Jackson, *Quasi-States*.

[23] Pierre Englebert, *State Legitimacy and Development in Africa* (Boulder, CO: Rienner, 2000).

provision is part of a neo-patrimonial bargain that serves to consolidate state authority by increasing the ties that bind the government to citizens. These theories suggest increasing public good provision can facilitate state consolidation.[24]

In Afghanistan, the plans for strengthening state support relied heavily on aid effectiveness. Policymakers hoped that as aid produced local quiescence, state-builders at the national level could proceed to "get the institutions right" by strengthening ministerial capabilities in Kabul. Together, creation of new political organizations and provision of public goods promised a new kind of political "modernization" whereby individuals would shed their local loyalties and even customary practices and develop esteem for the national state. In the years before 2007, it was hoped that this two-pronged strategy of large-scale institutional reform and aid at the local level would build allegiances to the government, thereby helping the government break the vicious cycle of promising but never producing improvements in provision of important goods and services. In addition, institutional strengthening of various ministries would ensure capacity to produce in the long term. That was the plan.[25]

After several years of pouring billions of dollars in assistance, the renewed Taliban insurgency provided fairly clear evidence this approach had not yielded the desired results.[26] The Taliban regrouped in neighboring Pakistan and began a full scale insurgency in southern and eastern Afghanistan that eventually spread throughout the country, intent on toppling the Afghan government.[27] A renewed Taliban had a mission: not only was it fighting to return the country to principles of shariat, but it sought to rid the country of the new Western presence. Most importantly, the Taliban made its case by pointing to ongoing corruption in the Government of Afghanistan, which had been unable to deliver on its promise to help the Afghan people.[28]

---

[24] For a fuller explanation of the relationship between revolutionary threat, economic development, and public goods see Jennifer Brick Murtazashvili, "Coloured by Revolution: The Political Economy of Autocratic Stability in Uzbekistan," *Democratization* 19, no. 1 (2012): 78–97.

[25] For an articulation of this "two-pronged" approach to strengthening fragile states by the World Bank, see Sarah Cliffe, Scott Guggenheim, and Markus Kostner, "Community-Driven Reconstruction as an Instrument in War-to-Peace Transitions" (Washington, DC: World Bank, 2003).

[26] Some observers have argued that aid levels during this period were very low and that the rebellion emerged as a result of the absence of aid. Based on my fieldwork, I did not sense that most people in rural areas shared this view. As has already been illustrated, most informants could detail several large scale projects that had affected their communities by the time of this field research in 2007. This was before the largest amounts of civilian and military assistance came to communities through "surge" funding.

[27] Sarah Chayes, *The Punishment of Virtue: Inside Afghanistan after the Taliban* (New York: Penguin, 2007).

[28] Sandy Gall, *War Against the Taliban: Why It All Went Wrong in Afghanistan* (New York: Bloomsbury Publishing, 2012).

Growing sense of corruption among Afghan bureaucrats at all level and the inability of aid to be delivered effectively undermined state-building efforts. Analysts observed that it was efforts to extend the state – and the corruption that accompanied such efforts – that was a driver of the renewed insurgency.[29]

Around 2006 there was a change in the state-building strategy. After witnessing an uptick in fighting in the southern and eastern parts of the country, a new approach emerged from an unlikely source: The U.S. military. Unlike the planners in Kabul or in Washington, the boots on the ground in the Afghan countryside began to understand that efforts to build the state in Kabul, which appeared to be corrupt at its core, sparked a backlash among those in rural areas. To fight the Taliban, military operations began to partner increasingly – and often in an ad hoc manner – with customary leaders and tribal elders in the countryside – leaders they realized were far more important for maintaining the legitimacy of their operations than the cooperation of local bureaucrats, who were either paralyzed to inaction or corrupted by the centralized system of government. The evolving approach in Afghanistan was also being refined elsewhere. While the U.S. appeared to be stuck in an Afghan quagmire, U.S. efforts in Iraq appeared to be turning around at this time. The Sunni or Anbar awakening in Iraq appeared to be based on the ability of the U.S. military and coalition partners to effectively partner with tribal structures in Iraq.[30] There appeared to be a growing consensus among Americans involved in counter-insurgency efforts in Afghanistan that customary authority could be engaged effectively to defeat the growing Taliban insurgency.

Many of these soldiers advocated for a new strategy, posting calls and ideas for change on blogs and internet sites, such as *Long War Journal* or *Small Wars Journal*. One of the most well-known pieces from this period was written by U.S. Army Major Jim Gant, who after several tours in Afghanistan argued that it would be impossible to win the war effort unless the U.S. military worked more closely with "tribes" or customary leaders. In his view, if forces spent more time gaining support of customary leaders, who were in his view the legitimate representatives of the people, they would be more likely to defeat the Taliban. His analysis was premised on the notion that customary leaders were often victims of Taliban attacks and thus predisposed to oppose insurgents. In his widely circulated think-piece, *One Tribe at a Time*, Gant outlined a new plan for fighting the Taliban insurgency based on Tribal Engagement Teams who would embed in villages and gain the trust of villagers at this level. As Gant explained, "with the central government still weak and corrupt, the tribes are the only enduring source of local authority and

---

[29] Sarah Chayes, *Thieves of State: Why Corruption Threatens Global Security* (New York: W. W. Norton & Company, 2015).
[30] Lynch, "Explaining the Awakening."

security in the country."[31] One writer went so far as to proclaim, "It's the Tribes, Stupid!"[32]

Commanders in the U.S. military who served both in Afghanistan and Iraq, including Generals David Petraeus and Stanley McChrystal, understood that tribal and other customary governance structures were important sources of information as well as loyalty. Indeed, the centerpiece of this new approach to war efforts in Afghanistan was outlined in the new U.S. Army Counterinsurgency Field Manual.[33] Official doctrine in the manual called for soldiers to actively engage the "human terrain" in their communities, with a special focus on "traditional" authority. The field manual includes instructions on how to develop analytical tools so that soldiers can better understand their operational environments. In addition, David Kilcullen, an advisor to Petraeus and former member of the Australian military, wrote an influential book on counterinsurgency that reflected these changing views. Kilcullen's *The Accidental Guerilla* stressed the importance of engaging with customary and tribal structures to defeat insurgent Islamic fundamentalists, including the Taliban in Afghanistan.[34] Counterinsurgency and state-building, in this view, were mutually reinforcing processes.

Like those in the development community, those in the U.S. military believed that provision of public goods to citizens was critical to winning hearts and minds. Yet a key difference was that the military engaged with customary governance and even sought to strengthen it when doing so promised to help fight a rising insurgency. The military had no ideological objection of working directly with customary leaders if such efforts helped win "hearts and minds." Unlike many of the state-building efforts by international organizations and NGOs, military efforts were far more comfortable negotiating the difficult "human terrain" of customary organizations in the countryside. Instead of viewing customary governance as adversaries to their efforts, as was the case among many in the aid community, the military took a different approach recognizing that gaining support of maliks and even mullahs would help channel the will of the population. In addition, during this second phase of state-building efforts, the amount of aid allotted to the U.S. and NATO military forces increased substantially.

---

[31] Ann Scott Tyson, "Jim Gant, the Green Beret who could win the war in Afghanistan." *The Washington Post*, January 15, 2010, www.washingtonpost.com/wp-dyn/content/article/2010/01/15/AR2010011502203.html.

[32] Writer Steven Pressfield has an online blog where he edited many of the arguments these soldiers, including Major Gant, made about tribes www.stevenpressfield.com/vblog.
He posits that understanding the "tribal mindset" is crucial to winning the "War against Terror."

[33] Nagl et al., *The U.S. Army/Marine Corps Counterinsurgency Field Manual.*

[34] David Kilcullen, *The Accidental Guerrilla: Fighting Small Wars in the Midst of a Big One* (New York: Oxford University Press, 2009).

Taking cues from the field manual, efforts to "win hearts and minds" in rural Afghanistan involved building small scale infrastructure projects. Counterinsurgency strategy was not an ideological pursuit of democratization and there was no concerted push to establish democracy at the village level. The Counterinsurgency Field Manual makes no mention of democracy. Rather, it only mentions that the population is interested in "political participation" and may take up arms because it has been denied a political right.[35] In fact, some soldiers, such as Gant, individually argued that customary governance in Afghanistan *is* democratic – or at least more democratic than the alternative offered by the government. He wrote, "What about democracy? A tribe is a 'natural democracy.' In Afghan shuras and jirgas (tribal councils), every man's voice has a chance to be heard. The fact that women and minority groups have no say in the process does not make it less effective or less of a democracy to them. Asking them to change the way they have always conducted their business through their jirgas and shuras just does not make sense."[36]

This leaves us with two fundamentally opposing views of customary organizations. On one hand, the international donor community largely viewed them as obstacles to the consolidation of a democratic state. On the other hand, a chorus in the military viewed gaining allegiance of such authority as key to defeating the Taliban. The findings presented in earlier chapters illustrate the general effectiveness of customary organizations at the village level. Although most theories of the state have long assumed that they are an obstacle to a consolidating state, it may be the case that those who participate in customary organizations in Afghanistan may be socialized in ways that make them more likely to accept a rational bureaucracy and even democracy. They may be a complement, rather than an obstacle for new governments.

CUSTOMARY GOVERNANCE, FOREIGN AID, AND THE STATE: HYPOTHESES

The perspectives described in the previous section, which suggest a deep irreconcilability between customary order and the demands of a modern state, can be formulated as hypotheses regarding the relationship between customary organizations and the state. The sociological and modernization perspectives view state building and consolidation as a largely linear progression in which a rational-legal state subjugates or replaces customary order.[37]

---

[35] Nagl et al., *The U.S. Army/Marine Corps Counterinsurgency Field Manual*, 3–12.

[36] Maj. Jim Gant, *One Tribe at a Time: A Strategy for Success in Afghanistan* (Los Angeles: Nine Sisters Imports, Inc., 2009), 15.

[37] This view is also echoed in the U.S. Army/Marine Counterinsurgency Field Manual *The U.S. Army/Marine Corps Counterinsurgency Field Manual*. In chapter 3 of the Field Manual, pages 10–11, authority is defined as "legitimate power associated with social positions. It is justified by

Similarly, academic and popular accounts of state–society relations in Afghanistan suggest a fundamental conflict between customary or tribal organization and the demands of a modern state, leading to a fairly clear hypothesis regarding the relationship between customary organizations and a rational-legal state:

Hypothesis 1 (ungovernability hypothesis): Presence of customary organizations, or the degree to which individuals interact with customary organizations, will be negatively associated with support for the central government.

Modernization theories posit that customary organizations inhibit effective state development and in order for progress to be achieved, such archaic relics of the past must be swept away. In Afghanistan, the rationale for creating CDCs was largely based upon the presumption that introducing democratically-elected community decision-making bodies was a "viable alternative to the traditional local governance structure[s]."[38] These scholarly and policy perspectives suggest the following hypothesis:

Hypothesis 2 (democratic deficit hypothesis): The presence of customary organizations, or the degree to which individuals interact with customary organizations, will be negatively associated with support for democratic values.

The literature earlier suggests that by providing public goods, the state can reduce the return to organized violence as well as demonstrate to citizens the positive functions of a modern and effective state. According to this perspective, once individuals see that the state can provide public goods, they may be more willing participate in state-related activities, pay taxes, or at least cease resisting the state. In order to achieve calm, the state has to commit credibly to its promise to provide public goods. These observations suggest that support for the state will be higher when public goods provision is greater:

Hypothesis 3 (public goods hypothesis): Individuals who perceive they are receiving increased public goods from the state will exhibit higher levels of state support.

State-provided public goods are perhaps the most direct way to prove to citizens that the state is competent and capable of improving the lives of its citizens. Failed states, however, are defined in part by their inability to provide public goods.[39] As the state is largely unable to carry out basic functions, it must rely on third-parties such as international donors and NGOs to provide

---

the beliefs of the obedient." Then the manual describes the three ideal-types of Weberian authority (rational–legal, charismatic, and traditional).

[38] NSP Afghanistan Website (Page Title: "The most important achievement of the NSP to date") www.nspafghanistan.org/Default.aspx?Sel=103.

[39] Robert I. Rotberg, "The Failure and Collapse of Nation-States: Breakdown, Prevention, and Repair," in *When States Fail: Causes and Consequences* (Princeton, NJ: Princeton University Press, 2004), 1–49.

public goods in its absence. Aid can fill a governance gap when the government is unable to provide public goods. In many situations, foreign assistance substitutes for formal government in the countryside. The perspective on aid and democracy mentioned earlier suggests that when individuals are aware of aid to their communities, they will be more likely to support the central government as they realize that aid agencies are working at the behest of and in cooperation with the state:

Hypothesis 4 (foreign aid hypothesis): Awareness of international donor assistance will be associated with higher levels of individual support for the state.

Each of the perspectives described earlier offers hypotheses that are informed by important theories regarding the process by which state authority is consolidated. At the same time, evidence presented in previous chapters shows that customary organizations are not as obdurate or authoritarian as they are sometimes depicted in the Afghan context. The presence of fairly effective customary organizations at the village level suggests alternative hypotheses. I found few reasons to believe that customary organizations, or the individuals who support them, simply despise state authority. For example, one of the most important jobs of the malik is to liaise with the state. Rather than undermine cooperation with the state, the presence of customary organizations serves to facilitate cooperation with the state thus giving communities the ability to represent their interests to and bargain with the state. Furthermore, norms of deliberation and growing expectations among citizens that customary governance after 2001 serve citizens rather than elites suggested that they may not be a source of anti-democratic values, and in fact, be associated with support for norms commonly associated with democracy. My alternative hypotheses are as follows:

H1a. Presence of customary organizations will be positively associated with stronger individual support for the state.

H2a. Presence of customary organizations will be positively associated with individual support for democratic norms and values.

The earlier chapters showed that customary organizations are able to provide many small-scale public goods that do not exhibit large fixed costs, are spread out over a large geographic area, require the cooperation of just a few communities or a single community to produce, given a politically stable environment. This implies the effect of foreign aid will be conditional. Specifically, when individuals are aware of foreign aid distributed for small scale public goods or when they perceive improvements in the provision of such small scale goods, such provision will not be associated with increased support for the state. On the other hand, when communities receive larger scale public goods through aid or indicate that they feel improvements in such sectors, they will be more likely to support the state since it is precisely these larger-scale public goods that communities have difficulty providing on their own. These observations can be recast as the following hypotheses:

H3a, H4a. Foreign aid and public good provision is conditional: perception of improvements in the provision of small-scale public goods will not be associated with increased support for the state and democracy, while perceived improvements in the provision of larger-scale public goods will be positively associated with support for the state and democracy.

CUSTOMARY GOVERNANCE AND STATE BUILDING

To test these hypotheses, I use survey data commissioned by the Asia Foundation and the USAID in Afghanistan. The survey is a nationally-representative sample of 6,200 respondents. The purpose of the survey was to provide insight into public perceptions of the government, security, development, democracy, media and other issues in the country. The analysis here, as in Chapter 4, focuses solely on the rural subpopulation of 5,209 households in 566 villages, the primary sampling unit, across rural Afghanistan. The survey data were collected during the same period when the bulk of my village-level qualitative data were collected. Summary statistics for all variables in this chapter can be found in the Appendix B at the end of the book.

Assessing the ungovernability hypothesis

In the analysis of the ungovernability hypothesis, the dependent variable is support for the state, which is the assessment of central government performance measured on a scale of one to four. In the context of Afghanistan, it is fair to say that those who have a positive assessment of central government performance support the state, while those assess who have a negative assessment of performance are less supportive of the state.

At the time the survey was administered, individuals had fairly positive assessments of the performance of the central government, as most Afghans were still fairly optimistic about the future of the country. Only four percent said the government was doing a very bad job, while 16 percent said the government was doing a somewhat bad job. A majority of the population, nearly 56 percent, said the government was doing a somewhat good job and a quarter of the population said the government was doing a very good job.

As the dependent variable is measured on a scale from one to four, the empirical analysis utilizes an ordered logit model. Estimation takes into account the unique design of the public opinion survey, including clustering of villages as well as population sampling weights.

The key independent variables measure the presence as well as the effectiveness of customary organizations at the village level. The shura variable is constructed from a survey question in which respondents were asked to agree or disagree (on a scale of one to four) as to whether their village shura or jirga is accessible to them.[40] Of the rural population, 40 percent believe their shuras are accessible, 46 percent somewhat agree, 10 percent disagree somewhat, while only 4 percent of the population strongly disagree that their village councils are accessible. A measure the effectiveness of shuras and jirgas was also included in the models. Specifically, the survey asked whether villagers believe their shuras or jirgas are fair and trusted. The inclusion of this variable in the model allows us to assess not only the presence of customary organizations, but also to explore whether perceptions of effectiveness of customary organizations relate to state support. Of the respondents, 32 percent strongly agreed that their shuras or jirgas are fair and trusted, 49 percent somewhat agreed, 16 percent disagreed somewhat, while only 3 percent strongly disagreed.[41]

In addition to the shura/jirga measures, the models include two additional variables measuring the presence of other customary bodies. The best available indicator measuring the presence of maliks and mullahs in a community is captured by responses to questions asking villagers whom they rely on for information in their community. In rural Afghanistan, just over 13 percent said maliks are a source of local information, while 11 percent said they got most of their information from mullahs. The other important organizational variable of interest is presence of a CDCs in communities. Thirty seven percent of respondents said they had a CDC in their community.

In addition to variables of theoretical interest models control for income, education, gender (whether the respondent was a female), age, and region (the same controls used in similar models in Chapter 4). The results of the statistical analysis are in Table 6.1. In model 1, the dependent variable is assessment of central government performance (described earlier). The findings of this model show that access to customary organizations either has no association with or is positively associated with assessments of central government performance. Individuals who receive information from their mullah or malik are more likely to have a positive assessment of central government performance. These variables are both statistically significant at the 1 percent level. The accessibility of a shura or jirga is not positively or negatively associated with perceptions of central government performance. Most importantly, accessibly to shuras or jirgas does not have the negative effect suggested by the ungovernability hypothesis. In fact, respondents who trust their shura or jirga are more likely to give their government high marks for performance (at the .05 level). These results suggest that customary organizations do not hinder and in some situations actually serve to increase how individuals perceive the performance of the central government. Higher

---

[40] See Chapter 4 for a longer discussion of the construction of this variable.
[41] In pairwise tests, the accessibility of shuras/jirgas was not correlated to whether individuals perceive them as fair and trusted.

TABLE 6.1: *Relationship between Customary Organizations and State Support, Democratic Values*

Dependent Variables	Central Government Performance	Is Afghanistan Moving in the Right Direction	Is Your Vote Influential	Would You Tolerate a Friend in an Opposing Political Party	Opposition Is Good for Afghanistan	Do You Support Equal Rights for Women?
	Model 1	Model 2	Model 3	Model 4	Model 5	Model 6
Info from Mullah	0.569***	0.001	0.037	-0.096	0.216*	-0.125
	[0.149]	[0.130]	[0.133]	[0.144]	[0.122]	[0.116]
Info from Malik	0.287***	-0.032	-0.118	0.004	0.139	0.021
	[0.104]	[0.102]	[0.122]	[0.119]	[0.105]	[0.120]
Shuras/Jirgas Fair or Trusted	0.158**	0.108*	-0.001	0.109	0.136*	0.152**
	[0.069]	[0.058]	[0.073]	[0.073]	[0.071]	[0.066]
Shuras/Jirgas Accessible	0.115	-0.068	0.164**	0.147*	0.213***	0.246***
	[0.076]	[0.052]	[0.065]	[0.079]	[0.068]	[0.065]
CDC in Community	-0.041	0.055	-0.027	0.296**	0.008	0.163*
	[0.095]	[0.083]	[0.105]	[0.115]	[0.094]	[0.098]
Income	-0.123***	-0.006	-0.042	0.044	-0.037	-0.015
	[0.033]	[0.033]	[0.036]	[0.043]	[0.036]	[0.036]
Education	0.050**	0.025	0.029	-0.002	0.027	0.052**
	[0.021]	[0.018]	[0.025]	[0.022]	[0.021]	[0.022]
Female	0.316***	0.354***	0.237*	0.026	-0.005	0.365***
	[0.118]	[0.099]	[0.126]	[0.133]	[0.117]	[0.125]
Age	-0.026	-0.263	-0.326	0.046	0.106	0.056
	[0.240]	[0.241]	[0.295]	[0.272]	[0.260]	[0.265]
Listen to Radio	0.125	0.394***	0.301***	0.213**	0.287***	0.323***
	[0.086]	[0.079]	[0.098]	[0.098]	[0.088]	[0.087]

(continued)

TABLE 6.1 (continued)

Dependent Variables	Central Government Performance	Is Afghanistan Moving in the Right Direction	Is Your Vote Influential	Would You Tolerate a Friend in an Opposing Political Party	Opposition Is Good for Afghanistan	Do You Support Equal Rights for Women?
	Model 1	Model 2	Model 3	Model 4	Model 5	Model 6
τ_1	-2.135***	-0.022			-1.857***	-2.685***
	[0.403]	[0.304]			[0.378]	[0.447]
τ_2	-0.305	1.186***			-0.682*	-0.765*
	[0.386]	[0.308]			[0.350]	[0.437]
τ_3	2.434***				1.379***	1.180***
	[0.391]				[0.361]	[0.409]
Constant			0.531	-2.018***		
			[0.345]	[0.405]		
Observations	4508	4347	4488	4439	4481	4581
Villages	565	564	565	564	565	565

Heteroskedasticty robust standard errors that correct for correlation of error terms within PSUs in brackets. Estimation also accounts for region, survey design including household weights and population sampling units. The baseline response in each model is a negative response to the specific question. Models 1,2,5,6: Ordered logit coefficients. Models 3 and 4: Logit coefficients.
* Significant at 10%; ** significant at 5%; *** significant at 1%.

trust for shuras and jirgas is associated with more positive views of central government performance.

Statistical tests were also conducted on two other dependent variables that serve as proximate measures for state support: whether individuals believe Afghanistan is moving in the right direction (model 2) and whether individuals believe their vote in national elections is influential (model 3). State-building efforts in Afghanistan had early success with the administration of two national elections: presidential elections in 2004 and parliamentary elections in 2005. Given security challenges and local sensitivities in Afghanistan, respondents might be hesitant to rate the government poorly in such a direct manner as a public opinion poll. Respondents who might be hesitant to criticize the government may be more likely to express their preferences using these two alternative dependent variables. Of the rural subpopulation, only 26 percent believed the country was moving in the wrong direction, 27 percent believed the country was moving neither in the right nor the wrong direction, while over 45 percent said the country was moving in the right direction. Once again, nearly a majority expressed an optimistic view about the progress of the country at that time. Rural Afghans also believed that their votes for national elections had an influence: nearly 76 percent of the rural population believed their vote matters, while 24 percent disagreed. It is important to note that this survey was taken before the massively fraudulent national elections between that captured national attention between 2009 and 2014.[42]

The ungovernability hypothesis can also be rejected using these two alternative measures of state support. In models 2 and 3, most of the organizational variables of interest are not statistically significant – but this lack of statistical significance is important in disproving the ungovernability hypothesis (which predicts a negative relationship that is statistically significant). In model 3, once again customary organizations are positively associated with individuals believing their vote is influential. Accessibility to shuras and jirgas is positively associated with individuals believing their vote in Afghan elections is influential.

In addition to rejecting the democratic deficit hypothesis, presence of a CDC in a community is not positively associated with assessments of central government performance or beliefs that Afghanistan is moving in the right direction. This finding is important as many in the foreign donor community, contended that the informal elections supposedly held in CDCs promote and sustain democratic values not previously shared by villagers. The analysis here demonstrates that CDCs do not seem to deliver on their promise to increase support for the central government.

---

[42] There is widespread evidence that elections prior to 2009 were similarly corrupt, but they did not capture national public opinion in the same manner or threaten the stability of the state as the 2009 and subsequent elections.

Assessing the democratic deficit hypothesis

To analyze the democratic deficit hypothesis, the statistical models consider three different types of democratic norms as dependent variables: whether an individual would tolerate a friend who was a supporter or member of an opposing political party (model 4), belief in opposition as being good for Afghanistan (model 5), and support of equal rights for women (model 6). Tolerance for members of other political parties captures support for freedom of association, which is one of the main features of democracy. In general, the survey showed that most in rural Afghanistan did not appear to be amenable to having friends in opposing political parties: only 36 percent of the rural population would accept such a notion, while 74 percent disagreed. This lack of tolerance is largely due to the fact that political parties were synonymous with the armed militias that brought havoc and violence to the country over the course of the past three decades. Tolerance for opposition is also a key feature of democracy. Afghans sampled were far more optimistic in terms of viewing opposition as being good for the country: 43 percent strongly agree that that opposition is good for Afghanistan, 41 percent somewhat agree, 10 percent disagree somewhat while only 6 percent strongly disagree. Finally, gender equity is central to modern democracies. Afghans express some desire that all genders should share equal rights under the law: 61 percent strongly agree, 29 percent somewhat agree, 8 percent somewhat agree and just 2 percent strongly disagree.

The democratic deficit hypothesis implies that participation in customary organizations undermines democratic norms. Hence, we would expect that the presence of a shura or jirga would be negatively associated with tolerating a friend in an opposing political party, believing opposition is good for Afghanistan, as well as support for gender equity. Similarly, individuals who receive their information from maliks or mullahs are also expected to exhibit less support for norms associated with democracy.

Contrary to the democratic deficit hypothesis, the presence of shuras or jirgas is associated with stronger beliefs in democratic norms. Individuals who have access to a shura or jirga are more likely to tolerate friends in opposing political parties (in model 4 this variable is significant at the 10 percent level) and to believe political opposition groups are good for the future of Afghanistan (in model 5 this variable is significant at the 1 percent level). Most surprisingly, access to customary organizations is strongly associated with support for equal rights for women: in model 6, accessibility to shuras or jirgas is positively associated with support for equal rights for women (the variable is significant at the 1 percent level). The quality of customary governance also matters: when shuras or jirgas are fair and trusted, individuals are also more likely to believe that opposition is good for Afghanistan (model 5 variable is significant at the 10 percent level) and to support equal rights for women (model 6, variable is significant at the 5 percent level).

CDCs fare a little better in these models in that they seem to be more positively associated with increased support of democratic values than support for the central government. The presence of CDCs in a community is positively associated with some democratic values, such as whether an individual would tolerate a friend in a political party (in model 4 the CDC variable is significant at the 5 percent level) as well as whether an individual supports equal rights for women (significant at the 10 percent level). However, the overall association of CDCs with democratic values is lower than that of customary organizations. The findings question the basic rationale upon which CDCs were founded – that they were needed to fill a democratic deficit in the countryside.

Explaining the findings

The correlations above are informative, but we also need to understand the reasons for these findings. There are three main reasons why customary organizations serve to enhance support for the state and democratic values. First, customary organizations in Afghanistan historically have played a central role in the consolidation and legitimation of Afghan governments. The Loya Jirga has played an important role in supporting the state, not only during the inception of the Afghan state in 1747, but also in the post-2001 period. Thus, customary organizations and their representatives underpin even the formal constitutional system.

Of course, Afghanistan has been the site of many rebellions against the state. Yet the state per se was not what fueled the flames of protest, but rather, the kinds of policies pursued by the government. When state consolidation occurred gradually and was built upon local consent, as it did during the long peace of the Musahiban, the state and customary organizations worked together. Zahir Shah understood that reforms must be undertaken with careful consultation of the people and without haste. The expansion of the state during his reign was slow but deliberate and it generally met little resistance in the countryside.

Second, and most importantly, it appears that customary organizations embody values and norms that are largely consistent with those values in a representative democracy. Village councils represent the deliberative soul of communities. In fact, the term shura is derived directly from the Quran and literally translates as "consultation." The concept of shura has legitimacy in Afghan customary law, but also in Islamic law and practice. Sura 42 of the Quran is devoted to the topic of shura or consultation. Sura 42, verse 38 calls upon all Muslims to engage in consultation (shura) with other members of the community in matters of local affairs. The Prophet Mohammad is instructed to engage in regular consultation (shura) with his followers in Sura 3. Moreover, as we saw in Chapter 3, maliks typically enjoy the consent of the governed – they are not headmen. They are typically first among equals, and in most villages they must work for the citizens in order to maintain legitimacy and stay in power, especially in the political environment in rural communities found after 2001. In light of these customary norms, it is perhaps less surprising that the presence of a customary council does not undermine, and may even increase, support for both the state and democracy.

Third, customary organizations facilitate regular interactions with the government, as mediated through the relationship between maliks and woluswals. Although historically the state has been weak and formally centralized, citizens developed mechanisms to deal with the government, mainly through informal institutions that govern relations between village representatives and their district governors. The malik system has endured, representing community interests to the government at the local level throughout the past centuries. The system persisted under the monarchy, under communist rule, and during the civil war. Despite traumatic dispersion of local populations during the war, communities preserved this organization – not out of a romantic desire to maintain communal norms – but because it fulfilled a very important role. While villagers believe that maliks represent their interests, government officials expressed a belief that maliks are their partners in governance. Since rural residents who have access to maliks may have better access to the government, the presence of a customary organization is more likely to increase their belief in the virtues of formal government and democracy than those who do not have such relations.

PUBLIC GOODS, FOREIGN AID, AND STATE BUILDING

In contrast to the ungovernability hypothesis, which posits customary order as a source of opposition to the state, the public goods and foreign aid hypotheses seek to explain ways state-building efforts can increase support for the government. In the models that follow, perception of central government performance is the dependent variable. The key independent variables, in addition to measures of public goods provision (service delivery) and foreign aid, are the presence of a shura or jirga and a CDC in a community. Control variables are identical to those in the previous models.

In addition to testing hypotheses, the statistical analysis in this section also provides a robustness check on the analysis of the previous section. Many of the models in this section are similar to the previous set except for the inclusion of additional variables for public goods and foreign aid. One way to assess robustness of findings is to see whether the statistical relations hold when additional theoretically relevant variables are included in the models. In addition to finding little support for the public goods and foreign aid hypotheses, the results indicate that the conclusions regarding customary organizations and CDCs hold when additional variables are considered.

Public goods, foreign aid, and the state

To measure the availability of public goods, the analysis disaggregates perceived individual assessments of public goods across sectors. Individuals were asked to evaluate the availability of public goods in the following sectors: drinking water, irrigation water, availability of jobs, electricity supply, security situation, medical care, education, as well as freedom of movement. The responses are dichotomous, indicating perceptions of positive or negative availability of a range of public goods. The baseline in each model is a negative response (zero) to this dichotomous variable.

Another key variable asks individuals whether they are aware of aid in their community across the following domains: drinking water, irrigation water, road construction, healthcare, demining, demobilization, agricultural aid, mosque construction, as well as humanitarian assistance.[43] Awareness of aid is distinct from (and not correlated with) perceptions of the availability of goods in their area in these sectors. I assume that an overwhelming majority of aid channeled to communities is funded by international or external sources. While there are a few Afghan organizations implementing aid projects in Afghanistan, most of their funding comes from foreign donor assistance, as during this period the government did not have a substantial self-financed development budget nor were local NGOs effective in raising revenue from local donors. The vast majority of assistance to rural areas was implemented by foreign NGOs, contractors, as well as international military forces through Provincial Reconstruction Teams. Given the overall context of state weakness, the government relied almost entirely on third parties to implement its own projects (important exceptions included the army, police, teachers, and some health care workers).

To disentangle the effects of foreign aid and assistance on individual communities, I estimated these relationships using four distinct models presented in Table 6.2. The baseline model (model 7) is almost identical to the estimation in the previous section. It examines the relationship between various measures of customary organizations and assessments of central government performance. Model 8 includes individual assessments of access to public goods and services in their community across a range of sectors in addition to the variables in the baseline model. In Table 6.3 at the end of the chapter, I present correlation coefficients between these variables measuring public goods.

The results indicate that when individuals have positive assessments of their access to jobs, security, education, and freedom of movement they are likely to

---

[43] Demobilization aid is commonly referred to as disarmament, demobilization, and reintegration (DDR). It is assistance provided to combatants that encourages them to give up their weapons and provides assistance for them to reintegrate back into civilian life. Because the primary data source is a public opinion survey, these are measures of perceptions of improvements rather than measures of actual improvements. During the several years of NATO intervention in Afghanistan there were many national programs aimed at demobilizing combatants. In these programs, such as the Afghanistan New Beginnings program, former combatants were given money to turn in their weapons. Many informants were keenly aware of these programs. One former male combatant in his late 50s in Guldara District even complained, "If the Americans hadn't asked us to turn in our weapons, I would be out there killing those Taliban myself. They only coming back because they took our weapons." Kabul-Guldara-Village 2-#5.

TABLE 6.2: *Public Goods, Aid, and Central Government Performance*

Dependent Variable: Central Government Performance

	Model 7	Model 8	Model 9	Model 10
Info from Mullah	0.569***	0.608***	0.608***	0.633***
	[0.149]	[0.154]	[0.152]	[0.157]
Info from Malik	0.287***	0.252**	0.263**	0.217*
	[0.104]	[0.106]	[0.110]	[0.111]
Shuras/Jirgas Accessible	0.115	0.111	0.095	0.103
	[0.076]	[0.076]	[0.077]	[0.077]
Shuras/Jirgas Fair and Trusted	0.158**	0.148**	0.123*	0.117*
	[0.069]	[0.069]	[0.069]	[0.070]
CDC in Community	−0.041	0.002	0.004	0.036
	[0.095]	[0.096]	[0.096]	[0.098]
Drinking Water Available		0.001		−0.006
		[0.105]		[0.104]
Irrigation Water Available		0.135		0.082
		[0.096]		[0.098]
Jobs Available		0.379***		0.297***
		[0.089]		[0.094]
Good Electricity Supply		−0.066		−0.097
		[0.113]		[0.111]
Good Security Situation		0.406***		0.408***
		[0.109]		[0.112]
Good Medical Care		0.126		0.122
		[0.092]		[0.091]
Education Available		0.301***		0.283***
		[0.098]		[0.103]
Good Freedom of Movement		0.188*		0.215**
		[0.103]		[0.107]
Drinking Water Aid			−0.081	−0.091
			[0.098]	[0.096]
Irrigation Water Aid			0.301***	0.257**
			[0.105]	[0.104]
Road Construction Aid			−0.171*	−0.195*
			[0.100]	[0.102]
Healthcare Aid			0.058	0.018
			[0.092]	[0.087]
Demining Aid			0.049	0.032
			[0.099]	[0.096]
Demobilization Aid			0.314***	0.281***
			[0.106]	[0.106]
Agricultural Aid			−0.186*	−0.14
			[0.101]	[0.103]
New Mosque Aid			−0.09	−0.124
			[0.097]	[0.098]

	Model 7	Model 8	Model 9	Model 10
Humanitarian Aid			0.154	0.058
			[0.099]	[0.100]
τ_1	−2.135***	−1.687***	−2.585***	−2.177***
	[0.403]	[0.417]	[0.389]	[0.406]
τ_2	−0.305	0.198	−0.678*	−0.22
	[0.386]	[0.405]	[0.374]	[0.396]
τ_3	2.434***	3.017***	2.127***	2.650***
	[0.392]	[0.417]	[0.382]	[0.409]
Observations	4508	4356	4130	4017
PSUs	565	562	552	550

Ordered Logit Coefficients. Heteroskedasticty robust standard errors that correct for correlation of error terms within PSUs in brackets. Estimation accounts for survey design including household weights and population sampling units. Models control for income, education, gender, region, age, and whether individual listens to radio. The baseline response in each model is a negative assessment of central government performance.
* Significant at 10%; ** significant at 5%; *** significant at 1%.

have a more positive assessment of central government performance. From this model, it is clear that the kinds of public goods that are positively associated with central government support are the larger-scale goods which the case studies of Chapter 5 suggested communities had a more difficult time providing on their own. In contrast, access to smaller scale public goods, such as availability of drinking water, is not associated with positive assessments of central government performance. One reason may lie in the ability of communities to provide such access without outside intervention.

Model 9 includes several measures of individual awareness of foreign aid across a range of sectors (discussed above). Due to concerns of collinearity between aid and perceptions of improved public goods (e.g., drinking water aid may be correlated to perceptions of improved drinking water), model 9 estimates whether such assistance is positively associated with perceptions of central government performance. Correlation coefficients for the aid variables are presented in Table 6.4 at the end of this chapter. Model 10 includes variables measuring perceptions of the availability of public goods together with the aid variables. The inclusion of both sets of variables (the public good and foreign aid variables) has no effect on the significance of variables of theoretical interest, thus ruling out collinearity concerns.

All models include measures of the presence and effectiveness of customary institutions. The inclusion of public goods and aid variables does not substantially affect the significance of the variables of interest from the models in the previous section. As the dependent variable is categorical, ordered logit models are used to estimate coefficients, taking into account the survey design, including clustering and population weights. The analysis also controls for the same control variables in the previous section.

The findings in model 10 illustrate that improvements in jobs, security, education, and freedom of movement are still positively correlated with positive assessments of central government support. In terms of the aid variables, model 10 reveals that only demobilization assistance and assistance rebuilding irrigation systems are positively associated with central government performance. Other forms of assistance that one might expect to be correlated with support of the state (and those most often employed by those providing development assistance), such as drinking water, agricultural assistance, or even assistance to build new mosques, have no positive association with how individuals assess the performance of the central government. The bottom line is that it is primarily the provision of larger-scale public goods that are most associated with support for the central government.

Explaining the findings

The findings here are broadly consistent with other empirical research in fragile states that explore the consequences of development assistance in efforts to attain stabilization. Research in Iraq has found that only a very small sub-set of aid projects under very specific conditions yielded decreases in violence.[44] Similar research on Afghanistan found that there was no relationship between development assistance and a reduction of violence.[45] Qualitative field research found that international assistance exacerbated violence and damaged support for the international effort.[46]

This research departs from previous analysis in that instead of looking at measures of violence, it examines perceptions of the state. In my own interviews in Afghanistan, individuals rarely associated aid with strong central government performance. Rather, they viewed persistent aid and NGO projects as a symptom of government failure and state weakness rather than the mark of government success. Many older people recalled when the government could provide some services – without the assistance of so many international NGOs – thereby measuring the current state as a weaker than predecessors.

The presence of aid organizations did not engender a sense of confidence among most people. Negative views toward NGOs was something

---

[44] Berman, Shapiro, and Felter, "Can Hearts and Minds Be Bought?"; Eli Berman et al., "Modest, Secure, and Informed: Successful Development in Conflict Zones," *American Economic Review* 103, no. 3 (2013): 512–17.

[45] Tiffany Chou, "Does Development Assistance Reduce Violence? Evidence from Afghanistan," *Economics of Peace and Security Journal* 7, no. 2 (2012): 5–13. Similarly, Berman et. al. find no relationship between unemployment and violence in Afghanistan. The logic behind development assistance to Afghanistan and other fragile states is based on the notion that development assistance increases opportunity costs to violence. They find no evidence for this assumption in Afghanistan. See "Do Working Men Rebel? Insurgency and Unemployment in Afghanistan, Iraq, and the Philippines," *Journal of Conflict Resolution* 55, no. 4 (2011): 496–528.

[46] Fishstein and Wilder, "Winning Hearts and Minds?"

I consistently faced as a researcher in the countryside, as most individuals with whom I spoke believed I had come to their village (at least at first) to conduct an assessment for an aid project. Many believed that NGOs serve as replacements for, not as complements, to the government. Consequently, there is little reason to expect that a blanketing of foreign assistance would be positively associated with support for the central government. Evidence from survey data supports these field observations. According to the Asia Foundation Survey, respondents had far higher levels of approval for the Afghan National Army and Afghan National Police in absolute terms (at 88 percent and 83 percent respectively), than they did for international NGOs who have a 69 percent approval rating. Local NGOs have a 59 percent approval rating (among the lowest of all public organizations discussed in the survey).

As we saw in the previous chapter, individuals seem to call upon the state to provide goods that are difficult for individual or groups of communities to provide without external assistance, because they typically exhibit high fixed costs. It is difficult, if not impossible, for most villages to build a school on their own because of the small size of Afghan communities (the average size of a village is 432 people according to the Central Statistics Office[47]) and their low average level of income. Security and freedom of movement are public goods that require cooperation of a large numbers of communities across a vast physical space, making it difficult for communities to organize these goods on their own. The Hobbesian state of nature occurs in the absence of security and freedom of movement. Individuals may be able to provide order within their communities, but the best functioning local enforcement and punishment mechanisms will not protect small communities from encroachments by large-scale insurgency groups such as the Taliban or expropriation by warlord groups. Freedom of movement implies the ability to move outside the boundaries of an individual community, to travel freely to access markets, education, and government offices. Once again, the provision of freedom of movement implies third party enforcement across communities.

Once we take into account citizen demands, we should not be surprised that availability of jobs, the security situation, education availability, and freedom of movement were the only categories of public goods that are positively linked with increased support for the state. These are precisely the goods that communities have a difficult time providing on their own. The qualitative evidence in the previous chapter helps us better understand these results.

CONCLUSION

Lloyd and Susan Rudolph once argued that "the misunderstanding of modern society that excludes its traditional features is paralleled by a misdiagnosis of

---

[47] Central Statistics Office, CSO 2003–2004 *Population Statistics: 388 Districts* (Kabul, Afghanistan: Central Statistics Office, 2004).

traditional society that underestimates its modern potentialities."[48] Their perspective shows the way "traditional" forms of governance can exist alongside
"modern" state law, in contrast to many of the predictions of modernization
theory and the democratization ethos.

Several of the findings presented in this chapter are anticipated by the
insights of the Rudolphs. First, participation in or support of customary organizations does not undermine support for the central government, a finding
which casts doubt on a long tradition in political economy and popular
accounts of state–society relations assuming that there is an inherent irreconcilability between customary and rational-legal order. Second, the presence of
customary organizations is positively associated with those norms and values
that sustain a modern democratic state. As it turns out, those who are more
closely associated with customary organizations are more likely to support
democratic values, such as tolerance of opposition, the right of women to
participation in the political process, and perceptions that their vote matters.
Third, public goods provision and foreign aid are not panaceas that generate
support for the central government.

There are several policy implications. One is that efforts to replace or
weaken customary authorities during periods of reconstruction may actually
undermine state-building efforts. In Afghanistan, customary decision-making
procedures appear to enhance democratic values rather than detract from them.
As such, tapping into them – rather than seeking to displace them – may
enhance the stability of the state in the long run.

A second policy implication is that efforts to build state support through
public goods provision are more likely to be effective when they promote larger
scale public goods that individual communities are unable to provide on their
own. Legitimacy can be improved through aid to the extent aid is targeted to
public goods communities cannot provide. Aid projects that provide people
with small scale investments such as water pumps may be desirable for economic development or improving public health but it would be a mistake to
think that such spending is "winning hearts and minds."

This chapter illustrates the relationship between customary organizations
and the state (and aid) in the aggregate. The next chapter explores these
relationships as they played out at the district level. Exploring the relationship
between communities at the state through interviews and field observations will
further help us interpret the statistical results in discussed in this chapter as well
as help us understand how individuals in communities across the country have
experienced the Afghan state.

---

[48] Lloyd Rudolph and Susanne Hoeber Rudolph, *The Modernity of Tradition: Political Development in India* (Chicago: University of Chicago Press, 1967), 5.

Statistical appendix to Chapter 6

TABLE 6.3: *Correlation Coefficients of Variables Measuring Improvements in Public Goods and Services*

	Improved Drinking Water	Improved Irrigation	Improved Job Availability	Improved Electricity	Improved Security	Improved Medical Care	Improved Education Available
Improved Drinking Water	1						
Improved Irrigation	0.2033	1					
Improved Job Availability	0.1415	0.0865	1				
Improved Electricity	0.1555	0.0669	0.2122	1			
Improved Security	−0.0152	0.096	0.1821	0.1597	1		
Improved Medical Care	0.1468	0.12	0.1675	0.1819	0.2178	1	
Improved Education Available	0.1352	0.0908	0.1242	0.1493	0.2349	0.2936	1
Improved Freedom of Movement	−0.0073	0.1372	0.1173	0.1525	0.3777	0.1903	0.2647

TABLE 6.4: *Correlation Coefficients of Variables Measuring Presence of Aid in Communities*

	Drinking Water Aid	Irrigation Aid	Roads Aid	Healthcare Aid	Demining Aid	Demobilization Aid	Agricultural Aid	New Mosque Aid
Drinking Water Aid	1							
Irrigation Aid	0.2796	1						
Roads Aid	0.2882	0.2134	1					
Healthcare Aid	0.1069	0.0647	0.2433	1				
Demining Aid	0.0562	0.126	0.146	0.1613	1			
Demobilization Aid	0.0039	0.0876	0.1429	0.1337	0.451	1		
Agricultural Aid	0.113	0.1674	0.098	0.1526	0.1567	0.1842	1	
New Mosque Aid	0.1309	0.0882	0.1678	0.1007	0.092	0.0983	0.2032	1
Humanitarian Aid	0.1058	0.1086	0.1796	0.2066	0.1028	0.1502	0.174	0.1898

7

Federalism, Afghan style

Despite the highly centralized government established in the 2004 Constitution, I found that governance in practice involves extensive power sharing between district governors and self-governing, village-based customary organizations. This chapter analyzes the nature of power sharing between the state and customary authorities in rural Afghanistan by describing its characteristics as well as specifying the conditions for its emergence, maintenance, and breakdown.

In this chapter, I characterize the power-sharing relationship between woluswals and maliks as constituting a de facto federal relationship. These power-sharing relationships – based entirely on informal norms – are a source of political stability in an overall environment of institutional weakness. However, they are inconsistent with the Weberian ideal whereby a uniform set of rules begin in the capital and penetrate political institutions down to the lowest level of political organization. State-building efforts in Afghanistan have sought to implement the uniform system called for in the Constitution, but such efforts have been unsuccessful because they are not in step with local norms or expectations of the political role government should play in society. This chapter shows that efforts to strengthen the state that focus on implementing such hierarchies have missed an opportunity to strengthen the state by failing to recognize relationships that already link villages and the state.

This is not the first study analyzing synergies between the state and villages. Based on fieldwork in Northern Afghanistan in the 1970s, Thomas Barfield analyzed the relationship between the state and villages, describing state relations with villages as a "weak link on a rusty chain."[1] The fall of the Taliban

---

[1] Thomas J. Barfield, "Weak Links on a Rusty Chain: Structural Weaknesses in Afghanistan's Provincial Government Administration," in *Revolutions and Rebellions in Afghanistan: Anthropological Perspectives*, ed. M. Nazif Shahrani and Robert Canfield (Berkeley: University of California, 1984), 170–83.

brought new opportunities to consider local governance in Afghanistan.[2] However, this is perhaps the first study to consider systematically the relationships Barfield contemplated prior to decades of civil war. The evidence that follows hows that there is no longer a formal chain that links villages to the state, although communities and district government officials recognize that it is in their interest to build such linkages. As a result, many districts governors together with community partners forged effective collaborative relationships and developed norms of respect for the autonomy of each other in their respective spheres of authority. Rather than a rusty chain, it shows that the links between communities and the state are incredibly strong in some areas and incredibly weak in others. This chapter explains variation in the strength of this chain.

Although there have been very few studies documenting ties between district and customary governance, several analyze relations between formal and informal systems of governance in Afghanistan. Most scholars who have looked at this relationship considered the relationship between customary authority and the state in terms of the rule of law, considering the interplay between customary law and state courts in promoting justice.[3] However, these studies generally confine the role of customary organizations as lawgivers or mediators rather than as governing structures, thereby neglecting the broader political balance of authority between customary representatives and the state.

Another perspective on center-local relations focuses on the extent of warlord governance at the provincial level, showing how warlords can make effective governors.[4] Through extensive fieldwork, Dipali Mukhopadhyay illustrated the ways former warlords often become effective "strongman

---

[2] Studies of local governance include works such as Schetter, *Local Politics in Afghanistan*; as well as several policy reports such as Sarah Lister and Hamish Nixon, "Provincial Governance Structures in Afghanistan: From Confusion to Vision?" (Kabul: Afghanistan Research and Evaluation Unit, 2006), Hamish Nixon "Subnational State-Building in Afghanistan" (Kabul: Afghanistan Research and Evaluation Unit, April 2008), Jennifer Brick "Final Report: Investigating the Sustainability of Community Development Councils in Afghanistan" (Kabul: Afghanistan Research and Evaluation Unit, 2008),and Douglas Saltmarshe and Abhilash Medhi "Local Governance: A View from the Ground" (Kabul: Afghanistan Research and Evaluation Unit, 2011).

[3] Barfield, "An Islamic State Is a State Run by Good Muslims: Religion as a Way of Life and Not an Ideology in Afghanistan"; Noah Coburn, *Informal Justice and the International Community in Afghanistan* (Washington, DC: United States Institute of Peace Press, 2013); Christine Noelle-Karimi, "Village Institutions in the Perception of National and International Actors in Afghanistan," Amu Darya Series (Bonn, Germany: Center for Development Research, University of Bonn, 2006); Noelle-Karimi, "Jirga, Shura and Community Development Councils: Village Institutions and State Interference"; M. Nazif Shahrani, "The Future of the State and the Structure of Community Governance in Afghanistan," in *Fundamentalism Reborn?: Afghanistan and the Taliban*, ed. William Maley (New York: NYU Press, 1998), 212–42.

[4] Giustozzi, *Empires of Mud*; Roger Mac Ginty, "Warlords and the Liberal Peace: State-Building in Afghanistan," *Conflict, Security & Development* 10, no. 4 (2010): 577–98; Mukhopadhyay, *Warlords, Strongman Governors, and the State in Afghanistan*.

governors."[5] Several high profile strongman governors have used their informal authority to provide public goods. Their power is critical to understand the success of certain cities such as Herat, Jalalabad, and Mazar-e Sharif. Although warlords remain important players in many regions, warlords typically do not play the most important role in mundane activities of day-to-day governance at the village level: their impact has been felt most in urban centers.

Finally, several studies consider how local decision-making procedures, including the extent to which "traditional" actors participate in the allocation of funds for development projects, influence outcomes such as government legitimacy and access to development projects.[6] Village-based customary organizations sometimes distribute aid, although their raison d'etre is governance, not aid distribution (and as noted earlier, aid creates rentier effects in communities). For this reason, this chapter focuses on the relationship between customary representatives and higher levels of government, rather than confining analysis to their consequences within villages or how they respond to tasks given to them by outsiders. Instead, the task is to understand their legitimacy in the spheres of governance citizens have carved out for them.

The findings in this chapter clarify an important missing link in the study of the Afghan state by considering political dynamics at the very lowest level of formal governance in the country.[7] Specifically, it helps explain findings in the previous chapter: that customary representatives and state officials are not necessarily locked in a zero-sum conflict. Rather, they serve different purposes and can coexist in what is for all intents and purposes a system of political power sharing. Theories of state formation postulate that the persistence of informal organizations and norms frustrate efforts to consolidate state institutions, viewing customary organizations as "parallel" forms of governance that compete with the state.[8] Yet in rural Afghanistan – a country that seems, at first glance, to be an exemplary case of conflict between customary and "rational" order – customary representatives and state officials often govern alongside one another, casting doubt upon such pessimistic perspectives about power sharing between "traditional" and "rational" political order.

---

[5] Mukhopadhyay, *Warlords, Strongman Governors, and the State in Afghanistan.*

[6] Andrew Beath, Fotini Christia, and Ruben Enikolopov, "Winning Hearts and Minds through Development Aid: Evidence from a Field Experiment in Afghanistan," Working Paper (Center for Economic and Financial Research (CEFIR), 2011).

[7] Noah Coburn explores similar dynamics in a thoroughly documented ethnography of a single village in Kabul Province. See Noah Coburn, *Bazaar Politics: Power and Pottery in an Afghan Market Town* (Stanford University Press, 2011).

[8] Everett Einar Hagen, *On the Theory of Social Change: How Economic Growth Begins* (Homewood, IL: Dorsey Press, 1962); Ronald Inglehart and Wayne E. Baker, "Modernization, Cultural Change, and the Persistence of Traditional Values," *American Sociological Review* 65, no. 1 (2000): 19–51; Gunnar Myrdal, *Economic Theory and Under-Developed Regions* (London: G. Duckworth, 1957); Gunnar Myrdal, *Asian Drama; an Inquiry into the Poverty of Nations* (New York: Twentieth Century Fund, 1968).

THE FORMAL STRUCTURE OF GOVERNMENT
IN POST-TALIBAN AFGHANISTAN

Although much has changed in terms of the formal structure of government since 2001, the way individuals at the local level experience the state has not altered much from previous eras. In fact, most issues pertaining to local governance in the 2004 Constitution are based on the 1964 Constitution, when Zahir Shah proclaimed the country to be a constitutional monarchy. The structure of subnational governance was not modified to accommodate democratic interests, but instead represents deep continuities with Afghanistan's authoritarian past. Despite a democratic veneer at the national level – with elections for the President and the National Assembly – the state maintains an almost identical, centralized system of sub-national governance as it had in the past, where all local officials are appointed by and beholden to the central government.[9] This means that all provincial and district governors are appointed by the government in Kabul with no input from citizens they are to serve.

The Constitution calls for elected provincial, district, and village councils at the subnational level. Despite this, the only sub-national elections implemented since 2004 have been for members of provincial councils. Yet provincial councils have virtually no oversight over the far more powerful provincial governors who are appointed by the president. Moreover, they have been given token responsibilities such as drafting provincial development plans for donor funds or producing provincial budgeting exercises that simply serve as recommendations to higher levels of government that actually draft budgets. As a result, most informants I spoke with rarely turned to these councils to resolve important issues of governance – and most could not name a provincial council member when asked. Even if elections for district and village councils were to be held, it is not clear what role they would have in checking the authority of government officials, as these councils would face similar constraints.

Each of the thirty four provinces has a governor appointed by Kabul. Provincial governors can be powerful actors if they can draw on an existing political base in their province. This has been true of Atta Mohammad Noor in Balkh Province, who has been able to consolidate his authority based on his existing legitimacy as a high-ranking officer in the Northern Alliance. Similarly, Ismail Khan, who served as the governor of Herat Province from 2001 to 2004, was able to affect development in his province due to enormous local legitimacy acquired from his time commanding jihadi fighters against the Soviets as well as his resistance to the Taliban. At one point, Ismail Khan even declared himself to be the "Amir of Herat." His power was so strong that Karzai chose to name him Minister of Water and Power in 2004 in an effort to weaken his autonomy, while bringing him closer to Kabul. Although these high profile cases are noted

---

[9] See Article 137 of the Constitution of the Government of the Islamic Republic of Afghanistan.

by many analysts, most provincial governors do not have such strong independent sources of power and legitimacy. Many are not even from the provinces
they serve, they are rotated around the country in order to keep them weak by
preventing them from developing strong relations with constituents.

   During the height of the NATO surge, provincial governors attracted enormous attention from international donors and NATO forces. However, district
governors, who serve directly beneath provincial governors, are the true face of
the state in the countryside and typically received substantially less assistance.
When individuals in rural Afghanistan seek state assistance, usually the district
governor and his staff are the office of first resort. There are around 400 district
governments in Afghanistan.[10] District government represents the lowest level
of formal government in a country that has between 20,000 and 40,000
villages.[11] Districts operate below the province level. In rural Afghanistan, there
is no formal level of government in place lower than district government.[12] As
we saw earlier, this is nothing new in Afghanistan – formal government in the
countryside has never existed below the district level.

   At the district level, government officials report directly to provincial governors. The governors, in turn, report to the president. The system is so
centralized that district governors typically have little say in who serves on
their staff.[13] In addition, the selection process for district governors is far from
clear. In countries that maintain centralized systems of government, it is not
unusual for the dynamics behind the selection of local officials remain
opaque.[14] Although exact figures have been difficult to come by, based on my
observations as well as interviews with government officials responsible for
appointing district governors in Kabul, district governors are usually not from

---

[10] Although the exact number is not clear – even to government officials in the government agency
   responsible for administering local government. Kabul-Kabul City-#38.

[11] Estimates of the number of villages vary substantially. One reason is that donor funds are
   allocated based on the number of villages in a district; therefore officials have incentives to
   inflate the numbers in their district. Thus, when aid programs were announced, the number of
   villages essentially doubled in national statistical data from 20,000 to 40,000.

[12] The Constitution establishes municipalities with mayors that are to be elected (although these
   elections have never been held). The precise number of municipalities in Afghanistan is also
   unknown, as their number has proliferated since 2001. This is due to the fact that the Constitution states that municipalities are the only sub-national body that is able to raise and retain
   revenue. All other sub-national entities – including provinces and districts – do not have the right
   to retain tax revenue. Principles of centralism require that all subnational revenue is sent to
   Kabul where it is then re-distributed by planners back to subnational entities.

[13] This was a common complaint registered by many district governors and district government
   officials I interviewed during the course of this study.

[14] Melanie Manion, *Retirement of Revolutionaries in China: Public Policies, Social Norms, Private
   Interests* (Princeton, NJ: Princeton University Press, 1993); Melanie Manion, "The Electoral
   Connection in the Chinese Countryside," *The American Political Science Review* 90, no. 4
   (1996): 736–48.

the districts where they serve.[15] They serve for indefinite periods of time and can be quickly removed and rotated from one district to another, or removed from government entirely. Indeed, it was not unusual for woluswals to serve in one district before rotating to another district. For example, several woluswals I interviewed were on their third rotation as a district governor, having previously served in two other districts in the same province.

It is important to note that in many districts of the country, woluswals do not have offices and rarely visit their districts. This is typically the case in districts wrought by violence and insurgent activity as district governors are high-profile targets for Taliban. In such conflict-ridden districts, it is not the woluswal that represents the face of the state to villagers, but instead this is the job the district security commander who is the chief of police in the district.[16] In insecure districts, security personnel have a far higher profile than do their civilian counterparts. All of the districts I visited at the time were secure: they had government offices. Several years later, many of the districts visited were no longer secure and were the site of heavy violence.

Although the Constitution calls for elected district councils, it neither specifies their mandate nor their responsibilities. Furthermore, the Constitution does not mandate popular elections of district governors, which makes it even less clear what kind of oversight, if any, these elected councils might have over woluswals who are appointed by the executive if they were to be held. More than a decade after the ratification of the 2004 Constitution, it was not clear if the constitutionally-mandated village or district council elections would ever come to fruition.[17] Thus, subnational governance seems to exist only as a "constitutional fiction." Center–local political relations, both formal and informal, are summarized in Table 7.1.

Despite a highly centralized formal structure, the international community began to take local government more seriously in the years after ratification of the new constitution, in particular as military and political strategists in the United States began to view local politics as key to the counterinsurgency effort.[18] Beginning around 2006, donors began partnering with a range of Afghan ministries to create ad hoc district councils throughout the country. However, there was not a single approach to creating these councils, and most served as vehicles to distribute and set priorities for development assistance rather than as an actual level of government. In fact, some were created for the

---

[15] This supposition is based almost entirely on anecdotal evidence. Even the government office responsible for district governance in Afghanistan could not confirm the number of districts in the country, let alone the birthplaces of district governors.

[16] The security commander is an employee of the Ministry of Interior, the ministry responsible for the Afghan National Police.

[17] Kabul-Kabul City-#41.

[18] Kilcullen, *The Accidental Guerrilla*; Nagl et al., *The U.S. Army/Marine Corps Counterinsurgency Field Manual*.

TABLE 7.1: *Political Representation in Afghanistan*

Level	Number of Units	Formal Political Representative	Accountability Mechanism	Key Informal Players
Province	34	Executive Authority: Provincial Governor	President	Warlords
		Legislative authority: Provincial Council	Elections	
District	~400	Executive Authority: District Governor	Provincial governor, president	Warlords Commanders Khans
		Legislative Authority: District council:	Elections have not yet been held	Maliks Mullahs
Village	20,000 to 40,000	Executive Authority: None	Elections have not yet held	Maliks Shura
		Legislative Authority: Village council		Mullahs Commanders

sole purpose of delivering aid as a counterinsurgency measure.[19] Faced with a rising insurgency, such efforts were mainly concerned with buying loyalty rather than governing. The "traditional" leaders who participated in these councils often received a healthy stipend, leading to intense competition between community members as to who might constitute an "elder."[20] As a result, the "traditional" councils created by such efforts might be hardly recognizable as such by district residents.[21] Thus, these district government programs were best described aid projects, rather than a fundamental change in political relationships between customary order and the state.

Counterinsurgency strategy in Afghanistan sought to promote local governance by partnering with traditional authority it viewed as more legitimate than state-supported sources. When such strategies "promoted" traditional authority to facilitate military objectives, governance outcomes that resulted seemed to have undermined the very authority they sought to promote by altering incentives with vast amounts of cash or by calling on such authority to mediate issues

---

[19] Frances Z. Brown, "The US Surge and Afghan Local Governance" (Washington, DC: United States Institute of Peace, 2012); Saltmarshe and Medhi, "Local Governance: A View from the Ground."

[20] Katja Mielke, "Constructing the Image of a State: Local Realities and International Intervention in North-East Afghanistan," in *Local Politics in Afghanistan: A Century of Intervention in Social Order*, ed. Conrad Schetter (New York: Columbia University Press, 2013), 1–20.

[21] Shahmahmood Miakhel and Noah Coburn, "Many Shuras Do Not a Government Make: International Community Engagement with Local Councils in Afghanistan" (Washington, DC: United States Institute for Peace, 2010).

beyond their legitimate scope.[22] The governance that resulted was similar to outcomes observed with the CDCs: ephemeral successes or failures that were highly contingent on outside resources.

THE FEDERAL DILEMMA IN AFGHANISTAN

On paper, the post-2001 Afghan government appeared to be anything but a federation. In the most general sense, a federation is defined by power sharing between multiple levels of government. More precisely, a federal system has three distinct characteristics: geopolitical division, sub-units with independent bases of authority, and governments at each level with the capacity to directly govern citizens within its jurisdiction.[23] Based on each of these dimensions, formal government is extremely centralized. However, if we recognize that the system of customary governance serves as a de facto level of government, then Afghanistan can be described as a de facto federation. Customary governance operates at the village level, which is distinct from district and provincial jurisdictions; sources of customary organizational authority are usually independent of the state, as its origins lie in custom and tradition; finally, customary authority has the capacity to carry out a mandate within its own sphere.

Scholars interested in Afghanistan have long understood the country is beset with independent sources of regional and customary authority beneath a weak state.[24] The extent to which these governance systems remain after decades of war is unclear. The previous chapters demonstrate that there is a system of governance at the village level, which satisfies the jurisdictional requirement of a federal system. In addition, villages in Afghanistan are typically self-governing and autonomous from the state. Autonomy is a critical because it is one of the requisite features of a federal system. Customary authorities do not receive a mandate from the state, but from members of the community. Finally, the previous chapters provided substantial evidence that customary organizations are often successful in providing public goods. These dimensions are summarized in Table 7.2.

De facto federalism in Afghanistan hinges on power sharing at the district level – between villages, represented by customary authority, and the state at its lowest level of authority. Power sharing is the mutual recognition by both the state and customary authority to act within their distinctive spheres.

---

[22] Conrad Schetter, "Afterword: Trajectories of Local Politics in Afghanistan," in *Local Politics in Afghanistan: A Century of Intervention in Social Order*, ed. Conrad Schetter (New York: Columbia University Press, 2013), 265–74.

[23] Jenna Bednar, *The Robust Federation: Principles of Design* (New York: Cambridge University Press, 2008), 18–19.

[24] Richard Tapper, "Ethnicity, Order and Meaning in the Anthropology of Iran and Afghanistan," in *Le Fait Ethnique En Iran et En Afghanistan*, ed. Jean-Pierre Digard (Paris: Editions du CNRS (Colloques Internationaux), 1988), 21–34; Barfield, *Afghanistan*.

TABLE 7.2: *Afghanistan's De Facto Federation*

Dimension of Federalism	Satisfied?
Geopolitical division	*Yes.* Customary organizations have jurisdictional authority at the village level, while formal state authority operates at the district and provincial levels.
Sub-units with independent bases of authority	*Yes.* Customary authorities derive legitimacy from custom and tradition, while the state derives its authority from the constitution.
Governments with capacity at each level	*Yes.* Customary governance provides public goods, and the nature and characteristics of those goods typically differ from those provided by district governors.

Theories of self-enforcing federalism explain the extent to which these informal norms of power sharing, embodied in these three characteristics of federalism described above, emerge as well as why they break down. The notion of self-enforcing federalism begins by observing that federations are inherently unstable because they seek to balance authority between multiple levels of government.[25] In order to persist, a federation must overcome its central dilemma, which is assuring that the central government is powerful enough to provide public goods, yet not so strong as to use its strength to expropriate citizen wealth or engage in predatory behavior.[26]

In Afghanistan, the "federal bargain" involves an implicit promise by district governors to provide public goods (such as honest brokering of disputes, basic security, and to forgo corruption) in exchange for information from maliks regarding security issues. Drawing on insights from theories of stability and breakdown of formal federations, several conditions must be satisfied in order for informal power-sharing arrangements to prevail in the Afghan countryside.

First, district governors must be strong enough to provide public goods. One of the reasons for a central government is to obtain economies of scale in provision of public goods.[27] Economies of scale in public goods provision is the central reason provided in demand-side explanations for increasing centralization of state authority and a main rationale as to why local power brokers accept such centralization.[28] An implication of the public goods rationale is

---

[25] Jenna Bednar, "Federalism as a Public Good," *Constitutional Political Economy* 16, no. 2 (2005): 189–205.
[26] Rui de Figueiredo and Barry Weingast, "Self-Enforcing Federalism," *Journal of Law, Economics and Organization* 21, no. 1 (2005): 103–35.
[27] Barzel, *A Theory of the State*; North and Thomas, *The Rise of the Western World: A New Economic History*.
[28] Hechter, *Containing Nationalism*.

that there are few reasons for communities to accept a "higher political power" unless district governors can deliver on promises to provide public goods.

Second, district governors must be constrained from expropriating wealth from communities. Public officials have few incentives to forgo predation unless leaders are constrained either by constitutional authority or can somehow tie their own hands.[29] Numerous and overlapping constraints on central governments yield more effective governance.[30] The presence of these constraints is expected to translate into more effective public goods provision.

Third, customary representatives require both incentives and capacity to uphold their end of the bargain. As village leaders are "rational," they will have a tendency to act in bad faith.[31] Villages can be a source not just of cooperation, but also of conflict between competing groups.[32] For example, decentralized delivery of aid to communities need not lead to improvements in aid provision, because aid can be captured by village elites.[33] When customary leaders cannot be trusted, or when they have short time horizons due to factors such as political uncertainty, power sharing may not emerge at all.

These approaches to federalism, applied to Afghanistan, suggest that power sharing – or de facto federalism – between the state and customary organizations depends on the ability of district governors to provide public goods, constraints on district governors, as well as constraints on village leaders. Unlike most studies of federations, which focus on stability or breakdown of such national systems, this approach recognizes that federal bargains often occur locally. Some federal arrangements may be stable, while others may collapse.

Studies relying on ethnographic data face challenges in measuring outcomes and explanatory variables. The dependent variable here is a successful federal bargain, which is measured by provision of public goods by the district governor, respect for community autonomy by district governors, and by customary leaders sharing information with district governors regarding security. These outcomes are measured qualitatively rather than quantitatively with conclusions discerned from dozens of interviews in each district. The independent variables, which include constraints on district governors and customary representatives, are also measured using field data.

---

[29] Levi, *Of Rule and Revenue*; Weimer, *Institutional Design*.
[30] Bednar, *The Robust Federation*.
[31] Samuel Popkin, *The Rational Peasant* (Berkeley, CA: University of California, 1979).
[32] Agrawal and Gibson, "Enchantment and Disenchantment."
[33] Pranab Bardhan, Maitreesh Ghatak, and Alexander Karaivanov, "Wealth Inequality and Collective Action," *Journal of Public Economics* 91, no. 9 (2007): 1843–74; Benjamin A. Olken, "Monitoring Corruption: Evidence from a Field Experiment in Indonesia," *Journal of Political Economy* 115, no. 2 (2007): 200–49.

A NOTE ON METHODS

A great deal of the data on government behavior discussed later was gained from direct observations and interviews in government offices. To gain access to villages for research, I obtained permission from the provincial and district governors of each respective area after informing them of the general vicinities where data would be collected. Using formal channels was important for two reasons. First, government officials in Kabul were adamant that local officials in the countryside could guarantee my well-being and as a result would be responsible for my security. I was not entirely convinced of this rationale, believing instead that corrupt government officials who had advance knowledge of my movements could put me and my Afghan colleagues in greater – not less – risk. Second, in order to understand how government works, relying up on the formal permission system provided an opportunity for me to actually exercise the bureaucracy. Using the official channels allowed me to spend valuable time waiting in government offices, observing processes, getting a sense of the tone of government officials, as well as engaging in informal interviews with people who had come to visit government offices. Thus, the process by which I gained access to a new province or district was not merely a matter of courtesy, but an opportunity to gain insight into how levels of government relate to one another beginning in Kabul and descending all the way down to the lowest level of government.

The bureaucratic process began with obtaining a letter from IDLG in Kabul informing provincial governors of the purpose of my visit. Upon arriving in a new province, I would present the letter of permission from IDLG to the deputy provincial governor. The deputy governor would then provide instructions about how I was to enter each district – these officials would either call each district governor or provide me with a set of introductory letters that I would then relay to the governor of each district targeted as part of this study.

It was clear from observing these interactions and the tone of conversations that provincial governors clearly viewed district governors as their subordinates rather than peers. In most cases, the deputy provincial governor wrote sealed letters (often sealed in melted wax with a stamp) that they handed to me to give to each district governor, instead of calling them. Poor telecommunications and cell phone access in many areas outside provincial capitals meant the government was still dependent upon pen and paper. I strongly preferred the written method, as the letter delivery process allowed me to observe interactions between district governors and citizens prior to formal introductions. If a phone call was made, district governors could anticipate my arrival. In these cases, they often prepared in some way, making it more likely that they might change their behavior in anticipation of observation. For obvious reasons, I had greater concerns about my own security when someone knew in advance of my travels to or from a particular location, especially to remote areas. In the few instances when district governors were warned by provincial governors of my impending visit, they would often gather maliks or CDC members from communities at their office. In most cases, however, I showed up to district government offices unannounced, which allowed me to observe state-society relations as they played out in these offices.

Saturdays are important as the first working day of the week in Afghanistan, but this is also the day when woluswals are most likely to convene meetings with maliks or other village representatives. For this reason, I entered each new district on Saturdays. Savvy woluswals understood that cooperation with maliks could yield information about security threats in the district. For example, a farmer in Qarabagh District, Kabul Province described regular meetings between the woluswal and maliks in his district:

> I think they discuss security issues because maliks are very important. Maliks are representatives to the government ... I know all the maliks gather every week. They exchange their ideas with each other. [Each] malik is responsible to report on his village every week during this weekly meeting. He should talk about everything that is happening in his village.[34]

These Saturday visits also afforded me the opportunity to speak with several maliks at one time, as well as to meet the individual maliks whose villages had been previously selected for research. When fortunate enough to stumble upon these weekly meetings, I could then approach specific maliks from villages I had preselected for research at the conclusion of their meeting with the woluswal to ask for permission to conduct research in his community. There was no instance where a malik refused access to his community.

Upon entering communities, I was surprised by the degree of openness with which most Afghans were willing to discuss their attitudes toward the government. Initially, I had anticipated politics to be a taboo and sensitive topic and had planned to ask only indirect questions about relationships with formal state authorities. Yet in almost every interview, informants were more than eager to share their widely-varying views of local government officials.

Women proved more than willing to discuss politics, although gaining rapport required some adjustment to interviewing techniques. During the first few rounds of interviews I conducted early on in the project, it was clear that many female informants were generally hesitant to speak critically of anyone – including the district governor or government officials. After the pilot phase of the field work, I redrafted interview guides for female informants so as to elicit knowledge of issues and behavior more generally, rather than asking about their perception of an individual or a particular situation. As with other issues discussed in previous chapters, when I sensed that an informant was reticent to discuss their own situation, I asked about the situation of their neighbors to elicit a more general response. Individuals often felt far more at ease discussing issues of their neighbors. In the vast majority of cases, despite

---

[34] Kabul-Qarabagh-Village 2-#6.

asking about neighbors, informants would instead talk about their own condition and that of their family.

Although many informants spoke candidly, there were also important challenges measuring the extent to which district governors uphold the federal bargain (which is to provide public goods), as well as using these interviews to understand the structure of constraints on both government officials and customary representatives. In interviews with district governors, for example, it would be surprising for a district governor to admit they do not care much about what is happening in villages (that they shirk on provision of public goods), or volunteer that they extend little effort to solve problems of the people in their district. It was also helpful to find alternatives to simply asking informants about their interactions with their woluswal. To counter this difficulty, I utilized observational techniques to gauge the effectiveness of district government performance.

As a rule of thumb, the responsiveness of woluswals to communities petitioning them to provide public goods they cannot provide on their own was reflected in the lines outside their offices. Usually, long lines outside of district administration offices corresponded with interview evidence that these same government officials were responsive to the constituents they were supposed to serve: when maliks and citizens told me their district governor was responsive, I also tended to observe long lines outside the district governor's office. On the other hand, empty hallways and the absence of lines to visit government officials corresponded to perceptions of weak or even corrupt government performance among citizens. Despite the fact that people visiting the woluswal were there to register a complaint and were generally unhappy, I reasoned that they would not expend time and energy to travel far distances to government offices unless they expected solutions from the district governor. In other words, the expected benefit to citizens of such visits should exceed the costs to embark upon such journeys.

For example, when I visited the district administration office in Shibar District, Bamiyan Province (a case discussed in greater detail later), there were several groups of elders from different villages who descended upon the government office in hopes of resolving a dispute that had emerged between several villages. The scene outside the government office was tense, with groups of elders from several communities perched in opposing positions glaring at one another. When I arrived at his office, the woluswal asked one of the community groups meeting with him in his office to wait outside momentarily so that I could interview him and his staff. Subsequent interviews with villagers in their communities suggested that individuals were actually very satisfied with this particular woluswal. The district government office was alive with activity. While there were long lines, such lines were a testament to a responsive government – one that actually provides public goods and services.

In contrast, in Karokh District, Herat Province (another case discussed later), the district governor's office was virtually empty, aside from several maliks whom the woluswal had summoned after learning of my visit. There were no bureaucrats in their offices or citizens waiting to speak with the woluswal about particular issues. Lack of activity in the woluswal's office reinforced the sentiments of informants, which was that this particular governor was unresponsive to citizen needs. In other words, longer lines equated better government performance – which is a finding that one would only understand through immersion in this particular context of governance.

Physical features of waiting areas, and even the presence of a tea service available to constituents, were another way to gauge the responsiveness of a district governor. In those districts where the district governor received high marks for responsiveness, the waiting area outside the district governor's office usually had a good number of chairs, tea service, and a courteous staff person who would register names and complaints. In these cases, the government official responsible for receiving citizen complaints and requests was polite and well-mannered. In cases where relations between the communities and the local government was more tenuous, there was typically no tea service, and no official to register citizen complaints or even to organize citizens as they approached government offices. In these districts, the only interface between citizens and the state was a gruff collection of Afghan National Police officers who greeted citizens at the entrance to government offices. In such districts, the police took cues from their district governors: they did not listen to concerns, but were there to simply cast citizens away.

By combining village-level interviews with observational evidence from seventeen district government offices, the case studies provide a fairly thorough account of the informal ties that bind Afghans to their district governors. With these methodological notes in mind, I now turn to the case studies.

DE FACTO FEDERALISM IN RURAL AFGHANISTAN

Four representative case studies constructed from interviews, focus-group discussions, and field observations illustrate the dynamics of stability and instability of de facto federal relations.[35] The first case illustrates stability of de facto federalism, while the three other cases illustrate various ways such norms break down. While I discuss three cases of failure later, around half of research districts enjoyed successful power sharing.

These cases were selected from a universe of seventeen cases (one from each district visited). There were nine cases of successful power sharing. This case of successful power illustrates the key features of power-sharing in rural Afghanistan as well as how customary governance operates. There were eight

---

[35] Interviews and focus group discussions in each district were conducted with the district governor (or his deputy), other district government officials, representatives of non-governmental organizations, and male and female villagers in two villages in each district. See Appendix A for a full discussion of field methods.

cases that involved breakdown of power sharing. The three cases were selected because they illustrate three different mechanisms of breakdown: in the first case of failed power sharing, district governors were unconstrained; in the second, the district governor was too weak; in the third, customary governance structures broke down. In addition, the third case demonstrates breakdown and reassertion of power sharing.

Governing together: Federal norms in Guldara District, Kabul

Although the center of Guldara District is a 45-minute drive north of Kabul, much of the district is isolated due to mountains sweeping across the western side of the district. The district population is around 25,000, split between Tajiks and Pashto-speaking Kuchi nomads who settled in the district long ago. Tajiks live in the mountainous areas on the district's western edges; Kuchis reside on the flat arid land in the east. Many Tajiks served as fighters in the anti-Soviet, anti-Taliban Northern Alliance.

The district experienced heavy fighting during decades of war. Entire villages in the district were destroyed by Soviet rockets during the jihad against Soviet forces. In the late 1990s, Taliban forces burned down entire villages in the Tajik areas as they feared these areas harbored fighters sympathetic to the Northern Alliance. While most of the homes had since been rebuilt, charred remains of some still stood untouched, serving as a constant reminder of the war. Almost every interview with women was met with tears as they recalled the immense suffering the district witnessed. As one malik put it, "We should rename our district ranjdara ("valley of suffering") not Guldara ("valley of flowers").[36]

Despite communal and ethnic differences in the district, informants from both of the major ethnic groups articulated their interests to elders and local customary councils. People in Guldara typically referred to these councils as "white-beard councils" (shura-ye rish safidan) or simply "white beards." These councils provided a forum for individuals, including those with different social identities, to deliberate on matters such as marriage, provision of public goods, and so on.

Residents seemed very satisfied with their maliks, largely because they were responsible for selecting them. In one Kuchi village, residents said they selected their malik in the past several months due to the death of a previous malik. The new malik was only 32 years old. He came from a fairly poor family that had a reputation for community service and fairness. The malik said that the villagers asked him to take the position because he was one of only a few in the village that could read and write as a result of his training in a religious madrasa. The malik openly doubted whether he could serve effectively because he was so

---

[36] Kabul-Guldara-Village 1-#4.

young and came from a poor family, but the people promised they would help him out if he chose to represent their interests to the government.[37]

In a Tajik village several kilometers away, located in a geographically remote mountainous area, the malik was about 55 years old and had served in his capacity for 28 years. His family immigrated to Pakistan in the mid-1990s when the Taliban came to power. When his family returned to Guldara after the fall of the Taliban, individuals selected him once again to represent their interests to the new government. In his case, the malik position was hereditary within the family, passed down from his grandfather through his father and on to him.[38] This Tajik malik described his work resolving conflicts and providing security to the community:

> We had some conflicts with [the Kuchi] tribes who had good relations with the Taliban. Our people suffered a lot under the Taliban. But eventually, we solved our problems with this neighboring community and now have good relations with them . . . Sometimes they have disputes in their village and they will call me over for my advice and I even work with them to help them resolve their internal issues now.[39]

The Kuchi malik claimed jurisdiction over eleven very small communities, while the Tajik malik in the mountainous territory oversaw twenty five similarly small villages. The communities in this area were so small, they could hardly be described as separate villages.

The young malik in the Kuchi community believed his most important responsibility was to represent the interests of the community effectively to the government. Among these responsibilities, he said was to visit the district government office to exchange information about security. At these meetings, the woluswal would also inform the maliks know about government and other aid projects that should begin work in the village and seek their input.[40] During the course of my field research, I observed several instances where NATO and coalition force representatives met with district governors together with maliks to discuss how they intended to distribute aid projects (it was unclear whether their advice was heeded).

The woluswal understood maliks to be an arm of the state. While they were selected by residents, he saw them as part of the government despite the fact that there is no law or piece of legislation in Afghanistan that mandates their selection. Like many woluswals, he viewed the introduction of the malik to him after community selection as a contract signifying community ties to the state:

> We have divided our districts into five parts or five valleys. Every division has one representative. The five representatives of these valleys meet with each other once a month. . . . They are a formal part of the government. The maliks in our district have a stamp, which I issue to them. They come frequently to the district center to discuss some village problems with us and we try to help them as much as we are able. . . . They

---

[37] Kabul-Guldara-Village 1-#4.   [38] Kabul-Guldara-Village 2-#5.
[39] Kabul-Guldara-Village 2-#5.   [40] Kabul-Guldara-Village 1-#4.

[maliks] are registered in the government, but they don't have a government salary. They just work for the people and they want to serve the people. Look at me. I don't have money for gas for my own car, and I still work for the people! There is no alternative.

There is no formal law or statute that requires maliks to have stamps or to represent community interests to the state. This is a practice, however, that occurs with remarkable regularity throughout the vast majority of districts I visited.[41] The district governor's division of his district into five sub-units was not called for by law, but entirely a management strategy he developed on his own. A malik shared a similar story:

We are formal [representatives to the state] but we don't sit in the woluswali [government administration building]. We do our work in the villages. In Guldara we have a shura of maliks. In the district there are eleven maliks. At these meetings we discuss important issues like security with the woluswal.[42]

The exchange of information for basic services lies at the heart of the relationship between district governors and maliks. According to the malik of the Tajik village, "We have a shura of maliks that meets regularly with the woluswal. At that meeting we talk about security issues. There are other kinds of councils that talk about projects and things like that. But the maliks talk about security issues."[43] In exchange, residents can all upon the woluswal to resolve conflicts when problems transcend several communities. A young woman described the conflict resolution process, explaining how communities first try to resolve disputes on their own, but can also call on the district governor when village-level negations reach an impasse:

The local government does help the people resolve problems in the village. If there is a conflict in the village the people initially go to the malik. If the malik cannot resolve the issue they go to the local government. The parties who have complaints are sent to the woluswal to resolve their issue. The malik asks that the parties to the conflict write letters discussing their situation to the woluswal. .... People in the village have a limit on the amount of water they can use. Sometimes people in the villages nearby use too much water. People downstream in the neighboring village then become angry. When this happens, elders from the two villages meet and discuss the issue. In this village [downstream] there are also many land disputes. Sometimes people are using other people's land. When this happens, villagers get angry and they go to the elders. ..."[44]

From my interview with him, the woluswal created an impression that he was widely respected by both ethnic groups, despite the fact that he was Tajik and a former Northern Alliance commander who fought both the Soviets and the Taliban. Since the picture painted by the wolusal of his own administration was

[41] In some districts, the woluswal recognized the thumbprint of the malik in lieu of a formal stamp.
[42] Kabul-Guldara-Village 2-#5.   [43] Kabul-Guldara-Village 2-#5.
[44] Kabul-Guldara-Village 2-#3.

quite rosy, it was important to explore the nature of this relationship with informants at the village level.

The woluswal appeared to have developed a reputation for bringing groups together. For example, the governor resolved political tension between the Tajiks and the Pashtun Kuchi population. The Kuchi group was no longer nomadic, but had adopted sedentary lifestyle more many decades before and settled in the area. After the collapse of the Taliban regime, these Kuchis fled to Pashtun-majority Laghman before seeking refuge in Nangarhar Province in Eastern Afghanistan closer to the Pakistani border where other Kuchi nomads had fled. The Kuchis, fearing retribution from the Tajik population who had assumed local control, were hesitant to return to Guldara. They feared that the Tajik communities, who were in control of the local government, would associate them with the Taliban and seek revenge.

While the woluswal could have grabbed the vacated land, houses, and resources for himself and his former fighters, he chose to serve as an honest broker in this conflict. According to various accounts, his actions immediately eased tensions. The woluswal explained that the land the Kuchis cultivated was of little interest to the Tajik population whose agricultural expertise did not equip them to tend to the dry, arid land where the Kuchis settled. The Tajiks in Guldara, he insisted, specialized in cultivating rain-fed, mountainous land. Several times in the early days after he came to power, the woluswal urged the Kuchi population to return to the area and claim their houses and their land. After they did not immediately heed these calls, the woluswal himself tracked down the Kuchi community Nangarhar Province, visiting them personally and urged them to return to the area. Although the Kuchi alliance with the Taliban left a fear of retribution from the Tajiks who had control of the district government, the actions of the district governor helped communities overcome the legacy of the war.

The story of his personal interest in achieving harmony in the district was echoed and repeated by many informants. The villagers in the Kuchi Pashtun areas remarked on the evenhandedness, and even compassion, of the Tajik woluswal. The statement from a Pashtun male elder represents the sentiment of villagers in the area:

We have a shura in our village where we resolve small disputes ... Sometimes we go to the woluswal and sometimes the woluswal comes here. We like the woluswal. Even though he is Tajik he has worked very nicely on our behalf. He made peace among the people and he has helped everyone. When he sees an old man carrying water up the mountain he will always stop and help him. He is an example of a very good person.[45]

The productive relationship between government and customary officials helped reduce the threat of violence in the region. Because the governor was trusted by each of these groups, both sides were willing to share information

---

[45] Kabul-Guldara-Village 1-#5.

about security threats in the areas.[46] Although Guldara District sat on the verge of conflict and chaos when the Karzai Government came to power in 2001, the woluswal acted quickly to diffuse tension, and would ultimately maintain his position for several years, despite the fact that he was clearly a partisan in the previous conflict.

Although the governor painted a wonderful picture, I had a hard time believing what seemed to be a fairy tale of reconciliation. Such skepticism informed the interviews with informants throughout the district. In interviews in this district, I did not refer to the district governor or try to verify the story directly, but used a technique to elicit oral histories by asking informants to discuss where they were during the war. Responses to this open-ended question elicited stories about family and community events that transpired during decades of conflict. The question did not specify which war, but instead informants were free to talk about the period when the intensity of fighting and conflict was most dire in their area. From a series of observations in the community, it appeared that the story told by the woluswal was grounded in reality. I heard the same story over and over again from villagers, almost exactly as the district governor had told it. In fact, the district government office was quite abuzz in this district, despite the fact that the district and its population were relatively small. Instead of meeting in the district government office, as was typically the case, the district governor of Guldara regularly received visitors in his home.

In this community, I sensed that individuals truly wanted an end to the conflict and wanted to stop the bitterness that had embraced Afghanistan. For example, a focus group discussion with women in the Tajik community quickly turned sober. Upon asking where they were during the war, several women began weeping. One young woman recalled how her fiancé had been killed by the Taliban and as a result, she married the brother of her fiancé. Another older woman described how she had lost a son and her husband during the fighting. They pointed to the charred remains of several homes in the area where people had died during the war. They said these homes are constant reminder of the pain in their community.

This case illustrates de facto federalism at work in Afghanistan. There are two different levels of government, each with the authority to act within their defined jurisdictional area of authority. Moreover, the relationship between the two levels is one of reciprocity whereby the district government provides larger-scale public goods in exchange for information from villages, represented by customary agents. This relationship, which is robust and common throughout the countryside, is based entirely on de facto power-sharing arrangements.

This case also illustrates why district–village power-sharing can be effective. First and foremost, the woluswal was able to deliver on promises to resolve disputes. His effectiveness brought different groups to the table. The woluswal

[46] Kabul-Guldara-Village 1-#4.

was also constrained, in part because he was from the district he served. As a result, he understood that transgression on his part would almost certainly result in retribution against his family. In the language of political economy, he appeared to have had longer time horizons. From my observations, when woluswals are not from the district they govern, they typically have a smaller personal stake in maintaining stable political dynamics. Finally, the maliks were also constrained. By all accounts, villagers had a say in who represented them to the government. They selected their representatives based on merit (the Kuchi malik was one of few in the village who could read and write, and the Tajik malik had a reputation for fairness); thus, they had incentives to work for citizens.

Unconstrained Woluswals: Karokh District, Herat Province

The governance situation in Karokh District, Herat Province, proved to be quite different from Guldara. Karokh, which has around 90,000 people, is a majority Tajik region, although there are significant Uzbek and Pashtun communities. Rather than shared governance, this case illustrates how lack of constraints on the district governor can lead to a breakdown of the kind of propitious relationships observed in Guldara.

In this district, customary governance was quite effective in dealing with issues arising within the village, although the institution of village representative appeared to have evolved in the past several decades. The arbabs of the district, which is the title used in Herat to refer to the village representative, differed historically from those in Guldara, as village representatives were typically large landholders. Historically, the arbabs were similar to the large khans present in some parts of the country prior to the 1970s, with many ruling with an iron fist. More generally, it appeared that arbabs in previous generations gained their authority from a combination of charisma, competence, and wealth. During the reign of Daud, the arbabs were appointed by the government and lost much of their legitimacy.

Despite these efforts to tie the arbab to the state, migration and other factors seemed to have weakened the position of the arbabs vis-à-vis society. In an effort to collectivize agriculture under Communist rule, the Soviet-backed government assassinated many arbabs or forced them to flee, so that they faced fewer obstacles in their efforts to collectivize agriculture.[47] The civil war in the 1980s also destabilized old power relations.

While the term arbab persisted, an arbab was no longer a large landholder. The system transformed because the wealth aspect of the arbab seemed to matter far less than charisma and competence. Barfield comes to a similar conclusion. Reflecting on fieldwork conducted in the 1970s, Barfield explains

---

[47] Male, *Revolutionary Afghanistan*.

that "Arbabs were usually literate men with business interests outside of the village; often they held urban property. Links to a larger world were important because they dealing with government officials required a greater sophistication and experience than most villagers had." They could command authority "only when he acted on behalf of the government as its agent."[48] Yet in conducting fieldwork after the Taliban regime fell, Barfield concluded that the old landholding-based system had broken down.

I came to a similar conclusion regarding changes in the arbab system, in that villagers explained it was no longer viewed as an arm of the state. Yet I also found that these informal systems remained important and had not been replaced by provincial or district government officials. In post-2001 Afghanistan, the role of the arbabs in Karokh were similar to those of the maliks in Guldara. Villagers used the same vocabulary as in Guldara to describe their role in society. They were selected by the same methods and served to represent community interests in the district government. In a focus group discussion, an arbab said that contemporary arbabs in Karokh are now more accountable than they were in the past.[49] In the same discussion, another arbab indicated that they are empowered and constrained by the people, describing the situation as follows: "Everything is in the hands of people themselves, they can select an arbab and fire him from his post."[50]

In addition to mediating disputes, one of the primary functions of the arbabs is to represent community interests to the woluswal. According to the arbab:

[In] every community, the arbabs work to resolve issues of the people. We are representatives of the people in the community. The woluswal is unable to see all the villages. We visit the woluswal from time to time and when we go there we discuss the problems of our communities. We try to resolve the problems [in our communities] ourselves. If we are unable to resolve the problems ourselves, then we go to the woluswal.[51]

A young man described how customary organizations in the village work together to resolve even the smallest of disputes and how such organizations protect individuals from predatory behavior among government officials at the district government office:

The arbabs, together with the elders, the shura, and the mullahs resolve problems. This past spring I had a fight with another guy in our village. We beat each other up. He beat me and I punched him in his face. Then the arbabs came and resolved the dispute. They did not allow us to go the woluswal to try to fix the problem because they knew it would cost us a lot of money to fix the issue there.[52]

---

[48] Thomas J. Barfield, "Continuities and Changes in Local Politics in Northern Afghanistan," in *Local Politics in Afghanistan: A Century of Intervention in Social Order*, ed. Conrad Schetter (New York: Columbia University Press, 2013), 135–6.
[49] Herat-Karokh-District Center-#1.   [50] Herat-Karokh-District Center-#1.
[51] Herat-Karokh-District Center-#1.   [52] Herat-Karokh-Village 1-#5.

One of the reasons arbabs work on behalf of their constituents is an understanding that if they do not act in good faith, they can be removed. Just as much
as the community depends upon the arbab for his services managing disputes,
providing government documents and information, and liaising with the outside world, arbabs, too, are dependent upon their constituents for support, and
in many cases for a salary as well.

Unlike Guldara, relations between the district governor and maliks were not
cordial in Karokh. Citizens described the government as corrupt and extractive.
When villagers had disputes, they relied on their arbabs to resolve them
internally, but only in the most extreme cases would they venture to the
woluswal. Many informants indicated that resolving disputes would be more
costly if they appealed to the government. According to the same man who was
party to the fight:

> The people are not happy to go to the woluswali. If they try to go there, they know
> they'll have to spend a lot of money. ... All of them [government officials] are corrupt.
> When the woluswal first arrives and is new, they are good for a few days, but then they
> just become corrupt. For example, this woluswal put small girls like 13 years old in
> prison for ransom, but he claims to be a mujahed [one who engages in jihad], but still he
> did things like this! If there is a problem they'll just fill the books and take money. You
> see, our local government cannot resolve our problems or address our needs.[53]

A woman in one of the villages in described how the incompetence of the
district governor led residents to avoid dealing with the government altogether:

> In our village we resolve issues like fights and other things. But if we can't resolve these
> issues we should go to the woluswal. But thankfully, we haven't had any issue in the past
> two years where we had to go to the woluswal. Now the arbab tries to resolve issues
> between several villages. But last year there was a fight between two villages over water.
> Instead of going to the woluswal, we went all the way to Herat City [about thirty miles
> away] to discuss the issue with the provincial government because we didn't want to go
> to the woluswal. We had to take it to a higher level because somebody in one of the
> villages was injured in this dispute. It was serious.[54]

A male informant felt that the woluswal would just side with whoever paid him
more money:

> People commonly solve their problems inside the village rather than referring their issues
> to the woluswal. The arbab represents the people, so he is the one who really solves the
> people's problems in the villages. Not long ago, some sheep vanished from our village.
> The arbab, along with the elders in our village resolved this issue instead of going to the
> woluswal. People don't go to the woluswal anymore. If we go there it takes a long time
> for things to get resolved and they just waste our money. People don't have the time or
> the energy to go to the woluswal and just waste time and money for nothing.[55]

---

[53] Herat-Karokh-Village 1-#5.   [54] Herat-Karokh-Village 1-#2.
[55] Herat-Karokh-District Center-#1.

My visit to the governor's office provided insight into the absence of an effective federal bargain. As mentioned earlier, I would only enter a district after first informing the district governor. In Herat Province, the deputy governor not only provided me with a written introductory note (contained in a sealed and stamped envelope describing the purpose of the research) to be delivered to the district governor, but he also called the district governor a few hours before I was to have an introductory meeting. The deputy provincial governor informed the woluswal that, among other things, I was interested in meeting with arbabs in the district.

In what turned out to be a harbinger, upon arrival in the district government office in Karokh, I could not find a single government official working in the office. There were no lines to see government officials. Unlike other communities, the reception area where district governor staff made tea and served those waiting was barren.

My Afghan colleagues were able to locate a group of arbabs who had been apparently summoned by district authorities in an adjacent building. From the beginning of our meeting, the atmosphere was extremely tense. As the arbabs had already gathered, we decided to hold a focus group discussion in the space provided by the district government staff. During this discussion with the arbabs, the woluswal placed one of his staff members outside the door to eavesdrop on the conversation. The arbabs were aware of this and whispered critical comments about the woluswal. Despite the tension, the arbabs did not appear too fearful of being overheard by government staff. It seemed that they viewed the district governor not only as corrupt but as incompetent and not sophisticated in his corruption.[56]

Eventually, when the woluswal arrived in his office several hours later, he echoed the important role of the arbabs in solving disputes in the community:

When there is any problem in the village, people refer first to their arbab and if he can't solve their problem he comes to me and we solve it in the woluswali. ... Yes, he has stamp, but doesn't have salary. People collect some wheat for the arbab and give him a small tribute annually. ... The small disputes and cases are solved in the villages. For example when people fight over irrigation water or land, people can solve these internal disputes in their villages. When there is an inheritance dispute and they can't solve the problem in the village, they come to us and we refer them to the Amlak Department [an agency in the Ministry of Finance responsible for registering land titles]. So we refer this issue to the Amlak to solve the problem. When there is a murder case, first they come to woluswali then we solve the case through courts. Whatever problem the people have in the village, the arbab comes to woluswali as the representative of the people. Then we discuss the problem and solve the problem.[57]

The woluswal also mentioned the use of the court as well as the Amlak Department to adjudicate disputes, although I was unable to corroborate the

---

[56] Herat-Karokh-District Center-#1.   [57] Herat-Karokh-District Center-#3.

claim by the woluswal that people actually used formal courts to resolve disputes during interviews in communities.

Interestingly, this was the only district that seemed to be collecting property taxes among those that I visited. Informants said that the Amlak Department, which was at that time the agency within the Ministry of Finance responsible for defining and taxing land parcels, was collecting land taxes.[58] This was surprising given the fact that the Afghan Government had yet to implement a policy on collecting land taxes, as land tenure in the country is far from secure and is often undefined or disputed.[59] In Karokh, villagers said they were paying land taxes to the district government, seemingly unaware that such taxation was not yet mandatory. While many thought this was the official policy of the government, it was the only district out of the seventeen where I conducted research that villagers spoke of paying any kind of land tax to the state.

More generally, informants did not speak of any good that came from relations with the district governor. Many villagers complained of unresolved disputes, hesitated to share information about security issues, and bemoaned the fact that they had stopped cultivating opium without receiving any kind of compensation in return. Several farmers claimed the district governor promised to give them money to stop growing opium, but never followed through on this promise, probably keeping all the money promised for himself. The following response sums up the feelings of informants in the district:

> We want to resolve our disputes in our village through our elders. We never allow the people to go to the woluswal. We have an elder's shura and we never allow the woluswal to participate in our meetings or to learn about our problems. If something happens in the village we should always go through the elders first. ... The woluswal is only looking out for himself. He's only looking to create problems for the people. He tries to use the arbabs for his own purposes. But we don't let it happen. Our people have made our own council by ourselves and it belongs to us, not to the government. The arbab belongs to us, not to the government![60]

In Karokh, the main obstacle to power sharing was the absence of constraints on the woluswal. Several informants argued that the woluswal engaged in corruption because he was not from the district. He was from another district in Herat and had already served as woluswal in two other districts in the province. He knew he would be rotated out shortly and thus, had short time horizons. Due to the absence of ties to the community, residents believed he faced no incentive to serve the people.

[58] In 2011, the authority of the *Amlak* was transferred to a new office, *Arazi*, which was housed in the Ministry of Agriculture, Irrigation, and Livestock.

[59] Stanfield et al., "Rangeland Administration in (Post) Conflict Conditions: The Case of Afghanistan."

[60] Herat-Karokh-Village 1-#4.

Weak Woluswals: Guzara District, Herat Province

The district center of Guzara, also in Herat District, is 5 kilometers from Herat City, but significant portions of the district extend 70 kilometers from the center. There are eighty villages in this district that has a population of close to 125,000. In the years immediately following 2001, Guzara District appeared to be one of the safest in Afghanistan. The chaos of war, however, had disguised a decades-old conflict between two Pashtun tribes that the government had been unable to resolve, but not for want of trying. The situation in Guzara District illustrates how power sharing can break down when district governors are too weak to provide security. For power sharing to work, district governors have to provide public goods, such as basic security. When district governors are too weak to do so, groups may overwhelm the district governor. In Guzara, warring communities left a district government that was stuck in the bubble of its district government office, having virtually no area to govern.

According to the district governor, a feud between two Pashtun qawms – the Alizai and the Popalzai – over land and other issues cut through the district. Subsequently, external political actors had taken advantage of these disagreements, providing both sides with weapons.[61] The woluswal conveyed the nature of the conflict:

In the northern part of our district our people have security problems. There is a dispute going on between two tribes – the Alizai and Popalzai. These two qawms have a lot of weapons. They fight with each other a lot. We don't even know what they are fighting about anymore. They are killing each other. Many times I have asked for help from the Governor of Herat so that someone can help me solve this problem. But our problem has not been solved. These two qawms are both armed. The government cannot control them.[62]

The district governor said there was an imminent security risk due to the fact that parties from both sides were stopping cars along the main road to the north. He also said that just the week before two Afghan social organizers from an NGO implementing the NSP in the district were kidnapped in one of the villages in this area and held in a well underground for two days before being rescued by the police.

Due to security concerns, the district governor did not give me permission to visit villages in the district. Of the seventeen districts I visited, this was the only district where official permission was refused. As result, I was restricted to conducting research in the district governor's compound, relying on participant observation and interviewing people who had business with the government to collect evidence. I spent significant time with the security commander in the district who was in charge of the local police. He also

---

[61] Herat-Guzara-District Center-#4.   [62] Herat-Guzara-District Center-#1.

described the nature of the qawm conflict in the north, believing the conflict was originally over a land dispute but it then took a more political turn, with each side receiving arms from outside political factions who wished to maintain a foothold in the area. Among prime targets in these attacks were the maliks from individual communities. It seemed that both communities were engaged in and endless tit-for-tat strategy to inflict pain on one another.

Competition created an anarchic situation, thus providing an opening for anti-government militias to operate in the area. While I was speaking to the security commander, a signature green pickup truck belonging to the Afghan National Police sped up to the office of the security commander. In the back of the pickup truck were two young men, lying face down in the bed of the truck with their hands handcuffed behind their backs. They were from one of the dueling qawms and were under "arrest" as they were accused of beating up a malik from the other qawm (I was unable to figure out from which of the qawm the arrested man came). Apparently, these kinds of beatings and robberies had plagued both sides for the past several years.

The district security commander said the conflict between the communities had been going on for several decades. The maliks did not have the capacity to govern because the customary system was under siege by armed commanders. Thus, they were neither able to provide services within their communities, nor were they able to represent community interests to the state.

The unruliness in the district made Guzara an undesirable spot to be designated woluswal. According to the district governor, there had been a revolving door of people in his position, each unable to impose order upon the warring parties. He had just come to power two months before. He said he was one of the few district governors to have taken and passed a civil service exam, which was intended to create a new cadre of competent bureaucrats. The instability signaled that the government was unable to deal with even basic problems, such as intra-communal conflict, and so if a group was looking to launch an insurgency, Guzara would be an ideal spot, as the government had almost no connections to the communities in the district.

Indeed, the district governor said that there was another conflict brewing in the district – a new insurgency led by a Tajik by the name of Ghulam Yahya. Apparently Yahya was formerly allied with Ismail Khan, a famous Northern Alliance "warlord" in the region. During the 1990s, Yahya was the mayor of Herat City. After 2001 he had a post in the provincial government as the head of the office for the Ministry of Public Works. Sometime in 2006, Yahya was fired from this position. Publically humiliated and facing allegations of corruption, he now found himself without sources of patronage he had long relied upon when he worked for the government. Angry with his former patrons, Yahya fled with a few followers to his native area in mountainous area in the eastern part of the district. According to the district governor:

We have difficulties in the north, south, east, and west of this district. In the east there is a village named Ghulam Yahya and there are some problems there. Recently, the Yahya people have been upset with the government. Before Ghulam Yahya had a governmental position but he lost that job. Now he doesn't have a job and is angry with the government.[63]

As a Tajik, Yahya was not party to the existing tribal disputes taking place between the Pashtun sub-tribes. Rather, the anarchy resulting from internecine feuds created an opening for Yahya and his followers to set up camp in the district. After setting up small bases in the mountains, Yahya claimed to invite followers of the anti-Government commander Gulbuddin Hekmatyar as well as the Taliban to the district. In search of fame, Yahya told Al Jazeera, who did a television story on him, that he allowed Arab fighters safe passage in an out of the area.[64] This Al Jazeera broadcast labeled him salaciously (and incorrectly) as a Tajik Taliban to provide evidence that the insurgency in Afghanistan had gained followers among non-Pashtuns in Afghanistan.

In February 2008, Ghulam Hazrat, the woluswal of Guzara whom I interviewed, was shot and killed along with his young son, allegedly by followers of Ghulam Yahya. Yahya was eventually killed as well.

In this district, the woluswal was not strong enough to provide basic law and order. While arbabs may have been willing to cooperate and the district governor wanted to provide security, the government had no capacity to reciprocate. The de facto federal bargain broke down as warring groups overpowered and weakened arbabs and ultimately overwhelmed the district government.

Breakdown and reassertion of Weak Maliks: Shibar District, Bamiyan Province

The history of public administration in Shibar District demonstrates how instability can undermine power-sharing relations, but at the same time illustrates how it can reemerge over time. Although maliks in the district were nearly completely annihilated by the Communist-backed government, leading to a breakdown of power-sharing relations between district governors and communities, communities later resurrected the malik system, albeit under another name. Ultimately, communities and district governors reinstituted norms of power-sharing that existed prior to the 1978 Saur Revolution.

The population of Shibar District is close to 30,000. Most of the population is either Sunni Tajik or Shia (Twelver) Hazara, but there is a significant population of Ismailis (Sevener) who also describe themselves as Hazara living

---

[63] Herat-Guzara-District Center-#1.
[64] "Afghan mayor turns Taliban leader," October 17, 2008, *Al Jazeera* English Service, www.aljazeera.com/news/asia/2008/10/2008101738154o6492.html

in two river valleys. As was the case in Karokh, the Soviet-backed Communist government systematically executed or exiled arbabs and other notable community leaders during their rule. The executions in this district, however, were far more extreme. In Karokh, the weakening of the arbabs seemed to make them more accountable to their citizens, while in Shibar, the elimination of arbabs meant that communities lost the sole vehicle available to them that allowed them to coordinate community action against an increasingly aggressive state. In the 1980s, communities were ravaged by Communist governments as well as anti-Communist warlords. In the 1990s, the Taliban imposed a particularly harsh social order on the non-Sunni population in the country, including the jizya, a tax imposed on non-Muslims, which the Taliban imposed because they consider Shia and Ismailis to be infidels.[65]

A female elder described the "old" system under the arbabs and compared it to the chaos that ensued during decades of war:

He [the arbab] was very respectful of the people. When the arbab used to walk from one place to another, the boys who would sit on the land or under a tree would be quiet because they respected the arbab lot. If someone did anything wrong in the village, the arbab would fine them. ... His presence was good. At least people in the village were afraid of someone. This was good. It kept order in our village. The young people respected them. ... During the war with the mujahideen, the warlord groups, and commanders harassed the people a lot. These mujahideen were always asking for money from the people. ... The people didn't respect these warlords.[66]

There was general disdain among the population for the systematic assassination of the arbabs by the Communist-backed government. Villagers throughout Bamiyan Province had acute recollections of this experience. As a result of these assassinations and mass migration outwards during the war, the social structure that facilitated local leadership broke down.

Though village leaders were decimated during the war, communities reconstituted customary governance as they did elsewhere upon return to their communities in the early 2000s. In Shibar, village leaders were no longer referred to as arbabs according to a middle-aged male farmer:

The leaders of our villages are just called rais (leader). That is the word the people give to these people. In the past, they were called arbab. The government did not give the name arbab to these people. This is something the people chose themselves.

Individuals in Bamiyan province no longer spoke of maliks or arbabs, but instead spoke of rais ("leader") or namayenda ("representative") who were selected by the people to represent their interests to the formal government. In a

---

[65] For more information about Taliban atrocities against the Hazara population during the 1990s see Human Rights Watch, "Afghanistan: The Massacre in Mazar-I Sharif" (New York: Human Rights Watch, 1998); Human Rights Watch, "Massacres of Hazaras in Afghanistan" (New York: Human Rights Watch, 2001).

[66] Bamiyan-Shibar-Village 1-#2.

neighboring village they simply referred to their village leader as an elder, "There is a man in our village who owns a little more land than everyone else. He is our elder and he solves our disputes in our village." An illiterate male farmer in the same village painted a picture of dispute resolution and appeal processes very similar to those in Guldara or Karokh:

In our village, we have an elder .... Everyone in our village has faced some challenges in life. They go to this elder. He resolves the disputes for them. He resolves any issues facing the village. If the people in the village aren't satisfied with the decision of the elder, then they go to the woluswali for help.[67]

Once the post-2001 government formed in districts throughout the country, newly-appointed woluswals began to search for organizations and individuals to work with who could fill the void left by arbabs in those areas where they were executed (and where security was stable enough for the government to establish its own authority). Many new government officials – although not all – seemed well aware of their limitations and distrust of government officials due to recent experiences. The woluswal in Shibar, for instance, was well aware that he could not directly rule the villages and thus relied on self-organized and emergent village namayenda. He understood that to govern effectively, he must share is power with community members.

Here as in elsewhere, the heart of the relationship involved sharing information in exchange for provision of public goods, such as resolution of disputes. The woluswal recognized that his ability to stay in power was dependent upon maintaining local order – especially safety from anti-government insurgents such as the Taliban. The government in this area did not have the resources to police every hill and valley in the mountainous region, so the woluswal relied upon information passed on by the population:

We do not have the arbab structure in the villages any longer. For example, if I want to inform the people of the villages that you will go to their village—then I will contact a village elder. ... Also, people are coming directly to me. The old men who were sitting here before you were having a dispute, but you came so I told them to wait outside. ... If there are problems we then gather the elders of the village. If there is a dispute between the people then I will contact with the elders. Also, if I want to rebuild secondary roads between villages then I contact them and invite them to the woluswali and then they tell the people in the villages of the plans. ... If we want to talk about poppy issues—I collect the elders. Even I discuss security issues with the elders and they help me.[68]

Similarly, citizens expected the woluswal to resolve conflicts and disputes that they were unable to resolve on their own. A female in her early 30s described a conflict over irrigation water in her community that led to violence:

Last year in our valley, there was a land conflict between two families. There was a lot of fighting between the two families and they beat each other up. It all started when water

---

[67] Bamiyan-Shibar-Village 1-#6.　　[68] Bamiyan-Sayghan-District Center-#1.

overflowed and flooded one family's land. One man blamed his neighbor for the flood on his land and then they fought. During the fight, the sister of one of the guys getting beaten showed up. She saw this fight and jumped on her brother and tried to pull him away. She jumped on him and thought she could stop the fight. The man who was beating her brother had scissors and stabbed the woman in the chest. She did not die but [eventually] she went to the woluswal and he helped them find a solution. The woluswal came and fined the man who stabbed this woman 50,000 Afghani [$1000].[69] When they took the girl to the hospital she received treatment. Now she is back in the village but her condition is very poor. She has really deteriorated.[70]

The government resolved this dispute, but did not use the rule of government law to resolve it.[71] This case was not recorded in official records, nor was the punishment meted out accordance to the criminal codes of the Government of the Islamic Republic of Afghanistan. Although individuals appealed to the government, individuals did not expect the government to apply the criminal code or formal law to the situation. Instead, they expected him to administer justice using norms of fairness and restorative justice embodied in customary law. The fine went to compensate the family of the injured woman. No one served any time in prison. The woluswal was able to establish a punishment that satisfied both parties.

In addition to solving disputes between families that communities were unable to resolve, individuals felt that the local government was best positioned to protect people from outside intruders. In the majority Ismaili Iraq Valley, villagers described how "Tajiks" came from Bamiyan Center, the provincial capital, to their valley to steal stones and sand for construction purposes. They would drive their trucks into the area at night:

In Iraq Valley there was fighting in the desert between Tajiks from Bamiyan Center and Hazara people about two or three months ago. The Tajik people wanted to take sand away from the area. The Hazara people did not want this to happen. They said that the sand belonged to them. They started fighting with each other. One of the Tajik men received a serious injury to his head when he was struck with a piece of wood. The men in our village went to the woluswali to complain about their actions. The woluswal then invited some rish safidan from both of the villages. After a while they came to an agreement. The woluswal said that the man who beat the Tajik man would have to pay a fine. I don't know how much money they should pay, but he had to pay a fine.[72]

A male elder told of the conflict in much the same way:

For example, we had a dispute in the woluswali yesterday. There is a river which is part of our valley. Some people from Bamiyan City were coming and taking the stones from

---

[69] This fine went to the family of the woman who was stabbed, not to the government.
[70] Bamiyan-Shibar-Village 1-#1.
[71] If the government used the criminal code, the accused would have gone to jail for this crime and would not have paid a fine.
[72] Bamiyan-Shibar-Village 1-#2. This story was confirmed in several other interviews in the village.

the river. They use these stones to build their homes there. Once we told them that they should not take these stones from this area because if a flood were to come, the lack of stones would destroy our land. These stones help prevent our land from getting destroyed when there is a flood. After a while, we heard that they were taking the stones during the night. We could hear their trucks. Some people from our village went and asked them why they are taking our stones. They promised not to take them again, but then both sides got into a big fight with one another. The skull of one person from our village was cracked. Two people from Bamiyan were injured as well. The people in our village put the [injured people from] into their car and drove to see the woluswal. The woluswal said that if we want to settle this dispute, he can help us. Otherwise, he said, he could refer the case to the courts in Bamiyan City. Both sides agreed to resolve the issue with the assistance of the woluswal. He sat the elders down (from the village and elders representing the people in Bamiyan City) and brought the injured parties before all present. We actually haven't resolved the issue yet, but the woluswal is working on it.[73]

The woluswal did not involve the police or court system to bring official charges against any of the party, but created an open and transparent hearing of the issue before members of both communities. He used restorative justice and customary law. The woluswal said that if the parties refused to abide by solution they had developed with him then he would send both sides to provincial authorities to use official courts – a far more costly and time consuming process. Both the parties to the dispute and the government believed that it was in their interest to rely on speedy informal justice provided by the district governor than on courts – which they perceived as far more corrupt than the district governor. Residents appreciated that the woluswal sought to resolve the dispute without involving the "government."

The appeals process in Shibar, whereby individuals took disputes to the district governor for resolution that they were unable to resolve on their own, was quite common throughout many of the districts I visited. When individuals approached district governors to resolve disputes, they very rarely expected – or desired – the formal government official to apply formal government law. Instead, the expectation of most involved was that district governors would simply serve to mediate disputes and apply customary law.

Governance in Shibar District came full circle. Informal norms of power-sharing that had long existed in the district broke down during the war, enabling a series of governments to expropriate wealth and govern ruthlessly. After the fall of the Taliban regime in 2001, power-sharing reemerged as villages reorganized themselves. Self-organization allowed communities to represent their interests to the state, but perhaps most importantly, provided a bulwark to protect communities from government predation.

---

[73] Bamiyan-Shibar-Village 1-#7.

THE SIGNIFICANCE OF DE FACTO FEDERALISM

Although the case studies only considered a single case of effective power sharing, this outcome was not unusual, occurring in around half of the districts visited during fieldwork. In these districts, customary representatives petitioned the government to help provide certain public goods and in exchange provided governors with information. In districts where relations between customary representatives and the government were poor, it was usually because woluswals were unconstrained, although it could also happen because customary authority broke down either due to violence or because they became predatory. Villagers in these districts believed that corrupt district governors were responsible for violating the implicit social contract that woluswals provide certain public goods in exchange for communities to cede some of their autonomy to the district governor.

These informal norms of power sharing provide insight into the political foundations of insecurity in Afghanistan. Erosion of constraints on district governors and weakening of village-based customary governance contributed to insecurity. When district governors are predatory and unconstrained, villagers cease cooperation with the government in security affairs, while the breakdown of customary governance means that district governors are deprived of a mechanism to call on citizens to provide information regarding insurgent activity. The breakdown of these federal norms helps us understand one reason why the security situation in the country has deteriorated in the years following 2001. If district government officials are predatory and unwilling to respect citizen rights, then communities will withdraw from their willingness to cooperate with the state. Maintaining and strengthening these power-sharing norms is a potentially important way to improve state-building prospects in the country.

CONCLUSION

The self-governance approach pioneered by Elinor Ostrom anticipated the power of customary organizations in Afghanistan to govern village affairs despite profound state weakness.[74] In nearly every village visited, informants reported that they were able to provide small-scale public goods, building projects and resolving conflicts without the help of the state or aid projects. Simultaneously, customary organizations interact with the state in important ways. Vincent Ostrom wrote that scholars of federalism should pay less attention to "forms of government and what governments are supposed to do, and a much greater preoccupation with the languages and cultures of covenanting societies and about the patterns of order in covenanting societies."[75]

---

[74] Ostrom, *Governing the Commons*; Ostrom, *Understanding Institutional Diversity*.
[75] Vincent Ostrom, "Where to Begin?" *Publius* 25, no. 2 (1995): 59.

As anticipated his insights into the "covenanting society," formal political relations in Afghanistan tell us little about governance in practice. Rather than centralization, governance in Afghanistan is much closer to a federation, one in which customary representatives of villages govern together with formal officials at the district level.

The case studies presented in this essay illustrate why power-sharing and de facto federalism works and when it breaks down. In a little more than half of the seventeen districts visited, I found robust cooperation between customary and formal officials, usually when district governors were from the region where they governed and villagers had a say in selecting their representatives. Unfortunately, these relationships often breakdown, oftentimes because the woluswals lacked ties to the community. This suggests that accountability of district government is important to sustaining a cooperative relationship between communities and district officials as the district level. Finally, given the ubiquity of customary governance, efforts to create new formal village government may be unnecessary.

Customary authorities have been the primary target of communists, mujahi-deen warlords, and the Taliban, because of the legitimacy they possess. The Taliban, during their formal rule from 1996 to 2001, worked to undermine customary governance and promote their own network of village based-religious leaders. In post-2001 Afghanistan, in areas it contests, the Taliban has continued its assault on customary authority assassinating local notables in large numbers. The cases here show that villagers are adept at reconstituting and regenerating these informal relations – both within their communities and between the community and the state – once violence ceases, which bodes well for the future of de facto federalism.

The presence of these informal relationships and their general stability suggests that a formal federation could work in the country. In particular, the evidence shows that prospects for state building may improve by closing the gap between formal constitutional structures and political relations as they are actually practiced. Such a narrowing of the gap between the formal rules and those in practice could likely strengthen these norms of power sharing, and in the process improve prospects for peace in a country that has too often ignored the virtues of federalism.

8

Conclusion

There are so many sad people here in this village who have lost their sons, brothers, mothers, and sisters during the war. Nothing could make them feel better. Even if someone gave them money, the money would not make them feel better. The people in our village say that it is better to be a beggar than to lose your loved ones in this war. I lost my husband during the war (*she was crying*). We were really depressed. I would rather be poor and hungry just to have my family with me. Food and everything else is meaningless to me without my loved ones around. Sometimes I think that all of this is the work of Allah. But those who are alive should pray to keep their spirits alive and to keep them with Allah...I pray to Allah to bring peace to our people who have suffered for so long.
– Widow, Shibar District, Bamiyan Province[1]

Afghanistan has never had a particularly strong state. There have been periods in its history when the state has exerted its authority in hopes of imposing order on the countryside. A history of resistance to these incursions by the central government from "traditional" authority contributes to a belief that such authority is inconsistent with the demands of a modernizing society.

This book has examined both the scope and limits of customary governance in rural Afghanistan. It has shown that customary order in Afghanistan is not inherently opposed to the state. Rather, individuals represented through customary leaders have opposed an unconstrained and extractive state guided by a vision of modernization that had little role for the customary basis of village life in the political regime. This book has also shown that the strength of customary authority, rather than an obstacle to state effectiveness, served to constrain the authority of the state, and in the process, improved the ability of communities and formal officials to govern together. These findings show that customary governance in

---

[1] Bamiyan-Shibar-Village 1-#3.

Afghanistan plays an important role mediating the relationship of the state to its people while also providing a check on frequently abusive governmental authority that electoral democracy has been unable to provide in the post-2001 period.

Inherent tension between customary authority and central government authority does not explain persistent state weakness. A history of resistance to incursions by the central government from traditional authority contributed to a belief that such authority is inconsistent with the demands of a modernizing and democratizing society. While rural communities often resisted authoritarian central governments in Kabul, it is important to keep in mind that the goals of state building have typically oscillated between intrusive "modernization" efforts and cultural "reform." Throughout Afghan history, citizens were rarely invited to collectively deliberate the contours of what role the state should play in society. Rather, a centralized state sought to impose reforms yielding extraction, taxation, or exertion of social control at the cost of local autonomy. The problem is not so much the existence of a central state that motivated customary resistance, but rather, the actions of an unconstrained, highly extractive one guided by a vision of modernization. During the post-2001 period, this sentiment was strengthened as the state-building project pumped billions of dollars into the coffers of the central government and organizations contracted on its behalf.

Michael Hechter explained that in some situations traditional and customary authorities accepted and even welcome centralizing states because with them came the promise of improvements in governance.[2] In contrast with this optimistic scenario, one in which economies of scale in public goods provision increases access to fruits of the good life, citizens were offered little in return for accepting central authority except more of the same. The historical lesson we should draw from Afghanistan is that failure to build a coherent state lies not so much with customary orders and their "backward" ideas, but with states throughout much of the developing world that have existed largely unconstrained. In Afghanistan, the drive for state capacity to speed along a "late developer" and lack of meaningful constraints on the central government yielded a polity in tatters after decades of civil war.

Disregard of customary authority is not a relic of the past. Information about the state of customary governance in Afghanistan was hard to come by in the early days after September 11, 2001, when plans for governing the country had to be quickly established. Despite lack of information about the economic, political, and social landscape in the countryside, international planners and some factions within the Afghan government operated by a set of assumptions that quickly became memes, some of them contradictory, to guide development planners and strategists for the next decade. Primary among these memes was the notion that customary organizations and self-governing communities were obstacles to state consolidation and political development. Others argued that customary authority

---

[2] Hechter, *Containing Nationalism*.

was no longer an obstacle to state consolidation, as it had withered away during decades of conflict. Others argued – with no sound empirical evidence – that the creation of new donor-supported alternatives would enhance governance outcomes.

This book cut through these perceptions to paint a clearer picture of the governance situation in Afghanistan. Fieldwork in rural areas demonstrated that rural Afghanistan has remained far from lawless. More importantly, fieldwork provided insight into why there is order despite formal state weakness. Customary organizations remain an important source of public goods in the countryside because they are characterized by a set of institutional constraints that yield legitimacy. This legitimacy yields capacity. Moreover, the evidence here illustrates citizen interactions with customary authority are actually associated with increased support for the state. Most people interviewed for this book saw a need for the central government, but questioned whether it could be effective when it attempted to rule them directly and without any real consultation.

From the outset, this book promised a more thorough accounting of the context within which state building has occurred in Afghanistan. It also promised insight into problems of state building and governance more generally. Now that we have a firmer understanding of the Afghan case, it is appropriate to consider the broader implications of the study.

RETHINKING "TRADITIONAL AUTHORITY"

The findings of this book suggest the need for both social scientists and policy-makers to rethink how they approach traditional and informal authority, not only in the Afghan context, but in fragile and failed states more generally. Modernization theory predicted the demise of traditional authority throughout the developing world. Although largely discredited, some it its central tenets are alive and well today among the international development community and academia where well-intentioned practitioners and scholars prioritize democracy and ballot boxes in an effort to move conflict-plagued countries quickly to a liberal democratic order untethered from feudal and traditional "chiefs" or "headmen."

Despite decades of donor assistance and democracy building around the world to promote development, traditional authority remains alive and well and poorly understood. From Libya to Somalia, from Pakistan to Yemen, to Iraq and Mali and beyond, "tribes" and "traditional" authority continues to thrive.

Yet there is also a vast diversity to traditional authority. As a result of Western colonialism in some contexts, traditional authority emerged as an instrument of elites and promotes inequalities because they were once used as an instrument of colonial indirect rule. In some contexts, such authority remained a primary vehicle for public goods provision or an important source of political legitimacy. In other contexts, customary authorities have emerged been a source of resistance against terrorists, and consequently have become the prime target of al Qaeda and other takfiri groups.

This diversity of experience suggests the challenges in offering generalizations regarding traditional authority. Indeed, generalizing from the Afghan context to other countries in the developing world may prove difficult, because the internal politics of Afghanistan was never subject to direct colonial control. Future research needs to carefully consider what role, if any, customary authority plays in the maintenance of social order in countries characterized by prolonged violent conflict. It is clear that decades of efforts to bring modernization, democratization, and development to much of the world have failed to yield desired outcomes. It may be the case that such efforts, along with prolonged conflict in some contexts, led individuals to rely more on their communities than on the state, thus strengthening self-governing mechanisms rather than weakening them.

To my surprise, traditional authority in Afghanistan endured but it evolved during the decades of conflict. It became more responsive to the needs of citizens who were no longer willing to tolerate pre-war authoritarianism – either from government officials or their customary leaders. It was the grueling and heartbreaking experiences of war and conflict – not elections and state-building efforts – that transformed Afghans from subjects of states to citizens. War changed individual attitudes and expectations of the state. It put to rest decades of authoritarian rule. When individuals returned home to their communities after decades of displacement, they understood that they could not return to old ways of governance, but instead reshaped previous organizations using an updated set of rules.

Rather than making any assumptions about the nature of "traditional" authority, a lesson from this study is that it is important to open the black box of informal authority to understand the rules-in-use by citizens and leaders. In Afghanistan, a major finding of this study was not only the persistence of customary authority despite its perceived decline, but its dynamic and increasingly deliberative aspects. Customary authority in Afghanistan governs well when leaders and citizens abide to norms of power sharing and checks and balances outlined in the informal constitution. When the constitution falls apart, customary leadership governs poorly. The surprise of this research was the extent to which community members increasingly demanded accountability from such authority. In this regard, a central lesson is the importance of continuing to approach traditional authority as a subject of research, rather than as a set of assumptions. To understand the role such authority plays in politics, scholars must open the black box of tradition to understand the rules governing the traditional realm.

GOING LOCAL: SELF-GOVERNANCE AS AN INSTRUMENT OF STATE BUILDING

There are several implications from this study that might help improve prospects for rebuilding states after protracted conflict. One is that outsiders or local authorities seeking to analyze or even build states emerging from conflict must train their eyes to understand the ways in which communities learned to cope in the absence of an effective state. Prolonged civil conflict may not lead to utter social destruction, but instead to a strengthening of self-governance. Although in many instances the self-governing mechanisms that emerge may be far from optimal coping mechanisms in the eyes of liberal peacebuilders, they remain legitimate in the eyes of the individuals who have constituted them. This is especially true of customary authority. No country – no matter how ravaged by war – is ever an institutional tabula rasa.

State-builders and scholars can only take self-governance more seriously if the study of local governance and administration return to the mainstream fold of comparative politics. For various reasons, comparative politics and international relations tend to focus on national-level politics or the work of external actors – especially in countries emerging from conflict. Although national politics is clearly important, it paints an incomplete picture. If building states is the ultimate objective, then understanding how the state is experienced at the local level should be a primary concern of political scientists and policy scholars.

To the extent local politics are considered in studies of state building, it is an improvement over top-down, state-centric perspectives. At the same time, when local politics is brought into the politics of state building, it is mainly in the form of organizations such as warlords and donor-sponsored development innovations. Despite quite obvious differences, however, both are tied to war. Customary organizations and other self-governing mechanisms tend to be overlooked because they because they are usually not tied to war and thus left out of the calculus of local politics.

Warlords and other violent nonstate actors receive the bulk of attention when scholars do explore levels below the national level in conflict environments. Scholars have used local settings to show patterns of insurgent organization or to illustrate how warlords can govern. Yet exploring such dynamics often tells us little about "mundane" day-to-day governance in weak states. In Afghanistan, warlords are but one actor in local politics and they mainly exist at the district or regional level, rather than in villages. Analysis that proceeds by considering warlords can only provide a very limited picture of governance.

Going local also requires us to move beyond analysis of donor projects. Enormous attention has been paid to the efforts by international organizations to promote CDD programs and manifold other NGO-sponsored initiatives. The logic behind such programs in many ways is an embodiment of the decentralization ethos, that by bringing programs closer to people and directly involving them in project selection they will be more likely to select something that helps them than alternatives suggested by donors or their own government.

The paradox of CDD programs is that in an effort to decentralize decision-making they have become manifestations of a one-size fits all approach to development.[3] By 2012, the World Bank had supported CDD activities in more than 94 countries around the world.[4] Although such programs are decentralized in that they encourage local ownership, their approach often creates decision making through parallel governance structures. Afghanistan is no better example of this, where the decentralized approach to governance paradoxically undermined existing sources of local governance. It is critical for these programs to take better account of the local politics in order to improve their effectiveness.

In recent years scholars have paid more attention to such donor phenomena because they have developed cutting-edge tools to study them. In fact, the scholarly study of the political economy of development has increasingly been dominated by sophisticated randomized controlled trials that seek to understand the impact of donor assistance programs around the world. Such impact evaluations are enormously important to understand the impact of aid programs, but they turn our attention to the things we can "control" and manipulate through research and away from the incredibly messy things that seem impossible to conceptualize and measure. The focus on the programmatic evaluation of community development schemes and randomized control trials throughout much of the developing world has resulted in a loss of focus on local and village politics. As a result, we know more about aid programs and the role of international organizations in Afghanistan than we do about local political factors that have much more of a role in day-to-day governance of communities. Many scholars have come to believe that the study of aid projects in villages is the study of local politics. It is often no more than the study of Potemkin village politics – politics organized and paid for by outside community organizers and their international patrons. Analysis of aid projects frequently views state building as a technical problem, rather than understanding it as a fundamentally political endeavor.

It would be foolish to deny the importance of organizations tied to war, both those that are part of fighting (warlords) and those promoting peace (community development). Yet customary organizations have been around but have also been evolving for centuries. For decades, development specialists and scholars have understudied such phenomena because they believed that with rapid urbanization and the emergence of megacities, such authority would wither away. It seems that such calls are always premature. Furthermore, in urban areas there is evidence that such authority tends to reproduce itself through new sets of self-governing mechanisms. In weakly institutionalized environments, new forms of customary authority emerge – as what constitutes custom is constantly evolving. Customary governance and other forms of self-governance may not be a panacea but it is important to understand their

---

[3] Pritchett and Woolcock, "Solutions When the Solution Is the Problem."
[4] Susan Wong, "What Have Been the Impacts of World Bank Community-Driven Development Programs? CDD Impact Evaluation Review and Operational and Research Implications" (Washington, DC: World Bank, 2012).

capacities and limitations. Unfortunately, the state-building process has too often ignored such phenomena in efforts to bring people a more powerful state.

Elinor Ostrom described the importance of taking a diagnostic approach to solving policy problems rather than transplanting panaceas to a new context. One of the tasks of government and assistance efforts should be attention to the organizational landscape in countries where they intervene, speaking to people directly in order to understand how the ways they overcome collective dilemmas in the absence of the state. Outsiders need to assume that individuals can overcome such dilemmas, despite enormous hardship. Such exercises would take self-governance seriously. By doing so, efforts to rebuild states can work with organizations that may be locally effective and legitimate, thus reducing the cost of building new governance institutions. Instead of assuming a tabula rasa, those wishing to build and assist fragile states should begin by asking what citizens want from state rather than making assumptions about positive consequences of its ubiquity.

POWER IN RESTRAINT

Liberal peacebuilding descends on countries around the world with incredibly noble desires to build expansive state institutions and provide a wide assortment of positive rights during times of great donor attention and seemingly endless funds. In the "golden hour" immediately following the cessation of conflict eager international "partners" develop strategies, equip ministries with new plans, and set into motion the march to achieve lofty goals.[5] Almost every post-conflict or peacebuilding endeavor begins with this renewed sense of optimism. Eventually, donors and implementers return home, become tired, frustrated, and turn their attention elsewhere. NGO workers and security contractors then pack up their bags and head for the next new and inevitably more hopeful adventure. Citizens of these countries remain saddled with the institutional residues and dashed hopes of such great aspirations that are embedded in local public policies and programs promoted by donors, along with the tax bill to pay for them.

One of the problems with the "hearts and minds" or the service delivery approach to state building is that it often promises citizens a state much larger than the government and the donor community can afford. It sees the solution to the maladies of long-suffering individuals in the state. After promising so much, fragile states are often left with a shell of a government that is bound to starve for revenue and resources as donors depart. To feed itself, the state will once again look to the people to provide revenue, potentially setting in motion dynamics that enabled conflict in the first place.

---

[5] Dobbins, *The Beginner's Guide to Nation-Building.*

Setting realistic expectations is essential for the state-building process to be credible in the eyes of citizens. As Francis Fukuyama observed, well-meaning international patrons fail to distinguish between the scope and the strength of states.[6] Ambitious state builders hope to bring "Denmark to Djibouti" by promising citizens a vast range of services in return for legitimacy.[7] The construction of national-level institutions intent on creating welfare states from scratch are increasingly embedded in new constitutions of post-conflict states. These constitutions promise an assortment of affirmative rights many advanced industrial democracies still struggle to provide. Great expectations are part of the liberal peacebuilding project.

The Constitution of the Government of the Islamic Republic of Afghanistan is a good example of the kind of excessive optimism about scope of the state that Fukuyama discusses. It promises universal health care, education, the right to shelter, and a litany of other rights. It created a powerful state with few meaningful constraints on its authority. Those who supported the centralized state argued that a strong executive was needed not only to fight insurgents but also to provide public goods.[8] By overpromising, such efforts inevitably under deliver and ultimately undermine faith in the international project, but more importantly they directly undermined trust in the government such efforts sought to strengthen.

An alternative vision of state building after (or even during) conflict is to discard with the notion of "winning hearts and minds" through infrastructure and capacity, replacing it with an attempt to gain legitimacy through government *restraint*. Individuals in rural Afghanistan did not seem eager to cede local autonomy to a distant government that had a very limited track record of working on behalf of citizens. Instead, I found many cases when individuals were willing to obey state rule when individual leaders – woluswals – acted in good faith and were willing to tie their own hands (discussed in Chapters 6 and 7). These individual woluswals demonstrated state capacity through self-restraint. Legitimacy was not gained through the onslaught of foreign NGOs and their Land Cruisers or through massive amounts of assistance. So many people I spoke with for this book told me that they began to respect the government when the government did not take too much from citizens, when it resolved disputes fairly among communities.

The key ingredients to local stability in Afghanistan was not service delivery or vast resources, but local leadership and the rule of law – a hardworking

---

[6] *State-Building: Governance and World Order in the 21st Century* (Ithaca, NY: Cornell University Press, 2004).

[7] Pritchett and Woolcock, "Solutions When the Solution Is the Problem."

[8] It was not only president Karzai who sought a strong presidency after 2001. The US government also promoted a strong presidency believing that a weak presidency or a parliamentary system would yield an "endless crisis of power." See Wikileaks, "Ambassador's April 6 Meeting with French Ambassador," April 13, 2003, https://wikileaks.org/plusd/cables/03KABUL955_a.html.

district governor who could partner with reliable customary leaders. The rule of law did not necessarily mean a "good" governor must apply punitive state laws, but was more respected when he applied restorative, customary law. Attitudes toward the government changed when cooperation between these groups emerged. Nobel Prize winning economist Roger Myerson noted the service delivery model of state-building and counterinsurgency is not destined to build stability. He argues this can only be facilitated by effective and legitimate political leadership and not by providing public goods and services alone.[9] One of the great tragedies of post-2001 Afghanistan is that there were cadres of leaders waiting in rural areas who were generally supportive of the central government and who had re-organized themselves. I found that communities resuscitated customary governance not out of a cultural disposition toward communalism, but out of self-interest and self-preservation. Rather than having a part in governance, communities were confronted with identical forms of bureaucratic centralization coupled with a desire to manicure community governance into a form (the CDCs) that could be manipulated and controlled through funds from the central government and international donors. These were patterns that people in rural areas had seen for decades. This book explains why efforts to create new forms of governance in rural areas actually undermined it in the long run.

The Afghan state may have some success by trying to do less – a lot less. This could be accomplished the renegotiation of a more limited government that may help the state regain the trust of citizens while slowly providing some public goods. Certainly, states emerging from conflict require increased capacity, but the broad scope promoted by the international donor community and gladly welcomed by Afghan politicians who were supported by its largesse is not sustainable and has run its course. The drive to build state capacity does not necessarily produce the rule of law, especially when it is established without constraints. International largesse did not yield sustainable public goods, but fueled fraud and corruption in almost every faction of society by spending billions of dollars society had no ability to absorb.

The historical problem in Afghanistan – and seemingly one that continues today – is a government that has been unconstrained in its behavior with its own citizens. Although the country is formally democratic, there are few checks and balances on government authority at the local level due to the fact that the government remains committed to the principles of centralism. The Afghan constitution provides almost no authority to local governors and citizens have no democratic oversight over officials appointed by Kabul. The 2004 Constitution painted democratic bodies with no authority onto of the rotting corpse of the old authoritarian constitution. The district governors who I found villagers

---

[9] Roger B. Myerson, "A Field Manual for the Cradle of Civilization Theory of Leadership and Lessons of Iraq," *Journal of Conflict Resolution* 53, no. 3 (2009): 470–82.

respected most were respected not because they observed the rule of state law, but because they willingly flaunted it. Instead of sending disputants to state courts, district governors sought negotiated settlements that parties viewed as more fair, less time consuming, and far less costly (in terms of bribes) than state courts.

One way to avoid these challenges is by strengthening power-sharing at local levels. Power sharing between customary representatives and district governors is a reality in many communities in the Afghan countryside, although these relations are mediated entirely through informal norms. I found them to be quite regularized despite the messiness of customary authority. Customary organizations do not exist to undermine the state, but to hold it accountable to citizens. Constitutional reforms that more closely align the state's parchment institutions with informal norms of decentralized governance could enhance prospects for an effective, limited state.

A limited government – both in Afghanistan and elsewhere – could be characterized by more modest goals and a willingness to incorporate existing social organizations into formal channels and also acknowledging that it is best to stop short of formalizing them (see later). By harnessing existing local capacity or social capital (rather than assuming its complete absence), the state would be able to economize on village-level resources and invest in public goods most demanded by citizens. In addition to decentralization, a more limited government would also stress negative rights, focusing on civil liberties and what the state cannot do to its citizens, rather than on positive rights associated with building quick state capacity.

This could be facilitated by administrative decentralization of budgetary and other decision making and direct election of district government officials – including district governors and district councils. Some may argue that decentralization will only breed corruption and weak government control. It is unlikely that anything can be worse that the corruption and weak governance experienced by many Afghans in the years after 2001. The heavily centralized system of government in a situation of strong de facto decentralization yields enormous tension that can only be resolved by a greater push toward centralization (which many Afghans would resist) or decentralization. The move towards elected district governors remains a long way off, as provinces must first move in this direction.

Another alternative to the service delivery model, characteristic of both liberal peacebuilding and counterinsurgency efforts to generate government legitimacy, is to focus on the rule of law prior to engaging in massive service delivery. It is clear from the evidence in this book that government legitimacy emerged when local leaders – both government and customary – were willing to tie their own hands and respect citizens. The service delivery model emboldened the state with resources and a drive for capacity. Capacity without constraints in a context of conflict and donor excess yielded a government that was increasingly distant from its citizens. Capacity and public goods did not win hearts and minds in the long run, as the state teetered on collapse with the withdrawal of international forces. In the districts where citizens describe restraint of government officials, there was a stronger willingness for individuals to support the government. Government officials were frequently constrained by the presence of customary authority – that often – but not always – served as a check on government power.

IMPLICATIONS FOR STATE BUILDING IN AFGHANISTAN

What do these findings suggest for the future of local government in Afghanistan? How can formal government take self-governance seriously? One possible way forward would be to reconsider plans to implement formal village government in the country.

The question of local government in Afghanistan is far from resolved. There is no formal representation of villages to the state, despite a constitutional mandate that calls for formal village councils. By the end of the Karzai administration, ministries within the Afghan government were still feuding for control of the village governance portfolio. MRRD sought to formalize the CDCs as the village councils called for in the constitution, estimating that it would need to create and sustain 40,000 CDCs as part of this effort (by comparison the much larger United States has 25,000 local governments). These bodies were created with little thought as to how they might be sustained in the in the long run. Creating formal government is costly. It is difficult to understand how this level of formal government will be sustainable, as the government has been almost entirely dependent on outside donor funds (more than $2 billion since 2003 to support the NSP alone) to support the effort. Finally, while some within the Afghan government sought to formalize the CDCs as a result of their desire to link villages to the government, I found very little evidence that citizens had any desire for their villages to be directly linked to the state. Very few informants desired the presence of formal government organizations in their communities. Instead, they sought to have a state but a state they could approach on their own terms. Many Afghans in rural areas regularly engage with the state, but this engagement occurs (and did so historically) at the district level.

Most districts in Afghanistan are quite small. Most have populations of fewer than 40,000. Very few have more than 100,000 residents. Given the inability of the government to provide rudimentary public goods and services, it is highly unlikely that the government will ever be able to support the level of government called for in the Constitution. If village councils were to be formalized, then they would require all the entrapments of the state – salaries, offices, and of course red tape. This is an ambitious undertaking, to put it mildly, in one of the world's weakest and poorest states. The task is even more daunting considering that district governments have not been established in some places and where they have been established, they remain extraordinarily weak.

The long-term consequences of such a decision, if taken seriously, could have long-term implications for the nature of the state. It would lead to an extension of government unprecedented in Afghan history, with formal bureaucracy present in every community in the country. The empowerment of these bodies would then enable the tentacles of the state to descend into each community. Based on the evidence in this book, this would likely undermine local representation rather than improve the quality of local decision-making. Decisions about the fundamental organization of the state and the size of government made under donor duress, while the country was basking in largesse from international supporters, is likely to yield ineffective government in the long run.

Given the incredibly small size of villages in Afghanistan, it is uncertain whether formal village government is necessary to produce outcomes that can improve the lives of citizens, ensure political control, or generate political order. In Afghanistan, it makes sense for government to stop at the district level – where it has always stopped and cede village governance to self-governing mechanisms. It would encourage political contestation at the district level, the precise level of governance where many issues remain unresolved and where self-governing mechanisms are less effective. This does not mean formalizing customary authority as a means of indirect rule or supporting it financially. The most successful local governance outcomes I found in rural Afghanistan occurred when district governors respected community desires – however imperfectly those desires were represented – and the government, in turn, earned the respect of communities and generated cooperation.

***

State building is incredibly complex. Solutions in Afghanistan will be challenging to achieve and they will not happen overnight. They require a long term commitment by the people to the government – and a commitment by the government to its people. One way to proceed is by recognizing the incredible aptitude of Afghans to govern themselves. War and violence does not equate community anarchy and disorder. There is substantial order even in an otherwise anarchic situation. Hopefully this book leaves no doubt of the various ways Afghans have come together to govern themselves in spite of state weakness, as well as the profound significance of village governance and local politics as the primary site of state construction.

Appendix A

Research design and fieldwork appendix

This book is based on more than 300 original interviews and focus group discussions along with careful field observations collected in more than thirty villages across rural Afghanistan. It is the first research, to my knowledge, that adopts a comparative, nationwide approach to local governance and customary institutions in post-2001 Afghanistan and is the first large-scale, independent study of customary institutions since the Soviet invasion of 1979. This research appendix discusses both the research design as well the way in which data for this project were collected.

To collect this data, I assembled a team consisting of male and female Afghan researchers to conduct interviews and focus groups under the auspices of a Kabul-based research organization, the AREU a well-established research organization in Afghanistan that is known for conducting qualitative research.[1] The original interview and focus group data came from thirty two villages collected across seventeen districts in six of the thirty four provinces of Afghanistan.

Together we interviewed community-identified village leaders (typically customary leaders), local government officials, religious officials, and randomly selected villagers, including an equal sample of both men and women on local governance, in three languages: Pashto, Dari, and Uzbek.[2] The members of the research team, who represented a variety of ethnic, tribal, and geographical groups, were each fluent in the two main languages of Afghanistan, Dari and Pashto. During fieldwork, I communicated and conducted interviews in two local languages, Dari and Uzbek. In addition, I usually introduced the research

---

[1] The group initially consisted of four researchers but expanded to six during the course of the investigation.

[2] Research was also conducted in Turkmen-speaking communities. These interviews were conducted in Dari, a language that serves as an effective *lingua franca* in Afghanistan.

team to the community and participated and led interviews in nearly all of the villages in the sample. We also interviewed dozens of officials from local and international non-governmental organizations (NGOs), donors, diplomats, as well as government officials at several ministries at the national and sub-national levels.

The original qualitative data were collected on four separate trips to Afghanistan, beginning in 2005, totaling nearly 20 months of research in Afghanistan. The first three trips, each between one and two months, allowed me to plan research and ascertain whether conducting such research was even viable. The fourth trip was for a period of eleven months, concluding in February 2008. After initial field research was complete, I made three additional trips to Afghanistan in 2011 and 2012, spending approximately an additional three months in country.

The research provinces were selected because they captured Afghanistan's regional and ethnic diversity. Research provinces were: Kunduz (northeast), Balkh (north), Kabul (capital), Bamiyan (central highlands), Herat (West), and Nangarhar (East). Originally, Kandahar was chosen a research site but a rapidly deteriorating security situation did not allow for me to conduct research safely in rural communities. Kunduz in the northeast replaced Kandahar as a research province.

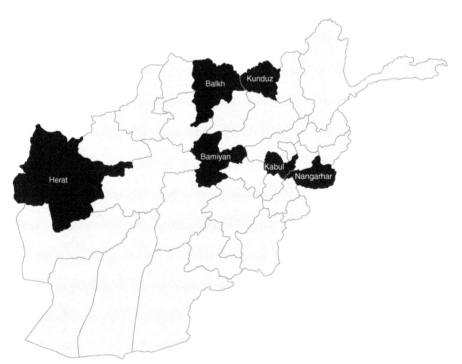

MAP A.1 Research Provinces

TABLE A.2: *Fieldwork Locations*

Province	District
Kunduz	Hazrati Imam Sahib
	Khanabad
Balkh	Nahri Shahi
	Dawlatabad
Kabul	Paghman
	Guldara
	Qarabagh
Bamiyan	Panjab
	Sayghan
	Markaz-i Bamiyan (Bamiyan Center)
	Shiber
Herat	Karokh
	Anjil
	Pashtun Zarghun
	Guzara[3]
Nangarhar	Behsod
	Surkhrod

In each province, two to four districts were selected for in-depth village-level research. Districts were selected in order to capture geographic as well as ethnic diversity within provinces. In each province, I wanted to examine at least one district that was close to the provincial capital (where populations are frequently concentrated) as well as one that was farther away. This was not always possible. For example, in Nangarhar province (which is close to the turbulent Pakistani border) my Afghan colleagues did not feel safe travelling to remote districts, so we studied districts closer to the provincial capital. If a province was ethnically diverse, I wanted to make sure that the district selection captured this diversity.

The same case selection logic applied to villages selected for research in each district. In each district I selected one village close to the district center and one that was farther away. Distance to district center correlates with access to state services. If there was ethnic diversity in a district, I selected villages that captured district diversity. In some cases this was achieved by studying villages that had diverse populations. In other cases, diversity was captured by selecting villages where I could identify single groups living (e.g., Ismaili populations in certain provinces are concentrated in specific villages).

To my surprise, the independent variables that I thought would capture divergent outcomes in the research design (ethnicity and distance to a district

---

[3] Research was cut short in Guzara district due to a deteriorating security situation.

center) did not yield variation on the dependent variable – a range of governance outcomes specific to the empirical chapters in this book. I was quite astonished by the uniformity of the importance of customary governance across ethnic groups, a pattern that became clear from my initial pilot interviews in Kabul province (as discussed in the Preface). As the book illustrates, sets of institutional factors explains the ability of local governing organizations to generate public goods. These were not correlated with ethnicity or other factors. The strength of customary governance is also reflected in most public opinion surveys of Afghanistan, but prior to my field research it was not a trend that scholars or observers had identified as continuing to play an important role in governance outcomes.

We visited villages without the presence of any security personnel, and so we were only able to visit districts that were at the time considered safe for such travel. We were able to conduct research in each of the villages we selected with the exception of one district, Guzara in Herat Province. The district governor denied our access to communities because several conflicts brewing in the district made it unsafe for research (I discuss important reasons why I relied on permission of governors to conduct research in Chapter 7). Tragically, the violence in Guzara district escalated, and the district governor who warned us not to visit his villages was himself shot dead, along with his young son, just a few months after my visit to his district.

In each village, we conducted between six and twelve interviews and focus group discussions. We also took field notes and detailed observations regarding each informant in addition to descriptions of community life. Due to security constraints and the inability to stay in a given community for a long period of time, conclusions are colored by conversations in local mosques, bazaars, schools, street gossip, and chit-chat as sources of triangulation.

In order reduce bias upon entering villages and also to ensure that my research team was welcome in a community, in a first visit to each village I would ask community members to identify their community leader. We did not want to give a title to the village leader, but instead wanted to know from community members who they thought was the leader of their community. After being led to this individual (or individuals), we could ascertain his or her title or position (as these titles varied by village and by region). In nearly all cases, we were directed toward a customary leader. In some instances, as a foreigner I would be introduced to a member of a donor-supported village group while Afghan colleagues would be introduced to a customary leader. I sought to conduct research with the village-identified leader at the very beginning of research in each community as a way to gain permission to conduct research in each community. In tightly-knit communities, word of outsiders traveled fast.

Gathering information about how governance works in a fragile state or how – or if – members of a community can provide public goods under such conditions is a delicate task. When asking questions about authority and power structures in communities, questions were crafted in ways to elicit individual experiences with a wide range of actors in communities rather than asking directly whether certain bodies were present or played a role in communities. Instead of asking "what role does your CDC play in your community?" or "Is your mullah active in your community?" we asked questions about experiences in village life to get a sense what role, if any, different actors and organizations played in village governance.

I found that informants were much more at ease when faced with questions about their neighbors or other villagers rather than when they were called upon to directly reflect upon their own experiences – especially in the very beginning of an interview or discussion. For example, as I sought to understand who people turn to when they want to settle disputes, we asked informants about their neighbors: "Have your neighbors been involved in any disputes recently?" Inevitably, as part of the story they would discuss the organization or mechanism the neighbor worked with to settle the dispute, thus providing crucial information about the way disputes might be solved in a village. Most of the time, informants were much more eager to speak about their own problems – and even insist upon it – rather than those of their neighbor or those happening in their community. After several days of fieldwork, we were then able to get a fairly good picture of how public goods are provided and by whom. We could sense the conflicts and fissures in the communities.

During the research we took great care to be sensitive to conflict and the ravages of war. We opened interviews by asking informants about where they had traveled during the war – as so many Afghans migrated internally as well as to neighboring countries. Opening interviews with this seemingly simple question usually resulted in informants vividly recounting their life experiences in ways that shed light on their personal travails as well as those of their entire community. Because many Afghans had been the subject of seemingly endless donor-sponsored community assessments and "mobilization efforts," I did sense a fatigue from some informants about having to sit through another interview where they were to detail problems in his or her community. Using oral histories and talking about the past eventually leading up to the present day seemed to present a new set of questions to most research participants. From what I could ascertain, aid and donor agencies did not ask these kinds of questions so it created an atmosphere that focused on the individual and their experiences rather than on the specific informational desires of my research.

Despite the struggles of daily life in much of rural Afghanistan, to the best of my recollection, *every single informant* we approached during the course of our research agreed to be interviewed. Such a high response rate would be largely unthinkable in most other parts of the world. I believe it was made possible only because of the face-to-face nature of our fieldwork, but more than anything by the enormous care with which we entered communities and introduced the research.

Although we traveled with no security personnel, security considerations certainly came into play. During the time of research, most of the districts selected for visits were relatively secure. There was minimal presence of insurgent groups in these areas. We used extreme caution and never announced when or if we would return to a community, as repeated and expected visits were more likely to lead to put the research team at risk. Due to security considerations, we did not usually sleep in the villages where we conducted research. Instead, we slept in nearby district centers, only staying overnight in villages that were more than a two hour drive from a given district center.

The fact that the districts selected were "safe" certainly suggests bias in site selection. Although there may be some selection bias and thus something unique about the areas where these data were collected, several years later about half of the districts where I was able to conduct were no longer secure. They are under Taliban control or intensely contested. Upon return visits to Afghanistan for follow-up research, I could not travel to several of the districts selected.

The inability to stay for long period of time in communities presented limitations on the ability to collect data. This was further hampered by the fact that interviews or meetings with many key informants could not be made in advance. As a result, we spent significant time trying to track down informants who may have been working in a bazaar or in far-away fields. The time spent trying to find informants also produced interesting stories and insights, as they led to more observations with unexpected people in the communities we engaged.

To deal with these access challenges, we worked very closely together to make the best use of our time in communities. Upon entering a community we broke up into two groups (men and women) and conducted two interviews or focus group discussions simultaneously. After theses initial interviews we would share stories and discuss what we had found. As we conducted interviews in a community, we would strive to triangulate findings to identify inconsistencies in stories as well as key individuals who might be mentioned frequently in our interviews but who were not on our list of key informant interviews. This frequent triangulation was essential to figure out, very quickly, the sources of conflict and contestation in a community. Furthermore, as a large group we often had disagreements over how to interpret our interviews and observations in individual communities. These disagreements were extremely useful, as seeing a single community through several perspectives helped create balance in the findings. They also ensured that we left no stone unturned in our community visits.

A shortcoming of evidence drawn from interview and focus group discussions, as opposed to extended participant observation, is that information is based on what people intentionally communicate. Unlike traditional ethnographic methods, interview data does not afford the researcher an opportunity to observe what is happening over time, or to figure out the "hidden transcript" that may go unsaid. However, in cases where there were issues or complaints brought up by individual community members that could be linked to an observable outcome, such as failed aid project, we made sure to examine the physical object described (typically this was an aid project that did not work, such as a collapsed retaining wall or broken generator).

Many of the interviews were not typical semi-structured interviews. Instead, they ended up as focus group discussions or group interviews because in most households, it was difficult to interview just one person at a time. When we asked to speak with a single individual, this individual typically led us to the guest room or mehmankhana. Once seated, the informant was typically joined by other members of the family or even neighbors. This was especially true when interviewing women, where crowds of as many as twenty women would gather to participate in our discussions.

Presence of additional individuals usually posed little problem for the research. In most instances, the presence of friends or family resulted in more engaging and even jovial conversations. We were very attentive to dynamics in conversations that might lead to some informants from speaking earnestly. If we sensed an uncomfortable situation or touched on an issue that would be difficult for an individual to speak about before others (as often happened between mother-in-laws and daughter-in-laws), we would typically break up the conversation so that one part of the group could go to another room or elsewhere.

It was not unusual for an outspoken person to dominate conversation. Typically, if one individual tried to dominate the conversation in a focus-group setting, one team member would ask that individual for a tour of the village or ask to see something specific that came up during the course of the interview. As a foreigner, I was often the one to ask the outspoken individual for the community tour. It enabled us to continue the conversation by removing a dominant informant in a way that allowed them to save face as they were seen as so important as to give guests a special introduction to the community. These one-on-one guides were also an important and invaluable source of data, as I was typically given a tour of the community school, shown some of the development projects, taken to see the village mosque, or given a history of the village that was difficult to obtain in a seated interview setting.

We also conducted interviews at the district, provincial, and national levels with government leaders, NGO representatives and "social organizers," as well as with journalists and others who could provide information about the area. We transcribed all village- and district-level interviews in English as soon as possible after concluding them by compiling notes taken by a note-taker present in each interview as well as the recollections of individuals conducting the interview. Given cultural sensitivities, it was not possible to record interviews. Notes from informational interviews, such as with inter-national donors, were not directly transcribed as conversations but instead remained as notes.

As the areas I selected for research were under government control, I made sure to work through the formal government channels to gain official permission to conduct research in villages (this process is described in Chapter 7). Following such procedures was a surprisingly important step in gaining the trust of informants in villages. I gained permission to conduct research in each province and district selected from government officials. The Ministry of Interior (and later the Independent Directorate for Local Government after it took responsibility for local government functions from the Ministry of Interior) provided a letter of introduction that was addressed to provincial governors in the six provinces where I conducted research. Upon entering a new province, I presented the letter of introduction from the Ministry in Kabul to the provincial governor (although I met with his or her deputy in all cases) who in turn alerted the selected district governors that research would be conducted in that area. In most cases, this introduction was done by letter. Usually, in each provincial capital I obtained a set of sealed letters by the deputy governor of the province – one for each of the districts selected for research in that province. Upon entering each new research district, I would hand the district governor the letter from the provincial governor that provided his blessing to conduct research in the district. Using this formal channel of permission also gave me an easy entrée to conducting interviews with the district governor and his staff. Waiting for long hours in government offices along with many other Afghans, also provided important sources of participant observation that helped me understand how individual Afghans relate to the government and allowed me the chance to obtain small background interviews to understand why they visited government offices.

It was a priority to communicate to all key informants at both the government and the community level that the research was not part of an aid project that would result in the provision of a community development project or any other kind of assistance. Residents in rural areas frequently expect that outsiders, especially foreigners, come to provide some kind of material assistance to the individual or community. As a foreigner not affiliated with a military agency, most Afghans assumed I was an aid worker and was visiting to find a location and partner for a new project. Because most assumed I was there to provide aid, discussions would begin with praises of international aid and assistance. Usually, it did not take long to convince most informants that I was not there to implement a project, but was instead there for other purposes. Beginning interviews with questions that elicited oral histories were an extraordinarily useful tool in turning attention away from aid and development projects.

Appendix B

Statistical Appendix

TABLE B.1: *Summary Statistics: Asia Foundation Survey of the Afghan People*

Mean	Survey Question/Description	Estimate	Std. Err.
Variables Related to Village Organizations			
*Shuras/jirga*s Accessible	Do you agree, agree somewhat disagree somewhat, or strongly disagree that a local *jirga* or *shura* is accessible to you?	3.218	0.024
Shura/Jirga Fair/ Trusted	Do you agree(=4), agree somewhat (=3), disagree somewhat (=2), or strongly disagree (=1) that your local *jirga*s or *shura*s are fair and trusted?	3.104	0.023
CDC in Village	Community Development Councils have been established as part of the National Solidarity Program and members of the Council are representatives of various groups in your community. Tell me; are you aware of such an institution formed in your neighborhood/settlement?	0.368	0.015

(*continued*)

TABLE B.1 (*continued*)

Mean	Survey Question/Description	Estimate	Std. Err.
Info From *Malik*	If you wanted to find out about something important happening in your community, who outside your family, would you want to tell you? [Do not read potential responses out loud] 1=*malik*, 0=other	0.134	0.007
Info from Mullah	If you wanted to find out about something important happening in your community, who outside your family, would you want to tell you? [Do not read potential responses out loud] 1=mullah, 0=other	0.108	0.007
Dependent Variables: Chapter 3			
Central Government Performance		3.024	0.022
Afghanistan Moving in the Right Direction	Generally speaking, do you think things in Afghanistan today are going in the right direction, or do you think they are going in the wrong direction? (3=right direction, 2=some in right, some in wrong direction, 1=wrong direction)	2.199	0.021
Is Your Vote Influential	Do you think that voting can lead to improvement in the future or do you believe that no matter how one votes, things never change? (1= Vote can change things, 0= Things are not going to get better)	0.760	0.011
Would You Tolerate a Friend in an Opposing Political Party	Suppose a friend of yours supported a part you do not like, Would you accept that , or would it end your friendship? (1=would accept it, 0=would end friendship)	0.334	0.014
Opposition is Good for Afghanistan	It is a good thing that the government should allow peaceful opposition. Do you agree (=4), somewhat agree (=3), disagree somewhat =2), disagree strongly (=1)?	3.190	0.027

Mean	Survey Question/Description	Estimate	Std. Err.
Do you Support Equal Rights for Women?	The new constitution says mean and women have equal rights, including the right to vote. What do you think about this statement? Do you agree or disagree? (Wait for response and then ask) Strongly or somewhat? Do you agree (=4), somewhat agree (=3), disagree somewhat =2), disagree strongly (=1)?	3.503	0.021
Dependent Variables: Chapter 4			
Individual Need Help Resolving Dispute	In the past two years, have you had a dispute or formal case that you couldn't' settle with the other part and had to go to a state court or village/neighborhood based *shura/jirga* to resolve?	0.175	0.009
Community Involved in Formal Dispute	Sometimes people and communities have problems, related to an issue that concerns everybody in their area, that they can't resolve on their own and they have to ask for the help of a government official or government agency. In the past five years, has your community had such a problem in your area that you had to ask for help or cooperation to resolve it?	0.155	0.008
Do You Fear for Your Personal Safety?	How often do you fear for your own personal safety or security or for that of your family these days? (1=Often, 2=sometimes. 3=Rarely.4= Never)	2.302	0.030
Victim of Crime	Have you or anyone in your family been the victim of violence or a criminal act in your home or community in the past year? (1=yes, 0=no)	0.171	0.008

(*continued*)

TABLE B.1 (*continued*)

Mean	Survey Question/Description	Estimate	Std. Err.
Dependent Variables: Chapter 5			
	I would like to ask you about today's condition in the village/ neighborhood where you live. Would you rate the availability (insert item here) as good or bad in your area?		
Education Available	1=good, 0=bad	0.710	0.014
Electricity Supply Available	1=good, 0=bad	0.226	0.013
Freedom of Movement	1=good, 0=bad	0.698	0.014
Irrigation Water Available	1=good, 0=bad	0.611	0.015
Jobs Available	1=good, 0=bad	0.284	0.013
Security Situation	1=good, 0=bad	0.631	0.015
Clean Drinking Water	1=good, 0=bad	0.619	0.015
Individual Characteristics			
Age	How old were you on your last birthday? 1=18–24 years, 2=25–34 years, 3=35=44 years, 4=45=54 years, 6=55–64 years, 7=Over 65 years old	0.338	0.002
Female	Indicates whether respondent is female	0.500	0.022
Income	For statistical purposes only, we need to know your average monthly household income. Will you please tell me which of the following categories best represents your average total family income? (1to 9 scale)	2.961	0.046
Listen to Radio	Do you listen to the radio at least once a week?	0.714	0.011
Education	What is the highest level of school you completed (1 to 7 scale)	2.388	0.050
Female		0.500	0.022
Trust People	Generally speaking, would you say that most people can be trusted or that you need to be very careful in dealing with people?	.4134303	.0121264

TABLE B.2: *NRVA Summary Statistics*

Mean	Survey Question/Description	Estimate	Std. Err.
Village Level Variables			
Shura	Presence of customary council in the community (Male *shura*, female *shura*, mixed gender *shura*, tribal *shura*, elders, *jirga*)	0.731	0.009
CDC	Presence of NSP Community Development Council in the community (measured as 1 if there is one of the following: male CDC, female CDC, mixed gender CDC)	0.291	0.009
Household Level Variables			
Altitude (meters)	Altitude of household (in meters)	1410.882	18.574
Income	Household Income (ln)	0.291	0.009
Household Head Literate	Based on whether household head could read a piece of text	.2946322	0.007
Years in Village	Number of years family has lived in the village	25.13153	.299458
Variables Related to Land Disputes			
Dispute Resolved	Whether the land dispute was resolved	0.491	0.031
Land Dispute	Have you had a dispute over the ownership of this dwelling and associated land	0.026	0.001
Deed to Land	Do you have a deed (evidence of ownership document) registered or recorded anywhere for this house and associated land?	0.525	0.009

Appendix C

List of Interviews and Focus Groups

Interview	Type of Data	Gender	Age of Informant(s)	Occupation	Ethnicity
Balkh-Dawlatabad-Village1-#1	Interview	Female	Middle aged	Widow; homemaker	Pashtun
Balkh-Dawlatabad-Village1-#2	Interview	Female	Approx. mid 20s	Homemaker	Pashtun
Balkh-Dawlatabad-Village1-#3	Focus Group	Family	Mixed	Husband, wife, and married daughter	Pashtun
Balkh-Dawlatabad-Village1-#4	Interview	Male	Middle aged	Farmer	Uzbek
Balkh-Dawlatabad-Village1-#5	Interview	Male	Approx. early 50s	Farmer	Hazara
Balkh-Dawlatabad-Village1-#6	Focus Group	Three Males	Mixed	One elder and two mardikar	Pashtun
Balkh-Dawlatabad-Village1-#7	Interview	Male	Approx. early 30s	Farmer	Uzbek
Balkh-Dawlatabad-Village1-#8	Interview	Male	Middle aged	Farmer	Uzbek
Balkh-Dawlatabad-District Center-#1	Interview	Male	Approx. 30	Foreign NGO employee	Uzbek
Balkh-Dawlatabad-District Center-#2	Interview	Male	Middle aged	District Governor	Uzbek
Balkh-Dawlatabd-Village2-#1	Focus Group	Six Females	Mixed	Three generations of a household	Hazara
Balkh-Dawlatabad-Village2-#2	Interview	Female	Approx. 60	Homemaker;	Tajik
Balkh-Dawlatabad-Village2-#3	Focus Group	Two males	Approx. early 50s	Qaryadar and his neighbor	Hazara
Balkh-Dawlatabad-Village2-#4	Interview	Interview	Approx. 18	School teacher	Hazara

Balkh-Dawlatabad-Village2-#5	Interview	Female	Approx. 30	Homemaker	Tajik
Balkh-Dawlatabad-Village2-#6	Interview	Male	Approx. 60	Farmer	Turkmen
Balkh-Provincial Capital-#1	Interview	Female	Approx. 50	International NGO employee	Tajik
Balkh-Provincial Capital-#2	Interview	Male	Approx. 50	Provincial MRRD employee	Tajik
Balkh-Provincial Capital-#3	Interview	Male	Approx. 40	Provincial NSP office director	Uncertain
Balkh-Provincial Capital-#4	Interview	Male	Middle aged	Afghan NGO employee	Tajik
Balkh-Provincial Capital-#5	Interview	Male	Approx. early 30s	International NGO employee	Pashtun
Balkh-Provincial Capital-#6	Interview	Male	Middle aged	Mayor, Mazar-e Sharif	Tajik
Balkh-Provincial Capital-#7	Interview	Female	Middle aged	Provincial Council Member	Tajik
Balkh-Provincial Capital-#8	Interview	Female	Approx. late 30s	Provincial Council Member	Tajik
Balkh-Provincial Capital-#9	Interview	Male	Middle aged	Provincial Council Member	Tajik
Balkh-Provincial Capital-#10	Focus Group	Mixed	Mixed	NGO employees	Mixed
Balkh-Nahri Shahi-Village 1-#1	Interview	Female	Middle aged	Homemaker; CDC participant	Hazara
Balkh-Nahri Shahi-Village 1-#2	Interview	Female	Middle aged	Biology teacher	Tajik
Balkh-Nahri Shahi-Village 1-#3	Interview	Male	Approx. 55	Qaryadar	Tajik

(continued)

(continued)

Interview	Type of Data	Gender	Age of Informant(s)	Occupation	Ethnicity
Balkh-Nahri Shahi-Village 1-#4	Focus Group	Male	Mixed ages	CDC participants	Pashtun
Balkh-Nahri Shahi-Village 1-#5	Interview	Female	Approx. 18	Student	Pashtun
Balkh-Nahri Shahi-Village 1-#6	Interview	Female	Approx. 30	Homemaker	Tajik
Balkh-Nahri Shahi-Village 1-#7	Interview	Male	Approx. 65	Shopkeeper; Mosque caretaker	Pashtun
Balkh-Nahri Shahi-Village 3-#1	Interview	Male	Approx. 60	Government employee	Pashtun
Balkh-Nahri Shahi-Village 2-#1	Interview	Interview	Approx. 45	Homemaker; CDC participant	Tajik
Balkh-Nahri Shahi-Village 2-#2	Interview	Female	Middle aged	Seamstress	Tajik
Balkh-Nahri Shahi-Village 2-#3	Interview	Female	Middle aged	Homemaker; mother of seven	Tajik
Balkh-Nahri Shahi-Village 2-#4	Interview	Male	Approx. 65	Former Qaryadar; now head of CDC	Tajik
Balkh-Nahri Shahi-Village 2-#5	Interview	Male	Approx. 45	Qaryadar	Tajik
Balkh-Nahri Shahi-Village 2-#6	Interview	Male	Approx. 50	Farmer	Pashtun
Balkh-Nahri Shahi-Village 2-#7	Interview	Male	Middle aged	Farmer	Pashtun
Balkh-Nahri Shahi-Village 3-#1	Interview	Female	Approx. late 40s	Qaryadar	Tajik
Balkh-Nahri Shahi-District Center-#1	Focus Group	Four males	Mixed	District governor and his staff members	Mixed

Location	Method	Gender	Age	Role	Ethnicity
Bamiyan-Provincial Capital-#1	Interview	Male	Middle aged	International NGO employee	Uncertain
Bamiyan-Provincial Capital-#2	Interview	Male	Approx. 30	International NGO employee	Pashtun
Bamiyan-Provincial Capital-#3	Interview	Male	Middle aged	Head of Shura-ye Mardomi	Hazara
Bamiyan-Provincial Capital-#4	Interview	Male	Middle aged	Deputy Provincial Governor	Hazara
Bamiyan-Bamiyan Center-Village 1-#1	Interview	Female	Middle aged	CDC participant	Hazara
Bamiyan-Bamiyan Center-Village 1-#2	Interview	Female	Approx. 60	Grandmother	Hazara
Bamiyan-Bamiyan Center-Village 1-#3	Focus Group	Male	Middle aged	Engineer; Head of CDC	Hazara
Bamiyan-Bamiyan Center-Village 1-#4	Interview	Male	Approx. 45	Uncertain	Hazara
Bamiyan-Bamiyan Center-Village 1-#5	Interview	Female	Approx. 60	Grandmother	Hazara
Bamiyan-Bamiyan Center-Village 1-#6	Interview	Male	Approx. 60	Head of CDC	Hazara
Bamiyan-Bamiyan Center-Village 2-#1	Focus Group	Five women	Between 18–25	Literacy course instructor	Hazara
Bamiyan-Bamiyan Center-Village 2-#2	Interview	Woman	Approx. 30	Housewife	Hazara
Bamiyan-Bamiyan Center-Village 2-#3	Interview	Woman	Approx. 45	Head of Female CDC	Hazara
Bamiyan-Bamiyan Center-Village 2-#4	Interview	Woman	Approx. 50	CDC participant	Hazara
Bamiyan-Bamiyan Center-Village 2-#5	Interview	Woman	Approx. 55	Housewife	Hazara

(continued)

(continued)

Interview	Type of Data	Gender	Age of Informant(s)	Occupation	Ethnicity
Bamiyan-Bamiyan Center-Village 2-#6	Interview	Woman	Approx. 50	Housewife	Hazara
Bamiyan-Bamiyan Center-Village 2-#7	Interview	Male	Approx. 60	Haji; CDC participant; War veteran	Hazara
Bamiyan-Bamiyan Center-Village 2-#8	Focus Group	Male	Four men (ages 30–45)	CDC participants	Hazara
Bamiyan-Bamiyan Center-Village 2-#9	Interview	Male	Approx. 70	Farmer; Haji	Hazara
Bamiyan-Bamiyan Center-Village 2-#10	Focus Group	Male	Both young men age 18	Students	Hazara
Bamiyan-Panjab-Village 1-#1	Interview	Woman	Approx. 27	Housewife	Hazara
Bamiyan-Panjab-Village 1-#2	Interview	Woman	Approx. 45	Housewife	Hazara
Bamiyan-Panjab-Village 1-#3	Focus Group	Two women	18 and 45 (her mother)	Student and her mother	Hazara
Bamiyan-Panjab-Village 1-#4	Interview	Female	Middle age	Housewife	Hazara
Bamiyan-Panjab-Village 1-#5	Focus Group	Three women	Middle aged	Housewife	Hazara
Bamiyan-Panjab-Village 1-#6	Interview	Male	Middle aged	Farm laborer	Hazara
Bamiyan-Panjab-Village 1-#7	Focus Group	Four males	Middle aged	Farmers	Hazara
Bamiyan-Panjab-Village 1-#8	Focus Group	Two males	Both around 20 years old	Farm laborers	Hazara

Location	Method	Participants	Age	Role	Ethnicity
Bamiyan-Panjab-Village 1-#9	Focus Group	Four males	All over age 60	Elders	Hazara
Bamiyan-Panjab-District Center-#1	Focus Group	Five women	Ages 21–40	NGO employees	Hazara
Bamiyan-Panjab-District Center-#2	Focus Group	One male	Approx. 35	NGO employees	Hazara
Bamiyan-Panjab-District Center-#3	Interview	One male	Approx. 50	District Governor	Hazara
Bamiyan-Panjab-Village 2-#1	Interview	One female	Approx. 45	CDC participant	Hazara
Bamiyan-Panjab-Village 2-#2	Interview	One female	Approx. late 40s	CDC participant	Hazara
Bamiyan-Panjab-Village 2-#3	Focus Group	Three females	Middle aged	Housewives	Hazara
Bamiyan-Panjab-Village 2-#4	Interview	One female	Middle aged	Housewife	Hazara
Bamiyan-Panjab-Village 2-#5	Focus Group	Two females	Approx. 50 and 30 years old	Mothers	Hazara
Bamiyan-Panjab-Village 2-#6	Interview	Male	Approx. 80	Mullah	Hazara
Bamiyan-Panjab-Village 2-#7	Interview	Male	Approx. 30	Qarbalayi	Hazara
Bamiyan-Panjab-Village 2-#8	Interview	Male	Approx. 25	Farm laborer	Hazara
Bamiyan-Panjab-Village 2-#9	Interview	Male	Approx. 25	Farmer	Hazara
Bamiyan-Sayghan-Village 1-#1	Interview	Female	Middle aged	CDC participant/Housewife	Tajik
Bamiyan-Sayghan-Village 1-#2	Interview	Female	Approx. 40	CDC participant/Housewife	Tajik

(continued)

Interview	Type of Data	Gender	Age of Informant(s)	Occupation	Ethnicity
Bamiyan-Sayghan-Village 1-#3	Interview	Female	Middle aged	Housewife	Tajik
Bamiyan-Sayghan-Village 1-#4	Interview	Male	Approx. 60	Malik	Tajik
Bamiyan-Sayghan-Village 1-#5	Focus Group	Male	Approx. 30–40	CDC participant	Tajik
Bamiyan-Sayghan-Village 1-#6	Interview	Male	Approx. 32	Farmer	Tajik
Bamiyan-Sayghan-Village 2-#1	Interview	Male	Approx. 50	Malik	Tajik
Bamiyan-Sayghan-Village 2-#2	Interview	Male	Approx. 60	Mullah	Tajik
Bamiyan-Sayghan-Village 2-#3	Interview	Male	Approx. 45	Cook at NGO	Tajik
Bamiyan-Sayghan-Village 2-#4	Interview	Male	Approx. 25	Farmer	Tajik
Bamiyan-Sayghan-Village 2-#5	Interview	Male	Approx. 50	NGO employee	Tajik
Bamiyan-Sayghan-Village 2-#6	Focus Group	Females	Approx. 40	Housewives	Tajik
Bamiyan-Sayghan-District Center-#1	Interview	Male	Approx. 45	District Governor	Tajik
Bamiyan-Sayghan-Village 2-#7	Interview	Female	Approx. 20	Literacy teacher	Tajik
Bamiyan-Shibar-District Center-#2	Interview	Male and Female	Female approx. 25, male approx. 30.	NGO employees	Hazara
Bamiyan-Shibar-District Center-#1	Focus Group	Four Males	Approx. between 18–35	NGO employees	Mixed

Location	Interview Type	Gender	Age	Role	Ethnicity
Bamiyan-Shibar-District Center-#3	Interview	Male	Approx. 60	District Governor	Tajik
Bamiyan-Shibar-Village 1-#1	Interview	Female	32	School teacher	Ismaili
Bamiyan-Shibar-Village 1-#2	Interview	Female	Approx. 60	Housewife	Ismaili
Bamiyan-Shibar-Village 1-#3	Focus Group	Females	Mixed	Homemakers	Ismaili
Bamiyan-Shibar-Village 1-#4	Interview	Female	Approx. 30	Homemaker	Ismaili
Bamiyan-Shibar-Village 1-#5	Focus Group	Three Males	Approx. 35–50	Mullah, Namayenda, and CDC participant	Ismaili
Bamiyan-Shibar-Village 1-#6	Interview	Male	Approx. 40	Farmer	Ismaili
Bamiyan-Shibar-Village 1-#9	Interview	Male	Unknown	Farmer	Ismaili
Bamiyan-Shibar-Village 1-#7	Interview	Male	Approx. 75	Village Elder	Ismaili
Bamiyan-Shibar-Village 1-#8	Interview	Male	Approx. 45	Farmer	Ismaili
Bamiyan-Shibar-Village 2-#1	Interview	Female	Approx. 50	Housewife	Hazara
Bamiyan-Shibar-Village 2-#2	Interview	Female	Middle aged	Housewife	Hazara
Bamiyan-Shibar-Village 2-#3	Interview	Male	Approx. 40	Shopkeeper	Hazara
Bamiyan-Shibar-Village 2-#4	Interview	Male	Approx. 50	Kalantar	Hazara
Bamiyan-Shibar-Village 2-#5	Interview	Male	Middle aged	School teacher	Hazara

(continued)

Interview	Type of Data	Gender	Age of Informant(s)	Occupation	Ethnicity
Bamiyan-Shibar-Village 2-#6	Interview	Female	Approx. 55	Homemaker	Hazara
Bamiyan-Shibar-Village 2-#7	Interview	Female	Middle aged	Homemaker	Hazara
Herat-Anjil-District Center #1	Interview	Male	Approx. 50	District Security Commander	Pashtun
Herat-Anjil-District Center #2	Interview	Male	Approx. 40	District Governor	Tajik
Herat-Anjil-Village 1-#1	Interview	Female	Approx. late 20s	Homemaker	Pashtun
Herat-Anjil-Village 1-#2	Interview	Female	Middle aged	Homemaker; CDC participant	Pashtun
Herat-Anjil-Village 1-#3	Interview	Male	Unknown	Farmer	Pashtun
Herat-Anjil-Village 1-#4	Interview	Female	Approx. late 30s	Homemaker	Pashtun
Herat-Anjil-Village 1-#5	Focus Group	Female	Early 20s–late 30s	Homemakers	Tajik
Herat-Anjil-Village 1-#6	Interview	Male	Middle aged	CDC participant	Pashtun
Herat-Anjil-District Center #3	Focus Group	Mixed	Approx. 25–50	Members of a district-wide environmental shura	Mixed
Herat-Anjil-Village 2-#1	Interview	Female	Elderly	Homemaker; spiritual leader	Aimaq
Herat-Anjil-Village 2-#2	Interview	Male	Approx. 40	Malik	Tajik

Herat-Anjil-Village 2-#3	Interview	Male	Approx. 50	"Doctor"; responsible for all NGO activity in community	Tajik
Herat-Anjil-Village 2-#4	Interview	Male	Middle aged	CDC member, Sayed	Tajik
Herat-Anjil-Village 2-#5	Interview	Male	Approx. early 30s	Farmer	Hazara
Herat-Anjil-Village 2-#6	Interview	Female	Middle aged	CDC participant	Tajik
Herat-Anjil-Village 2-#7	Interview	Female	Middle aged	Homemaker	Hazara
Herat-Anjil-Village 2-#8	Interview	Female	Approx. 20s	Homemaker	Tajik
Herat-Provincial Capital - #1	Interview	Male	Approx. 50	Provincial Government Official	Tajik
Herat-Guzara-District Center-#1	Interview	Male	Approx. 40	District Governor	Tajik
Herat-Provincial Capital #2	Interview	Male	Approx. 65	Deputy Provincial Governor	Tajik
Herat-Provincial Capital #3	Focus Group	Mixed	Approx. 30–50	NGO employees	Tajik
Herat-Provincial Capital #4	Interview	Male	Middle aged	Provincial Line Ministry Representative	Tajik
Herat-Provincial Capital #5	Interview	Male	Approx. late 20s	Provincial MRRD director	Tajik
Herat-Provincial Capital #6	Interview	Male	Approx mid. 20s	Provincial MRRD employee	Tajik
Herat-Karokh-District Center-#1	Focus Group	Six Males	Approx. 35–70	Maliks and other community members	Tajik

(continued)

(*continued*)

Interview	Type of Data	Gender	Age of Informant(s)	Occupation	Ethnicity
Herat-Karokh-District Center-#2	Focus Group	Two males, one female	Approx. 25–40	International Organization Employees	Tajik
Herat-Karokh-District Center-#3	Interview	Male	Approx. 45	District Governor	Tajik
Herat-Karokh-Village 1-#1	Interview	Female	Approx. 50s	Female CDC participant	Tajik
Herat-Karokh-Village 1-#2	Interview	Female	Age 65	Homemaker	Tajik
Herat-Karokh-Village 1-#3	Interview	Female	Approx. 50	Literacy teacher	Tajik
Herat-Karokh-Village 1-#4	Interview	Male	Approx. 30s	Policeman	Tajik
Herat-Karokh-Village 1-#5	Interview	Male	Age 29	Shopkeeper	Tajik
Herat-Karokh-Village 1-#6	Interview	Male	Approx. 50	Village Elder	Tajik
Herat-Karokh-Village 2-#1	Interview	Female	Approx. late 30s	Female	Aimaq
Herat-Karokh-Village 2-#2	Interview	Male	Unknown	Only literate person in village; CDC participant	Aimaq
Herat-Karokh-Village 2-#3	Interview	Male	Approx. mid 40s	Farmer	Aimaq
Herat-Karokh-Village 2-#4	Interview	Male	Approx. 65	Farmer	Aimaq
Herat-Karokh-Village 2-#5	Interview	Male	Approx. 30	Farmer	Aimaq
Herat-Pashtun Zarghun-Village 1-#1	Focus Group	Two females	Approx. 40 and 65	CDC participant and mother-in-law	Pashtun

Herat-Pashtun Zarghun-Village 1-#2	Interview	Female	Approx. 30s	Homemaker	Pashtun
Herat-Pashtun Zarghun-Village 1-#3	Focus Group	Two females	Approx. 35 and 45	Homemaker	Pashtun
Herat-Pashtun Zarghun-Village 1-#4	Interview	Male	Approx. 40–45	Arbab	Pashtun
Herat-Pashtun Zarghun-Village 1-#5	Interview	Male	Approx. 50	Farmer	Tajik
Herat-Pashtun Zarghun-Village 1-#6	Interview	Male	Approx. early 20s	Farm laborer	Pashtun
Herat-Pashtun Zarghun-Village 1-#7	Interview	Male	Approx. early 60s.	Mirab	Pashtun
Herat-Pasthun-Zarghun District Center-#1	Interview	Male	Approx. mid 50s	Head of District Government Administration	Tajik
Herat-Pasthun-Zarghun District Center-#2	Interview	Male	Approx. mid 30s	International NGO employee	Tajik
Herat-Pasthun-Zarghun District Center-#3	Interview	Male	Approx. mid 40s	District Police Commander	Pashtun
Herat-Pasthun Zarghun-Village 2-#1	Interview	Female	Approx. mid 50s	Homemaker; CDC participant	Pashtun

(continued)

(continued)

Interview	Type of Data	Gender	Age of Informant(s)	Occupation	Ethnicity
Herat-Pasthun Zarghun-Village 2-#2	Interview	Female	Approx. mid-30s	Homemaker	Pashtun
Herat-Pasthun Zarghun-Village 2-#3	Interview	Female	Unknown	Homemaker	Pashtun
Herat-Pasthun Zarghun-Village 2-#3	Interview	Male	Approx. 40s	Arbab	Pashtun
Herat-Pasthun Zarghun-Village 2-#4	Interview	Male	Approx. mid 50s	Government worker; CDC treasurer	Pashtun
Herat-Pasthun Zarghun-Village 2-#5	Interview	Male	Approx. 60	Farmer; larger landowner	Pashtun
Herat-Pasthun Zarghun-Village 2-#6	Interview	Male	Approx. 40	Farmer	Pashtun
Herat-Pasthun Zarghun-Village 2-#7	Interview	Male	Approx. mid 30s	NGO employee	Pashtun
Kabul-Guldara-District Center-#1	Focus Group	Six males	Approx. 20–40	NGO Social organizers	Mixed
Kabul-Guldara-District Center-#2	Interview	Male	Approx. mid 50s	District Governor	Tajik
Kabul-Guldara-District Center-#3	Interview	Female	Early 30s	Homemaker; mother	Pashtun
Kabul-Guldara-Village 1-#1	Interview	Female	Late 20s	Wife of Malik	Pashtun
Kabul-Guldara-Village 1-#2					

ID	Method	Gender	Age	Occupation	Ethnicity
Kabul-Guldara-Village 1-#3	Focus Group	Three females	Approx. mid 20s-mid 40s	CDC participants	Pashtun
Kabul-Guldara-Village 1-#4	Interview	Male	Age 32	Malik	Pashtun
Kabul-Guldara-Village 1-#5	Interview	Male	Age 53	Farmer	Pashtun
Kabul-Guldara-Village 1-#6	Interview	Male	Approx. mid 50s	Farmer	Pashtun
Kabul-Guldara-Village 1-#7	Interview	Female	Unknown	Homemaker	Pashtun
Kabul-Guldara-Village 1-#8	Interview	Male	Approx. mid 40s	Farmers	Pashtun
Kabul-Guldara-Village 2-#1	Interview	Female	Approx. mid 50s	CDC participants	Tajik
Kabul-Guldara-Village 2-#3	Focus Group	Three females	Approx. mid 30s-mid 50s	Homemakers; Mother of martyr	Tajik
Kabul-Guldara-Village 2-#2	Interview	Interview	Approx. mid 50s	Homemaker	Tajik
Kabul-Guldara-Village 2-#4	Interview	Female	Approx. mid 40s	Homemaker	Tajik
Kabul-Guldara-Village 2-#5	Interview	Male	Age 55	Malik	Tajik
Kabul-Guldara-Village 2-#6	Interview	Male	Age 77	Farmer	Tajik
Kabul-Guldara-Village 2-#7	Interview	Male	Middle aged	Farmer	Tajik
Kabul-Guldara-Village 2-#8	Interview	Male	Approx. 25	Shepherd	Tajik
Kabul-Paghman-Village 1-#1	Interview	Female	Unknown	Homemaker; CDC participant	Pashtun

(continued)

(continued)

Interview	Type of Data	Gender	Age of Informant(s)	Occupation	Ethnicity
Kabul-Paghman-Village 1-#2	Interview	Male	Age 48	Former 'jihadi'	Tajik
Kabul-Paghman-Village 1-#3	Interview	Male	Age 51	Farmer	Tajik
Kabul-Paghman-Village 1-#4	Interview	Male	Approx. mid 60s	Mason	Tajik
Kabul-Paghman-District Center-#1	Interview	Male	Approx. mid 40s	Head of district government administration	Tajik
Kabul-Paghman-District Center-#2	Interview	Male	Approx. mid 20s	Afghan NGO employee	Tajik
Kabul-Paghman-District Center-#3	Interview	Male	Approx. mid 50s	District Governor	Pashtun
Kabul-Paghman-Village 2-#1	Interview	Male	Approx. mid 40s	Security guard for local commander	Pashtun
Kabul-Paghman-Village 2-#2	Interview	Male	Age 45	Farmer	Pashtun
Kabul-Paghman-Village 2-#3	Interview	Female	Approx. mid 50s	Homemaker	Pashtun
Kabul-Paghman-Village 2-#4	Interview	Male	Unknown	former mujahed; farmer	Pashtun
Kabul-Paghman-Village 2-#5	Interview	Male	Approx. early 40s	unemployed	Pashtun
Kabul-Qarabagh-District Center-#1	Interview	Male	Approx. early 30s	Afghan NGO employee	Tajik
Kabul-Qarabagh-Village 1-#1	Interview	Female	Approx. late 50s	Homemaker; widow	Pashtun
Kabul-Qarabagh-Village 1-#2	Interview	Female	Middle aged	Homemaker	Pashtun

Kabul-Qarabagh-Village 1-#3	Interview	Female	Approx. late 60s	Homemaker	Pashtun
Kabul-Qarabagh-Village 1-#4	Interview	Male	Middle aged	Malik	Pashtun
Kabul-Qarabagh-Village 1-#5	Interview	Male	Middle aged	Former commander	Pashtun
Kabul-Qarabagh-Village 1-#6	Interview	Male	33 years old	Shopkeeper	Pashtun
Kabul-Qarabagh-Village 2-#1	Interview	Female	Middle aged	Homemaker	Pashtun
Kabul-Qarabagh-Village 2-#2	Interview	Female	Approx. mid 60s	Homemaker; Mother of CDC participant	Pashtun
Kabul-Qarabagh-Village 2-#3	Interview	Female	Approx. 50	Homemaker; widow	Pashtun
Kabul-Qarabagh-Village 2-#4	Focus Group	Two males	Age 25 and Approx. 32	Malik and his brother	Pashtun
Kabul-Qarabagh-Village 2-#5	Interview	Male	Approx. age 40	Farmer	Pashtun
Kabul-Qarabagh-Village 2-#6	Interview	Male	Approx. 45	Farmer	Pashtun
Kabul-Qarabagh-Village 2-#7	Interview	Male	Middle aged	Unemployed	Pashtun
Kunduz-Imam Sahib-Village 1-#1	Interview	Female	Approx. late 30s	Homemaker; CDC participant	Uzbek
Kunduz-Imam Sahib-Village 1-#2	Interview	Female	Approx. mid 60s	Midwife	Uzbek
Kunduz-Imam Sahib-Village 1-#3	Interview	Female	Middle aged	Homemaker	Uzbek
Kunduz-Imam Sahib-Village 1-#4	Interview	Male	Approx. early 30s	Commander	Uzbek

(continued)

(*continued*)

Interview	Type of Data	Gender	Age of Informant(s)	Occupation	Ethnicity
Kunduz-Imam Sahib-Village 1-#5	Interview	Male	Middle aged	"Doctor"	Uzbek
Kunduz-Imam Sahib-Village 1-#6	Interview	Female	Approx. mid 40s	Homemaker	Uzbek
Kunduz-Imam Sahib-Village 1-#7	Interview	Male	Unknown	Metal worker	Uzbek
Kunduz-Imam Sahib-Village 1-#8	Interview	Male	Approx. early 70s	Shopkeeper	Uzbek
Kunduz-Imam Sahib-District Center-#1	Interview	Female	Approx. mid 40s	International NGO employee	Pashtun
Kunduz-Imam Sahib-District Center-#2	Interview	Male	Middle aged	District Governor	Pashtun
Kunduz-Imam Sahib-District Center-#3	Interview	Male	Middle aged	International NGO employee	Tajik
Kunduz-Imam Sahib-Village 2-#1	Interview	Female	Middle aged	Female CDC participant	Pashtun
Kunduz-Imam Sahib-Village 2-#2	Interview	Male	Approx. late 30s	Arbab	Pashtun
Kunduz-Imam Sahib-Village 2-#3	Interview	Male	Age 43	Farmer	Pashtun
Kunduz-Imam Sahib-Village 2-#5	Interview	Female	Middle aged	Homemaker; Mother of nine children	Pashtun
Kunduz-Imam Sahib-Village 2-#4	Interview	Female	Approx. mid 40s	Widow	Pashtun
Kunduz-Imam Sahib-Village 2-#6	Interview	Female	Approx. early 50s	Homemaker	Pashtun
Kunduz-Imam Sahib-Village 2-#7	Interview	Male	Age 30	Farmer	Pashtun

Location	Type	Gender	Age	Occupation	Ethnicity
Kunduz-Imam Sahib-Village 2-#8	Interview	Male	Approx. 65	Mardikar	Pashtun
Kunduz-Khanabad-Village 1-#1	Interview	Female	Approx. mid 40s	Homemaker	Tajik
Kunduz-Khanabad-Village 1-#2	Interview	Female	Approx. late 50s	Homemaker; Widower; former CDC participant	Tajik
Kunduz-Khanabad-Village 1-#3	Interview	Female	Approx. late 30s	Homemaker	Tajik
Kunduz-Khanabad-Village 1-#4	Focus Group	Two females	Approx. early 20s	Two sisters	Tajik
Kunduz-Khanabad-Village 1-#5	Interview	Male	Middle aged	Arbab/mirab	Tajik
Kunduz-Khanabad-Village 1-#6	Interview	Male	Approx. 40	Farmer	Tajik
Kunduz-Khanabad-Village 1-#7	Interview	Male	Approx. 30	Unemployed; Handicapped	Tajik
Kunduz-Khanabad-Village 1-#8	Interview	Male	Approx. age 50	CDC participant	Tajik
Kunduz-Khanabad-District Center-#1	Interview	Female	Approx. early 30s	Afghan NGO employee	Tajik
Kunduz-Khanabad-District Center-#2	Interview	Male	Middle aged	Head of district government administration	Tajik
Kunduz-Khanabad-Village 2-#1	Interview	Female	Approx. early 50s	School teacher	Tajik
Kunduz-Khanabad-Village 2-#2	Interview	Male	Approx. 50	Farmer	Hazara
Kunduz-Khanabad-Village 2-#3	Interview	Female	Approx. mid 60s	Homemaker	Ismaili
Kunduz-Khanabad-Village 2-#4	Interview	Female	Approx. early 30s	Homemaker	Hazara

(continued)

Interview	Type of Data	Gender	Age of Informant(s)	Occupation	Ethnicity
Kunduz-Khanabad-Village 2-#5	Interview	Male	Middle aged	Teacher	Hazara
Kunduz-Khanabad-Village 2-#6	Interview	Female	Approx. mid 40s	Teacher	Hazara
Kunduz-Khanabad-Village 2-#7	Interview	Male	Approx. mid 50s	Farmer	Hazara
Kunduz-Provincial Capital-#1	Interview	Female	Approx. early 30s	Provincial MRRD employee	Pashtun
Kunduz-Provincial Capital-#2	Interview	Female	Middle aged	Afghan NGO employee	Pashtun
Kunduz-Provincial Capital-#3	Interview	Male	Approx. early 50s	Head of provincial MRRD office	Pashtun
Kunduz-Provincial Capital-#4	Interview	Male	Age 25	Provincial MRRD employee	Pashtun
Kunduz-Provincial Capital-#5	Interview	Male	Approx. early 30s	Afghan NGO employee	Unknown
Kunduz-Provincial Capital-#6	Interview	Male	Approx. early 40s	Afghan NGO employee	Pashtun
Kunduz-Provincial Capital-#7	Focus Group	Mixed; seven people	Approx. early 20s–mid 50s	Foreign NGO employees	Mixed
Nangarhar-Behsod-District Center-#1	Interview	Male	Approx. mid 30s	Foreign NGO employees	International
Nangarhar-Behsod-District Center-#2	Interview	Male	Approx. mid 20s	Foreign NGO employees	Pashtun
Nangarhar-Behsod-District Center-#3	Interview	Male	Middle aged	Foreign NGO employees	Pashtun
Nangarhar-Behsod-Village 1-#2	Interview	Female	Approx. 60	Homemaker	Pashtun

Nangarhar-Behsod-Village 1-#3	Interview	Female	Middle aged	Homemaker	Pashtun
Nangarhar-Behsod-Village 1-#1	Interview	Female	Approx. mid-60s	Homemaker; mother of 11	Pashtun
Nangarhar-Behsod-Village 1-#4	Interview	Female	Approx. 55	Homemaker	Pashtun
Nangarhar-Behsod-Village 1-#5	Interview	Male	Age 32	Malik	Pashtun
Nangarhar-Behsod-Village 1-#6	Interview	Male	Approx. early 20s	Farmer	Pashtun
Nangarhar-Behsod-Village 1-#7	Interview	Male	Approx. early 70s	Farmer	Pashtun
Nangarhar-Behsod-Village 2-#1	Interview	Female	Approx. 18	Literacy teacher	Pashtun
Nangarhar-Behsod-Village 2-#2	Interview	Female	Approx. mid 20s	Homemaker; CDC participant	Pashtun
Nangarhar-Behsod-Village 2-#3	Interview	Male	Approx. mid 60s	Malik	Pashtun
Nangarhar-Behsod-Village 2-#4	Interview	Male	Approx. 45	Farmer; bird keeper	Pashtun
Nangarhar-Behsod-Village 2-#5	Interview	Male	Approx. early 60s	Mullah	Pashtun
Nangarhar-Behsod-Village 2-#6	Interview	Female	Approx. 24	Homemaker	Pashtun
Nangarhar-Behsod-Village 2-#7	Interview	Female	Approx. 35	Seamstress	Pashtun
Nangarhar-Behsod-Village 2-#8	Interview	Male	Approx. 45	Teacher	Pashtun

(continued)

Interview	Type of Data	Gender	Age of Informant(s)	Occupation	Ethnicity
Nangarhar-Provincial Capital-#1	Interview	Female	Approx. late 20s	Foreign NGO employees	Pashtun
Nangarhar-Provincial Capital-#2	Interview	Male	Approx. late 40s	Journalist	Pashtun
Nangarhar-Provincial Capital-#3	Interview	Male	Approx. early 50s	Engineer; Head of provincial NSP office	Pashtun
Nangarhar-Provincial Capital-#4	Interview	Male	Approx. mid 40s	Deputy provincial governor	Pashtun
Nangarhar-Provincial Capital-#5	Interview	Male	Middle aged	Mayor of Jalalabad City	Pashtun
Nangarhar-Sorkhrod-Village 1-#1	Interview	Female	Approx. 45	Homemaker	Pashtun
Nangarhar-Sorkhrod-Village 1-#2	Interview	Female	Middle aged	Homemaker	Pashtun
Nangarhar-Sorkhrod-Village 1-#3	Interview	Male	Approx. age 60	Malik	Pashtun
Nangarhar-Sorkhrod-Village 1-#4	Interview	Male	Middle aged	Mullah; religious instructor	Pashtun
Nangarhar-Sorkhrod-Village 1-#5	Interview	Male	Approx. late 40s	Trading merchant	Pashtun
Nangarhar-Sorkhrod-Village 1-#6	Interview	Female	Approx. mid 40s	Homemaker	Pashtun
Nangarhar-Sorkhrod-Village 1-#7	Interview	Male	Approx. early 20s	Farmer	Pashtun
Nangarhar-Sorkhrod-Village 2-#1	Interview	Female	Middle aged	Homemaker; mother of 13	Pashtun

Nangarhar-Sorkhrod-Village 2-#2	Focus Group	Three Females	One respondent in early 20s; others middle aged	Homemaker; CDC participant	Pashtun
Nangarhar-Sorkhrod-Village 2-#3	Interview	Male	Approx. mid 40s	Malik; teacher	Pashtun
Nangarhar-Sorkhrod-Village 2-#4	Interview	Male	Middle aged	CDC participant; farmer	Pashtun
Nangarhar-Sorkhrod-Village 2-#5	Interview	Female	Approx. late 60s	Seamstress	Pashtun
Nangarhar-Sorkhrod-Village 2-#6	Interview	Male	Approx. 30	Teacher	Pashtun
Nangarhar-Sorkhrod-Village 2-#7	Interview	Male	Middle aged	Mardikar	Pashtun
Nangarhar-Sorkhrod-District Center-#1	Interview	Female	Approx. late 20s	Foreign NGO employees	Pashtun
Nangarhar-Sorkhrod-District Center-#2	Interview	Male	Middle aged	District Governor	Pashtun
Herat-Guzara-District Center-#2	Interview	Male	Approx. 50	District Security Commander	Tajik
Herat-Guzara-District Center-#3	Focus Group	Two Males	Approx. 50	District court officials	Tajik
Herat-Guzara-District Center-#4	Interview	Male	Approx. 65	Amlak official	Tajik
Herat-Guzara-District Center-#5	Focus Group	Mixed	Approx. 25–40	International organization employees	Tajik
Herat-Guzara-District Center-#6	Interview	Female	Approx. 25	Woman seeking government assistance	Tajik
Kabul-Paghman-Village 2-#6	Interview	Male	Approx. mid 50s	Malik	Pashtun

(*continued*)

(*continued*)

Interview	Type of Data	Gender	Age of Informant(s)	Occupation	Ethnicity
Kabul-Paghman-Village 2-#7	Focus Group	Females	Approx. mid 20s-mid 30s	Homemakers	Pashtun
Kabul-Paghman-Village 2-#8	Interview	Female	Approx. mid 60s	Homemaker	Pashtun
Kunduz-Imam Sahib-District Center-#3	Interview	Male	Approx. 40	District-level MRRD representative	Pashtun
Kunduz-Khanabad-Village 2-#8	Interview	Male	Approx. mid 30s	Arbab	Hazara
Kabul-Kabul City-#1	Interview	Male	Approx. early 70s	Former national minister	Tajik
Kabul-Kabul City-#2	Interview	Male	Approx. mid 40s	MRRD official	Tajik
Kabul-Kabul City-#3	Interview	Female	Middle aged	Foreign Advisor, MRRD	International
Kabul-Kabul City-#4	Interview	Male	Middle aged	Foreign Advisor, MRRD	International
Kabul-Kabul City-#5	Interview	Female	Middle aged	Advisor, World Bank	International
Kabul-Kabul City-#6	Interview	Female	Middle aged	Advisor, World Bank	International
Kabul-Kabul City-#7	Interview	Female	Approx. early 30s	NGO implementing NSP	International
Kabul-Kabul City-#8	Interview	Female	Approx. early 40s	NGO implementing NSP	International
Kabul-Kabul City-#9	Interview	Male	Middle aged	NGO implementing NSP	International
Kabul-Kabul City-#10	Interview	Male	Middle aged	NGO implementing NSP	Tajik
Kabul-Kabul City-#11	Interview	Male	Approx. early 60s	NGO implementing NSP	International
Kabul-Kabul City-#12	Interview	Female	Approx. late 30s	NGO implementing NSP	International
Kabul-Kabul City-#13	Interview	Female	Approx. late 20s	NGO implementing NSP	International

Kabul-Kabul City-#14	Interview	Female	Approx. early-30s	NGO implementing NSP	International
Kabul-Kabul City-#15	Interview	Female	Approx. mid 40s	NGO implementing NSP	International
Kabul-Kabul City-#16	Interview	Female	Approx. mid 20s	NGO implementing NSP	International
Kabul-Kabul City-#17	Interview	Male	Approx. early 30s	NGO implementing NSP	International
Kabul-Kabul City-#18	Interview	Male	Approx. mid 40s	UN development agency official	International
Kabul-Kabul City-#19	Interview	Male	Approx. early 30s	UN official	Pashtun
Kabul-Kabul City-#20	Interview	Male	Approx. early 60s	UNDP official	International
Kabul-Kabul City-#21	Interview	Male	Middle aged	U.S. Government official	International
Kabul-Kabul City-#22	Interview	Male	Approx early 30s	U.S. Government official	International
Kabul-Kabul City-#23	Interview	Male	Middle aged	IDLG official	Pashtun
Kabul-Kabul City-#24	Interview	Male	Approx. mid 50s	Ministry of Interior official	Pashtun
Kabul-Kabul City-#25	Interview	Male	Approx. mid 60s	Ministry of Tribal Affairs official	Pashtun
Kabul-Kabul City-#26	Interview	Female	Approx. early 40s	Constitutional Lawyer	Qizilbash
Kabul-Kabul City-#27	Interview	Male	Middle aged	German government official	International

(continued)

Interview	Type of Data	Gender	Age of Informant(s)	Occupation	Ethnicity
Kabul-Kabul City-#28	Interview	Female	Approx. mid 30s	British government official	International
Kabul-Kabul City-#29	Interview	Male	Approx. mid 40s	IDLG official	Hazara
Kabul-Kabul City-#30	Interview	Female	Approx mid 40s	UN agency official	International
Kabul-Kabul City-#31	Interview	Male	Approx. late 30s	Japanese government official	International
Kabul-Kabul City-#32	Interview	Male	Middle aged	Japanese government official	International
Kabul-Kabul City-#33	Interview	Female	Age 41	International NGO employee	International
Kabul-Kabul City-#34	Interview	Male	Approx. mid 40s	International security expert	International
Kabul-Kabul City-#35	Interview	Male	Approx. early 40s	Political Scientist, Kabul University	Pashtun
Kabul-Kabul City-#36	Interview	Male	Approx. late 40s	IDLG official	Pashtun
Kabul-Kabul City-#37	Interview	Male	Approx. late 30s	Independent Elections Commission Official	Pashtun
Kabul-Kabul City-#38	Interview	Male	Approx. early 40s	IDLG official	Pashtun
Kabul-Kabul City-#39	Interview	Male	Approx. early 40s	US Embassy official	International
Kabul-Kabul City-#40	Interview	Male	Approx. late 30s	Independent Elections Commission Official	Pashtun

Kabul-Kabul City- #41	Interview	Male	Approx. late 50s	Program Manager	International
Kabul-Kabul City- #42	Interview	Female	Approx. late 30s	Program Manager	International
Kabul-Kabul City- #43	Focus Group	Males	Approx. late 20s–Mid-50s	Program Managers	International
Kabul-Kabul City- #44	Interview	Male	Approx. early 30s	MRRD official	Pashtun

Works cited

Acemoglu, Daron. "Why Not a Political Coase Theorem? Social Conflict, Commitment, and Politics." *Journal of Comparative Economics* 31, no. 4 (2003): 620–52.

Acemoglu, Daron, and James Robinson. *Why Nations Fail: The Origins of Power, Prosperity, and Poverty.* New York: Crown Business, 2012.

Acemoglu, Daron, and James A. Robinson. *Economic Origins of Dictatorship and Democracy.* New York: Cambridge University Press, 2006.

Acemoglu, Daron, Simon Johnson, and James A. Robinson. "The Colonial Origins of Comparative Development: An Empirical Investigation." *The American Economic Review* 91, no. 5 (2001): 1369–1401.

Acemoglu, Daron, Tristan Reed, and James A. Robinson. "Chiefs: Economic Development and Elite Control of Civil Society in Sierra Leone." *Journal of Political Economy* 122, no. 2 (2014): 319–68.

"Afghanistan's Nation Building." *The Washington Post*, July 20, 2010, sec. Opinions.

"Afghans Question Reconstruction Scheme." *Institute for War and Peace Reporting*, June 23, 2015. www.iwpr.net/global-voices/afghans-question-reconstruction-scheme.

Agha, Sayyed Mohammad Akbar. *I Am Akbar Agha: Memories of the Afghan Jihad and the Taliban.* Berlin: First Draft Publishing GmbH, 2014.

Agrawal, Arun, and Clark C. Gibson. "Enchantment and Disenchantment: The Role of Community in Natural Resource Conservation." *World Development* 27, no. 4 (1999): 629–49.

Agrawal, Arun, and Sanjeev Goyal. "Group Size and Collective Action Third-Party Monitoring in Common-Pool Resources." *Comparative Political Studies* 34, no. 1 (2001): 63–93.

Ahmed, Akbar S. *Pukhtun Economy and Society.* New York: Routledge, 1980.

 The Thistle and the Drone: How America's War on Terror Became a Global War on Tribal Islam. Washington, DC: Brookings Institution Press, 2013.

Akhmedzyanov, A., and V. Baykov. "Afghanistan Begins a New Life." *Moskva Za Rubezhom*, June 1, 1978, FBIS Daily Report, FBIS-SOV-78-111 edition.

Alesina, Alberto. "Joseph Schumpeter Lecture: The Size of Countries: Does It Matter?" *Journal of the European Economic Association* 1, no. 2–3 (2003): 301–16.

Alesina, Alberto, and Eliana La Ferrara. "Who Trusts Others?" *Journal of Public Economics* 85, no. 2 (2002): 207–34.

Alesina, Alberto, and Enrico Spolaore. "On the Number and Size of Nations." *Quarterly Journal of Economics* 112, no. 4 (1997): 1027–56.

The Size of Nations. Cambridge, MA: MIT Press, 2005.

Alesina, Alberto, and Romain Wacziarg. "Openness, Country Size and Government." *Journal of Public Economics* 69, no. 3 (1998): 305–21.

Alesina, Alberto, Reza Baqir, and William Easterly. "Public Goods and Ethnic Divisions." *Quarterly Journal of Economics* 114, no. 4 (1999): 1243–84.

Alesina, Alberto, William Easterly, and Janina Matuszeski. "Artificial States." *National Bureau of Economic Research Working Paper Series* No. 12328 (June 2006).

Allan, N. J. R. "Defining Place and People in Afghanistan." *Post Soviet Geography and Economics* 42, no. 8 (2001): 545–60.

"Rethinking Governance in Afghanistan." *Journal of International Affairs* 56, no. 2 (2003): 193–203.

Anderson, Jon W. "There Are No Khāns Anymore: Economic Development and Social Change in Tribal Afghanistan." *Middle East Journal* 32, no. 2 (1978): 167–83.

Andersson, Krister, and Elinor Ostrom. "Analyzing Decentralized Resource Regimes from a Polycentric Perspective." *Policy Sciences* 41, no. 1 (2008): 71–93.

Andreoni, James. "Why Free Ride?: Strategies and Learning in Public Goods Experiments." *Journal of Public Economics* 37, no. 3 (1988): 291–304.

Andreoni, James, and Rachel Croson. "Partners versus Strangers: Random Rematching in Public Goods Experiments." In *Handbook of Experimental Economics Results*, ed. Vernon L. Smith and Charles R. Plott, Volume 1:776–83. New York: Elsevier, 2008.

Ansary, Tamim. *Games without Rules: The Often-Interrupted History of Afghanistan.* New York: PublicAffairs, 2012.

Arnoldy, Ben. "Afghanistan War: Successful Foreign Assistance Lets Afghans Pick Their Project." *Christian Science Monitor* July 28, 2010.

Arthur, William Brian. *Path Dependence.* Ann Arbor, MI: University of Michigan Press, 1994.

Arzaghi, Mohammad, and J. Vernon Henderson. "Why Countries Are Fiscally Decentralizing." *Journal of Public Economics* 89, no. 7 (2005): 1157–89.

Asia Foundation. *Afghanistan in 2007: A Survey of the Afghan People.* Kabul, Afghanistan: The Asia Foundation, 2007.

Autesserre, Severine. *Peaceland: Conflict Resolution and the Everyday Politics of International Intervention.* New York: Cambridge University Press, 2014.

The Trouble with the Congo: Local Violence and the Failure of International Peacebuilding. New York: Cambridge University Press, 2010.

Axelrod, Robert. *The Evolution of Cooperation.* New York: Basic Books, 1984.

Azoy, G. Whitney. *Buzkashi: Game and Power in Afghanistan.* 3rd edition. Long Grove, IL: Waveland, 2011.

Baland, Jean-Marie, and Jean-Philippe Platteau. "The Ambiguous Impact of Inequality on Local Resource Management." *World Development* 27, no. 5 (1999): 773–88.

Baldwin, Kate. "Why Vote with the Chief? Political Connections and Public Goods Provision in Zambia." *American Journal of Political Science* 57, no. 4 (2013): 794–809.

Banerjee, Abhijit, Lakshmi Iyer, and Rohini Somanathan. "History, Social Divisions, and Public Goods in Rural India." *Journal of the European Economic Association* 3, no. 2–3 (2005): 639–47.

Banks, Jeffrey S., and Eric A. Hanushek, eds. *Modern Political Economy*. Cambridge: Cambridge University Press, 1995.

Bardhan, Pranab. "Decentralization of Governance and Development." *The Journal of Economic Perspectives* 16, no. 4 (2002): 185–205.

Bardhan, Pranab, and Dilip Mookherjee. "Decentralizing Antipoverty Program Delivery in Developing Countries." *Journal of Public Economics* 89, no. 4 (2005): 675–704.

Bardhan, Pranab, and Jeff Dayton-Johnson. "Unequal Irrigators: Heterogeneity and Commons Management in Large-Scale Multivariate Research." In *Drama of the Commons*. Washington, DC: National Academies Press, 2001.

Bardhan, Pranab, Maitreesh Ghatak, and Alexander Karaivanov. "Wealth Inequality and Collective Action." *Journal of Public Economics* 91, no. 9 (2007): 1843–74.

Barfield, Thomas J. *Afghanistan: A Cultural and Political History*. Princeton, NJ: Princeton University Press, 2010.

"An Islamic State Is a State Run by Good Muslims: Religion as a Way of Life and Not an Ideology in Afghanistan." In *Remaking Muslim Politics: Pluralism, Contestation, Democratization*, ed. Robert W. Hefner, 213–39. Princeton, NJ: Princeton University Press, 2004.

"Continuities and Changes in Local Politics in Northern Afghanistan." In *Local Politics in Afghanistan: A Century of Intervention in Social Order*, ed. Conrad Schetter, 131–45. New York: Columbia University Press, 2013.

"Culture and Custom in Nation-Building: Law in Afghanistan." *Maine Law Review* 60, no. 2 (2008): 348–73.

"Problems in Establishing Legitimacy in Afghanistan." *Iranian Studies* 37, no. 2 (2004): 263–93.

The Central Asian Arabs of Afghanistan: Pastoral Nomadism in Transition. Austin, TX: University of Texas Press, 1982.

"Weak Links on a Rusty Chain: Structural Weaknesses in Afghanistan's Provincial Government Administration." In *Revolutions and Rebellions in Afghanistan: Anthropological Perspectives*, ed. M. Nazif Shahrani and Robert Canfield, 170–83. Berkeley: University of California, 1984.

Barkey, Karen. *Bandits and Bureaucrats: The Ottoman Route to State Centralization*. Ithaca, NY: Cornell University Press, 1994.

Barnett, Michael, and Christoph Zuercher. "The Peacebuilder's Contract: How External Statebuilding Reinforces Weak Statehood." In *The Dilemmas of Statebuilding: Confronting the Contradictions of Postwar Peace Operations*, ed. Roland Paris and Timothy D. Sisk, 23–52. New York: Routledge, 2009.

Barrett, Scott. *Why Cooperate?: The Incentive to Supply Global Public Goods*. New York: Oxford University Press, 2007.

Barth, Fredrik. *Political Leadership among Swat Pathans*. London: Athlone Press, 1959.

Barzel, Yoram. *A Theory of the State: Economic Rights, Legal Rights, and the Scope of the State*. New York: Cambridge University Press, 2001.

Bates, Robert H. *When Things Fell Apart*. New York: Cambridge University Press, 2008.

Beath, Andrew, Fotini Christia, and Ruben Enikolopov. "Empowering Women through Development Aid: Evidence from a Field Experiment in Afghanistan." *American Political Science Review* 107, no. 3 (2013): 540–57.

Randomized Impact Evaluation of Afghanistan's National Solidarity Programme. Washington, DC: The World Bank, 2013.

"Winning Hearts and Minds through Development Aid: Evidence from a Field Experiment in Afghanistan." Working Paper. Center for Economic and Financial Research (CEFIR), 2011.

Beattie, Hugh. "Effects of the Saur Revolution in the Nahrin Area of Northern Afghanistan." In *Revolutions & Rebellions in Afghanistan: Anthropological Perspectives*, ed. M. Nazif Mohib Shahrani and Robert L. Canfield, 184–208. Berkeley, CA: Institute of International Studies, University of California, Berkeley, 1984.

Bednar, Jenna. "Federalism as a Public Good." *Constitutional Political Economy* 16, no. 2 (2005): 189–205.

The Robust Federation: Principles of Design. New York: Cambridge University Press, 2008.

Beissinger, Mark R. *Nationalist Mobilization and the Collapse of the Soviet State.* New York: Cambridge University Press, 2002.

Berman, Eli, Jacob N. Shapiro, and Joseph H. Felter. "Can Hearts and Minds Be Bought? The Economics of Counterinsurgency in Iraq." *Journal of Political Economy* 119, no. 4 (2011): 766–819.

Berman, Eli, Joseph H. Felter, Jacob N. Shapiro, and Erin Troland. "Modest, Secure, and Informed: Successful Development in Conflict Zones." American *Economic Review* 103, no. 3 (2013): 512–17.

Berman, Eli, Michael Callen, Joseph H. Felter, and Jacob N. Shapiro. "Do Working Men Rebel? Insurgency and Unemployment in Afghanistan, Iraq, and the Philippines." *Journal of Conflict Resolution* 55, no. 4 (2011): 496–528.

Berman, Sheri. "From the Sun King to Karzai: Lessons for State Building in Afghanistan." *Foreign Affairs* 89 (2010): 2.

Besley, T., R. Pande, and V. Rao. "Just Rewards? Local Politics and Public Resource Allocation in South India." *The World Bank Economic Review* 26, no. 2 (2011): 191–216.

Billaud, Julie. *Kabul Carnival: Gender Politics in Postwar Afghanistan.* Philadelphia, PA: University of Pennsylvania Press, 2015.

Boone, Catherine. *Political Topographies of the African State: Territorial Authority and Institutional Choice.* New York: Cambridge University Press, 2003.

Bowles, Samuel, and Herbert Gintis. "Social Capital and Community Governance." *The Economic Journal* 112, no. 483 (2002): F419–36.

Braithwaite, John, and Ali Wardak. "Crime and War in Afghanistan Part I: The Hobbesian Solution." *British Journal of Criminology* 53, no. 2 (March 1, 2013): 179–96.

Brautigam, Deborah A., Mick Moore, and Odd-Helge Fjeldstad. *Taxation and State-Building in Developing Countries: Capacity and Consent.* New York: Cambridge University Press, 2008.

Brinkerhoff, Derick W., ed. *Governance in Post-Conflict Societies: Rebuilding Fragile States.* New York: Routledge, 2007.

"Rebuilding Governance in Failed States and Post-Conflict Societies: Core Concepts and Cross-Cutting Themes." *Public Administration & Development* 25, no. 1 (2005): 3–14.

"State Fragility and Governance: Conflict Mitigation and Subnational Perspectives." *Development Policy Review* 29, no. 2 (2011): 131–53.

Bromley, Daniel, and Glen Anderson. *Vulnerable People, Vulnerable States: Redefining the Development Challenge.* New York: Routledge, 2012.

Brown, Frances Z. *The US Surge and Afghan Local Governance.* Washington, DC: United States Institute of Peace, 2012.

Bunce, Valerie. *Subversive Institutions: The Design and the Destruction of Socialism and the State.* New York: Cambridge University Press, 1999.

Byrd, William A. *Lessons from Afghanistan's History for the Current Transition and Beyond.* Washington, DC: United States Institute of Peace, 2012. www.usip.org/sites/default/files/SR314.pdf.

Carey, John M. "Parchment, Equilibria, and Institutions." *Comparative Political Studies* 33, no. 6–7 (2000): 735–61.

Carter, Lynn, and Kerry Connor. *A Preliminary Investigation of Contemporary Afghan Councils.* Peshawar, Pakistan: Agency Coordinating Body for Afghan Relief (ACBAR), 1989.

Central Statistics Office. *CSO 2003–2004 Population Statistics: 388 Districts.* Kabul, Afghanistan: Central Statistics Office, 2004.

Chabal, Patrick, and Jean-Pascal Daloz. *Africa Works: Disorder as Political Instrument.* Bloomington, IN: Indiana University Press, 1999.

Chambers, Robert. "The Origins and Practice of Participatory Rural Appraisal." *World Development* 22, no. 7 (1994): 953–69.

Chandrasekaran, Rajiv. *Little America: The War within the War for Afghanistan.* New York: Knopf, 2012.

Chartier, Gary. *Anarchy and Legal Order: Law and Politics for a Stateless Society.* New York: Cambridge University Press, 2013.

Chauvet, Lisa, and Paul Collier. *Development Effectiveness in Fragile States: Spillovers and Turnarounds.* Oxford: Center for the Study of African Economies, Oxford University, 2004.

Chayes, Sarah. *The Punishment of Virtue: Inside Afghanistan after the Taliban.* New York: Penguin, 2007.

Thieves of State: Why Corruption Threatens Global Security. New York: W. W. Norton & Company, 2015.

Chou, Tiffany. "Does Development Assistance Reduce Violence? Evidence from Afghanistan." *Economics of Peace and Security Journal* 7, no. 2 (2012): 5–13.

Clapham, Christopher. "The Challenge to the State in a Globalized World." *Development and Change* 33, no. 5 (2002): 775–95.

Cliffe, Sarah, Scott Guggenheim, and Markus Kostner. *Community-Driven Reconstruction as an Instrument in War-to-Peace Transitions.* Washington, DC: World Bank, 2003.

Coburn, Noah. *Bazaar Politics: Power and Pottery in an Afghan Market Town.* Stanford, CA: Stanford University Press, 2011.

Informal Justice and the International Community in Afghanistan. Washington, DC: United States Institute of Peace Press, 2013.

Coghlin, Tom. "Afghans Accuse Liam Fox of Racism; Karzai Angry at Reference to 'Broken 13th-Century Country.'" *The Times*, May 24, 2010.

Collier, Paul. *The Plundered Planet: Why We Must–and How We Can–Manage Nature for Global Prosperity*. New York: Oxford University Press, 2010.

Wars, Guns and Votes. New York: HarperCollins, 2009.

Collier, Paul, and Anke Hoeffler. "Greed and Grievance in Civil War." *Oxford Economic Papers* 56, no. 4 (2004): 563–95.

Coll, Steve. *Ghost Wars: The Secret History of the CIA, Afghanistan, and Bin Laden, from the Soviet Invasion to September 10, 2001*. New York: Penguin, 2004.

"Corruption Hampers Development in Afghan Districts." *Institute for War and Peace Reporting*, November 14, 2014. https://iwpr.net/global-voices/corruption-hampers-development-afghan-districts.

Coyne, Christopher. *After War: The Political Economy of Exporting Democracy*. Palo Alto, CA: Stanford Economics and Finance, 2007.

Coyne, Christopher J. "Reconstructing Weak and Failed States: Foreign Intervention and the Nirvana Fallacy." *Foreign Policy Analysis* 2, no. 4 (2006): 343–60.

Crews, Robert D., and Amin Tarzi, eds. *The Taliban and the Crisis of Afghanistan*. Cambridge, MA: Harvard University Press, 2008.

Crile, George. *Charlie Wilson's War*. New York: Grove Press, 2004.

Deaton, Angus. *The Analysis of Household Surveys*. Washington, DC: World Bank Publications, 1997.

De Figueiredo, Rui, and Barry Weingast. "Self-Enforcing Federalism." *Journal of Law, Economics and Organization* 21, no. 1 (2005): 103–35.

Deutsch, Karl Wolfgang. *The Nerves of Government*. New York: Free Press, 1963.

Diamond, Jared. *The World Until Yesterday: What Can We Learn from Traditional Societies?* New York: Viking Adult, 2012.

Díaz-Cayeros, Alberto, Beatriz Magaloni, and Alexander Ruiz-Euler. "Traditional Governance, Citizen Engagement, and Local Public Goods: Evidence from Mexico." *World Development* 53 (2014): 80–93.

Dixit, Avinash K. *Lawlessness and Economics: Alternative Modes of Governance*. Princeton, NJ: Princeton University Press, 2004.

Dobbins, James. *The Beginner's Guide to Nation-Building*. Washington, DC: RAND Corporation, 2007.

Dorronsoro, Gilles. *Revolution Unending: Afghanistan, 1979 to the Present*. New York: Columbia University Press, 2005.

Dupree, Louis. *Afghanistan*. Princeton, NJ: Princeton University Press, 1973.

Easterly, William. *The White Man's Burden: Why the West's Efforts to Aid the Rest Have Done So Much Ill and so Little Good*. New York: Penguin Press, 2006.

Echavez, Chona. *Does Women's Participation in the National Solidarity Programme Make a Difference in Their Lives? A Case Study in Kabul Province*. Kabul: Afghanistan Research and Evaluation Unit, 2012.

Edwards, David B. *Before Taliban: Genealogies of the Afghan Jihad*. Berkeley, CA: University of California Press, 2002.

Heroes of the Age: Moral Fault Lines on the Afghan Frontier. Berkeley, CA: University of California Press, 1996.

Eisenstadt, Shmuel Noah. *Traditional Patrimonialism and Modern Neopatrimonialism*. Beverly Hills, CA: Sage Publications, 1973.

Elias, Norbert. Norbert Elias on Civilization, Power, and Knowledge: Selected Writings. ed. Stephen Mennell and Johan Goudsblom. *Heritage of Sociology*. Chicago: University of Chicago Press, 1998.

Elphinstone, Mountstuart. *An Account of the Kingdom of Caubul and Its Dependencies in Persia, Tartary and India*. London: Longman, Hurst, Rees, Orme, and Brown, 1815.

Elster, Jon, Claus Offe, and Ulrich K. Preuss. *Institutional Design in Post-Communist Societies: Rebuilding the Ship at Sea*. New York: Cambridge University Press, 1998.

Emadi, Hafizullah. *Dynamics of Political Development in Afghanistan: The British, Russian, and American Invasions*. New York: Palgrave Macmillan, 2010.

Englebert, Pierre. *State Legitimacy and Development in Africa*. Boulder, CO: Rienner, 2000.

Ensminger, Jean. *Making a Market: The Institutional Transformation of an African Society*. New York: Cambridge University Press, 1992.

Ertman, Thomas. *Birth of the Leviathan: Building States and Regimes in Medieval and Early Modern Europe*. Cambridge: Cambridge University Press, 1997.

Esteban, Joan, and Debraj Ray. "Conflict and Distribution." *Journal of Economic Theory* 87, no. 2 (August 1999): 379–415.

Etzioni, Amitai. "Bottom-up Nation Building." *Policy Review* no. 158 (2009): 51–62.

Evans, Peter. *Embedded Autonomy: States and Industrial Transformation*. Princeton, NJ: Princeton University Press, 1995.

  "Government Action, Social Capital, and Development: Reviewing the Evidence on Synergy." In *State-Society Synergy: Government and Social Capital in Development*, 178–209. Berkeley, CA: University of California at Berkeley, 1997.

Evans, Peter, and James E. Rauch. "Bureaucracy and Growth: A Cross-National Analysis of the Effects of 'Weberian' State Structures on Economic Growth." *American Sociological Review* 64, no. 5 (1999): 748–65.

Evans, Peter, Dietrich Rueschemeyer, and Theda Skocpol. *Bringing the State Back In*. New York: Cambridge University Press, 1985.

Fearon, James D. "Domestic Political Audiences and the Escalation of International Disputes." *The American Political Science Review* 88, no. 3 (1994): 577–92.

Fearon, James D., and David D. Laitin. "Ethnicity, Insurgency, and Civil War." *American Political Science Review* 97, no. 1 (2003): 75–90.

  "Explaining Interethnic Cooperation." *The American Political Science Review* 90, no. 4 (December 1996): 715–35.

Feiock, Richard C. "Metropolitan Governance and Institutional Collective Action." *Urban Affairs Review* 44, no. 3 (2009): 356–77.

  Metropolitan Governance: Conflict, Competition, and Cooperation. Washington, DC: Georgetown University Press, 2004.

  "Rational Choice and Regional Governance." *Journal of Urban Affairs* 29, no. 1 (2007): 47–63.

Feiock, Richard C., and John T. Scholz, eds. *Self-Organizing Federalism: Collaborative Mechanisms to Mitigate Institutional Collective Action Dilemmas*. New York: Cambridge University Press, 2009.

Ferguson, James. *The Anti-Politics Machine*. Minneapolis, MN: University of Minnesota Press, 1994.

Firmin-Sellers, Kathryn. "The Politics of Property Rights." *The American Political Science Review* 89, no. 4 (1995): 867–81.

The Transformation of Property Rights in the Gold Coast: An Empirical Study Applying Rational Choice Theory. New York: Cambridge University Press, 1996.

Fishstein, Paul, and Andrew Wilder. *Winning Hearts and Minds? Examining the Relationship between Aid and Security in Afghanistan*. Medford, MA: Feinstein International Center, Tufts University, 2012.

Franck, Peter G. *Afghanistan between East and West*. Washington, DC: The National Planning Association, 1960.

Friedman, David. "A Theory of the Size and Shape of Nations." *The Journal of Political Economy* 85, no. 1 (February 1977): 59–77.

Fukuyama, Francis. *Political Order and Political Decay: From the Industrial Revolution to the Globalization of Democracy*. New York: Farrar, Straus and Giroux, 2014.

State-Building: Governance and World Order in the 21st Century. Ithaca, NY: Cornell University Press, 2004.

"What Is Governance?" *Governance* 26, no. 3 (2013): 347–68.

Gaddis, John Lewis. *The Long Peace: Inquiries into the History of the Cold War*. New York: Oxford University Press, 1989.

Gall, Sandy. *War Against the Taliban: Why It All Went Wrong in Afghanistan*. New York: Bloomsbury Publishing, 2012.

Gambetta, Diego. *The Sicilian Mafia: The Business of Private Protection*. Cambridge, MA: Harvard University Press, 1996.

Gannon, Kathy. "Afghanistan Unbound." *Foreign Affairs* 83 (2004): 35.

Gant, Maj. Jim. *One Tribe at a Time: A Strategy for Success in Afghanistan*. Los Angeles: Nine Sisters Imports, Inc., 2009.

Geddes, Barbara. *Politician's Dilemma*. Berkeley, CA: University of California Press, 1996.

Gelman, Andrew, and Jennifer Hill. *Data Analysis Using Regression and Multilevel/Hierarchical Models*. New York: Cambridge University Press, 2006.

Ghani, Ashraf. "Islam and State-Building in a Tribal Society Afghanistan: 1880–1901." *Modern Asian Studies* 12, no. 2 (1978): 269–84.

Ghani, Ashraf, and Clare Lockhart. *Fixing Failed States: A Framework for Rebuilding a Fractured World*. New York: Oxford University Press, 2008.

Ginty, Roger Mac. "Warlords and the Liberal Peace: State-Building in Afghanistan." *Conflict, Security & Development* 10, no. 4 (2010): 577–98.

Giustozzi, Antonio. *Decoding the New Taliban: Insights from the Afghan Field*. New York: Columbia University Press, 2009.

Empires of Mud: War and Warlords of Afghanistan. New York: Columbia University Press, 2009.

Koran, Kalashnikov, and Laptop: The Neo-Taliban Insurgency in Afghanistan. New York: Columbia University Press, 2007.

War, Politics and Society in Afghanistan, 1978–1992. Washington, DC: Georgetown University Press, 2000.

Goodhand, Jonathan. "Aiding Violence or Building Peace? The Role of International Aid in Afghanistan." *Third World Quarterly* 23, no. 5 (2002): 837–59.

Goodson, Larry P. "Afghanistan in 2003: The Taliban Resurface and a New Constitution Is Born." *Asian Survey* 44, no. 1 (2004): 14–22.

Gorodnichenko, Yuriy, and Gerard Roland. "Culture, Institutions and the Wealth of Nations." Working Paper. Washington, DC: National Bureau of Economic Research, 2010.

"Which Dimensions of Culture Matter for Long-Run Growth?" *American Economic Review* 101, no. 3 (2011): 492–98.

Gregorian, Vartan. *The Emergence of Modern Afghanistan: Politics of Reform and Modernization*. Palo Alto, CA: Stanford University Press, 1969.

Greif, Avner. *Institutions and the Path to the Modern Economy: Lessons from Medieval Trade*. New York: Cambridge University Press, 2006.

Greif, Avner, and Guido Tabellini. "Cultural and Institutional Bifurcation: China and Europe Compared." *The American Economic Review* 100, no. 2 (2010): 135–40.

Greif, Avner, Paul Milgrom, and Barry R. Weingast. "Coordination, Commitment, and Enforcement: The Case of the Merchant Guild." *Journal of Political Economy* 102, no. 4 (1994): 745–76.

Grindle, Merilee S. *Going Local: Decentralization and the Promise of Good Governance*. Princeton, NJ: Princeton University Press, 2007.

"Good Enough Governance: Poverty Reduction and Reform in Developing Countries." *Governance* 17, no. 4 (2004): 525–48.

"Good Enough Governance Revisited." *Development Policy Review* 25, no. 5 (2007): 533–74.

Haber, Stephen, Noel Maurer, and Armando Razo. *The Politics of Property Rights Political Instability, Credible Commitments, and Economic Growth in Mexico, 1876–1929*. New York: Cambridge University Press, 2003.

Hagen, Everett Einar. *On the Theory of Social Change: How Economic Growth Begins*. Homewood, IL: Dorsey Press, 1962.

Hanifi, M. Jamil. "Editing the Past: Colonial Production of Hegemony through the 'Loya Jerga' in Afghanistan." *Iranian Studies* 37, no. 2 (2004): 295–322.

Hanifi, Shah Mahmoud. *Connecting Histories in Afghanistan: Market Relations and State Formation on a Colonial Frontier*. Palo Alto, CA: Stanford University Press, 2008.

Hechter, Michael. *Containing Nationalism*. New York: Oxford University Press, 2001.

Hechter, Michael, and Nika Kabiri. "Attaining Social Order in Iraq." In *Order, Conflict, and Violence*, ed. Stathis N. Kalyvas, Ian Shapiro, and Tarek Masoud, 43–74. New York: Cambridge University Press, 2008.

Heilbrunn, John R. "Paying the Price of Failure: Reconstructing Failed and Collapsed States in Africa and Central Asia." *Perspectives on Politics* 4, no. 1 (2006): 135–50.

Helmke, Gretchen, and Steven Levitsky. "Informal Institutions and Comparative Politics: A Research Agenda." *Perspectives on Politics* 2, no. 4 (2004): 725–40.

Herbst, Jeffrey. "African Militaries and Rebellion: The Political Economy of Threat and Combat Effectiveness." *Journal of Peace Research* 41, no. 3 (2004): 357–69.

States and Power in Africa: Comparative Lessons in Authority and Control. Princeton, NJ: Princeton University Press, 2000.

Hirschman, Albert O. *Getting Ahead Collectively: Grassroots Experiences in Latin America*. New York: Pergamon Press, 1984.

Hobbes, Thomas. *Leviathan*. ed. J. C. Gaskin. New York: Oxford University Press, 1998.

Horowitz, Donald L. *Ethnic Groups in Conflict*. University of California Press, 2000.

Howe, Herbert M. *Ambiguous Order*. Boulder, CO: Lynne Rienner Publishers, 2001.

Human Rights Watch. *Afghanistan: The Massacre in Mazar-I Sharif*. New York: Human Rights Watch, 1998.

Massacres of Hazaras in Afghanistan. New York: Human Rights Watch, 2001.

Humphreys, Macartan, Raul de la Sierra, and Peter Van der Windt. *Social Engineering in the Tropics: Case Study Evidence from East Congo*. Unpublished Manuscript, 2014.

Huntington, Samuel. *Political Order in Changing Societies*. New Haven, CT: Yale University Press, 1968.

Hyman, Anthony. *Afghanistan under Soviet Domination, 1964–83*. New York: Palgrave Macmillan, 1984.

Inglehart, Ronald, and Wayne E. Baker. "Modernization, Cultural Change, and the Persistence of Traditional Values." *American Sociological Review* 65, no. 1 (2000): 19–51.

International Legal Foundation. *The Customary Laws of Afghanistan*. New York: International Legal Foundation, 2004.

Jackson, Robert H. "Quasi-States, Dual Regimes, and Neoclassical Theory: International Jurisprudence and the Third World." *International Organization* 41, no. 4 (1987): 519–49.

Quasi-States: Sovereignty, International Relations, and the Third World. Cambridge: Cambridge University Press, 1990.

Jochem, Torsten, Ilia Murtazashvili, and Jennifer Murtazashvili. "Social Identity and Voting in Afghanistan: Evidence from a Survey Experiment." *Journal of Experimental Political Science* 2, no. 1 (2015): 47–62.

Kahl, Colin H. *States, Scarcity, and Civil Strife in the Developing World*. Princeton, NJ: Princeton University Press, 2006.

Kakar, M. Hasan. *Government and Society in Afghanistan: The Reign of Amir Abd Al-Rahman Khan*. Austin, TX: University of Texas Press, 1979.

The Pacification of the Hazaras of Afghanistan. New York: Asia Society, Afghanistan Council, 1973.

Kaldor, Mary. *New and Old Wars: Organized Violence in a Global Era*. Cambridge: Polity Press, 1999.

Kalyvas, Stathis N., and Laia Balcells. "International System and Technologies of Rebellion: How the End of the Cold War Shaped Internal Conflict." *American Political Science Review* 104, no. 3 (2010): 415–29.

Kandori, Michihiro. "Social Norms and Community Enforcement." *Review of Economic Studies* 59, no. 198 (1992): 63–80.

Kaplan, Robert D. *The Coming Anarchy: Shattering the Dreams of the Post Cold War*. New York: Vintage Books, 2001.

Kasfir, Nelson. "Domestic Anarchy, Security Dilemmas, and Violent Predation: Causes of Failure." In *When States Fail: Causes and Consequences*, ed. Robert I. Rotberg, 53–76. Princeton, NJ: Princeton University Press, 2004.

Khān, 'Abd al-Raḥmān. *The Life of Abdur Rahman, Amir of Afghanistan*. ed. Mir Munshi Sultan Mahomed Khan. Vol. 2. London: J. Murray, 1900.

Kilcullen, David. *Out of the Mountains: The Coming Age of the Urban Guerrilla*. New York: Oxford University Press, 2013.

The Accidental Guerrilla: Fighting Small Wars in the Midst of a Big One. New York: Oxford University Press, 2009.

King, Elisabeth. "A Critical Review of Community-Driven Development Programmes in Conflict-Affected Contexts." International Rescue Committee and Department for International Development, 2013.

King, Elisabeth, and Cyrus Samii. "Fast-Track Institution Building in Conflict-Affected Countries? Insights from Recent Field Experiments." *World Development* 64 (2014): 740–54.

King, Gary, Robert Keohane, and Sidney Verba. *Designing Social Inquiry: Scientific Inference in Qualitative Research*. Princeton, NJ: Princeton University Press, 1994.

Knight, Jack. *Institutions and Social Conflict*. New York: Cambridge University Press, 1992.

Krasner, Stephen D., and Carlos Pascual. "Addressing State Failure." *Foreign Affairs* 84, no. 4 (2005): 153–63.

Krasner, Stephen D., and Jeremy M. Weinstein. "Improving Governance from the Outside In." *Annual Review of Political Science* 17, no. 1 (2014): 123–45.

Kreps, David M., Paul Milgrom, John Roberts, and Robert Wilson. "Rational Cooperation in the Finitely Repeated Prisoners' Dilemma." *Journal of Economic Theory* 27, no. 2 (1982): 245–52.

Kuran, Timur. *The Long Divergence: How Islamic Law Held Back the Middle East*. Princeton, NJ: Princeton University Press, 2010.

Kyamusugulwa, Patrick M., and Dorothea Hilhorst. "Power Holders and Social Dynamics of Participatory Development and Reconstruction: Cases from the Democratic Republic of Congo." *World Development* 70 (2015): 249–59.

Laffont, Jean-Jacques, and Mathieu Meleu. "Separation of Powers and Development." *Journal of Development Economics* 64, no. 1 (2001): 129–45.

Lambton, Ann S. K. *Landlord and Peasant in Persia: A Study of Land Tenure and Land Revenue Administration*. New York: I.B.Tauris, 1991.

Larson, Anne M., Peter J. Cronkleton, and Juan M. Pulhin. "Formalizing Indigenous Commons: The Role of 'Authority' in the Formation of Territories in Nicaragua, Bolivia, and the Philippines." *World Development* 70 (2015): 228–38.

Leeson, Peter T. *Anarchy Unbound: Why Self-Governance Works Better than You Think*, New York: Cambridge University Press, 2014.

"An-arrgh-chy: The Law and Economics of Pirate Organization." *Journal of Political Economy* 115, no. 6 (2007): 1049–94.

"Better off Stateless: Somalia before and after Government Collapse." *Journal of Comparative Economics* 35, no. 4 (2007): 689–710.

"Efficient Anarchy." *Public Choice* 130, no. 1/2 (2007): 41–53.

The Invisible Hook: The Hidden Economics of Pirates. Princeton, NJ: Princeton University Press, 2011.

Lerner, Daniel. *The Passing of Traditional Society: Modernizing the Middle East*. Glencoe, IL: Free Press, 1958.

Levi, Margaret. *Of Rule and Revenue*. Berkeley, CA: University of California Press, 1989.

Lipset, Seymour Martin. "Some Social Requisites of Democracy: Economic Development and Political Legitimacy." *The American Political Science Review* 53, no. 1 (1959): 69–105.

Lister, Sarah, and Hamish Nixon. *Provincial Governance Structures in Afghanistan: From Confusion to Vision?*. Kabul: Afghanistan Research and Evaluation Unit, 2006.

Logan, Carolyn. "Selected Chiefs, Elected Councillors and Hybrid Democrats: Popular Perspectives on the Co-Existence of Democracy and Traditional Authority." *The Journal of Modern African Studies* 47, no. 1 (2009): 101–28.

"The Roots of Resilience: Exploring Popular Support for African Traditional Authorities." *African Affairs* 112, no. 448 (2013): 353–76.

Lowery, David. "A Transactions Costs Model of Metropolitan Governance: Allocation versus Redistribution in Urban America." *Journal of Public Administration Research and Theory* 10, no. 1 (2000): 49–78.

Lubell, Mark, Mark Schneider, John T. Scholz, and Mihriye Mete. "Watershed Partnerships and the Emergence of Collective Action Institutions." *American Journal of Political Science* 46, no. 1 (2002): 148–63.

Lynch, Marc. "Explaining the Awakening: Engagement, Publicity, and the Transformation of Iraqi Sunni Political Attitudes." *Security Studies* 20, no. 1 (2011): 36–72.

Macaulay, Stewart. "Non-Contractual Relations in Business: A Preliminary Study." *American Sociological Review* 28, no. 1 (1963): 55–67.

Maiwand, Safi. "Afghanistan: Local Reconstruction Effort Goes Awry." *Institute for War and Peace Reporting*, May 17, 2011. https://iwpr.net/global-voices/afghanistan-local-reconstruction-effort-goes-awry.

Male, Beverley. *Revolutionary Afghanistan*. London: Croom Helm, 1982.

Malkasian, Carter. *War Comes to Garmser: Thirty Years of Conflict on the Afghan Frontier*. New York: Oxford University Press, 2013.

Mamdani, Mahmood. *Citizen and Subject: Contemporary Africa and the Legacy of Late Colonialism*. Princeton, NJ: Princeton University Press, 1996.

Mampilly, Zachariah Cherian. *Rebel Rulers: Insurgent Governance and Civilian Life during War*. Ithaca, NY: Cornell University Press, 2011.

Manion, Melanie. *Retirement of Revolutionaries in China: Public Policies, Social Norms, Private Interests*. Princeton, NJ: Princeton University Press, 1993.

"The Electoral Connection in the Chinese Countryside." *The American Political Science Review* 90, no. 4 (1996): 736–48.

Mann, Michael. "The Autonomous Power of the State: Its Origins, Mechanisms and Results." *European Journal of Sociology/Archives Européennes de Sociologie* 25, no. 02 (1984): 185–213.

Mansfield, Edward D., and Jack L. Snyder. *Electing to Fight: Why Emerging Democracies Go to War*. BCSIA Studies in International Security. Cambridge, MA: MIT Press, 2005.

Mansuri, Ghazala, and Vijayendra Rao. "Community-Based and-Driven Development: A Critical Review." *The World Bank Research Observer* 19, no. 1 (2004).

Localizing Development. Washington, DC: World Bank, 2013.

Marx, Karl. *The Eighteenth Brumaire of Louis Bonaparte*. Chicago: C. H. Kerr, 1913.

Mashal, Mujib, and Jawad Sukhanyar. "Gunmen in Northern Afghanistan Kill 9 Local Aid Workers." The New York Times, June 2, 2015.

McChrystal, Stanley A. "It Takes a Network." *Army Communicator* 36, no. 2 (2011).

McGinnis, Michael Dean, ed. *Polycentric Governance and Development: Readings from the Workshop in Political Theory and Policy Analysis*. Ann Arbor, MI: University of Michigan Press, 1999.

McGinnis, Michael D., and Elinor Ostrom. "Reflections on Vincent Ostrom, Public Administration, and Polycentricity." *Public Administration Review* 72, no. 1 (2012): 15–25.

Meininghaus, Esther. "Legal Pluralism in Afghanistan." Working Paper. Amu Darya Series Paper No. 8. Bonn, Germany: University of Bonn, Center for Development Research, 2007.

Menkhaus, Ken. "Governance without Government in Somalia: Spoilers, State Building, and the Politics of Coping." *International Security* 31, no. 3 (2007): 74–106.

Miakhel, Shahmahmood, and Noah Coburn. *Many Shuras Do Not a Government Make: International Community Engagement with Local Councils in Afghanistan.* Washington, DC: United States Institute for Peace, 2010.

Mielke, Katja. "Constructing the Image of a State: Local Realities and International Intervention in North-East Afghanistan." In *Local Politics in Afghanistan: A Century of Intervention in Social Order*, ed. Conrad Schetter, 1–20. New York: Columbia University Press, 2013.

Mielke, Katja, Iskandar Abdullayev, and Usman Shah. "The Illusion of Establishing Control by Legal Definition: Water Rights, Principles and Power in Canal Irrigation Systems of the Kunduz River Basin, Afghanistan." In *Negotiating Local Governance: Natural Resources Management at the Interface of Communities and the State*, ed. Irit Eguavoen and Wolfram Laube, 181–210. Piscataway, NJ: Transaction Publishers, 2010.

Migdal, Joel S. *State in Society: Studying How States and Societies Transform and Constitute One Another. Cambridge Studies in Comparative Politics.* New York: Cambridge University Press, 2001.

Strong Societies and Weak States: State-Society Relations and State Capabilities in the Third World. Princeton, NJ: Princeton University Press, 1988.

Miguel, Edward, and Mary Kay Gugerty. "Ethnic Diversity, Social Sanctions, and Public Goods in Kenya." *Journal of Public Economics* 89, no. 11–12 (2005): 2325–68.

Milner, Helen V. *Interests, Institutions, and Information.* Princeton, NJ: Princeton University Press, 1997.

Ministry of Rural Rehabilitation and Development (MRRD). "National Solidarity Programme (NSP)." Islamic Republic of Afghanistan, April 2008. http://nspafghanistan.org/media/downloads/NSP_Brochure_April_2008.pdf.

Ministry of Rural Rehabilitation and Development and World Bank. *National Solidarity Program Operations Manual.* Kabul, October 2004.

Ministry of Rural Rehabilitation and Development (MRRD). "The Most Important Achievement of the NSP to Date," May 27, 2010. www.nspafghanistan.org/Default.aspx?Sel=103.

Moghadam, Valentine M. "Patriarchy, the Taliban, and Politics of Public Space in Afghanistan." *Women's Studies International Forum* 25, no. 1 (2002): 19–31.

Montesquieu, Charles De. *The Spirit of the Laws.* ed. Anne M. Cohler, Basia C. Miller, and Harold S. Stone. New York: Cambridge University Press, 1989.

Moore, Mick. "Between Coercion and Contract: Competing Narratives on Taxation and Governance." In *Taxation and State-Building in Developing Countries: Capacity and Consent*, ed. Deborah Brautigam, Odd-Helge Fjeldstad, and Mick Moore, 34–63. Cambridge: Cambridge University Press, 2008.

MRRD. *NSP-03nd Quarterly Report- 01st Mizan to 30th Qaws 1393 (23rd September to 21st December 2014).* NSP Quarterly Report. Kabul: Ministry of Rural Rehabilitation and Development, 2015.

Muḥammad, Fayẓ, and R. D. McChesney. *Kabul Under Siege: Fayz Muḥammad's Account of the 1929 Uprising.* Princeton, NJ: Markus Wiener Publishers, 1999.

Mukhopadhyay, Dipali. *Warlords, Strongman Governors, and the State in Afghanistan.* New York: Cambridge University Press, 2014.

Murphy, Kevin M., Andrei Shleifer, and Robert W. Vishny. "Industrialization and the Big Push." Working Paper. National Bureau of Economic Research, 1988.

Murtazashvili, Ilia, and Jennifer Murtazashvili. "Anarchy, Self-Governance, and Legal Titling." *Public Choice* 162, no. 3–4 (2014): 287–305.

Murtazashvili, Jennifer. "Gaming the State: Consequences of Contracting out State Building in Afghanistan." *Central Asian Survey* 34, no. 1 (2015): 78–92.

Murtazashvili, Jennifer Brick. "Bad Medicine." *Central Asian Affairs* 2, no. 1 (2015): 10–34.

"Coloured by Revolution: The Political Economy of Autocratic Stability in Uzbekistan." *Democratization* 19, no. 1 (2012): 78–97.

Survey on Political Institutions, Elections, and Democracy in Afghanistan. Washington, DC: Democracy International and United States Agency for International Development, 2015.

Myerson, Roger. "Constitutional Structures for a Strong Democracy: Considerations on the Government of Pakistan." *World Development*, Decentralization and Governance, 53 (2014): 46–54.

Myerson, Roger B. "A Field Manual for the Cradle of Civilization Theory of Leadership and Lessons of Iraq." *Journal of Conflict Resolution* 53, no. 3 (2009): 470–82.

Myrdal, Gunnar. *Asian Drama: an Inquiry into the Poverty of Nations.* New York: Twentieth Century Fund, 1968.

Economic Theory and Under-Developed Regions. London: G. Duckworth, 1957.

Nagl, John, David Petraeus, James Amos, and Sarah Sewall. *The U.S. Army/Marine Corps Counterinsurgency Field Manual.* Chicago: University of Chicago Press, 2007.

Newell, Richard S. *The Politics of Afghanistan.* South Asian Political Systems. Ithaca, NY: Cornell University Press, 1972.

Nixon, Hamish. *Subnational State-Building in Afghanistan.* Kabul: Afghanistan Research and Evaluation Unit, April 2008.

Noelle, Christine. *State and Tribe in Nineteenth-Century Afghanistan: The Reign of Amir Dost Muhammad Khan.* New York: Routledge, 1997.

Noelle-Karimi, Christine. "Jirga, Shura and Community Development Councils: Village Institutions and State Interference." In *Local Politics in Afghanistan: A Century of Intervention in Social Order,* ed. Conrad Schetter, 39–58. New York: Columbia University Press, 2013.

Village Institutions in the Perception of National and International Actors in Afghanistan. Amu Darya Series. Bonn, Germany: Center for Development Research, University of Bonn, 2006.

Nojumi, Neamatollah, Dyan Mazurana, and Elizabeth Stites. *After the Taliban: Life and Security in Rural Afghanistan.* New York: Rowman and Littlefield, 2008.

North, Douglass C. *Institutions, Institutional Change, and Economic Performance.* New York: Cambridge University Press, 1990.

North, Douglass C., and Robert Paul Thomas. *The Rise of the Western World: A New Economic History.* New York: Cambridge University Press, 1973.

North, Douglass C., John Joseph Wallis, and Barry R. Weingast. *Violence and Social Orders: A Conceptual Framework for Interpreting Recorded Human History.* New York: Cambridge University Press, 2009.

Oakerson, Ronald J., and Roger B. Parks. "The Study of Local Public Economies: Multi-Organizational, Multi-Level Institutional Analysis and Development." *Policy Studies Journal* 39, no. 1 (2011): 147–67.

Olesen, Asta. *Islam and Politics in Afghanistan.* 1st edn. Surrey, UK: Routledge Curzon, 1995.

Olken, Benjamin A. "Direct Democracy and Local Public Goods: Evidence from a Field Experiment in Indonesia." *American Political Science Review* 104, no. 2 (2010): 243–67.

"Monitoring Corruption: Evidence from a Field Experiment in Indonesia." *Journal of Political Economy* 115, no. 2 (2007): 200–249.

Olson, Mancur. "Dictatorship, Democracy, and Development." *The American Political Science Review* 87, no. 3 (1993): 567–76.

Power and Prosperity: Outgrowing Communist and Capitalist Dictatorships. New York: Basic Books, 2000.

The Logic of Collective Action: Public Goods and the Theory of Groups. Cambridge, MA: Harvard University Press, 1971.

Ostrom, Elinor. "A Diagnostic Approach for Going beyond Panaceas." *Proceedings of the National Academy of Sciences of the United States of America* 104, no. 39 (2007): 15181–87.

"Collective Action and the Evolution of Social Norms." *The Journal of Economic Perspectives* 14, no. 3 (2000): 137–58.

Governing the Commons: The Evolution of Institutions for Collective Action. New York: Cambridge University Press, 1990.

"Self-Organization and Social Capital." *Industrial and Corporate Change* 4, no. 1 (1995): 131–59.

"Social Capital: A Fad or Fundamental Concept?" In *Social Capital: A Multifaceted Perspective,* ed. Partha Dasgupta and Ismail Serageldin, 172–216. Washington, DC: World Bank, 2000.

Understanding Institutional Diversity. Princeton, NJ: Princeton University Press, 2005.

Ostrom, Elinor, Roger B. Parks, and Gordon P. Whitaker. "Do We Really Want to Consolidate Urban Police Forces? A Reappraisal of Some Old Assertions." *Public Administration Review* 33, no. 5 (1973): 423–32.

Ostrom, Vincent. "Where to Begin?" *Publius* 25, no. 2 (1995): 45–60.

Ostrom, Vincent, Charles M. Tiebout, and Robert Warren. "The Organization of Government in Metropolitan Areas: A Theoretical Inquiry." *The American Political Science Review* 55, no. 4 (1961): 831–42.

Pain, Adam, and Sayed Mohammad Shah. *Policymaking in Agriculture and Rural Development in Afghanistan.* Case Studies Series. Kabul, Afghanistan: Afghanistan Research and Evaluation Unit, 2009.

Palfrey, Thomas R., and Howard Rosenthal. "Participation and the Provision of Discrete Public Goods: A Strategic Analysis." *Journal of Public Economics* 24, no. 2 (1984): 171–93.

Panchanathan, Karthik, and Robert Boyd. "Indirect Reciprocity Can Stabilize Cooperation Without the Second-Order Free Rider Rroblem." *Nature* 432, no. 7016 (2004): 499–502.

Parks, Roger B., and Ronald J. Oakerson. "Local Government Constitutions: A Different View of Metropolitan Governance." *The American Review of Public Administration* 19, no. 4 (1989): 279–94.

"Metropolitan Organization and Governance." *Urban Affairs Review* 25, no. 1 (1989): 18–29.

Pejovich, Svetozar. "The Effects of the Interaction of Formal and Informal Institutions on Social Stability and Economic Development." In *Institutions, Globalisation and Empowerment*, ed. Kartik Chandra Roy and Jörn Sideras, 344–70. Northampton, MA: Edward Elgar Publishing, 2006.

Persson, Torsten, Gerard Roland, and Guido Tabellini. "Separation of Powers and Political Accountability." *Quarterly Journal of Economics* 112, no. 4 (1997): 1163–1202.

Peters, Gretchen. *Seeds of Terror: How Drugs, Thugs, and Crime Are Reshaping the Afghan War*. New York: Picador, 2010.

Platteau, Jean-Philippe. "Information Distortion, Elite Capture, and Task Complexity in Decentralised Development." In *Does Decentralization Enhance Poverty Reduction and Service Delivery?* ed. Ehtisham Ahmad and Giorgio Brosio, 23–72. Cheltenham: Edward Elgar Publishing, 2009.

Platteau, Jean-Philippe, and Frederic Gaspart. "The Risk of Resource Misappropriation in Community-Driven Development." *World Development* 31, no. 10 (2003): 1687–1703.

Popkin, Samuel. *The Rational Peasant*. Berkeley, CA: University of California, 1979.

Posner, Daniel. *Institutions and Ethnic Politics in Africa*. New York: Cambridge University Press, 2005.

Poullada, Leon B. *Reform and Rebellion in Afghanistan, 1919–1929; King Amanullah's Failure to Modernize a Tribal Society*. Ithaca, NY: Cornell University Press, 1973.

Pritchett, Lant, and Michael Woolcock. "Solutions When the Solution Is the Problem: Arraying the Disarray in Development." *World Development* 32, no. 2 (2004): 191–212.

Qian, Yingyi, and Barry R. Weingast. "Federalism as a Commitment to Preserving Market Incentives." *The Journal of Economic Perspectives* 11, no. 4 (1997): 83–92.

Rashid, Ahmed. *Taliban: Militant Islam, Oil and Fundamentalism in Central Asia, Second Edition*. New Haven, CT: Yale University Press, 2002.

Rauch, James E. "Choosing a Dictator: Bureaucracy and Welfare in Less Developed Polities." Working Paper. National Bureau of Economic Research, July 1995.

Reedy, Kathleen. "Elders and Shuras: Upholding Tradition or Disenfranchising the Population?" *Journal of the Spanish Institute for Strategic Studies*, 2012, 45–58.

Reeves, Madeleine. "The Ashar-State: Communal Commitment and State Elicitation in Rural Kyrgyzstan," unpublished manuscript.

Reno, William. *Warlord Politics and African States*. Lynne Rienner Publishers, 1999.

Ribot, Jesse C. "Authority over Forests: Empowerment and Subordination in Senegal's Democratic Decentralization." *Development and Change* 40, no. 1 (2009): 105–29.

"Decentralisation, Participation and Accountability in Sahelian Forestry: Legal Instruments of Political-Administrative Control." *Africa: Journal of the International African Institute* 69, no. 1 (1999): 23–65.

Robinson, James A., and Q. Neil Parsons. "State Formation and Governance in Botswana." *Journal of African Economies* 15, no. S1 (2006): 100–140.

Rodden, Jonathan A. *Hamilton's Paradox: The Promise and Peril of Fiscal Federalism*. New York: Cambridge University Press, 2005.

Roe, Allan, and Colin Deschamps. "Land Conflict in Afghanistan Building Capacity to Address Vulnerability." Issues Paper Series. Kabul, Afghanistan: Afghanistan Research and Evaluation Unit, 2009.

Ross, Michael. "Does Taxation Lead to Representation?" *British Journal of Political Science* 34 (2004): 229–49.

"Oil, Islam, and Women." *American Political Science Review* 102, no. 1 (2008): 107–23.

"The Political Economy of the Resource Curse." *World Politics* 51, no. 2 (1999): 297–322.

Rotberg, Robert I. "The Failure and Collapse of Nation-States: Breakdown, Prevention, and Repair." In *When States Fail: Causes and Consequences*, 1–49. Princeton, NJ: Princeton University Press, 2004.

When States Fail: Causes and Consequences. Princeton, NJ: Princeton University Press, 2004.

Rothstein, Bo. *The Quality of Government: Corruption, Social Trust, and Inequality in International Perspective*. Chicago; London: University of Chicago Press, 2011.

Roy, Olivier. *Islam and Resistance in Afghanistan*. Cambridge: Cambridge University Press, 1990.

"The New Political Elite in Afghanistan." In *The Politics of Social Transformation in Afghanistan, Iran, and Pakistan*, ed. Myron Weiner and Ali Banuazizi, 72–100. Syracuse, NY: Syracuse University Press, 1994.

Rubin, Barnett R. *The Fragmentation of Afghanistan: State Formation and Collapse in the International System*. 2nd edn. New Haven, CT: Yale University Press, 2002.

Rudolph, Lloyd, and Susanne Hoeber Rudolph. *The Modernity of Tradition: Political Development in India*. Chicago: University of Chicago Press, 1967.

Saikal, Amin. *Modern Afghanistan: A History of Struggle and Survival*. London: I.B.Tauris, 2004.

Salehyan, Idean, and Kristian Skrede Gleditsch. "Refugees and the Spread of Civil War." *International Organization* 60, no. 2 (2006): 335–66.

Saltmarshe, Douglas, and Abhilash Medhi. *Local Governance: A View from the Ground*. Kabul: Afghanistan Research and Evaluation Unit, 2011.

Samatar, Abdi Ismail. "Destruction of State and Society in Somalia: Beyond the Tribal Convention." *The Journal of Modern African Studies* 30, no. 4 (1992): 625–41.

Schetter, Conrad. "Afterword. Trajectories of Local Politics in Afghanistan." In *Local Politics in Afghanistan: A Century of Intervention in Social Order*, ed. Conrad Schetter, 265–74. New York: Columbia University Press, 2013.

"Introduction." In *Local Politics in Afghanistan: A Century of Intervention in Social Order*, ed. Conrad Schetter, 1–20. New York: Columbia University Press, 2013.

ed. *Local Politics in Afghanistan: A Century of Intervention in Social Order*. New York: Columbia University Press, 2013.

Schultz, Kenneth A. "Looking for Audience Costs." *Journal of Conflict Resolution* 45, no. 1 (2001): 32–60.

Schweber, Howard. *The Creation of American Common Law, 1850–1880: Technology, Politics, and the Construction of Citizenship*. New York: Cambridge University Press, 2004.

Scott, James C. *Two Cheers for Anarchism: Six Easy Pieces on Autonomy, Dignity, and Meaningful Work and Play*. Princeton, NJ: Princeton University Press, 2012.

Shahrani, M. Nazif. "Afghanistan's Alternatives for Peace, Governance and Develop-
ment: Transforming Subjects to Citizens and Rulers to Civil Servants." The
Afghanistan Papers. Waterloo, Ontario: The Center for International Governance
Innovation, 2009.
"Local Knowledge of Islam and Social Discourse in Afghanistan and Turkistan in the
Modern Period." In *Turko-Persia in Historical Perspective*, ed. Robert L. Canfield,
161–88. New York: Cambridge University Press, 2002.
"Marxist 'Revolution' and Islamic Resistance in Afghanistan." In *Revolutions
and Rebellions in Afghanistan: Anthropological Perspectives*, 3–57. Berkeley, CA:
University of California at Berkeley, 1984.
"State Building and Social Fragmentation in Afghanistan: A Historical Perspective." In
The State, Religion, and Ethnic Politics: Afghanistan, Iran, and Pakistan, ed. Ali
Banauazizi and Myron Weiner, 23–74. Syracuse, NY: Syracuse University Press, 1986.
"The Future of the State and the Structure of Community Governance in Afghanistan."
In *Fundamentalism Reborn? Afghanistan and the Taliban*, ed. William Maley,
212–42. New York: NYU Press, 1998.
The Kirghiz and Wakhi of Afghanistan: Adaptation to Closed Frontiers and War.
University of Washington Press, 2002.
Shahrani, M. Nazif, and Robert L. Canfield, eds. *Revolutions & Rebellions in Afghanistan:
Anthropological Perspectives*. Berkeley, CA: University of California Press,
1984.
Shalinsky, Audrey. *Long Years of Exile: Central Asian Refugees in Afghanistan and
Pakistan*. Lanham, MD: University Press of America, 1994.
Sinno, Abdulkader H. "Explaining the Taliban's Ability to Mobilize the Pashtuns." In
The Taliban and the Crisis of Afghanistan, ed. Robert D. Crews and Amin Tarzi,
59–89. Cambridge, MA: Harvard University Press, 2008.
Organizations at War in Afghanistan and Beyond. Ithaca, NY: Cornell University
Press, 2008.
Skaperdas, Stergios. "An Economic Approach to Analyzing Civil Wars." *Economics of
Governance* 9, no. 1 (2008): 25–44.
"The Political Economy of Organized Crime: Providing Protection When the State
Does Not." *Economics of Governance* 2, no. 3 (2001): 173–202.
"Warlord Competition." *Journal of Peace Research* 39, no. 4 (2002): 435–46.
Snyder, Jack L. *From Voting to Violence: Democratization and Nationalist Conflict*.
New York: Norton, 2000.
Solnick, Steven L. *Stealing the State: Control and Collapse in Soviet Institutions*.
Cambridge, MA: Harvard University Press, 1999.
Spruyt, Hendrik. *The Sovereign State and Its Competitors*. Princeton, NJ: Princeton
University Press, 1996.
Stanfield, J. David, Mohammad Yasin Safar, Akram Salam, and Jennifer Murtazashvili.
"Rangeland Administration in (Post) Conflict Conditions: The Case of
Afghanistan." In *Innovations in Land Rights Recognition, Administration, and
Governance*, ed. Klaus Deininger, Clarissa Augustinus, Stig Enemark, and Paul
Munro-Faure, 225–41. Washington, DC: The World Bank, 2010.
Suhrke, Astri. *When More Is Less: The International Project in Afghanistan*. New York:
Columbia University Press, 2011.
Tapper, Nancy N. *Bartered Brides: Politics, Gender and Marriage in an Afghan Tribal
Society*. New York: Cambridge University Press, 1991.

Tapper, Richard. "Ethnicity, Order and Meaning in the Anthropology of Iran and Afghanistan." In *Le Fait Ethnique En Iran et En Afghanistan*, ed. Jean-Pierre Digard, 21–34. Paris: Editions du CNRS (Colloques Internationaux), 1988.

"Introduction." In *The Conflict of Tribe and State in Iran and Afghanistan*, ed. Richard Tapper, 1–82. New York: St. Martin's Press, 1983.

Tavernise, Sabrina. "Afghan Enclave Seen as Model for Development." The New York Times, November 13, 2009.

Tendler, Judith. *Good Government in the Tropics*. Baltimore: Johns Hopkins University Press, 1997.

Tiebout, Charles M. "A Pure Theory of Local Expenditures." *The Journal of Political Economy* 64, no. 5 (1956): 416–24.

Tilly, Charles. *Coercion, Capital, and European States, AD 990–1992*. Cambridge: Blackwell, 1992.

The Formation of National States in Western Europe. Princeton, NJ: Princeton University Press, 1975.

"War Making and State Making as Organized Crime." In *Bringing the State Back In*, ed. Peter B. Evans, Dietrich Rueschemeyer, and Theda Skocpol, 169–86. New York: Cambridge University Press, 1985.

Tsai, Lily. *Accountability Without Democracy: Solidary Groups and Public Goods Provision in Rural China*. New York: Cambridge University Press, 2007.

Tsebelis, George. *Veto Players: How Political Institutions Work*. Princeton, NJ: Princeton University Press, 2002.

United Nations Assistance Mission in Afghanistan and United Nations High Commissioner for Human Rights. *Harmful Traditional Practices and Implementation of the Law on Elimination of Violence against Women in Afghanistan*. Kabul, 2010.

Varese, Federico. *The Russian Mafia: Private Protection in a New Market Economy*. New York: Oxford University Press, 2005.

Volkov, Vadim. *Violent Entrepreneurs: The Use of Force in the Making of Russian Capitalism*. Ithaca, NY: Cornell University Press, 2002.

Wade, Robert. *Village Republics: Economic Conditions for Collective Action in South India*. New York: Cambridge University Press, 1988.

Walle, Nicolas van de. *African Economies and the Politics of Permanent Crisis, 1979–1999*. New York: Cambridge University Press, 2001.

Wardak, Ali. "Building a Post-War Justice System in Afghanistan." *Crime, Law and Social Change* 41, no. 4 (2004): 319–41.

Warner, Gregory. "The Schools the Taliban Won't Torch." Washington Monthly, December 2007. www.washingtonmonthly.com/features/2007/0712.warner.html.

Weber, Max. *Economy and Society*. ed. Guenther Roth and Claus Wittich. Berkeley, CA: University of California Press, 1978.

Essays in Economic Sociology. ed. Richard Swedberg. Princeton, NJ: Princeton University Press, 1999.

The Vocation Lectures: Science as a Vocation, Politics as a Vocation. ed. David S. Owen and Tracy B. Strong. Translated by Rodney Livingstone. Indianapolis: Hackett, 2004.

Wedeen, Lisa. *Peripheral Visions: Publics, Power, and Performance in Yemen*. Chicago: University of Chicago Press, 2008.

Weimer, David, ed. *Institutional Design*. Boston: Kluwer Academic Publishers, 1995.

Weimer, David, and William Riker. "The Political Economy of Transformation: Liberalization and Property Rights." In *Modern Political Economy*, ed. Jeffrey S. Banks and Eric A. Hanushek, 80–107. New York: Cambridge University Press, 1995.

Weingast, Barry R. "The Economic Role of Political Institutions: Market-Preserving Federalism and Economic Development." *Journal of Law, Economics and Organization* 11, no. 1 (1995): 1–31.

"The Political Foundations of Democracy and the Rule of Law." *The American Political Science Review* 91, no. 2 (1997): 245–63.

Weyland, Kurt. "The Rise of Latin America's Two Lefts: Insights from Rentier State Theory." *Comparative Politics* 41, no. 2 (2009): 145–64.

White, C. M. N. "African Customary Law: The Problem of Concept and Definition." *Journal of African Law* 9, no. 2 (1965): 86–89.

Wikileaks. "Ambassador's April 6 Meeting with French Ambassador," April 13, 2003. https://wikileaks.org/plusd/cables/03KABUL955_a.html.

Wily, Liz Alden. *Land Rights in Crisis: Restoring Tenure Security in Afghanistan.* Issues Paper Series. Kabul: Afghanistan Research and Evaluation Unit, 2003.

Wolf Jr., Charles. "Market and Non-Market Failures: Comparison and Assessment." *Journal of Public Policy* 7, no. 1 (1987): 43–70.

Wong, Susan. *What Have Been the Impacts of World Bank Community-Driven Development Programs? CDD Impact Evaluation Review and Operational and Research Implications.* Washington, DC: World Bank, 2012.

World Bank. *Afghanistan: National Reconstruction and Poverty Reduction, the Role of Women in Afghanistan's Future.* Washington, DC: The World Bank, 2005.

Young, Crawford. *The African Colonial State in Comparative Perspective.* New Haven: Yale University Press, 1994.

Zoellick, Robert B. "The Key to Rebuilding Afghanistan." *The Washington Post,* August 22, 2008, sec. Opinions.

Index

CPSIA information can be obtained
at www.ICGtesting.com
Printed in the USA
LVHW042041270821
696290LV00008B/376